Rainbow On My Heart

Rainbow On My Heart

*A Memoir of the Early Years
of the Mission of
Sant Ajaib Singh Ji*

by

Kent Bicknell

Sant Bani Ashram, Sanbornton, N.H.
February 2002

Cover design by Todd Smith
All photos are by the author

Printed by The Sant Bani Press, Tilton, N.H.
Copyright © 2002 by Kent Bicknell

ISBN: 0-89142-049-5
Library of Congress Control Number: 2002102854

Contents

Preface vii

Introduction ix

Chapter One   Meeting the Saint 1

Chapter Two   Not a Leaf Stirs 51

Chapter Three   Going to Receive Sant Ji 87

Chapter Four   The First Tour 117

Chapter Five   South America 169

Chapter Six   Return to New Hampshire 201

Chapter Seven   Spiritual Vanity 213

Chapter Eight   Spiritual Surgery 225

Chapter Nine   The Ocean of Love 263

Chapter Ten   Epilogue 309

Preface

The story of the love of the Master cannot be told.
— Sant Ajaib Singh, *"Takle Man Oe Kirpal"*

The following account is a personal narrative of the early years of the mission of Sant Ajaib Singh, covering 1976 through 1979. Through what Sant Ji described as "luck," I was given the opportunity to travel with Him on tours to South America, and to stay in His house when He resided at Sant Bani Ashram in New Hampshire. From the beginning, Sant Ji encouraged me to learn Hindi — and while I never became fluent in the spoken word, I was able to write directly to Him and to read His letters to me. When Sant Ji's mission was in its earliest phases — before we even thought of it as a "mission" — I was given much access to Him.

Over the years I have shared some of these experiences, but much I held for myself. I was very happy to have the opportunities to serve Sant Ji, and I did not wish to be in the position of having divulged something that He would have preferred I had not. Selfishly, I liked being able to travel and live with Sant Ji, and did not wish to be replaced for being indiscreet.

The narrative is not a history *per se*, as it focuses on my growth and development. That, of itself, is of limited interest. The way that Sant Ji, the Master Teacher, taught me the lessons I needed is what readers may find instructive and inspiring. Master Kirpal Singh and Sant Ajaib Singh have never stopped showering Their love and infinite care down upon me. In the routine of my day-to-day life, it can be very easy to lose sight of the magic of the universe — of the divine forces at work behind the scenes. A focus of the book is the extraordinary power and reach of the Masters — Who come into this world to awaken us by showering Love and Grace upon us. The book stands as a testament to that — not just in my life, but in the lives of my family, friends, and both the Sant Bani Ashram and the Sant Bani School.

There is an abundance of detail in the book — the source of which is decidedly not a prodigious memory. For the past few years I have been transcribing hours and hours of personal cassettes and several written journals kept at the time — all of which served as the foundation for this account. Any errors or omissions are my own — for which I ask the reader's forgiveness.

The title of the book, *Rainbow On My Heart*, was suggested by a specific incident in June of 1977, in Vermont, described in Chapter Four. I think also of the Sant Bani School, whose beginnings were sealed with a double rainbow. This summer, while I was in the midst of working on the book, a freak storm swept by our cottage on Newfound Lake. As fast as the tempest came, it was gone, leaving behind a double rainbow that hung almost within reach. I hold these to be more than physical manifestations of the natural world. They are visual unfoldings of the covenants of God.

The narrative describes meeting Sant Ji in 1976, visiting the Ashram in India, and the First World Tour of 1977 (Chapters One through Six). Chapters Seven and Eight speak of my own misguided attempts to become truly spiritual, and Sant Ji's loving guidance directing me back to my old self. Chapter Nine centers on two areas: the unfolding of the English translation of the *Anurag Sagar* [*The Ocean of Love*] the great spiritual text of Sant Kabir Sahib; and the wonder of it all as shared with a nine year old boy, my son Chris. Chapter Ten is a short epilogue.

If this work provides any inspiration, credit must go to the extraordinary presences of Master Kirpal Singh Ji Maharaj, and Sant Ajaib Singh Ji. My gratitude to both of Them is unending. Thanks also to my family, Karen, Christopher, and Nicholas — who lived it with me and were supportive throughout. Raaj Kumar Bagga ("Pappu") has been an unerring friend from day one, and his service in translating all of the Satsangs, *darshans*, question and answer sessions, interviews, *et al,* is legendary. He may not wish our gratitude, but he has it in abundance. His suggestions, as well as those of Mr. A. S. Oberoi, were gratefully received and incorporated throughout the text (again, the errors are my own). Russell Perkins was also kind enough to read the book, offer commentary, and write an introduction. Russell, and his late wife Judith, lived through these times with me as well — as is most apparent in the narrative. Thank you. And to all of the other readers and listeners who have provided encouragement along the way — Robert and Wendy Schongalla, Jonathan Powell, Catharine Farkas, Lori Budington, Linda Turnage, Karen Gregg, Richard Hawley, Lane Zachary, Joe Gelbard, and Richard and Susan Shannon — as well as to every future reader — a hearty "thank you and Godspeed!"

KENT BICKNELL
November 6, 2001
Sant Bani Ashram
Sanbornton, NH

Introduction

It has been a remarkable and moving experience, reading this book of Kent's and reliving those marvelous days when the Master was young and the world was new; for that is what it seemed like to all of us who were privileged to be alive in those glorious days. In the days and months following our beloved Master Kirpal's passing, the sangat (or brotherood of disciples) hit bottom; a great many of us, myself included, succumbed to partisanship and polarization, during which we forgot entirely who we were and what we really wanted. Then our Master gave us Sant Ajaib, and suddenly we were flying: priorities righted, destination reaffirmed, the overwhelming reality and joy of darshan experienced once again. Kent has captured it all, and the intense personal focus he maintains throughout reflects accurately the intense personal focus with which all of us approach the Master: there is no other way to approach Him, really. Kent was privileged to do enormous amounts of seva and was given an immense personal blessing by Sant Ajaib Singh Ji, and his book comes as close to doing justice to the reality of that as any book can.

The esoteric teaching which in India is known as *Sant Mat* or "The Way of the Saints" is often summarized by the Masters of that teaching in three words, and Sant Ji often used them to anchor His satsangs. The three words are: *Satnaam*, *Satguru*, and *Satsang*. If we understand them and their significance, the assumptions and world-view that underlie Kent's account will be much clearer to us, and we will be able to appreciate his adventures more fully.

Satnaam:

This is the word the Masters use for the fundamental fact of the universe, the power which brought it into being and sustains it even now: the expression of God through which His Love comes to us. It is in actuality the True Name of God (*satnaam* literally translates as "true" or "original" name), the Word (as it is called in the Gospel of John) by which He names Himself. Other traditions and scriptures have other names for it, but they all know about it: the Chinese call it *Tao,* the Sufis *Kalma or Saute Sarmad,* the Hindu scriptures refer to it as *Nad* or *Udgit,* etc. It is referred to in the very beginning of the Bible: "**And God said, Let there be light.**" The

ix

"speaking" of God is His Word or Name, but that "speaking" is not an abstraction; it is an actual Sound which can be heard. And the Light which the Word produced can be seen. The Word is not something which only happened way back when; as the Gospel of John makes clear, it is the basic essential reality of every human being; indeed, of all life:

In the beginning was the Word, and the Word was with God, and the Word was God. He was in the beginning with God. All things came into being through him, and without him not one thing came into being. What has come into being in him was life, and the life was the light of all people. The light shines in the darkness, and the darkness did not overcome it. (John 1: 1-5)

The light shines in the darkness even now, and the darkness still is not overcoming it; and this is an eternal drama that every human being can experience within him/herself. And the Masters say that to experience it is in fact to solve the mystery of life.

Satguru:

But how to begin to approach this? If this is the ultimate Reality of our own selves, as the Masters say, why do we not know it? Why do we not live in the light of it? Bikha, an Indian saint of the sixteenth century, explains it this way:

None is poor, O Bikha;
Everyone has rubies in his bundle;
But how to untie the knot he does not know,
And therefore is he a pauper.

Still, as Master Kirpal used to say, "It is our *birthright* to become God." As human beings we are His children, made in His image, and He cannot help but love us, regardless of what we deserve or how bad we are. In Luke 15, Jesus tells three stories to illustrate the never-ending, never-taking-no-for-an-answer love of God: the lost sheep, the lost coin, the lost son. Because God loves us by virtue of our existence, and because He *wants* to bring us into His presence and show us what our heritage is so that we can see it for ourselves, He will do it; no matter how long it takes, how many repetitions of the Wheel, how much resistance we put up, He will eventually bring each one of us into His presence, because that is what is meant by "God is love." Rabia, the great Sufi mystic, said, "Love is the core of the universe." She meant exactly this: that love which is the heart of the universe will bring us to itself, and we will happily come. And the Master *(Satguru)* is the means that God uses to reach us.

Satsang:

But in order for the Master to reach us, there has to be something there to reach; as C. S. Lewis put it, "we cannot expect the gods to meet us face to face until we have faces." And this interaction between the Master and the disciple, the reaching out of the Master to the disciple and the disciple's response, is the esoteric meaning of "Satsang," or association with Truth. The real Master is Truth personified, and association with Him, no matter what the terms of that association may seem to be, will result in growth, deepening, and learning on the part of the disciple. The Master's methods here may be highly unorthodox; many stories which illustrate this point exist, for example the following from Rabbi Nachman of Bratslav:

A prince becomes mentally ill and feels that he has become a rooster. He insists on sitting "naked beneath the table to eat pieces of bread and bone." The king and his physicians despair of curing him, but a wise man comes along and offers to heal him. The latter takes off his own clothes and sits under the table with the prince. When the prince asks him what he is doing, the wise man says that he, too, is a rooster. "And they both sat together until they became used to each other." Finally, the wise man asks for a shirt, telling the prince, "You think that a rooster cannot wear a shirt? Even though he is a rooster, he can wear a shirt." And both of them put on shirts. After a while, he asks for pants and soon both of them are wearing pants. The same process is used to get the prince to eat regular food and, finally, to sit at the table. Nachman concludes his story by saying that every man who wishes to come closer to the worship of God is a "rooster, that is, enveloped in grossness. By the above technique, however, the *tzaddik* [holy man or Master] can gradually lift up the man, and bring him to the right way of serving God. (Herbert Weiner, *9 1/2 Mystics: The Kabbala Today, p.219*)

If we keep this story in mind while reading this book, many of the events Kent describes will resonate more clearly.

*   *   *

I did live through many of these adventures with Kent and his family, although of course I experienced them from my particular intense personal focus, which was not necessarily the same as Kent's. Nevertheless, I can

attest to the truth of the narrative, as well as its spiritual value. I would like
to comment especially on Chapter Seven, "Spiritual Vanity," and Chapter
Nine, on the *Anurag Sagar.*

Kent's experiences during his bout with spiritual vanity took us all, including him, by surprise at the time, and that was indeed a difficult time
for my late wife Judith and me, and for Sant Bani Ashram as a whole. It is
a mistake to assume that Kent was wholly responsible for that. It was my
job to monitor whatever was going on at the Ashram and deal with it, if
necessary, by communicating directly with the Master, as He made very
clear to me when I saw Him in September 1978. 1 did not do that, or anything like it; I basically gave up and retreated into a kind of ongoing fury
combined with a complete giving up, a ceding of the ground. It was a very
childish and unhelpful reaction, which made everything worse. Since then,
I have had a good deal of experience with this kind of thing; it is actually a
very easy thing to fall prey to. When you begin to experience the fruit of
prolonged regular meditation for the first time, it can be very heady. The
temptation to compare oneself with others is very hard to avoid. And although, as Kent points out, Sant Ji gave us very specific warning (in the
talk, "The Enemy Within," given to the Sant Bani sevadars in May 1977),
we were all very naive when it came to facing up to this and recognizing
it. Sant Ji has described the process exactly in the first chapter of *The
Jewel of Happiness,* in the story of the swan and the crane; and Master Kirpal
often referred to the fact that ego was the last thing to go, so that whatever
power or adeptness we acquired in the course of our meditations was apt
to be appropriated by the ego, and would strengthen it rather than be used
to rise above it. (A very important reason why "man-making," or spiritual
growth, has to accompany or even precede spectacular meditation experiences.) So, although failure was there, it was not the failure of one individual. Kent's honest and non-self-sparing account should benefit many
others who might otherwise have fallen into the same trap.

Regarding the *Anurag Sagar,* my experience with that great book
started when Pappu and Kent left off, but Kent's point, that it seemed like
the seva was doing them, was certainly experienced by me also. Sant Ji
handed me the translated manuscript, the fruit of the labor that Kent describes so vividly in Chapter Nine, on the first day of our stay in Quito,
Ecuador (the first day in the South American part of the 1980 Tour), and
told me I would have plenty of time to work on it, as I didn't speak
Spanish and so would have little to do in South America. He said I should
edit the manuscript carefully from the point of view of the English

language, notice every point that a Westerner might find hard to understand, and write an explanatory note at that point. He added that I could consult Him about points that were hard for me.

Over the next few weeks, I had many questions, and I went to Him two or three times a week with them; the darshan that I got while doing this made me very happy. He gave me complete answers, which are all incorporated into the Notes of that book (published as *The Ocean of Love: The* Anurag Sagar *of Kabir)*. But one day He said, "No. You cannot keep asking me these questions. *Be receptive.* You will know the answers; you won't need to ask me. Don't ask me any more questions about it." I was sad at this, but I quickly found that He was right: problem after problem came up, and each time, on reflection, I found that I did know the answer.

The entire job took many months, extending long after the 1980 Tour was over; I finished it finally in August 1981. At the very end, there was one question I did not know the answer to, and no matter how much I meditated on it, how receptive I could get, it would not come. I wanted to write the Master and ask Him, but he had told me not to! Finally, in desperation, I picked up the pen and began writing, something, anything: but *the second the pen touched the paper* I knew what the answer was. I realized then what I should have learned long before, and have experienced many times since, and to which Kent gives such eloquent testimony in the course of this book: the Master does not give orders without giving the Grace to obey them. It is what makes the Path a Reality.

RUSSELL PERKINS

CHAPTER ONE

Meeting the Saint

On August 21st, 1974, the disciples of the great spiritual teacher, Kirpal Singh Ji Maharaj, received the profound news that the Soul of their Beloved Master had parted from Its body in the phenomenon that the world calls "death." Those of us living at Sant Bani Ashram in central New Hampshire passed through all of the known stages of grief, and, as there was no clear Successor for the spiritual work, we entered a period of continuing on with our meditation and waiting. Others around the country, indeed, the globe, began to follow this or that person who stepped (or was pushed) forward to claim the spiritual reins of Sant Mat, the Science of the Soul. Time passed, and in February of 1976 various events converged to suggest that the moment was ripe for the appearance of the New Master.

Russell Perkins, who with his wife Judith, had given their house and land in New Hampshire to the service of the Master, received a clear command from Master Kirpal within. The deathless Inner Master ordered Russell to travel to India to find a disciple of Master's named Ajaib Singh.[1] Earlier we had heard that Ajaib Singh was very advanced in the practice of meditation.[2]

Russell, who has told his story in detail in his book, *The Impact of a Saint*, responded to this inner pull and, after an arduous journey with many roadblocks, succeeded in finding Sant Ajaib Singh (Sant Ji) in the rural village of 77 RB in the desert province of Rajasthan. Russell sent us a cable that said, "HAVE FOUND AJAIB SINGH – HE IS REAL – WE LOVE HIM" and we were giddy with excitement and anticipation. After months of confusion, this felt clear and right. Russell spent a few hours

---

[1] Russell Perkins, *The Impact of a Saint*, p. 149.
[2] See "A Possibility," in *Sat Sandesh*, October 1974 (pp. 28-32), an account by Arran Stephens of how he sought and found Sant Ajaib Singh Ji in September of 1974.

1

with Sant Ji, and then in March a group of three visited Him and spent the night.[3] They brought back similar testimony as to the quality of Sant Ji and His Life.

This saga of my journey really begins on the night Russell returned from India. As he told the story of his visit, of the joy of seeing the dancing, twinkling eyes of Kirpal in Ajaib, something in my heart began to sing and I wanted to go. Until that time I had felt no need to find the Successor. My personal life was going smoothly with no trauma, and I was content. The idea of going began as an emotional throb and gradually settled into a cold rational drive. Since I had no money, however, I directed my attention toward the Master Power inside and again began to meditate three (rather than two) hours daily.

I was rewarded – enough so that I was able to resign myself to the idea of not going to India. When Jane Counter came back from the group of three I talked to her and felt more inclined than ever to travel. The next day some totally unexpected finances arrived (from my wife's parents) and the door was thrown open for my trip. By the time I was ready to leave, two more from here were also ready – Robert and Wendy Schongalla. Robert was teaching at the Sant Bani School and Wendy was helping at the Ashram – as they both do today. Wendy's two daughters attended the School at that time. Wendy had applied for Initiation from Master Kirpal Singh Ji, but He left the body before responding to her request.

After the usual last minute scramble, with impossible snags and delays taken care of by Him, we left for Delhi and arrived on the morning of Thursday, April 1st, 1976. Raaj Kumar Bagga, "Pappu," who had been waiting for us for over three hours as our plane had been delayed, met us at the airport. We had been afraid we might not recognize each other, but it was instantly apparent to both parties who we were. Thus began a long and fruitful friendship with the person who was to serve as Sant Ji's translator and dedicated sevadar throughout His Mission.

We traveled through the complex maze that is New Delhi and arrived at the Bagga household. We were able to secure tickets for the train that evening to Ganganagar, the city in Rajasthan closest to Village 77 RB where Sant Ji was residing. I was excited at the thought of going

---

[3] The visitors were: Jane Counter and James Russell, disciples of Master Kirpal, and Ronnie Yow, a spiritual seeker who became one of Sant Ji's first Western disciples.

soon, yet in my mind I had a desire to visit Sawan Ashram – to see some old friends who were still residing in that sacred home of Beloved Master Kirpal Singh. I had spent several weeks at Sawan Ashram in 1970 and 1974, and had come to know some of the sevadars as real friends. The librarian had kindly allowed my four-year-old son, Christopher, and I to visit him often in his little room on the Ashram. Another man, a devoted disciple who lived at Sawan Ashram, had also been very sweet to me. His daughter developed a keen interest in attending the Sant Bani School – and we had corresponded about that possibility in the year and a half after the passing of Master Kirpal.

Pappu and I went over to Sawan Ashram in the afternoon, but for a variety of reasons felt less than comfortable. Our stay was not even five minutes, as we never went beyond the entrance gate of the Ashram. We left without making contact with anyone that I knew. Pappu remarked on how much things had changed and I agreed. For me there was no hint of the Master Power left at a place that had been so enchanting in my earlier visits.

We returned to the Bagga household and I was feeling quite distraught. After the interminable plane ride to India it was all too easy to become negative until I had had a chance to really rest. Pappu suggested I write my friends a letter but I was determined to return later that day to see them. I verbalized much of my feelings to Robert and Wendy, and they were very sweet and helpful. By that time I had made so much more out of it than it was, but with Master's Grace I meditated and it came to me quite clearly that Pappu was right. I would simply write a letter to my fellow disciples saying that I would come to see them on my return to Delhi next week. This is what I did, and then I was able to sleep for two hours. Upon awakening I felt refreshed and rested, and more receptive to His Will.

While reflecting on the whole incident, I came to feel that much of the negativity I experienced at Sawan Ashram that afternoon was due to my own paranoia and fears. As I wrote at the time, "I now feel I sent out negative vibes and got what I deserved/needed. When I go again I'll tell them who I am and why I've come – I must be open, honest, and loving to all." As Sant Ajaib Singh showed me later, however, it was simply better for me to move on. By the end of my time with Sant Ji, this trip to Sawan Ashram (and my plans to return) had played a dramatic role in demonstrating that the protection (*raksha*) of the Master is infinite.

Before I left for Ganganagar I had several good conversations with

Pappu's older brother Kulwant and his wife, Linda.[4] I had wondered how to behave around Pappu's father, Papa Ji, as I was afraid lest I do something wrong on a cultural level. I asked Linda (Papa Ji's daughter-in-law) about it and her advice to me was, "Do what is in your heart." This advice served me well at the Bagga house, and became the underlying principle for many of my actions on the entire trip.

Sant Ji had told Kulwant that if we wished, we could arrange for Him to move closer to a city – if that would make it easier for those wanting to come visit. Kulwant felt concern for the villagers regarding the effect of a steady stream of visitors. I had the feeling that we were at the beginning of something very big – a great mission. Reflecting on that, as well as on the love and kindness extended to the three of us by every member of the Bagga Family, left me feeling moved to my roots.

The journey from Delhi to Ganganagar was a new experience. We climbed aboard an overnight train pulled by a steam engine and entered our first class sleeper cabin. We thus had at least a semblance of the privacy so dear to Western hearts. The rhythm of the rails merged with the inner repetition of the Names of God, and we all drifted off.

The First Day – Friday, April 2nd, 1976

The next morning our eyes opened to a completely different terrain – the sandy countenance of a desert awakened to agriculture through an elaborate system of canals. The plaza outside the train station in Ganganagar was filled with all kinds of vehicles, animals, and people, and we were relieved to reach the apothecary shop of a Satsangi from where we were able to arrange a Jeep to take us to our final destination two and a half hours away.

Looking out the back of the Jeep there was little to see beyond the constant cloud of dust from our vehicle. And it was only when we stopped along the way – to give a ride to an elderly man and his daughter or to visit the Satsangi station master of a small train station – that our surroundings made full impact on my tired consciousness. Suddenly we arrived at the adobe compound, and drove through the arched doorway in the golden walls of mud and straw.

The place was very beautiful and peaceful, and full of God's loving

---

[4] Kulwant and Linda accompanied Russell to see Sant Ji on the February trip.

sweetness and service. Everyone rushed to make us feel welcome, and a small troop gave us tea, refilled our cups, and flicked at the flies so we would not be pestered by them. Sant Ji had not yet appeared. Someone suggested that we look at the new bathing area – just finished for our convenience – and while we were there, Sant Ji came. We met Him in the courtyard and were so very warmly received. He patted Robert's shoulder and Wendy's and tapped Pappu on the back as he bent to touch Sant Ji's feet. As if it were the most natural thing in the world (which indeed it became for me) I bent and touched His feet. In the years to come this became important for me on many levels, and I often felt unable to "begin" the spiritual work of a pilgrimage to Sant Ji unless I had touched His feet.

When Karen and I had gone to see Master Kirpal Singh Ji in February of 1974 we entered His sitting room to greet Him – and a Western friend we were with bent and touched His feet. I wanted to do that, but for whatever reason, I could not. Six weeks later, on the night we were to leave, Master Kirpal invited us all to sit with Him in a courtyard while He said goodbye to the travelers. I was sitting right in front of Him, staring up at His radiant face with a full moon shining over His shoulder. At one point He pushed His right foot out toward me so that it was almost in my lap. I looked down, hesitated, and then, with the index finger of my right hand, gently made contact with that black patent leather shoe. He did not react outwardly (I had been afraid He would cry out or jerk His foot away) and I felt a warm wave of goodness wash over me. Without doubt it had been the right thing for me to do at that moment. And two years later it felt right for me to touch the feet of Sant Ajaib Singh Ji.

Sant Ji was dressed in light pink clothing with a white turban. Over tea (prior to seeing Him) I had decided that it was all right to be skeptical and that I should be cautious. When we came in from the courtyard to sit, I found my mind caught in the "does He or doesn't He" syndrome. Is He really the Successor to my Master, Kirpal Singh Ji Maharaj? This was difficult because He kept looking right into my eyes and I felt like I had Him on trial. I just prayed, "Oh God, you can see my every thought so I have nothing to hide." He was very loving and sweet. After a short period my internal questions subsided. He really could and did look so much like I remembered Master Kirpal. And suddenly there was no doubt that, for me, both His face and His eyes were those of Master Kirpal. I told Him that although I knew that the outer form changed while the Master Power stayed the same, it seemed to me as if the outer form had stayed the same also. The first photos had not properly conveyed the physical likeness. It was very strong, as was the sense of being in the presence of a Realized Soul.

Someone showed Sant Ji a picture of Master Kirpal. After looking at it for a long time He asked, "Where did you get this picture of me?" Later in the trip I told Him that even though we had heard He had stopped wearing a white turban so the resemblance to Master Kirpal would not be so great, it did not work. He commented that He had tried to hide, but what could He do if the Master Power was directing everything? It was interesting that He was wearing a white turban at this first meeting – at which time I took no photos – as later He wore a pink one.

He asked which of us were initiated and for how long. He asked Wendy why she had not received the Naam, and she explained that she had wanted It, but Master Kirpal left His body before she could receive It. She added that although she was not initiated, all her desires had been answered. She told of meeting Robert and moving to the Ashram. She also said she knew Sant Ji was not giving Initiation, but that she had come for His help. After closing His eyes for several seconds, He told her that she could have Naam a year from the thirteenth of March past, as He was meditating full-time until then. He added that all her desires would be fulfilled.

We showed Him the letter from Russell, and Pappu translated it aloud. Sant Ji took it and put it away in His pocket. At some point I told Him that we were confused because we wanted to see Him, but we also did not wish to disturb His meditations. He said it was no disturbance and that someone who rises above cannot be bothered by anything. He later indicated that our coming was part of Master Kirpal's Plan. First a dear one from the West had come to find Him in 1974, after which Sant Ji had told people not to give His address to anyone. Then Russell came, and next the group of three, and now we were there. He said this was all Master's Plan unfolding. Those who go to Sach Khand see Master face-to-face and know. He was reminded of a Shabad by a Muslim Master which He had Pathi Ji, the singer, chant. It had to do with the Guru planting a seed in the mind which, when watered with meditation and Satsang, would become a fragrant blossoming tree. He told the story of Sawan Singh – how one day He was walking and suddenly a sweet fragrance entered His being. Then He met a sadhu and knew it had come from him. The sadhu said that the fragrance was there but very few smelled it. The implication was clearly that the Master Power is here for those who want it.

He told many stories about the physical sons of past Masters trying to become the Guru – through a written will, through force, and by various other means. They are really after money and property. He said that when the Guru comes forth for His mission, an organization comes up and the money starts coming in. When the money gets more than is needed, greed enters the organization and the Guru goes away. He told of the flesh and blood sons of Guru Nanak in relation to Guru Angad, Guru Amardas and Guru Ramdas. An especially moving story concerned the sons of Nanak, who came to Guru Ramdas and asked Him, "Why do you grow this long beard – are you trying to be the Guru?" His response was that He had grown His Beard to wipe the dust from their shoes, because they were the sons of Guru Nanak.

He said that one time Master Kirpal was to go in a car to Ganga-nagar, and He insisted that Sant Ji go also. They were alone, and Master explained many things about what follows after a True Guru leaves the body. Master told Sant Ji the story of the sun rising over Jullundur – how none of those surrounding Sawan Singh could recognize the spiritual import of what He was saying.[5] Master Kirpal related how someone wrote a new will when Sawan Singh was critically ill. Sant Ji told us that when Master Kirpal left the body, the people around Him initially said that no one there had been chosen for spiritual work – but within hours the same people were wrangling over it.[6]

---

[5] "During His last physical illness, Hazur [Sawan Singh] said one night, 'A strong Sun has risen. Can the people of Jullundur see it?' All the relatives around Him thought He was in a state of delirium . . . When S. Kirpal Singh came to see Hazur, the latter had a hearty laugh and repeated the question. S. Kirpal Singh replied, 'Sir, not only the people of Jullundur but even the inhabitants of America and other places can see that Sun at this time if Your Holiness were to open their inner vision.' Hazur was very happy to hear the apt reply and said, 'Kirpal Singh, you have replied my query correctly.' " As cited by Bhadra Sena, in *The Beloved Master: Some Glimpses from the Life of Sant Kirpal Singh Ji Maharaj* [1963], p. 49.

[6] In an extraordinary question and answer session given in India a decade later (February 26th, 1986), Sant Ji both referred back to and expanded upon incidents in this chapter. He said:

You know that all the perfect Saints who have come in this world up until now, They have always gone to the feet of Their Master, They have sacrificed a lot, They have made Themselves very pure, and They have devoted Themselves to Their Master very much. Those disciples who go within and who are able to carry on the work, when They were given the work of the continuation of the mission, They have always begged Their Master, "Master, this is a very heavy burden to carry. You Yourself do this work; we cannot do it." They have never claimed to be the Successor of Their Master and They have never wished to do the work after the Master leaves the body. But on the other side you will find also those people who have not perfected their meditation, who have not made their life pure, but still after the Master leaves the body they claim to be the successors of the Master. They even go to court and fight for the property of the Master. Because they have not done meditation, they do not know how heavy that burden is that they want to carry. I do not mean to criticize anyone by saying this; I am only telling you things which history has witnessed and what has happened with the Saints in the past and with Their Successors.

When Bhai Lehna, who later on became Guru Angad, came to Guru Nanak, Guru Nanak asked him, "What is your name?" He said, "Lehna." In Punjabi that means, "I have to take." Guru Nanak said, "If your name is Lehna and you have to take, then my job is to give to you." He embraced Bhai Lehna and afterwards He made him Guru Angad. Angad means "of my own body." When Guru Nanak told Guru Angad, "After me you will have to continue this work," he wept and said, "Master, this is a very heavy burden; I cannot carry it." But still Guru Nanak insisted and told Guru Angad that he would have to be His Successor. His sons Sri Chand and Lakhmi Das got upset at Guru Nanak and told Him, "He is our servant and you are giving him the Successorship and all our things?" Guru Nanak told Guru Angad, "Leave all this property here at Karturpur for them; you go to your own village of Kadur Sahib and do your work there."

When Guru Amardas went to His Master Guru Angad, He also served Him very wholeheartedly and He moulded His life according to the instructions of His Master. When Guru Angad Dev was about to leave the world, He told Guru Amardas, "After me you will have to do this work of giving Naam Initiation." Guru Amardas also said," It is a very heavy thing and I cannot do it." But still when Guru Angad insisted, He also had to do it. But here too Dasu and Datu, the sons of Guru Angad Dev, were opposing Guru Amardas. When Guru Amardas sat down to do the Satsang they came and kicked Him and said, "Are you in your senses? You used to be the servant in our home and now you have become the owner of our home?" At that time Guru Amardas did not get upset at them; He was the abode of peace and was very humble. He told them, "Forgive me, but I am an old person and my bones are very stiff, it is possible that when you kicked me you might have hurt yourself. So please forgive me." And He left all that property there and went to the place called Goindwal, where He started His work.

In the same way when Master Sawan gave the orders to Master Kirpal to do the work, He asked His dear ones to bring the register and count how many people He had initiated; When they told Him, He said, "Kirpal Singh, I have done half of your work. The other half you will have to do." So Master Kirpal wept and told Him, "No, you should do the other half also." But when Master Sawan Singh said, "No: this is your job and you will have to do it," Master Kirpal said, "Well, whatever You tell me I will do that. I am just the pipe; you will have to send the water. Whatever way you make me dance I will dance."

Master Kirpal had made a very beautiful house in the Dera of Master Sawan Singh and when Master Sawan Singh left this earthly plane Master Kirpal could not even look at the house which He had made Himself, He just bowed down to that place and peacefully left the Dera, and in the remembrance of His Master He went to the forest of Rishikesh where He did His devotion.

Regarding myself, you may have read in Mr. Oberoi's book that when Master Kirpal came to my ashram He told me that I should come with Him to His ashram and take care of the things there. I wept and said, "All my life long since my childhood, I have been waiting for You, and now when you have met me You want me to go and get involved in the bricks?" At my ashram we had so many bricks, and I told Him, "If you want to hit me in the head with bricks, here they are; You can hit me. I wanted only you and that is why I am content with you and I don't want anything else."

I have often told this story: that when Master Kirpal Singh was supposed to go from Kunichuk to Ganganagar he had me sit in His car with Him for two or two and a half hours. At that time He was not physically well, and I wanted Him to lie down in the back seat and I would go in my own car. But He said, "No: come with me in my car because I want to talk about something very important with you." I begged Him to lie down comfortably and I would go in my own car but still he insisted. He took me in His car with Him and then He started talking about the things which His Master Baba Sawan Singh had told Him when Baba Sawan Singh gave Him the orders to do the work of Naam initiation. He told me that there are many orders which the Masters give to the disciples and the disciples obey those orders even though they do not want to because it is for the good of the people. He said, "When my Master told me to do initiation, I told Him that I could not do that, but He insisted and said that I would have to do it. He told me, 'There will be many people who can explain the theory in a much better way, but it will be very difficult to find someone who will meditate and make others meditate. I don't want my teachings to be lost in the world; I am giving this job to you to make sure that my teachings remain alive and are given to the people. I am giving this work to you and you will have to do it.' "

When Master was telling me all these things which His Master had told Him, I got the hint that he was going to tell me the same thing, and I felt like opening the door and jumping out of that car. But He held me very tightly and

After a while Sant Ji ordered cushions for us all and I took the opportunity to slip to the floor. He insisted that I sit in my chair. He then told how He always tried to sit at Master's Feet but Master Kirpal insisted Sant Ji sit next to Him – even on the dais. I protested that He was clean and I was dirty, and He commented that it is easy to find God but difficult to become a man. God is looking for a true man. He said it was our love that would draw Him to America, and that Russell Sahib would make the arrangements.

At some point in this first meeting we gave Him all the printed material we had brought. There was a bound volume of *Sat Sandesh*, pictures of Master Kirpal on the rock at Sant Bani Ashram, a School brochure, the booklet of the Third World Tour, and other items. He looked at it all quite carefully. We explained about Master's house, the Satsang Hall, and other buildings in New Hampshire. I asked Him about taping what He had to say and taking photographs, and He answered, "As you please." He arranged to give Satsang at 8:00 p.m. that evening. He talked about the new washroom for us and how the next time we come there will be a bathroom for us (at that point we used the fields across the road). He mentioned that shortly before we came, the new manger collapsed on a sevadar. Although it took five hours to help the dear one out of the rubble, he was unharmed. And, He observed, we were coming here to the middle of the desert, even though we could have been enjoying wonderful facilities elsewhere.

Sant Ji said we should take *khanna* [food], and hearing that word, I repeated, "*Khanna*" and gestured toward Him, indicating that He was the only "food" we needed. Everyone laughed. As the hour and a half raced on He looked more and more and more like I remembered Master Kirpal, until He was that. His Eyes were amazing. At first I had some racing

---

He told me, even though I had refused earlier; but when He told me that time, Tai Ji, who was sitting in the front seat, said, "Just imagine how much the Sangat will lose if you refuse to do that, and remain inside." I said, "Yes, I know that. The dear ones will lose a lot." Then Master told me that I had to do this work. At that time I begged Master Kirpal, "Master, people criticized you and Master Sawan very much even though You are competent. You are filled with worldly knowledge and you are competent and Almighty. In the same way people will criticize me also, but I do not have any worldly knowledge or anything. How will I bear that? How will I do that?" Master told me, "When the bad people do not stop their bad deeds, why should the good people stop their good deeds? You will have to do this work."

(*Sant Bani Magazine*, July-August 1986, "In the Hands of Kirpal" pp.58 *ff*).

horrible thoughts – even as we looked at each other – but I just prayed to Master for help, and silently said how dirty I was. Sant Ji said He appreciated our coming so far and that now He could have our *darshan*.

We heard our first Satsang that evening, April 2nd. After Satsang Sant Ji asked about us – how was our arrival at Delhi, who was watching our children, etc.? He spoke of Russell and asked Pappu to write the translation of Russell's letter on the back of the page. He said that people were coming here for the true Peace – for *Shanti*. By His Grace we were allowed to sit on the floor that evening and from then on. Sant Ji always took great pains to make sure we were seated on cushions, however.

The Second Day – Saturday, April 3rd, 1976

"Wow!" I thought, "It is getting more and more amazing." I went to sleep at 11:15 p.m. and awoke at 4:15 a.m. for meditation. There were many Indians bedded down in our quarters. Later we discovered that our roommates were Sardar Rattan Singh and his friends, who had brought food for us on a tractor from their home twenty miles away – at Village 16 PS. In the morning we toured the gardens of Babu Ji, visited the village school, and saw the place where Arran Stephens had first met with Sant Ji.

Sant Ji came for darshan, and I was as ready as I could be. He was so gracious and beautiful, dressed in a pink turban with shimmering sparkles in it. I told Him how grateful I was to be there, and He said it was all Master working behind the curtain. We were meant to be brought there. Later I said I could not understand why God was giving one so unworthy as me so much, and He explained in a word, "Luck."

He was so accommodating and humorous about my picture taking (and they all came out). At one point as I gazed, He was overflowing as Master Kirpal and Baba Sawan Singh Ji. Sant Ji said that after bathing we should come to see Him about arranging for His tour to our country. He was so full of love. The carpet was made of burlap bags sewn together, the wicker chairs and footstools trimmed with old bicycle tires. Such furniture was made graceful by the love of the Lord.

We recorded that first morning session with Him – and it was published in the inaugural issue of *Sant Bani Magazine* under the title, "The Essence is Meditation."[7] He talked about chastity and His advice

---

[7] *Sant Bani Magazine*, July 1976, p.33

was sound and direct. Basically He said that when you start feeling the
pull toward *kam* [lust] then begin meditating. You have mind on one side
and Satguru on the other. If you divert your attention toward mind, then
you'll be the slave of mind; if you direct it toward the Satguru, then you
can get the Master. Meditation is just like lighting up a light in your
within, and if you are heading toward that light, it will go on increasing.
In the place that is full of light, no thief is going to come. The thief of
kam will not come to you if you are meditating properly. If you are
going to meditate regularly that will bring more love from the Master . . .
where there is kam, the soul comes down into the body, and when there
is anger, the soul spreads out. One who is desirous of lust, anger, greed,
etc. cannot do meditation. MEDITATION IS DONE ONLY BY THE
BRAVE PEOPLE. We have to give our heart to the Master. If you want
to be a true disciple of Master, then be away from this kam. And the way
to be away is through meditation. If you would give two and one half to
three hours in the morning and the same in the evening then you would
be happy and not be having these desires. If you do meditation properly,
you won't lose life fluid in dreams either. If you cannot be stable in this
plane, then what are you going to do in the inner planes, where there are
beautiful fairies and many other distractions?

I had heard my title, "Principal Sahib," a few times when Sant Ji had
been talking to Sardar Rattan Singh and his friends. Later I asked Pappu
what He had been saying. Pappu said that He had introduced Robert as a
teacher and me as a principal. He then told the villagers that nothing
could be gained by reading books, because we had also read the books of
the Master but still we were anxious and eager to have some radiation of
a holy man. He also mentioned that politicians and dignitaries such as
Indira Gandhi were being drawn to this path. Pappu told me that Indira
Gandhi got Naam two months before Master Kirpal left – that Sant Ji
also had said this.

The First Organizational Meeting
in the Room of Sant Ajaib Singh Ji

It is impossible to convey the experience of sitting with Him in the
room where He has been meditating for so long. We were there for an
hour and a half. We began by talking about an organization. Sant Ji had
asked, "What do you need at this end?" and my response was pretty

incoherent. Robert and Wendy were better able to convey some problems and issues we foresaw, besides which Sant Ji divined what we were
after and went into a very long explanation.

Sant Ji said that it was up to us to organize both in the States and
abroad, and that what we did would be of benefit to others coming after.
He said one of us could stay in India and organize. We made some
suggestions and He said to do it anyway we want. The point was He did
not want to be involved in the organization, in the money, or anything
like that. He said that people on the committee should be people we trust.
He spoke of how pained He was that He could not serve us better. He
said that after Russell had left He cried and said to Master that He (Sant
Ji Himself) was such a low and petty man, and He was sad that He could
not serve Russell better because Russell was the man sent by Master. He
spoke of how these villagers are farmers and are inconvenienced by
having to serve us. I asked about Indian laws regarding sending money
from the States. He said He did not know the laws, and that that was up
to us. He also said that, if we wished, He could move to an ashram closer
to a city – it was up to us to arrange things as we saw fit. It later became
clear that the most logical spot was right there, at 77 RB. That was
certainly what the villagers wanted. They had applied for electricity and
had plans for a Satsang Hall and more, so we heartily recommended it to
Him. We said we had a place in the States, Sant Bani Ashram, and He
said that He would come when we arranged it. We knew best about the
climate and other particulars. He said that He could not live with us
because of the language problem. We asked Him to come for a year or
so, and He replied that He would come for four to six months as soon as
we wanted after March 13th, 1977. Wendy suggested March 16th, because
that is her birthday, and Sant Ji laughed a lot.[8]

Sant Ji said the reason He would not initiate Ronnie[9] and Wendy yet
was because then they would want to stay and meditate for a long time,
and the facilities were not there. He said He would initiate in the
presence of Russell. He added that Pappu should also get Naam and be
available to come to the States for translating, if his parents would agree.
I asked him if it would be better to learn Hindi or Punjabi. He responded

---

[8] While we tried to arrange for Sant Ji to come prior to that date, it did not
happen. His first trip to the United States was in the spring of 1977, as He had
suggested it would be.

[9] Ronnie Yow was a member of the group of three who visited Sant Ji in
March of 1976.

that either was fine, as He spoke both. He added that Hindi would be better because it is more universal.

There were some things that were difficult to discern. It was clear that we were disrupting His routine – and thus His life. Ordinarily He was coming out of meditation just once a month, and now we were changing that. He reiterated that He was planning on meditating full time until March 13th of the following year. He explained that many people wanted Him to come here or there. After He had given Naam to more than two hundred souls, however, there had been so much propaganda against Him that He came to this place and resolved to stay hidden for one year. All of that made me feel like we ought to leave Him alone. Then again, I recalled that He had said that Master Kirpal had brought us there. He had told people not to give out the address but they did. It was definitely the Master's plan unfolding.

As He talked He outlined some points for the future. He said that those who come should be prepared to serve themselves, specifically mentioning that people needed to be able to prepare the food. The devotees should come in the middle of the month since that is when He was coming out to give Satsang. People should come in groups. We all wondered if a Jeep would make things much more convenient. Sant Ji said how He was pained that we had to pay the driver forty rupees per day to wait for us. He reiterated that Babu Ji's brother, who lived in nearby Gajsinghpur, had a Jeep, and that we should take the train to that place instead of Ganganagar. Sant Ji also mentioned that the station master there has Naam. We had already met that disciple when we were coming to 77 RB. As we talked more, Sant Ji mentioned that when He had to see the doctor for treatment for His Eyes, He took a camel cart rather than a Jeep so that it would not cost so much. Instead of a one-hour trip it had been a five-hour journey. His humility was overwhelming. He commented that we could have had wonderful accommodations at Sawan Ashram, but instead we were putting up with the inconveniences at 77 RB. This was because we wanted Truth – we wanted the Satguru.

He had given us such overwhelming responsibility for setting up an organization that I was scared. I told Him that sometimes we are given tasks by the Master and then we think those tasks are our own and we go off on our own will. I prayed that He would stop us if we ever did anything against His will. He said that we could check with Him before we made decisions – we could discuss things with Him. He said that starting an organization was hard – but also not hard, because we would get help from the Master.

Sant Ji told us how the villagers here were afraid that we would take Him away to the West. He related that at a very recent satsang of another guru in Ganganagar, Sant Ji had been spoken of in a negative way. The villagers at 77 RB did not like that, and made a joke that "the dogs were barking." Then they made a second joke, and said that those same dogs should be sent to bark in the West, so that we would not want Sant Ji to come there!

Sant Ji told us about a man nearby who had so much love that when the previous party of three came he brought food and other necessary items for their comfort. This turned out to be Sardar Rattan Singh Ji. Last night he again came in his tractor and brought items for us. He knew we were coming due to our cable. Sant Ji explained that Sardar Rattan Singh built a place where Sant Ji meditated the two years prior to Master Kirpal's leaving the body – at the village of 16 PS. He then asked if we would like to visit that spot tomorrow – it is twenty miles away. I asked if He would go also and He laughed and said He would. He is so gracious.

We appeared to be winding up, so I asked if I could say one more thing. He said okay. I wondered, would He be willing to say something, to give some message, for my wife? She was back home doing all the service and I was with Him getting the benefit of His presence. He was thoughtful and then asked, "Is she initiated?" I said that she was. Then He said, "MEDITATE!" and we all laughed uproariously. It was very beautiful. He asked how old my children were, and I said one and six. He held His Hands apart showing the length of a baby. He said, "I have love for your children." He turned to Wendy and said the same. Later He said He would see our children when He came to the Ashram.

At this point I could no longer distinguish as to Whom I was sitting in front of – Ajaib or Kirpal – and it did not matter. I asked Sant Ji if He would visit the Sant Bani School also when He came (after He said He would see our children). He said how could He not come? Heart speaks to heart. How could He refuse our love? He was so sweet about the photos. Earlier I had noticed (after the session in the morning) that I had been waiting to take photos until Sant Ji looked like Master Kirpal through my viewfinder). I thought how insulted I would be if an initiate of Baba Sawan was waiting to snap pictures until Master Kirpal looked like Baba Sawan. I decided simply to take pictures of Sant Ji, realizing that I would not be surprised if He then looked more like Master Kirpal. All I knew was that He certainly did to my physical eyes.

Evening Satsang on Saturday, April 3rd

I taped the Satsang in the evening, and He had me play the tape of the girls singing the devotional songs (*bhajans*). He said the villagers had never heard or seen a tape recorder before. He was laughing throughout. He gently chided one girl for moving closer to the recorder when I played it back.

This Satsang was the beginning of a series of events that amazed me. My receptivity was increasing to such an extent that I became fearful of the effect on my ego. It felt like everything was really clicking. There were so many ideas that I thought of (especially regarding organizational matters) that either Sant Ji asked me about and agreed 100%, or else He said them Himself without my saying anything. For instance, an idea had come to me while Sant Ji had been giving Satsang: since Russell had the Initiation instructions in English from Master Kirpal, and since Russell had been authorized to give Initiation, I wondered if Sant Ji could authorize him to convey the instructions to the hungering souls before Sant Ji came the next year? It was in my mind to ask Him that when, in a long discussion following Satsang, He Himself made the suggestion.

After Satsang we continued sitting in the dining area, enjoying the radiance. Pappu gave Sant Ji the copy of the English translation of His letter back to Russell. While He was looking at it I took a flash photo, and He laughed, and everyone laughed. I said, "For Russell Sahib" and they laughed more and He really, really laughed. He spent such a long time looking at every single word of the letter that it was astounding. When it was time to sign it, Robert got out a pen, but Babu Ji beat him to it. Sant Ji took Babu Ji's pen, worked the cap off, played with it a bit, chose not to use it – and then accepted the pen from Robert. He gave the letter to me to give to Russell.

He asked us how far the School was from the Ashram. We said that it was right on the Ashram. Then He asked how many families were living there and we said six or seven – twenty-seven people in all. He asked if Russell were the leader of the Ashram, and we said yes. I added that Master Kirpal had given that authority, that responsibility, to Russell, but that many times he had tried to give it back to Master. Master had always refused to take it. Sant Ji commented, "Master knows best."

I explained how Russell and Judith had bought the place to be away from crowds and to be in the countryside. They had wished to raise their children in a secluded spot, and now they were surrounded by people and they did not even live in the original Big House. They lived in a little house next door. Sant Ji said, "Russell is a very loving man – he really loves the Master." Then He spoke about how sad He was that when Russell came he only stayed a few hours, due to the Jeep driver. The fellow had to get back that same day. Sant Ji was very disappointed that Russell had not stayed at least a couple of days. He added that the next time Russell came he should visit for a week. He went on to reveal that when Russell came He would initiate those foreigners who accompanied him, and that afterwards Russell would be authorized to give Naam to people back in the States who wanted it. There was my whole idea, the groundwork for what I had thought was "my" scheme, which (of course) was the Master's all along.

I told Sant Ji that in Master Kirpal's lifetime Russell had already been authorized to convey the Naam for Master, and that at Sant Bani we had a copy of the Initiation instructions written in English by Master Kirpal. I wondered if, perhaps . . . well, my hint was clear: could He possibly authorize for Russell to begin right away? Sant Ji thought it was very funny and so did I. I felt like an advocate for those who had not yet received the Naam, and Sant Ji knew exactly what I was trying to do. He lovingly and humorously restated that Russell would be authorized to do this after he came here again. Earlier He had mentioned to us that one problem was that Pappu was not initiated, and therefore some of the translation would be lost. In this session He added that Pappu would have to be initiated very soon.

Sant Ji again stated that Russell would come, and that He would initiate those people who came with him. I remarked that Russell would like to come here soon. He repeated that Russell was a loving man, and added that He would very much like to see him. With a twinkle, He concluded, "Russell said I shouldn't hide myself away, so why is Russell hiding himself away?"

I could not believe that I would continue, but I muttered under my breath, "one step further," and I said, "But Sant Ji, Russell is a very poor man and he has just come to India," implying that it would be difficult to afford a ticket to come back. When Pappu translated, Sant Ji cracked up. He extended His Hand towards me as if to say, "What is this guy trying to pull?" It was very, very funny, and I felt like an intoxicated puppet. He added that when Russell wished to come, the money would be provided. When Russell did come again in May, Sant Ji told him that the reason He was so amused at what I had said, was because the Master within had already informed Sant Ji that Russell would be coming.

I went on to say that Judith, Russell's wife, would very much like to come, as well as his son Eric, adding that Eric was initiated. Sant Ji said that, as He had told us, it was good for groups to come; and they should come in the middle of the month and plan to stay from two to three days to a week. After all this He said, "I think that when Russell hears all I have been saying, he will come very soon," and we all laughed heartily. He said that He was mentioning all of these things about Russell because of our love for Russell – that he had praised us in the letter, saying we were co-workers and dear friends and devoted disciples.

By this time I felt so intoxicated with love and happiness that I did not even know where the floor was anymore. Sant Ji was laughing like anything. He decided to leave, and in a blink He was gone. Everyone – fifty Indians and the four of us – were just sitting and staring at each other. I was laughing, and the tears were rolling down my cheeks. Pappu finally said, "Look, if we don't move all these people will just sit here," – so we got up. After chatting a bit amongst ourselves we returned to the same room – now set up with classic Indian rope beds for the four of us. It had been a full and exhausting day – but in a most wonderful way. We drifted off at once, excited that the next morning we would be arising early to travel with Sant Ji (and many others) in the Jeep.

The Third Day – The Morning of April 4th, Sunday

I woke up at 2:00 a.m. feeling quite sick. It crossed my mind that perhaps it would be better for me to stay here, rest, and recover – and not make the journey to Village 16 PS. And then I realized that I would be better off sick in Sant Ji's presence than sick away from Him. I made the decision to go, took some aspirin, and felt much better at once. At breakfast I ate only fruit.

The Jeep ride was surprisingly pleasant given that there were ten of us in the vehicle. Sant Ji, the driver, Wendy, and Pappu sat in front, while Robert, Babu Ji, Pathi Ji, his daughter, Balwant ("Bant"), his niece, and I squeezed into the back. We navigated through canals, dust, jungle, cities, packs of wild dogs – and made it in an hour and a half. As we approached our destination, we passed the place, specially built for Sant Ji, where He stayed and meditated for two years. Shortly after, we arrived at the house of Sardar Rattan Singh, right in the middle of the simple village called "16 PS."[10]

At Sardar Rattan Singh's home we rested for a bit, and then Sant Ji led us on a walk back to the place where He had meditated a great deal. A few years later Sant Ji would choose this location to be His permanent home, and to develop it as a blessed spot from which many of us derived a great deal of spiritual benefit. At this time, however, there was only a small two-story building that covered the underground room where Sant Ji had done constant devotion. Sant Ji set a very brisk pace for the walk, about half a mile. We had rested, so I was in good shape. As we passed over the plowed fields I had my first experience of walking literally in the Footsteps of the Lord. Although in later years I shied away from doing this (and to this day I cannot say why or why not), I did it then because it came from my heart.

Sant Ji took us down into the room where He had sat for full-time meditation. It was very small and bare except for a wooden bench. He told us that wood was good to sit on for meditation. He also suggested that other Americans would like to visit here.[11] I said I was sure Russell would like to come, especially when he saw our photos. I took a picture of Him on the bench and as He came up the stairs. While we were down there, Robert – who also had felt somewhat ill – became faint and had to go upstairs. When we all came up he was lying in a room, being massaged by several of Sardar Rattan Singh's sons. Sant Ji looked on and I snapped a photo – much to the mirth of everyone.

The door to the underground room was locked again; and we went upstairs and sat in the room where Sant Ji had lived when He was not meditating. He pointed out that He had left everything behind, even the utensils. During the three-hour session that followed He told many funny stories, related incidents about His early life, and wove much gentle instruction into the conversation.

---

[10] The names of the villages are apparently based on the number of the canal that brings water to these otherwise arid parts of Rajasthan.

[11] While the next group in May did visit the Underground Room, the trips to 16 PS stopped after that. From what Sant Ji had said, I had assumed that each group would get to see it, but that did not seem to be happening. In 1981 Sant Ji relocated the Ashram from 77 RB to 16 PS, and stepping down to see that sacred spot at the end of the ten days of devotion became a high point for devotees from so many countries, including America.

Sant Ji said that His parents had died around the time of His birth.[12] He was an orphan and his great-aunt and uncle in town took Him in and raised Him as their own. He lived with them until He was twenty. His great-aunt asked Sant Ji to accept all of the lands and estate when she passed on, but He refused. He was asked to select someone to inherit everything, so He chose someone else to be the heir.

At some point before He left his "parents," they took Him to meet His first Master, Baba Bishan Dass.[13] The Master of Baba Bishan Dass was named Amoluk Dass and he had only two initiates: Baba Bishan Dass and Prince Bhupinder of Patiala State. Baba Bishan Dass, on the other hand, had only one initiate: Sant Ajaib Singh Ji. Baba Bishan Dass gave Him the first Two Charged Names and Sound instruction in the Path of True Devotion. When I questioned Sant Ji about some dates, as I wanted to be accurate in my reporting, He told me that He had no head for dates.

Sant Ji told us that Baba Bishan Dass once showed Him the spot of His (Ajaib's) cremation in His last life. Sant Ji asked how He could be sure that was the right spot, and Baba Bishan Dass told Him, "Dig and you will find the bones." Sant Ji paid ten rupees for the digging and found the bones[14] at quite a deep level.

Baba Bishan Dass told Sant Ji that He owed something to a woman in Sant Ji's hometown, and so Sant Ji served her for three years, from the age of seventeen to twenty. She was a wealthy lady, who owned many horses, ponies, and carts, but Sant Ji always carried heavy loads on His head instead of using the wagons. People wondered why He did this. Once a sadhu came through, and he could see that it was not really Sant Ji who was carrying the load – that this was payment of His debt and that God was helping.

Sant Ji told a story of a low woman who lived in the same town as Baba Bishan Dass. She was desirous of Sant Ji, and offered forty rupees to have Him, using another man as a go-between. A few days later the woman suffered a serious injury. The go-between became quite critical of Sant Ji and abused Him verbally – and subsequently lost all his

---

[12] See "A Brief Life Sketch of Sant Ajaib Singh" published as a separate booklet by Sant Bani Ashram and as part of the September 1981, *Sant Bani Magazine*.

[13] See the February 1980 issue of *Sant Bani Magazine*, pp. 23-24.

[14] Small pieces of bone – known as "flowers" in India – remain mixed in with the ashes after cremation.

property and wealth. Sant Ji said He saw that man after twenty years, and that the poor fellow was sorrowful and repentant. At this moment Sant Ji reminded us that it is very important not to criticize and abuse others – and asked us to give that message to Russell regarding the contents of whatever might be published in future magazines.

When Master Kirpal abandoned His physical body, Sant Ji left 16 PS and went to the village at 77 RB. He was weeping all the time. A disciple from the West came and met Him – and then Sant Ji left that place too, crying all the while. He wandered around in a disheveled state with no shoes and no turban, at times dressed only in a simple cloth wrap. It was at that time that Sant Ji's eyes were affected.

A Sub-divisional Officer (SDO) and another person found Him, and gave Him a room in a rest house. The villagers at 77 RB missed Him very much, so Pathi Ji went looking for Him and finally found Him after much travail.[15] It was very hard for Pathi Ji to get the SDO to give out much information about Sant Ji, but at last Pathi Ji found Him. Sant Ji returned to 77 RB where the villagers had built Him the compound that

---

[15] Pathi Ji's story is recounted by Mr. Oberoi in *Support for the Shaken Sangat*:

> It was at that place that Mr. Gurdev Singh, known as Pathi Ji, later found Him, after waiting at 77RB for His return for a long time. Having no news about Him he was compelled by his inner self to search for Him, and not come home until He was found.
> Pathi Ji recalled to me the tremendous difficulties he had to face, because Sant Ji had left no hint of where He was going. Where to search in the vast land was a big problem, but the inner power which impelled him to go, helped him and gave him confidence that his efforts would succeed. Accordingly, when Pathi Ji was led to the place by the inner power, Sant Ji expressed much surprise to find him there, and said that He had had a dream a day before, finding that the Sangat at 77RB was building a place for Him and were doing good seva, but were quarreling among themselves at times. This was exactly what had happened sometime before Pathi Ji had set out. Pathi Ji told me that after seeing Him, Sant Ji told him to go away, as He was absolutely unwilling to go there; but when Pathi Ji told Him that the entire Sangat was weeping due to His absence, and passing a difficult time, and would not bother Him at all if He returned there, Sant Ji relented, agreed to go and told Pathi Ji to go back and that He would come there Himself, indicating the date and approximate time when He should reach them. True to His word, Sant Ji arrived there while the Sangat was sitting together and waiting anxiously for Him, and He gave a Satsang immediately on arrival. (pp. 291-92)

we were staying in. And then Russell came to 77 RB. Sant Ji also mentioned that Master Kirpal had given Him the order to meditate full time for nine years.

Sant Ji referred again to the Western disciple who had first met Him, saying that he was a strong man. Sant Ji laughed as He told how that person had been ready to walk from Sri Ganganagar if he had had to. Sant Ji said that Master Kirpal had told that man from within that the Successor would be a bachelor, and so the disciple asked Sant Ji if He were married. Sant Ji continued, stating that Russell and that fellow had been brave to endure all of the hardships they encountered in their quest to find Sant Ji. Everyone laughed as Sant Ji related that when Russell had finally arrived with Kulwant and Linda, Kulwant, in confusion, had introduced Linda as Russell's wife, rather than his own.

Sant Ji proceeded to relate several hilarious stories about one of the sons of Sardar Rattan Singh who was present in the room. This son, Sathi, was a very handsome, tall, clean-shaven fellow. Sant Ji told us how Sathi really liked to sleep. Once a sadhu came through and Sathi and the sadhu had a sleeping contest. Sardar Rattan Singh's son was the winner after sleeping for two days straight. With a great deal of laughter and much good will flowing from the crowd seated on the floor, Sant Ji explained that much Master Power had been "wasted" in bringing Sathi to the Path – but that now he had served very devotedly for eight or nine years. He also told how Sathi had entered the Gurdwara twice with no head covering, and would only leave and get something for his head after Sant Ji ordered him to. Sant Ji then told us that when Sathi would come to visit Him, if the tractor were having mechanical trouble, Sathi would use the Master Power to make it go. Sant Ji concluded, "It is true – you ask him." We turned and looked at Sathi – who just grinned sheepishly and nodded his head.

It was some of the devotees gathered here who had been at Sri Ganganagar when the followers of another guru had criticized Sant Ji. The story was told again about the "barking dogs," and how they should be sent to the West so we would not want Sant Ji to come. It was stated that it is the nature of dogs to bark. I quoted, "A tree is known by the fruit it bears," and people were quick to point out that the abuse toward Sant Ji came before that guru had arrived. These people had a good deal of love and respect for the guru himself, so my comment was ill-timed to say the least. Sant Ji commented that if a man owns a dog, and the dog goes mad, then the owner is blamed.

Sant Ji told the story of the merchant, Makhan Shah, and Guru Teg

Bahadur (1621-1675), the ninth Guru in the Sikh line. Once Makhan Shah was on a ship that was caught in a fierce storm. The merchant promised God that he would give the living Saint a lot of gold coins if only his life would be spared – which it was. Later Makhan Shah went to see all of the so-called successors and finally came to Guru Teg Bahadur, the True One. After the merchant gave Him only one coin, the Guru showed him the scars on His back and asked for the balance promised – only to show Makhan Shah Who He really was.

I mentioned to Sant Ji that Russell had used this story quite recently as a means of encouraging hope. Then Wendy related the story of Russell's return from meeting Sant Ji. She said that Russell spoke of the trip in the evening and again the next day at Satsang, and how inspiring it had been for all of us. Sant Ji, referring to these statements, added that Russell should not be afraid to speak the truth as he sees it.

Sant Ji said that He was going to send a quotation to Russell from Mr. H. Chadda Sahib's book *Pita Poot* (*Father/Son*) that explained how the Guru Power could not come to the physical sons through the means of instruments like wills. He suggested that this would help in the article Russell was to write for the magazine *Sat Sandesh* – or for a separate article if that were how it was going to be published. At this point I mentioned how confusing it could be – that I had heard that at least two of the other so-called successors were giving experiences at initiation. Sant Ji's response was quite strong: "Don't believe what you hear from others – see for yourself." He said that Akbar once asked Birbal to define the difference between truth and untruth, and Birbal said it is the difference between eyes and ears. What you see you may accept as true; what you hear as untrue. He added, "If you see any truth here, you may speak about it. It is a service to the Master to continue this work." He concluded that we should not worry about what we hear, but ignore it.

I began to wonder if I should or should not visit Sawan Ashram on my return to Delhi. I decided not to ask Him, but He turned to me and said, "Do you have a question?" I told Him I had wished to see the fellow disciples of Master Kirpal who lived at Sawan Ashram, and with whom I had become friendly in 1974, while not mentioning that Pappu and I had already attempted to visit. Sant Ji told me that I could go to see them if I liked. This advice would change by the end of the trip based on a number of dynamics that unfolded, including a vivid dream I had early the next morning.

Sant Ji told another story about the Sub-divisional Officer. The SDO and Sant Ji were together, when a petty town official confronted them. He wanted Sant Ji to admit that "Radhasoami" was the highest name of God. Sant Ji was silent, but the SDO got "vibrations" from Him, and spoke for Him. Sant Ji said it was the same for Russell – if he feels moved to speak for Sant Ji, it is the Master Power working. He also said again that He would begin to initiate the hungry souls when Russell came. He added that those coming should not worry about the heat in May – that it would be all right to come whenever they could.

Sant Ji then asked if we liked mangoes and we were very enthusiastic. He said He would send some to Sant Bani when they were in season. I told the story (prefacing it by saying I had no idea if it were true or not) of Master Kirpal, Bibi Hardevi (Tai Ji) and the mangoes. I had heard that Master once took some mangoes from a fruit bowl Tai Ji had set out on a table for dignitaries. He proceeded to poke a small hole in each, suck out the juice, blow it back up, and replace it in the fruit bowl. Sant Ji said simply that eating mangoes in that manner was a common occurrence, and then He added that Master Kirpal had resurrected the mangoes. He said, "I also was a dead body until Master breathed life into me." He stated again, as He said often, that He was, "the sweeper of the dust of the Sangat's feet."

He talked in some detail about His trip to Sawan Ashram after Master left the Body. He mentioned that Chadda Sahib took Him in and gave Him some fruit and the book, *Pita Poot*.[16] He spoke about how He was mistreated at the Master's physical place. He wished to speak with people there, but He was told everyone was meditating. He sat outside the place of meditation, and He could hear people talking – while others came and went. Finally, He asked what kind of meditation were these disciples doing, that He could hear them talking all the time? After three hours, someone came out and asked Him to leave. At that time He was crying constantly. He went to a Gurdwara near the Red Fort. The priests there thought He was very holy and asked why He was weeping, and He answered that He was remembering the saints. He left and was taken in by someone for a time, and then He went back to 77 RB.

At this point Sant Ji mentioned that He always ate with Master Kirpal when They were together. On one of those occasions Master asked His age, but Sant Ji was afraid to answer because He knew that

---

[16] It was Mr. H. Chadda Sahib who recognized in Sant Ji's eyes the eyes of Beloved Master Kirpal when Sant Ji came to Sawan Ashram (see A. S. Oberoi's *Support for the Shaken Sangat*, p. 288).

there was a profound meaning to a Saint asking someone's age. Master Kirpal laughed and said, "Why are you afraid of my asking when people will be coming from America who will ask?" And in the March group a visitor had asked His age! When Master Kirpal told Sant Ji that He would have to do the spiritual work, Sant Ji replied that He was afraid. He did not want the abuse that He would receive at the hands of the disciples of the various so-called "successors." Master Kirpal embraced Him and said, "If a bad man will not leave off his bad habits, why should a good man leave off his good habits?" Tai Ji, the devoted disciple of Master Kirpal, told Sant Ji at that time that He must do this work so that others coming after would benefit.[17]

I mentioned that Mildred Meeh, a devoted teacher in the Sant Bani School, had had a dream of Sant Ji in which He said, "I don't like crowds." He responded by stating, "It is true." He also said that if dreams and visions are coming in the West, then it is the Master Power sending them. Referring back to the first long session we had with Him, He reminded us that to be protected from *kam* [lust] we should run behind the Master in meditation.

We left that blessed room, went downstairs and strolled out into the garden where Sant Ji pointed out the grove of mango trees – after which we headed back to Sardar Rattan Singh's house. On the way a disciple stopped in his Jeep and asked if Sant Ji wanted a lift, but He declined the offer. As we walked on Sant Ji made a joke, threw back His head, clapped His hands together, and roared with laughter.

We arrived back at the house at 7:15 p.m., and evening Satsang was scheduled for 8:00. I was dead tired and glad for the chance to rest. I had just fallen asleep when several people came into the room and said that Sant Ji had sent them because "Principal Sahib" should also have a rubdown like Robert had received. So I got a much-appreciated massage. At Satsang we sat right in front of Him, and I was so tired that I nodded off two or three times with my knees tucked up under my chin. I would snap awake and He would be looking at me with the gentlest, most loving smile in the world – that of a father to his toddler son.

During the Satsang, given in Punjabi with no translation, I had heard the terms *"Sardar," "Sat Sri Akaal," "Musalman,"* and *"Salaam-Sal-*

---

[17] In the summer of 1976 Tai Ji asked Sant Ji to please come to Sawan Ashram. Earlier she had asked Sant Ji if He were aware how much loss the Sangat had suffered by Sant Ji's not visiting Sawan Ashram? (See A. S. Oberoi's *Support for the Shaken Sangat*, p. 281).

aam," repeated several times, so I asked Pappu about it before we went to sleep. He said Sant Ji had told a story of the meeting between a Sikh and a Musalman. To greet each other the Sikh said, *"Sat Sri Akaal,"* but the Musalman said, *"Salaam-Salaam."* The Musalman insisted that the Sikh use "Salaam," and stated that he was superior. The Sikh asked in what way, and the Musalman said that his blood was made of milk. The Sikh invited him to get down off his camel to see if that were true, and proceeded to deliver a beating until the blood of the Musalman ran freely. It was not made of milk!

Again it was a very full day, and we went to bed quite exhausted.

The Fourth Day – Monday, April 5th

I awoke and meditated alertly from 4:30 to 6:30 a.m. – and then lay back on my bed and fell asleep. I had the following dream: We arrived back at 77 RB to find that a VW Bus had come while we were gone. Several people – some of whom I knew and others I did not – had come to the compound in it. Things were very confusing, as these people were making many demands on the villagers. In the dream I immediately felt the need of the kind of organization we had been talking about with Sant Ji in His room. Then the dream shifted and I was coming into the Doon Valley near the city of Dehradun – looking for the water tower that was the most visible edifice of Master Kirpal's divine project, Manav Kendra.[18] Instead I saw smog. I asked where the tower was, and people told me "right there" in the middle of the smog. Finally I saw the once brilliant tower – now faded and gray. I asked to see Miss Sati (a good friend – the principal of Master Kirpal's School, Manav Vidya Mandir) and was met with resistance from two big clean-shaven men who did not wear turbans. They began to put pressure on me verbally to accept another person as the "true" successor, and then, because I insisted only on seeing Miss Sati, they each grabbed an arm and began to twist them

---

[18] Manav Kendra was a service project begun in the twilight years of Master Kirpal's mission. Located in the Doon Valley (with the Himalayan Mountains as a backdrop), it was a model community that included a beautiful reflecting pool to inspire meditation, a residence for the elderly, a school for the young, a library with literature from all of the world's religions, a medical center, and a working farm where the animals were treated with kindness.

up behind my back. At this point I awoke. It was all quite vivid, and I related it in detail to Robert and Wendy.

After breakfast we began a day of many visits to nearby houses, with tea and Satsangs at each. From Sardar Rattan Singh's house, we first headed to the home of a retired police inspector, Mr. Khushi Ram. The itinerary included stops at the houses of Khushi Ram, Chiman Lal, and various other relatives of Sardar Rattan Singh. It had rained during the night, which was wonderful as it kept the dust down. Sant Ji said Master was celebrating our coming with rain.

I took the usual group photos at Sardar Rattan Singh's house and then a picture of the group around the Jeep. We left and started down the road – once again heading past "Sant Ji's Place." The Jeep had no rearview mirror and no outside mirrors either. Suddenly Sant Ji spoke briefly and the people in back with me turned, and looked down the road from where we had just come. Pathi Ji and his daughter began to speak loudly to the driver, who stopped the Jeep. As he began to back up, I saw two boys running after the Jeep. It occurred to me that Sant Ji had been the first to speak, and that was while He was looking straight ahead, so I asked Pappu what it was that Sant Ji had said. He had stated, "There are two boys running after the Jeep and we should stop and give them a ride."

It was only a few minutes later that I told Sant Ji about the pond at Sant Bani Ashram – how Master Kirpal had said in 1972 that we should develop the pond more, and then in 1974, He had explained that He meant we should make it bigger and deeper. He added that we "might find a spring there." When I told Sant Ji we had indeed found a spring, He replied that Saints know everything, but it is very rare that They reveal it. I realized that He had just given us a glimpse of His omniscience in stopping the Jeep to give the boys a ride. When we drew abreast of His place, He asked me if I had taken a picture of it. I had not, so we stopped and I snapped a lovely photo.

As we drove on, Sant Ji told us many more things about His life. After He mentioned that He had performed the austerity of sitting in the five fires – of sitting in a ring of four fires while the summer sun beat down overhead – I remarked that it reminded me of the story of Baba Kahan as related by Master Kirpal. I told the story Master Kirpal told about sending His brother, and then a friend, to see the ascetic, Baba Kahan. Baba Kahan abused the friend, hit him, even struck him with burning wood, but the fellow would not leave. Finally Baba Kahan asked, "What do you want?" and then Baba Kahan "made him to hear the Sound Current."[19] I mentioned that Master Kirpal kept a picture of Baba Kahan at His house on 207 Rajpur Road, Dehradun, and also that Master had said Baba Kahan was "a hard nut to crack." Sant Ji told us more of His experiences with Baba Bishan Dass.

He said that once He came to Bishan Dass with His beard tied up (as had become the fashionable style with Sikh gentlemen). Bishan Dass grabbed His beard and yanked it down, and then slapped Him twice in the face. Still, He always loved Baba Bishan Dass for making His life. Baba Bishan Dass told Him: "I was a hard nut to crack, but you were harder because you cracked me!" Sant Ji mentioned that He would spend ten months out of the year in the army, and two months with Baba Bishan Dass. Sant Ji gave all His pay to Bishan Dass, and with that money the latter built an ashram. Baba Bishan Das would not even allow Sant Ji to see the ashram Sant Ji had paid for, lest He think of it as His own. People called Sant Ji "mad" and laughed at the way He was treated by Baba Bishan Dass. There was always an old man outside Baba Bishan Dass's place, however, and that man would sing a verse about the diamond hidden within each of us. This gave Sant Ji the inspiration to continue coming to Baba Bishan Dass to find that precious wealth. As He had said, it was Baba Bishan Dass Who gave Him Initiation into the first Two Sacred Words, and had formed the basis for His spiritual life.

Finally Baba Bishan Dass told Sant Ji that He should stay at His own home and He would get the rest (of the Initiation) there. As Sant Ji did His devotional practices, the inner divine and Radiant Form of beloved Soami Ji began to come to Him in meditation. After some time, Soami Ji's Hair grew long and He became Master Kirpal. At some point Master Kirpal within embraced Sant Ji, and said He would come to see Sant Ji outwardly the next day, which He did. Master Kirpal came all alone to see Sant Ji. I asked Sant Ji when it was that this had happened. After giving it some thought, He said He could not remember, but that it was written down back at 77 RB, and added it was sometime before the Third World Tour (1972).

Sant Ji said that Master had been very specific that He would be working with Russell – to the extent that He had had Russell's name written on a piece of paper before He ever met Russell. I was scribbling in my notebook as we bounced along in the Jeep. At one point I jokingly

---

[19] From Master Kirpal Singh's talk, "How I Met My Master." See *Support for the Shaken Sangat*, pp. 97-98 for a transcript of the relevant section.

asked Pappu to tell Sant Ji that He should take care of what He said, because I was writing the book of His life, and He laughed heartily. He added that it was too bad there wasn't a camera when Master Kirpal had come to Him, because then we could see pictures of the meetings.[20] He laughed again, and repeated that, like a madman, He had no head for dates.

He mentioned that He had built a three-story ashram under Baba Bishan Dass' orders, and that an old friend and associate of Sant Ji's, Bachan Singh, had tried to break it down so people would not say that Sant Ji was mad. They began to say He was really crazy after Master Kirpal came. People verbally tried to force him to, "Leave that Kirpal!" With much amusement Sant Ji told us that He had said to Bachan Singh, "If I were to give you only 1% of the kind of treatment I got from Baba Bishan Dass, you would have left me by now!" He then added that it was all the blessing of the Master that we had arrived there.

The last account I remember from the short Jeep ride over to Khushi Ram's house was a "ghost" story. At one place Sant Ji had been staying, He began to be disturbed by people, especially women, who fussed over Him because He had no mother, father, children, etc. He went off to meditate in a graveyard. One girl came along and saw Sant Ji sitting still – not moving. She thought He was a ghost, and ran away.

Khushi Ram came in a car to meet the Jeep and we followed him to his home at PS 22, Post Office Raisinghnagar. When we arrived at the house I had the most incredible tea of my life. The table before us was heaped with plates of cashews, golden raisins, orange sections, biscuits, cookies, and diamond-like rock candy. Khushi Ram's sons and daughters waited on us hand and foot, twirling cloth fly-flickers and pouring tea. Sant Ji kept passing plates back and forth to Robert, Wendy, and me. At one point it crossed my mind to ask Him for extra rock candy for my family, but Wendy had the same thought and asked before me. He said that He already had some for our families back at 77 RB. After tea we posed for several group photos and then had a short Satsang. While we waited for our Jeep driver to return from getting his hair cut, we were introduced to more of Sardar Rattan Singh's extended family. They had climbed on the tractor and followed us over to Khushi Ram's house.

---

[20] At least two photographs exist of Master Kirpal and Sant Ji together. One was (apparently) taken at Kunichuk Ashram in 1972, and the other at an apothecary shop in Sri Ganganagar – see the first issue of *Sant Bani Magazine*, July 1976, p.11, and the cover of the November 1976, *Sant Bani Magazine*.

Wendy and I felt immediately close to a woman named Gangi, who was the sister of Sardar Rattan Singh. We had fun introducing ourselves, and making small talk that was less than intelligible.

Before we left, there was a joke about Khushi Ram and his wife. "Khushi" means "happy" and his wife's name also meant "happy" – so they were referred to as double happiness. Khushi Ram, an initiate of Sant Ji's for a few months only, certainly was a happy man.

The next stop was at Chiman Lal's house, in a small town. We had a Satsang in a room there. These Satsangs would always begin with Bant and her cousin singing a few bhajans, and then Pathi Ji would chant. Afterwards we were led back into a very small room where the five of us (Sant Ji, Pappu, Robert, Wendy and me) were served tea and assorted condiments. As I had been ill the day before I was trying to eat less, but at each stop we were offered so much food, and Pappu had indicated that it was best if we took at least something when served. At Chiman Lal's I ate what I could, but knew I should not have even one more bite. Wendy took the rest from me and split it with Pappu so that we would not leave any – and perhaps offend the gracious hosts. I was mildly concerned and said to Sant Ji that now I would be in Pappu and Wendy's debt. I told Him that I was afraid to eat more because I had been sick, but that now I felt like a new man. He told me very directly, "Eat less!"

The host brought Sant Ji His tea in a metal container with a graceful neck – the cover of which Sant Ji inverted to use as His cup. He poured His own tea, and laughingly asked if we would serve Him tea in a container like this at Sant Bani? I said that yes, we would. I made a note to buy one in Delhi (later, at 77 RB, the subject came up again and He told me not to buy one for Him). There was a small fan blowing on us in this room. Something caused me to relate to Sant Ji the story of Russell's telegram: how we (the Ashramites) were all anxious to hear from Russell and then the cable came: "HAVE FOUND AJAIB SINGH – HE IS REAL – WE LOVE HIM." I said we were dancing all around. Sant Ji responded, "That place (Sant Bani) is the Master's base" and then He added, "Russell didn't find Ajaib, he found Master."

We left and went to at least two more places, both of them connected to Sardar Rattan Singh. The latter was very poor before coming into contact with Sant Ji, but had prospered since. The first place was a quick stop – for a darshan only. Toasted cardamom seeds were passed around as *parshad*,[21] and while Sant Ji ate His seeds, Robert and I pocketed ours due to the state of our stomachs. On our way out I muttered something about how I thought cardamom might be a stimulant, and Robert said, "Sant Ji is probably giving us just what we need." We made our last stop (to see Sardar Rattan Singh's brother-in-law), and Satsang was held in a small room where Sant Ji sat on a beautifully draped sofa. I was sitting in a chair at the back of the room, and again began to feel my eyelids droop. Suddenly Robert's comment about the cardamom came back to me, and I ate a seed, shell and all. I was wide-awake for the rest of the Satsang.

After Satsang we went out onto a terrace where dinner was soon to be served. I saw Gangi (Sardar Rattan Singh's sister) and greeted her by name. Sant Ji really cracked up, and repeated her name several times. I had placed the accent on the wrong syllable, and He said it to her my way.[22] It was at this moment, with my heart full of love, that I said to Sant Ji, "I heard that You are wearing a colored turban so that You don't look so much like Master Kirpal, but for me it doesn't work." He laughed and said, "I tried to hide myself, but if the Master within is directing you, I cannot hide away."

This last stop was special for all of us because here we were allowed to serve the dinner to those who had been serving us. We took a tearful leave of Sardar Rattan Singh and his loving family. It was dark as the Jeep pulled away, about 8:45 p.m. on Monday, April 5th – the fourth day of our stay. The ride home was quiet, with the two girls singing occasional snatches of bhajans. We arrived back at 10:15 p.m. – which meant that we had been in His Presence for twelve straight hours. Amazingly enough, there were still another four hours to go.

We pulled into the compound at 77 RB and I was astounded to see, illumined by the headlights, several disciples of Master Kirpal from Delhi, – all of whom had been promoting the physical son of Master Kirpal, Sardar Darshan Singh, as the next Guru. Robert, who was sitting

---

[21] *Parshad* is anything that has been blessed by the Guru, and thus carries a special Grace, or charging. The Guru may choose to distribute *parshad* to the disciples in a variety of ways, including (and perhaps most often) in edible form, as here. The genesis of *parshad* lies in the Godman's sharing excess food with His/Her disciples.

[22] Later, at 77 RB, He taught me the proper way to say it – much to the amusement of the Sangat: Sant Ji: Gan—gí . . . Me: Gan'-gi . . . Sant Ji: Gan—gíí . . . Me: Gan—gíí and there was much laughter for all.

on the other side of the Jeep, said, "Look! There is Charles Feinman."
Charles was a disciple of Master Kirpal who lived near Sant Bani and
whose son attended the Sant Bani School. I had been aware when I left
New Hampshire that Charles had had an idea to come to India to unite all
of Master Kirpal's scattered disciples, and I wondered if that was what
was happening. I jumped to the conclusion that Charles had brought
these people with him from Delhi. I soon discovered that I was wrong,
and felt relieved to find that Charles had arrived on his own.

The Delhi visitors were a distinguished group, including a Western
disciple and two Indians who had been prominent during the Unity of
Man Conference in Delhi back in February of 1974. I was acquainted
with all of these people. Along with them were a woman, and an elderly
satsangi, both from Sri Ganganagar, and both of whom I did not know.
So the first part of my dream – the unexpected arrival of a group of
people, some of whom I knew and others whom I did not, had come true
– even if they had not arrived in a VW bus!

The contingent from Delhi had come early in the morning and spent
the day talking to the villagers about the various successors in relation to
Sant Ji. Sant Ji later told us these villagers knew nothing of all this
controversy. The woman, who knew Sant Ji well, had questioned the
villagers closely, asking in Whose Name was Sant Ji giving Naam
(Initiation). Bachan Singh, the devoted *sevadar*, knew that this woman
had been present when Master Kirpal had authorized Sant Ji to give the
Naam. When Bachan Singh asked her if her memory was so short that
she could not recall the order Sant Ji received from Master Kirpal, she
kept quiet.

The villagers had gathered in the room where Satsang was held (and
where we previously had slept and dined) and we all followed. Sant Ji
told me to sit right beside Him. He excused Himself and was gone with
the woman for half an hour. During this time the villagers were chanting
bhajans. When Sant Ji came back, a long discussion ensued. He was
silent throughout much of it, as the woman talked about Him. I could
feel in my heart that Sant Ji was being criticized, and it was so painful
that the tears began to stream down my cheeks. Sant Ji kept His eyes
closed, but would nod now and then as she spoke. After a while, my pain
was lifted and I began to bathe in the knowledge that the Satguru knew
all. Shortly after this I was certain that I was supposed to move. My role
in the drama had changed, so I moved to the back of the room and sat in
a chair. I found my notebook in hand, and at that moment the Westerner
began to ask his questions.

The first was what could Sant Ji recommend to "heal the artificial split in the Sangat." Sant Ji said He was not aware enough of the goings-on to comment on that. The fellow said that there was a group in the West that was trying to use Sant Ji to create a faction. Sant Ji asked him to explain, and the man said that there were hopes in the West that there will be a new Satguru – and the hope was that Sant Ji would be it. The Westerner asked, "Is Sant Ji aware that they are using Him as an instrument to create a split?" Sant said that He was keeping off both tracks – staying away from being pushed in the West or the East. In His response He made reference to a critical letter from a disciple in America that had been translated into Hindi and circulated in India.

At the mention of this letter, the visitors took the opportunity to blame Russell Perkins for the current state of the divided Sangat. They pointed out that the letter had been critical of Russell, not of Sant Ji. The letter took Russell to task for leaving out what was referred to as "an admittedly weak part of Sant Ji's story: that He had not visited Sawan Ashram during Master Kirpal's lifetime." Thus, they explained, the letter was critical of Russell, not of Sant Ji. Sant Ji politely disagreed. The Delhi people asked to see Sant Ji's copy of that particular letter, so He sent someone to get it. The result was delightful from my perspective, because when the person returned and handed the envelope to Sant Ji, there was no letter inside! Sant Ji played with the envelope for the next fifteen minutes or so, occasionally looking inside as if to see whether the letter had rematerialized.

One of the visitors started to ask another question, but by this time it was past midnight. Sant Ji asked all of the villagers to retire. The rest of us settled in for another two hours of talk. I had initially thought that I was not supposed to be taping, but at one point I changed my mind. I turned on the machine for fifteen minutes. Then I pressed the "STOP" button – as I was positive that there was no need to tape. In the morning the fifteen minutes I had recorded were blank.

Sant Ji had mentioned His trip to Sawan Ashram after Master Kirpal left the Body. The Delhi people were criticizing those currently in power at Sawan Ashram, and Sant Ji told them that He was very sorry when He heard that someone else was now at Sawan Ashram. He said that the rightful person to be at the head of Master's place was Master Kirpal's son, Sardar Darshan Singh.

At some point it came up that Sant Ji had given Initiation – and there was some confusion here. It was not clear if this was a reference to the

200 or so people that Sant Ji initiated a few months earlier, or to the souls Sant Ji had brought into Sant Mat during Master Kirpal's life-time.[23] At any rate the Westerner got very excited and demanded to know in Whose Name Sant Ji had done this since, according to him, Master Kirpal delegated that authority in the West only, and not in India. When the fellow found it was by Master Kirpal's authorization, he be-came frantic to know if Russell knew this, because, from his viewpoint, "Russell is obviously waiting for the moment to announce that Sant Ji is the Guru." Sant Ji said He could not recollect whether He had told Russell this or not.

The Western visitor also added the comment that people noticed that Russell had become more humble and careful since he got back from his visit to 77 RB. Sant Ji explained that He had told Russell not to publish critical comments, and that Russell had written a letter of apology. He told how He had mistakenly thought Russell wrote a letter that was quite critical in tone, and had taken him to task for backbiting. The visitors received this with uproarious laughter. Sant Ji said He had apologized to Russell when He came to know that Russell did not write that letter.[24] Sant Ji then asked, "When the author of that letter was talking about me, you didn't come to me to stop him; so if Russell is talking about me, why do you come to me to stop Russell?" There was no reply.

There was more talk coupled with much laughter, and their opinion of Sant Ji seemed to change. The elder Indians were becoming quite jolly in His presence. One of them tried to lean forward to touch Sant Ji's extended Feet, but His Feet moved like lightening, and the man missed. Several times I thought, "Satguru is the conductor" and smiled with happiness – and then Sant Ji would look across the room to me and break into a broad smile.[25]

---

[23] Sant Ji had, in fact, given the holy instructions for Initiation to a group in the presence of Master Kirpal in 1972. See A.S. Oberoi, *Support for the Shaken Sangat*, p 281: " . . . in 1972, when Supreme Father Kirpal had visited his [Sant Ji's] place, [and] made him initiate fifty persons in His presence, and ordered him to distribute the Truth, and also manage Sawan Ashram. And he [Sant Ji] had replied, 'I want you, not Ashrams and Deras. If You are not happy at Sawan Ashram, how can I be?' . . . After hearing him [Sant Ji], Hazur Maharaj Ji [Master Kirpal] had kept reserved and not said a word."

[24] *Sant Bani Magazine*, July 1976, p.16-17; *Impact of a Saint*, p. 161

[25] Twenty-five years later, Wendy Schongalla, a participant in the drama, observed, "When we were babies or young children, we bonded with our parents unconsciously – it just happened. But seated in that room with Sant Ji, we were

The session broke up in the wee hours – about 2:15 a.m. – but I was wide-awake. Pappu came over to me and expressed concern as to whether he would still get initiated the next day. Sant Ji had said that would happen, but Pappu thought the presence of unexpected visitors might interfere. I said, "Don't worry – you'll get It!" and at the exact moment I completed my sentence, we both heard Sant Ji call, "Pappu" on His way out the door. Pappu ran after Him – after a quick look at me. Our smiling faces reflected our love for each other and for Him! In half an hour Pappu returned, and was quite happy that Sant Ji had said he would receive Naam as planned. We retired grinning from ear to ear.

The Fifth Day – Thursday, April 6th

The next day the group from Delhi went to Sant Ji's room for an hour and taped a message from Him about Master Kirpal for a memorial book to be published in Hindi. The Western disciple asked that I convey his love to the Perkins Family, with a comment that Russell seems more willing to work together now. He went on to say that all we need to do is sit together in love. He then offered to do whatever he could to help unite us all – and I responded cautiously that we were all very busy. He threw his arm around Sant Ji, and said, "*Prem, prem, prem* [Love, love, love]." They took a bus from somewhere within walking distance and were gone by 8:30 a.m.

Pappu got the full Initiation soon after the visitors left. He was with Sant Ji – all alone – from 9 to 11:30 a.m. He floated back, bringing many oranges as parshad for all of us. He commented that Sant Ji had given him very much wealth. Pappu later told me that Sant Ji treated him like a son at the Initiation. He added, "I got some glimpse from Sant Ji that I am supposed to stay here and share in the life of these villagers." Sant Ji told him to learn how to drive. He asked Pappu to get a book of bhajans, and to learn to chant for the trip to the West.

Pappu and I went for a long walk, and our excitement grew as we anticipated another session with Sant Ji. Robert, Wendy, and I were to see Him again that afternoon. I had composed a letter to Sant Ji about the schedule Master Kirpal had used at Sawan Ashram, and we were intend-

---

able to experience the events of that trust-building <u>consciously</u>, which was such a great joy and comfort." From a personal conversation with the author, March 4th, 2001.

ing to go over that. Further, Pappu and I had discussed several more ideas that we wanted to talk over with Him. Specifically we wondered if any arrangements for future trips should be handled through Russell for now, and if Pappu should be the middleman for all correspondence. With those things in mind, we went to His room at 3:00 p.m. and spent the next four hours with Him. During that time we covered an amazing range of subjects.

I read the letter I had composed to Him – the text of which had flowed out of me at Sardar Rattan Singh's house. It had to do primarily with a schedule for meditations, food, and the times of meals. It was offered only as a description of how Sawan Ashram functioned for Western guests, and was in no way critical of 77 RB. He had asked me to write it, so I did. The schedule was copied down and left with Babu Ji. I hoped that others coming after (and Judith Perkins was very much in my mind) could help develop this more.

We had not yet mentioned the thought that Russell should make future trip arrangements, when Sant Ji asked that I record a "message to Russell." He proceeded to state that Russell should be responsible for making the arrangements for the groups to come. As for Pappu being the middleman (and we had not relayed that either), Sant Ji sent me to get the letter He had written to Russell so that He might add a postscript. He wrote that Pappu would be His "personal secretary." As I had just explained to Pappu the meaning of "P.S." (which I had used in the letter to Sant Ji), Pappu now smilingly told me that P.S. also meant "Personal Secretary!"

Sant Ji lovingly advised, "You should not try to remember all the words – it is the feelings in the heart that are important." Wendy later told me how relieved she had been to hear Sant Ji say that, because she had been trying to remember everything but couldn't – and consequently felt badly. I felt a twang in my heart, because I had been trying so hard to remember as much as I could. I asked her when He had said that, as I definitely had not heard it. She answered, "In His room, this afternoon" – and I realized that He must have said it when I had gone to retrieve the letter. I reasoned that as He had not said it to me, I should continue my effort to record as much as I could.

This marathon session with Sant Ji was absolutely incredible, and we were all beautifully stretched. I passed through states difficult to describe except that they never got lower than ecstatic joy. I was operating on a level of consciousness that I had never, ever operated on before. At one point I realized that we were all like Frodo: we had been given the ring, but we <u>could</u> do it, with His help.[26] And it was at this time that Sant Ji crossed out the "Sant" from His signature on His reply to Russell, and wrote "Dass" – "Servant."

As we continued, it felt as if we moved between the sublime and the ridiculous. Among other things, we discussed how to make pancakes. This began when we arrived in His room and He distributed parshad. He gave us cashews and raisins, and then He pulled out a huge bag of rock candy and said, "For your families!" We really laughed. He gave us whole apples. Pappu left to get something Sant Ji had requested, and He began talking to me in Hindi. He would say a word and I would repeat it – and then on to another word. We were laughing like anything. When Pappu returned, Sant Ji told me, "You will learn Hindi. I think it will be easy for you. For me I think it would be difficult to learn English." He asked if we wanted to eat and I said, "Yes. Whatever You want." He said, "No, no. Do you want to eat?" and I said, "Yes," so Wendy cut up apples and He took the sections and gave them to us.

Several times it was very clear to me that He was either pulling things out of us that we needed to say, or else He was just reading everyone's thoughts and going right into things. I mentioned that the next time I came, I would bring my wife and He asked, "You are coming again?" I thought "Oh God, I've invited myself." I had been looking for a positive response and had not gotten what I wanted. After feeling so in tune it was depressing to think that I had asserted, and gone against His Will. But at that moment I had been sorely wishing that my wife, Karen, could be there, sharing this with me.

He continued speaking mostly to Robert and Wendy – saying such amazingly beautiful things. The conversation had moved around to when He was coming and I said, "Remember, You are coming for Wendy's birthday, the 16th of March," and He really laughed. He asked her what she had on her birthday and she told Him about birthday cakes. She related that this time her daughters and Miriam Perkins had made a cake for her. Then He asked Robert what he had on his birthday. Robert answered that they had not celebrated his birthday together yet, but that a year ago they had met on his birthday. He was talking about how they had so much love for each other, and again my heart was heavy that

---

[26] In J. R. R. Tolkien's masterful saga, *The Lord of the Rings*, the tremendously important task of carrying the powerful ring back to its source is given to one of the most humble of characters, Frodo. Frodo is not a wizard, warrior, or elf, but one of the common-folk creatures known as Hobbits.

Karen was missing. I felt only one-half there.

Sant Ji looked at Wendy and said, "I am feeling in my heart that you are like my own dear daughter." And I thought, "Oh, I hope He will say that about Karen someday." He immediately turned to me and said, "Your wife is sending her love to me through Wendy, and I am sending love back to her." I started crying, and bowed down before Him, as the whole weight had been lifted in a flash. The love that was going between Him and us was just amazing. It was pouring out from Him and we were loving Him back. He dropped another hint that He may be at Sant Bani sooner than March 13th – in time to celebrate Wendy's birthday on the 16th. He asked such sweet questions: where did the plane stop, what kind and how many coats should He bring, what kind of farming did they do in America, and did they use irrigation canals?

Sant Ji asked about the Managing Committee of the Ashram. He specifically wanted to know who was on it, so I told him the five people (Russell, Judith, Gerald Boyce, Karen and me). Sant Ji wondered if He could be assured that no one on the committee would be part of a faction to divide the Sangat, and we said yes. He was pleased, and said that when He came He would only go to the places we wanted Him to go. If other people invited Him to different places, as He had just been invited to go to Delhi, then He would not go. He was curious as to where the different centers of Master Kirpal were in the US, and He wanted to know about the relations with Canada as well.

Sant Ji mentioned that Master Kirpal had told Him how some of the sevadars who were close to Master Kirpal had misused their positions. Once Master was left to sit in a car in the heat of the day for several hours while the sevadar who was with Him visited friends in a cool house. Hearing this I responded that Sant Ji had been telling us all of these stories about the mistreatment of Master Kirpal, and now I felt afraid, because He was putting us in the same position in relation to Him. Sant Ji said, "Yes, that is why I am telling you all of this. You should learn from it."

I decided I had to tell Sant Ji about the dream I had had at Sardar Rattan Singh's house. I observed that, just like in my dream, when we arrived back at the village there had indeed been a whole lot of visitors, some of whom I knew and some of whom I did not. Sant Ji remarked, "When you are traveling with or are near a holy man, the dreams that you have foretell the future." Then He added, "100%." He said that is what that dream was. I continued, "When I was sitting at Your Feet, I was crying because I thought they were abusing You, but then I knew that You were the Satguru and I became all happy and knew that You could take care of it." He said that I was crying because in my heart I was sensing that they (the Delhi people) were finding fault with Him, and indeed they were. But their opinion of Sant Ji had changed, and that is why I had stopped crying and was able to feel peace in my heart.

He explained that the people from Delhi had come to promote their candidate to succeed Master Kirpal. Before we had returned to 77 RB, the visitors were telling the villagers what was wrong with Sant Ji, as well as finding fault with Russell. While their opinion of Sant Ji had changed after they met Him and talked to Him, they also saw that they could not get Him to do what they wanted: to support their choice of a Successor. They were afraid of what was going to happen when Russell would begin to publicly support Sant Ji. They thought that if Sant Ji were to join together with the man they were promoting, Russell's support of Sant Ji would be support for their choice as well. However, as the evening went on, it had become more and more clear that Sant Ji would not cooperate with their plans.

During the late-night session, Sant Ji had told the visitors many stories of a disciple of Baba Sawan Singh called Mastana Ji – how he gave all of his wealth to the sons of Baba Sawan Singh and went away penniless. Baba Sawan Singh Ji kept making him wealthy, however, and he always gave away everything – motorcycles, shops of clothing, etc. He had so much money that the government people came to see if he had a printing press for making counterfeit bills. Whenever he needed money, he would just reach into his pocket and the money would be there. Much of the laughter during the evening had come from Sant Ji's narration of the amusing stories of Mastana Ji.[27]

---

[27] Sant Ji spoke of Mastana Ji many times over the next two decades. At a Satsang on August 14th, 1977 at Sant Bani Ashram in New Hampshire, He explained many details of the life of this devoted disciple of Baba Sawan Singh Ji: "Mastana Ji used to distribute a lot of money among the poor people; all day he would distribute new currency notes. That wealth kept on coming, and he would say, 'This is the treasure of Baba Sawan Singh.' Many times government people caught him and searched for the money, and they would think, 'Maybe he has a printing press' – but whenever they would search they would find only pebbles, and cushions full of pebbles, and nothing else." (*Sant Bani Magazine*, Oct/Nov 1977, pp. 11-12).

In a talk given at the SKA Retreat in Sampla, India, on December 13th, 1995, Sant Ji related the following: "I met with Mastana Ji many times at the

The visitors had asked if Sant Ji at least would come and sit on the dais with the one they were supporting when their guru came to the city of Ganganagar. Sant Ji politely said that He would not. They offered to send a vehicle to get Him, but Sant Ji still said no. When He refused all of those options, they asked Him again to come to Delhi. Sant Ji told them that He had much love for the man they were following. He added that if that guru came to 77 RB, Sant Ji would give him everything. Their guru was the physical son of Master Kirpal, after all, and Sant Ji loved him. As Sant Ji gently but persistently had refused to cooperate, the

---

feet of Baba Sawan Singh. During the Satsangs I had many opportunities to spend time with Mastana Ji. He was my old friend; we had a lot of love for each other. He was a lover in the true sense. He used to call Master Sawan Singh as Sawan the Emperor, and he used to remember Him with his every single breath . . . [Sant Ji speaks at length of the love of Mastana Ji – revealing along the way that it was actually Sant Ji Himself Who wrote the songs attributed to Mastana Ji – see footnote to Chapter Six, below].

"So dear ones, Mastana Ji used to say, 'All that you see here is the blessing, the grace, of Master Sawan Singh' – because Mastana Ji used to distribute money to the people. When He would do that, He would start in the morning, and He would go on distributing money to the people until late in the evening. Many times the Indian government officials tried to find where He was getting all the money from, and they even put Him into prison. They searched all His belongings, but they could not find any money; but still He was distributing to everyone. So He used to say, 'All that you see here is nothing but the blessings and grace of Master Sawan Singh.'

"He used to say, and He had this thing in writing also, 'If anyone says that he has given even one rupee to Mastana Ji, he can take back 1,000 rupees.' His own clothes were always torn, and I have seen that He used to wear torn shoes too. He used to say, 'The poor Mastana has only these things.' He used to show His torn clothes and torn shoes, and say, 'Such is the play of Master Sawan Singh: the poor Mastana doesn't have anything more than these torn shoes and the clothes.'

"One day very lovingly He told me, 'Look here, everything you see here is the grace of Master Sawan Singh. I have the blessings of Master Sawan Singh, but the Power Who is going to come to you by Himself, He has done the meditation. Sawan Singh is God Almighty, and the One Who is going to come to you, He is the Son of God. He has done so much meditation, He is such a big Power, that if He puts His hand like this in front of cannons blowing the fire, even the cannons would stop. When the time will come, that Power will come to your home by Himself and you have to appreciate Him.' " (from "To Become the Child of the Master," *Sant Bani Magazine*, Jan/Feb 1996).

visitors went to bed without hope of accomplishing any of their plans.

Sant Ji paused to ask us if the King's English were different than American English, because He had had trouble understanding the Westerner. He said that He could understand 25% of what Robert and I said to Him – but that He could not answer us in English. He also said that He could understand 25% of what Russell had said. Of Wendy and Linda, however, He could understand more – about 30%.

Sant Ji continued. As the visitors had not been able to convince Him last night, they had come up to His room for an hour in the morning. Sant Ji explained that He had considered inviting us up also, but He thought that they might criticize Russell more, and He wondered why we should have to hear all that. Besides, He felt that He was sufficient to absorb it all, and that He could defend Russell. When the woman complained that Russell was a "black marketer," Sant Ji had responded, "Well you have been benefiting from him for years, so now let me have some profit."

Sant Ji then told the visitors that He could show them within Who the Satguru was, and asked if any of them could show Him the same? They did not respond. As they saw that He still would not bend, they once more invited Him to Delhi, this time offering to proclaim both Sant Ji and their choice as the "true successors." Sant Ji asked them if they now had the power and authority to make Gurus? Sant Ji reminded us that Lord Kal, the Negative Power, was quite capable of creating illusionary experiences within.

Pappu brought up our question as to whether Sant Ji should be presented in *Sat Sandesh* magazine, or separately? Sant Ji responded, "Let it be separate until the point in time comes where the change seems right." [28] He said even those people who are now saying they have no need for a Successor – that Master Kirpal Singh inside is sufficient – He said that even they will have to come to recognize the Successor one day.

I commented that the visitors had left worried that Russell would start to say that Sant Ji had been authorized to do the spiritual work of Master Kirpal. Sant Ji asked me to explain, so I went on. I mentioned that Russell would come soon, and then Sant Ji would begin to give Initiation to Westerners. The mission in the West would begin – in fact it already had! As people began to hear more about it, critics would say

---

[28] *Sat Sandesh* was the monthly publication for the Mission of Master Kirpal and Russell Perkins was the editor. Sant Ji's advice here gave birth to *Sant Bani Magazine.*

that Sant Ji was just a simple village farmer who was being exploited by people like Russell, and that Sant Ji really knew nothing. Sant Ji listened to me very graciously and said, "Yes, in my heart I feel that the same thing will happen."[29]

---

[29] Ten years later, in the question and answer session from February 26th, 1986 cited in footnote #6 above, Sant Ji spoke of these early days as follows:

I had spent all my life sitting underground doing meditation and I did not know anyone in the world. You can ask Kulwant (Bagga), who is sitting here: I did not know the Bagga family. I had never known them. It was all the arrangement of Master Kirpal that He brought them into contact with me and everything happened. At first Kulwant came, and he did not speak very good English; then he brought Pappu, who at that time did not speak good English, and did not have any idea how to translate; I told him that he will get the initiation and everything will become all right. Later on he got the initiation and with Kirpal's grace everything was all right. He started doing the work of translation, and did it very well. When Kulwant brought him he told me, "We all are initiated by Master; he is the only black sheep in the family and had not got the initiation." So I told him to get initiation, and when with the grace of Master Kirpal he got it, you know how everything happened.

When we started thinking about the first tour one person came here, a very learned person, and asked me, "Why are you taking Pappu? He is just a kid, he does not speak very good English—how can he do a good translation?" I told him, "It is all in the hands of Kirpal: whomever He has chosen to go with me is going; I do not have any choice." Then another gentleman came from Delhi. He was a very learned man and spoke good English and he said the same thing. And he said, "You do not even know about the Westerners. Even God fears the Westerners, they are so smart; they will 'sell' you so you should be very careful with them." I mean to say that they tried in every possible way to intimidate me. I told him, "Go within and ask Master Kirpal Who has made all these arrangements. I cannot go against His wishes; whatever the Master has wanted I am doing." So they tried to stop me; they did not want that I should go out and give the message of my Master.

But I had His support and I told them, "I cannot go against the wishes of my Master. Whatever arrangements He has made I will abide by." I also told them, "You have said that in the West when someone goes to give a talk, if the audience does not like that they start saying, 'Stop this, shut up, stop this nonsense.' So if people do that, then I will have to face it, and what will I do? I will just keep quiet and come back." So then that dear one went, because he wanted that I should not go outside and I should just remain here. So I mean to say that this is

Sant Ji then said some really beautiful and personal things to all of us. He told us how He was going to feel it in His heart so much when we left, and that His heart would not be happy again until we were back with Him, or He was back with us. And He meant it – He really, really meant it. He said He wished that we were staying twenty days. He also said that He would arrange next time for us to go and meet many other devoted disciples like Sardar Rattan Singh, and share in their love. Wendy and Robert and I, we all felt that He would be very happy to come and live at Sant Bani Ashram for a time.

In the evening there was a wonderful Satsang, after which Charles Feinman showed pictures of his family. The dried fruits and nuts that Charles had brought were distributed as parshad – and Sant Ji made a joke, because an overweight fellow got a rich date. Sant Ji looked at me

---

all the grace of Master Kirpal, He has made all these arrangements; now you know that here is the same Pappu, and he is doing a very good work of translator, he can explain things very well to the dear ones. So all these things were arranged and done by Master Kirpal Himself.

When that dear one had come from Delhi and he was talking with me about all those things, Kent Bicknell was also here and he got very upset, he did not like the things which that dear one was saying to me. Because he was saying that Westerners can "sell" people and like that. So when Russell Perkins came to me the second time, I told him, "Some dear ones have come and have told me that I should be careful with Westerners because they can even sell a person." Russell Perkins said, "Yes, they are right; I will sell you. Now it is up to you to decide whether you want to come out with me or not."

The meaning of saying all these things to you is to just make you understand that God, our perfect Almighty Master, forgives our karmas only when we do some sacrifice, when we take some initiative to get His grace. When we give up name and fame and the things of the world, when we make our heart empty for the Master to come and reside, only then He resides within us. And when He comes within us, He brings all the prosperities of the world.

Guru Ramdas Ji Maharaj says that even if the Master offers all the material of the world, all the gold and precious things, to such a disciple, that disciple will not look at all that. He will only ask for the intoxication of the Lord, and for the darshan and the Naam of the Master.

I have often said that I always ask for darshan from the Master; I only ask for His love. Ever since my childhood, I was the devotee of love; and He gave me love. I did not ask for any worldly thing from Him." (Sant Bani Magazine, *July-August 1986, "In the Hands of Kirpal," pp.58 ff).*

and said slowly, "Sat . . . Sri . . ." and left the rest for me to finish, which I did, "Akaal!" Everyone laughed, and Sant Ji asked me to play the tape of the girls' bhajans, which all enjoyed.

The Sixth and Final Day – Wednesday, April 7th

Charles, Wendy, Robert, Pappu and I saw him from 8:00 to 10:00 a.m., before our Jeep was to leave at 11:00. I had given some BIC pens for the office work, and when we came in to Sant Ji's room He had one in His pocket. He looked at us with those twinkling Eyes and said, fingering His pen, "Now I'm an educated man!" Charles had a bag of toys he had brought that his family no longer needed, and asked Sant Ji to distribute them as needed. Sant Ji looked at each item carefully and, after returning most to Charles, gave a few to some sevadars. One fellow received a yellow stuffed bunny and Pathi Ji's wife, our cook, got a toy rolling pin. Sant Ji gave a magnet to Pappu. It was a very jolly time, at the end of which He distributed more parshad.

Sant Ji had a message for Sant Bani Ashram. He said that we should carry on the work in exactly the same way as when Master Kirpal was alive. He talked more about chastity and stressed the importance of making the home harmonious: "Have love and respect for your life companion – if you make each other life companions in the true sense, then that love is immortal." He referred to a bhajan of Guru Nanak that addressed the value of chastity – the benefits of preserving the vital fluid. One hundred drops of blood are needed to make a drop of life fluid – and 100 drops of life fluid are needed to make a drop of *ojas*, from which we may derive great spiritual benefit. Thinking of His comment to carry on the same way, I wondered if we were doing anything differently at Sant Bani. It came to me about the diary – how I was no longer showing it to Russell. I asked if I should and He said, "Yes, it is good to show the diary to someone else."

Then Charles asked about living at the Ashram in New Hampshire. Sant Ji said that first he must love and follow Russell. He continued, "When you get back, embrace him to show how much love you have for him." Charles asked if when he went to talk to Russell about problems, could he bring a third party with him, and Sant Ji said that there was no need to do that. Sant Ji told each one of us individually to love and cooperate with Russell.

Sant Ji sent His love to our families. He said He would be glad to see me in the School. I asked for a message for the School children, and He said that He sends His love to all – that they should wait for Him to come and He will meet them there. "Love is the true *Sandesh* (Message)," He added. He asked me when Russell would be coming, and I said mid-April or mid-May, probably the latter. He told Charles not to mix with people back in Delhi but to go home with us. As Sant Ji had His glasses on throughout the session, I expressed concern about His Eyes, but He said they were being treated and were all right.

Towards the end of our time Charles asked, "Did Master Kirpal leave early?" Pappu did not understand, so I paraphrased the question, "Some people say Master Kirpal left the Body fourteen years before He was supposed to, because those around Him did not love Him. Is this true?" When Sant Ji answered, "It is true," it was as if a knife had entered my heart. The only thing that kept me from dissolving in a huge puddle of emotion and guilt was knowing that I was sitting in the presence of my Old Friend (Master Kirpal) in His New Coat (Sant Ji).[30] Charles also asked if Sant Ji was still afraid of the work and He said, "Yes!" I silently wondered, "Why shouldn't He be? Master Kirpal's disciples failed in their love – Why will it be any different for Sant Ji?" And then I prayed, "God help us."

After a couple of hours we left His room to get ready to depart. I scribbled some notes in my book, closing with the entry, "P.S. I can't operate at this level for too much longer – I am very out of touch with my body." After writing that, I began to arrange my bags. I was packing furiously – literally like a madman. Wendy asked me if she could help, but I said no and went on with it. Just as I was finishing Charles asked me what time I had, because he had 10:25. I said I had the same, and he pointed out that we had 35 minutes to go, so why was I so frantic? I was still dazed, and just laughed and said, "Oh yeah." I zipped things closed and, leaving my bags on the bed, stepped out of the room right into the path of Pappu, who was hurrying to find me. "Come on – Sant Ji wants to see you," he said. I spent the rest of the hour till 11:00 with Sant Ji, and when I came down, my bags were in the Jeep.

One of the first things I noticed as I entered Sant Ji's room was that He was sitting on His bed instead of on the floor. This was really sweet for me, as I was able to look up into His face the whole time. Also He

---

[30] As Master Kirpal once commented regarding how to recognize His Successor: "Look here: When your friend comes with a different coat on, won't you recognize him?" *Sat Sandesh*, September 1974, p. 32.

did not have His glasses on, so He was just pouring His Eyes into mine the whole time. He told me so sweetly that since those people from Delhi had come, He had had a thought that perhaps it would be better if I did not go to visit Sawan Ashram after all. I immediately said, "I won't. I won't go," but there was also that pang in my heart, because I had written a letter to my old acquaintances saying that I would come on Tuesday or Wednesday. But I just told Him I would not go, and was willing to work it out in my own mind later. He drew more out of me, however, and I told Him that I would only do what He wanted and would not go to Sawan Ashram, but that my heart was still heavy because those people were expecting to see me, and they had been good friends. I asked if it would be all right to write a letter from Delhi and include some photos of my family, and He was really positive about it. He said, "Yes, a letter would be good . . . that would be good."

And then I told Him how I had gone before – when Pappu and I had gone. I told the whole story, and said that when we went there, someone was sitting on the dais giving Satsang, but I could not look at that person. I said I could not even stay because . . . and at this point I broke down crying at His feet. What I was trying to say was that I could not stay because Master Kirpal's home had changed for me. It was not the same – to the extent that it felt as if the Master Power had left that place. I finally got out the words, ". . . it changed." And He pulled me together while Pappu translated. He was just looking and looking into my eyes. He responded that He had had the same experience when He went there after Master had left the Body. They had turned Him out. When He said that, my heart was deeply soothed.

I suddenly recalled that He had told me that my dream foretold the future, 100%. That meant that the physical and verbal abuse I had dreamt of was yet to come. But until He made me see, I had not connected my proposed visit with the dream. I felt overwhelmed at so much protection. I recalled that I had planned to be very honest in Delhi, and to tell the people at Sawan Ashram exactly who I was, and that I just wanted to see my friends, not the person sitting at the head of the Ashram. And I also recalled that at Sardar Rattan Singh's place Sant Ji had told me I could visit if I wished. Obviously, at that time I was not ready to hear that I should not go.

He asked me if all these events would be communicated to Russell Sahib, and I said that yes, I would tell Russell everything. The air had been cleared and things had come sharply into focus. I told Him how happy I was that He had explained so much, because prior to coming, many of us had been somewhat confused. People from the West were visiting various persons claiming to be the spiritual successor of Master Kirpal, and returning with stories of much sweetness, strong meditations, and no rancor at the different places. And yet I had found nothing at Sawan Ashram – the place that had meant so much to me when Master Kirpal was in residence there.

Sant Ji observed that it was because of people's sojourns to various successors that the recent visitors had come up from Delhi. When those visitors first arrived, they had had a bad opinion of Sant Ji. After their position changed, they tried to scare Him away from Russell. Sant Ji informed them that His heart was in tune with Russell's heart from the moment they had met. He had had to ask them to stop criticizing Russell, because it had felt as if they were attacking His own body. Sant Ji told them that if they loved Him, they must love Russell as well. He pointed out that it is possible to kill someone with a sword that is sweet.

I brought up one more subject, that of disciples who wanted to live at the Ashram in New Hampshire. Sometimes people felt they had a right to live at the Ashram, arguing that it belonged to Great Master Kirpal, and not to any person. Thus they were offended if Judith and Russell told them they could not live there. I told Sant Ji we had formed the Managing Committee for this reason – to decide who could live at the Ashram. This alleviated the load on Russell and Judith. Now if we have to tell a family they cannot live here, it is not a personal decision from Russell, but a decision from the Committee. Sant Ji said, "Ah, hah . . . Ahhh-chah!" I asked if it was good to continue the use of the Managing Committee for this purpose, and He said, "Yes, it is good!" He said that we had to look at a family and decide if they could live on and contribute to the Ashram in a harmonious manner. We should think not only of the present, but could they continue like that in the future as well? He concluded that whatever the Committee decided would be fine.

My last session was almost over. I told Sant Ji that I was planning to write an account of this trip in Spanish for Dr. Molina. We stood up to go and He told me how much He loved me and how glad He was that I was on the Managing Committee. On our way down the stairs He told me that if He had known about the Managing Committee before, He would have used its name where He had been using Russell's. I said, "It's the same thing," and we laughed.

And this was the end of the six days at 77 RB. We had the usual group photos and I was so happy just looking at Him. Since I had fallen apart emotionally in His room, and He had had to put me back together, I was sure it would not happen again, so I simply basked in the bliss. He looked at me and I bowed down before Him. He raised me up and gave me a tremendous bear hug for a long time. He told me to get in the Jeep and I was in it like a shot! We left soon after, and my last memory is of Him stepping away from the crowd so that His pink figure was alone and contrasting against the mud walls of the compound.

Return to Delhi – Back in the "Real World" – April 8th and Beyond

We left on Wednesday for Delhi and got in from the overnight train on Thursday, the eighth of April. I was sure we would fly out that night, but at the downtown airline office the officials noticed our excursion fare dates, and said we could not fly out until Monday. I felt momentarily sunk until I got out on the street and heard one man say to another as they passed by me, "Sant Ji Kirpal," as clear as a bell. That lifted me, and I settled in for four more days at the wonderful Bagga house.

Pappu suggested I could phone or cable my contacts at Sawan Ashram, but Sant Ji had said a letter would be good so I wrote. I asked Pappu if I could give the Bagga address and he said yes. The letter said nothing about where I had been – only that I was at the Bagga house through Monday. On Sunday, Robert, Wendy, and Pappu's brother Jawahar, and sisters Vimal and Boya went to the Taj Mahal, so I was quite alone. My stay there was very peaceful, and this day most of all. Pappu's father, Papa Ji asked me to watch TV, so I did that for a time, and then excused myself. I lay on my bed, listening, and then heard a knocking at the gate out back.

I looked down from the balcony and saw my old acquaintances from Sawan Ashram. Responding to my letter they had come all the way over from Shakti Nagar on their bicycles. At first I was worried – were these two dear old friends the two men from my dream? My worry then turned into caution, and I was certain that the Satguru was taking care of all, and that these men had come out of love. We talked for an hour or so, and then they visited with Papa Ji as well.

They told me many stories about life at Sawan Ashram – basically what was once heaven had become a hell. As they talked their eyes filled with tears. I told them only what Russell had said in *Sat Sandesh* – that I had been to Rajasthan to see Sant Ji, that He was a holy man, and that I loved Him. I gave them the March *Sat Sandesh* – my last copy – which they never see anymore. That issue had the report of the Ruhani Satsang Board meeting in it. They had been led to believe that most disciples in the West were now following the man placed at the head of Sawan Ashram – and the magazine made it clear that the truth was far from that. There is little point in relating any more of the tales they told – but the love they expressed for me and the rest of their brothers and sisters in the West was what felt real. They peddled off, and I never saw them again.

I was bubbling over with happiness at having been so immersed in the presence of a Realized Soul, and anxious to share that with any who were willing to listen. My first thought was to attempt to call Karen from Delhi – not an easy task in April of 1976. With much perseverance and a great deal of luck one was connected with an operator who would "book" your call. Hours later it might come through. You needed to shout, as the audio quality was poor at best, and often you could hear the party on the other end or they could hear you, but the two events rarely coincided. The only private telephone to which we might have access was in the house of a relative of the Baggas, on the other side of Delhi. Papa Ji and I rode a scooter across the city to the phone and began the process. After several hours I got through, and, understanding that Karen could hear me, I did my best to blurt out the essence of those five magical days. I told her that Sant Ji was expecting Russell to come back soon, and that He had entrusted much work to Sant Bani Ashram.

I had other work to do in Delhi those four days, including starting a crash course in Hindi with my willing teachers, Pappu's younger brother and sisters. Late Monday evening, Robert, Wendy, and I said our laughing, crying, and loving "good-byes" to the ever-gracious Bagga family, and headed to the airport for our long flight back to our physical home, Sant Bani Ashram. On reaching the end of our time in India, the book was gently closed. If I could no longer be in the physical presence of a Godman, I was ready to be home.

CHAPTER TWO

"Not a Leaf Stirs nor a Twig Moves but by the Will of God"

Wendy, Robert, and I returned to Sant Bani and shared our delight in sitting at the Feet of the New Form of the All Powerful Sat Purush. We talked informally, at Satsangs, and at a slide show on a Saturday night a couple of weeks after our return. Plans were made for Russell's return, this time accompanied by Judith and their son Eric, who was fourteen at the time. Several others also wished to go, and in mid-May a caravan of seven adults and two infants left. Along with the Perkins Family, Sant Bani Ashram residents Susan Shannon (and Matthew, her one-year old son) and Susan Dyment were joined by Susan Winn and Alex Weiss (and her young son). An account of that trip was published in the July 1976 issue of *Sant Bani Magazine* (Vol. I, No. 1), with reminiscences by Russell, Susan Winn, and Susan Dyment.

I was in love with Sant Ji. Via the group I sent a brief letter in English, asking that He please allow my entire family to come to see Him as soon as possible. His reply, written out in block letters (by His personal secretary – Pappu) and signed by Sant Ji, was sweet and to the point:

> *77 RB P.O. Sangrana*
> *Dist SriGangaNagar*
> *23ʳᵈ May '76*

Satguru Kirpal's Beloved,
Dear Kent (Principal Sahib)

> *Received your loving letter. You have written that "either You come or let my family come soon." So my dear Principal Sahib with His Order I am coming in July. Put in more time for meditation. It is the Real & True Service (Seva).*
> *With His Love to you and your family,*
> *Yours*
> *Dass Ajaib Singh*

51

This was the first of many letters that Sant Ji wrote to me over the next twenty-one years. With love, respect, humility, and a touch of humor (quoting my demands back to me!), He gave me exactly what I needed in a very few words. It is so emblematic of Who He Was and Is.[1]

The plans were made for Sant Ji to come to America in the summer, and those of us who lived at or near the Ashram, and many of the students at the Sant Bani School, were very excited. Around the country a growing number of the disciples of Master Kirpal, as well as new seekers, were being drawn to Sant Ji by various routes. Some were pulled by inner experiences. Others were attracted by hearing about the pure and direct qualities of His life. Those who had met Him brought back a vibrant picture of a True Godman, humbly sitting in the desert of Rajasthan, Whose keenest desire was to be in the Lap of His Guru. The total effect – positive and magnetic – connected with people's hearts – and we made preparations for the upcoming tour.

Sant Ji, accompanied by Pappu for translation and Pathi Ji to chant and cook, was scheduled to come in July – but as we ran into various obstacles, the dates were moved to August. Securing visas for the United States was one of many challenges. After a phone conversation with Pappu, we decided that I should fly over to India to assist. I would bring the necessary letters of invitation for a face-to-face meeting with embassy officials, as well as enough cash for any incidentals that might arise. When I was certain the visa applications were complete, I called the U.S. Embassy in Delhi to offer whatever support I could.

Anne and Bob Wiggins provided the requisite multitude of financial documents for an affidavit of financial support, and the Ashram collected all of its official papers (such as the articles of incorporation). Anne Wiggins and I spent the day on Monday, August 9th, in a flurry of activity that included visiting banks, seeing a lawyer, and typing a ream of forms. I hurriedly packed, and Robert and Wendy took me to the airport that evening. We realized that we had not done enough as far as preparing the legal way for His coming, and my hopes began to be clouded with guilt and remorse. On the way to the airport Wendy commented, "It ought to teach us that we can no longer be children – just sitting back and waiting for the Master Power to do our work. If His Will

---

[1] I feel blessed to have received more than a hundred letters from Sant Ajaib Singh between 1976 and 1997. The majority of these were written in Hindi.

calls for action, then we must do it to the best of our ability." I had the sinking feeling that we had not done that.

The First Day – Wednesday, August 11th, 1976

The Master definitely worked His Grace at the London Airport. I had been alone in three seats from Boston to London, and, since I had seen the movie, there was nothing to distract me from remembrance and sleep. I stretched out and the Master's voice came to me on a mental level, "Do you not think I am with you?" In my head I responded, "Yes, Master," and received a response, "I am with you every step of the way." Somewhat at peace I drifted off, and awoke suddenly near London, feeling ill with acute nausea and an aching head. I made it off the plane to the bathroom in Heathrow, and was sick. I went to the medical station and a nurse politely said she would, "get something to settle the tummy" and told me I could rest in the transit lounge. A doctor saw me however, and wondered what was wrong. He took me to a small private room with a bed, and there he told me to lie down and rest. I did so for the remainder of my five hours in Heathrow. When I got up I felt much better, and later wondered if the whole thing had not been some kind of cleansing process. While seated in the plane I had been rehearsing over and over again my lines to the officials at the U.S. Embassy. I was able to meditate some as well, and had become more and more positive about the chances for success. I was determined not to fly back without Him!

We landed in Delhi and I was one of the first to exit the plane. I walked quickly through the sleepy airport towards the immigration area. Feeling confident and assured, I bee-lined over to a smiling man who, after taking one look at my passport, told me that I was not permitted to enter India – period! My heart went KLUNK! I begged, pleaded, and whined, but he said flatly that I could not enter India without a visa, owing to a new rule that required a visa if a foreigner wished to visit more than once in any six month period (and I had just come in April). They told me that I had to fly back to London immediately.

By now I was gathering a group of officials beyond the original immigration officer, and we continued to talk. For a moment there was slight hope for a 72-hour permit allowing me to come in, but that came to naught. I almost panicked, but I kept trying to remember the Master, thinking all the while that this must also be part of the plan. My head

filled with questions – was Pappu outside waiting for me, could I get a
message to him if he were, could I give him the vital papers I had with
me – and I attempted to operate through a sea of confusion. My luggage
had been lost in transit. Both cameras (movie and still), my clothes, and,
most important, several supporting documents about the Ashram were
apparently left in London. Master Kirpal used to say that, "Man proposes
and God disposes," and that certainly was what it felt like at the moment.

Finally someone suggested that I could go to Katmandu, Nepal and
get a visa at the Indian Embassy there (you cannot get a visa from within
the country that you need it for). It might even be possible to do this and
return to Delhi on the same day. I counted my money and found I had
just enough: $200 round trip to Katmandu and $900 for a return to New
York on Air India if required.[2] I booked for Katmandu, and then I was
able to telephone Pappu.[3]

Pappu had not received our telegram and therefore was not outside
waiting for me. Instead, he was surprised to hear I was in Delhi.
Actually, Pappu said, they had already obtained their visas with the help
of Dennis Huntington, an American who was staying in Dalhousie while
doing graduate work. It turned out that when I had been on the phone to
the embassy from New Hampshire, pleading their case, Sant Ji, Pathi Ji,
Pappu, and Dennis had been in another room talking to someone else.
The woman I spoke to ultimately signed their visas – so perhaps the
phone call had helped – but it was clear that the outer reasons that
compelled me to come were gone.

British Airways was willing to fly me back to Boston that same day,
but I felt I was supposed to be in India so I chose to head to Katmandu. I
called Pappu again and told him to book me for America on Sunday
night with them. Sant Ji wanted to know if He could come to the airport
and assist me, but I said I would be all right: I told them that I would be
back either that day or the next, and that I would get to the Bagga house
in the neighborhood of Bali-Nagar by myself.

I still thought that I was supposed to be there, but could not help but
wonder why. If I had known that this time I would need a visa to get into
India, then I would have been delayed in my departure from Boston, as it

---

[2] Although I already had a return ticket on British Airways, if the Indian
party were booked on a different airline then I would need to buy a new ticket to
accompany them.

[3] The Baggas had moved to a new house between April and August, and a
neighbor had a phone that could be used.

took several days to get an Indian visa in 1976. While I was very grateful that Sant Ji and the party had obtained U.S. visas, it seemed to mean that my presence was no longer required. As I sat quietly in the waiting room of Royal Nepal Airlines three things came to me quite clearly. First, I was supposed to be there. Second, the Master was with me every step of the way. Finally, time would clarify any residual confusion I had. As I mounted the portable steps on the tarmac, a feeling of rightness, sweetness and peace descended on me. On entering the plane I felt joy radiating – it was so clean and small with lovely Nepalese stewards and stewardesses. And of course the Master Travel Agent placed me in a cozy front section with a window seat for viewing the Himalayan grandeur. I was in His hands and happy for it, and laughed as I saw myself sitting on an airplane headed to Katmandu – so close to Everest. Who would have thought it?

Flying into Nepal was a visual feast. We flew over valleys, terraced lands, small houses connected by cart tracks – and all of it so much greener and more lush than India. We landed in Katmandu and I found I had to have a visa to get into Nepal! However, you could get a visa right there at the desk, but of course you needed a photograph of yourself. By signing a slip saying that I would present a photo when I left, I was able to get out of the airport. As the crowd of taxi hawks approached I put my hand on one fellow's shoulder and said, "You – I'm following you!" and went through the crowd. He was, as it turned out, a very nice young man named Naren, who spoke enough English that we could communicate well.

I arrived at the Indian Embassy and the man behind the desk said, "Yes sir, no problem. You may have visa." I told him I wanted to get it in an hour so I could get back and catch the plane to Delhi. He responded, "Not possible. Don't even consider it. Don't dream on it. One hour not possible. This afternoon . . . maybe." So there went all my hopes.

The Indian official then asked me what was my purpose in coming to India. I knew that the safest answer was merely to state that I was a tourist, but something compelled me to be more forthcoming. I told him that I had come to help these three friends from India obtain their visas to the U.S. (without bothering to mention they already had their visas – as it was why I came). I showed him the lawyer's letter, the School brochure and other material, all the while saying to myself, "I think this is what Master wants me to do." Suddenly the whole picture changed. I was no

longer a tourist, but something else. The man behind the counter had to
go speak to his superior. I was left wondering if I would get the visa, not
when. By this point my level of distress was high again. I did not know if
the extra $200 I spent for my round trip ticket to Katmandu would leave
me too short of cash for my ticket from Delhi to the States. All in all it
was very confusing.

The man was gone for about a half an hour. The phone rang in the
other room and I was asked to come in and say my name. The fellow on
the phone repeated my name into the receiver and hung up. I thought,
"Yikes, they have my passport and everything." I headed back to the
waiting room. After a while I was called back to the superior's office,
and what followed was this incredibly lucid discussion (from his end) on
the differences in education and culture of India and the United States.
He was a very sweet and beautiful person, and we talked for quite a
while. I said to myself, "Oh, so that's what Master had up His sleeve,"
because the exchange was quite positive. I was able to explain why I felt
it was essential to come 10,000 miles for spiritual guidance. He expressed an appreciation for the ancient cultures of India and the inquis-
itiveness and honesty of Western seekers. In the end he said that there
would be no problem in my getting a visa and that it would be ready for
me at four o'clock that afternoon.

I had to get three pictures for the visa application and one for exiting
the country, so my cab driver took me to a place that had a Polaroid
camera that took four pictures at once. I stopped by a travel agency to
see if I could get a flight in the afternoon, but that was not possible. I
naively asked about trains, and was told that trains did not reach
Katmandu. Realizing that I had to pass the night in Nepal, I asked the
agent to book me on the noon flight to Delhi the next day. She called the
airport, and when she told me that tomorrow's plane had 90 seats with
130 people wishing to be on it, I just about fell through my chair. I could
not believe it. As an alternative she booked me on a flight that ended in
Delhi after a series of short hops. The first was from Katmandu to
Benares – and that was the only one that was confirmed. All the rest
were "stand by." This was certainly a test for me. I was bone weary,
completely befuddled, and I absolutely did not know what to make of the
whole thing.

Naren, the driver, and I had looked at a number of hotels ranging
from a real fleabag that cost $3.50 a night (40 rupees) to a very nice one
for a little over $10. The latter had telephone service so I thought, "Well,
at least I can call Karen tonight, and tell her that they have their visas,

and that I'm in Katmandu – but not to worry!" As I had begun to feel more panicked about my return ticket, the thought of calling my U.S. travel agent to wire a ticket to me was also attractive. The draw of a phone grew until I found out that there was no such thing as a collect call from Nepal – you had to pay on the spot. I checked into a less luxurious hotel, the Mt. Malaku, and then headed to the Air India office to find the actual cost of a new ticket back to the States from Delhi. I was desperately trying to get a sense of my worrisome finances.

I entered the Air India office and one of the two fellows there politely told me it was closed from 1:00 to 2:00 for lunch. It was 12:55 and he was not eating. He was insistent however, so I left. It occurred to me to speak to British Airways, and the kind woman behind the counter at British allayed my fears. I did have enough to buy a ticket if I could not transfer my British Airways return over to Air India. I was about to leave when something inspired me tell her my plight, and she said, "Oh, I must be able to get you on that plane tomorrow." My emotions had been going up and down like a yo-yo, and they shot up again. I was very excited, thinking that maybe Master was going to get me on that direct flight after all.

I reviewed how quickly one learns to accept. I had been very upset that I had had to come to Katmandu in the first place; then I could barely believe that I could not fly out that same afternoon – nor even the next day. As all my plans kept crumbling, I would take a step back to what had been unthinkable, and be hoping for that. Suddenly I was ecstatic that I might indeed be able to get on the next day's direct flight to Delhi. No, she could not get me on it, but she discovered another plan. She thought the travel agent could book me the next day on a flight to Patna, then to Lucknow, and finally to Delhi. She felt I could be confirmed all the way through by 5:00 that evening. Although there was a five-hour layover in Patna, at least I could be relatively certain of arriving in Delhi tomorrow sometime. I went back to the travel agent and had her book me to Delhi on the Indian Airline flight via Patna and Lucknow. It was actually about $50 cheaper than the direct flight to Delhi – so that was a small compensation.[4] I dropped by the Indian Embassy and collected my passport, which fairly shone with its brand new visa.

My feet were aching as I arrived at my room on the fifth floor of the Mt. Malaku Hotel. I sat on the bed, looking out the window at fantastic cloud-topped mountains. In the foreground there were great Buddhist

---

[4] As it turned out I arrived back to the U.S. with $20 in my wallet.

pagoda-topped buildings scintillating everywhere. It was a visually gorgeous setting, but I had no idea on earth what I was doing there. By that time I had become so totally confused that, although I knew Master was working something, it was all way beyond me. While I tried to understand that the Master was sending me whatever I needed, I just could not make heads or tails of most of it. I was actually glad that I had not phoned anyone, as it would have been impossible not to convey a sense of worry. A bright note was that I tried my elemental Hindi on everyone with a pretty good degree of success. The only trouble was when they started talking back to me, and I would get lost in the velocity of the responses.

The Second Day – Thursday, August 12th, 1976

I awoke and sat for meditation in the early hours of the next morning, Thursday. At twenty minutes to four I opened my window and drank in the sounds of the awakening city of Katmandu. Buddhist monks beat on drums and rang tinkling prayer bells as they passed by on their way to *pujas* – morning prayers, and a pack of wild dogs howled in the distance. I continued the inner dialogue. I wondered if I had not been too excited about my role of being the person to come to India and facilitate with the visas? Had I been feeling like the Lone Ranger who would "save the day?" As pride does indeed go before a fall, was that what was happening? Or was this even a fall? I saw that I had had a conception of my role based on my first trip to His Feet. I had thought that I was going to be right in the thick of things, recording everything, taking notes, and, hopefully, being used like a puppet once again – and here I was in Nepal for Heaven's sake! I realized that it was wrong to assume anything, and that it would be terrible to force it, as I had been trying to do. I concluded that I really did not know much of anything, and that, as Baba Sawan Singh Ji had said, the Guru can get the work needed out of anyone – even from the stones. I brought nothing special to the task.

Later, after more sleep and a hot shower, I recalled that wonderful prayer from the *Jap Ji* of Guru Nanak: "If I may please Him, 'tis pilgrimage enough." I thought, "Well, if I fly to Patna and am stuck there for two days, or if I fly to Delhi and they have already left and I am stranded there for two weeks, or whatever happens to me, I pray that I do the best with it that I can. I pray to use it for my own growth, because that's what it's sent to me for." At that point I was definitely feeling much better – more at peace – and anxious to see what would unfold next. I was left with many questions (such as would my luggage have arrived in Delhi?[5]), but I sensed that I was being taught something that might take a long time to unfold. I was ready to go.

Before I left the hotel room, I took a last look at the dozens of rooftops covered with flowering gardens and the many pagodas crowned with gold. Beyond were the mountains – all around poking up through the mist – and I really did bid Katmandu a fond *adieu*. I headed off to the airport for what well could have been another day of frustrations and hassles.

I had no problem with the immigration officials in Katmandu, and boarded the plane for Patna at 2:00 p.m. It was an incredible flight, as we were carried by a turbo prop airplane that flew so low we had great views of the valleys, the mountains, and then the plains and rivers (including the Sacred Ganges) of India. Right next to me was a West German woman who had been living in India for a year, and then in Katmandu for the past four months. She was headed back to India to spend time with her guru. I was cautious (as talking about one's spiritual teacher to a disciple of another can quickly devolve into a "my guru is better than your guru" exchange), but we had a very pleasant conversation. We talked a lot about being on a spiritual path, its twists and turns, and when we parted in Patna, she was very happy to take a copy of *Sant Bani Magazine*. Somehow the experience leant more meaning to my circuitous route. Flying above the landscape of "Mother India" I was reminded that there is nothing like distance to get a better perspective. It felt like the frustration and confusion had drifted away into relative smallness. I realized that while Saints always have the distance, because Their seat is high above, for mortals like me accurate perspective most often came through more horizontal distance: the passage of time.

We landed in Patna and I felt so relieved to clear immigration and set legitimate feet in India. I was excited to be able to walk around during my long layover, and to foist my Hindi on unsuspecting souls. People really did appreciate the effort – even if the language as it emerged from my mouth was rather "broken." We headed to Lucknow in a Boeing 737, and everything I had ever heard about Indian Airlines (as opposed to Air India) seemed to manifest. It was the shortest, fastest take off I had ever

---

[5] My luggage had arrived, although reclaiming it from the Delhi airport was a saga in itself, requiring numerous visits to various authorities – each time signing my name several times in gigantic ledger books.

experienced. The nose lifted so quickly that it seemed like the tail would scrape the runway – and the couple behind me actually gasped. At five hundred feet we made a 30° bank to the left (the seatbelt sign flipped off after 10 seconds) and then we did a 30° turn back the other way. Suddenly the seat belt sign came on again as we headed up through a wall of thunderclouds – and the plane really banged around. We did make it to Lucknow, and then, after a similar take-off, we went on to Delhi.

By God's Grace I made it to the Bagga household on Thursday afternoon. As I approached the house, Satsang was just finishing and Sant Ji called me right to His room. He told me that He had been thinking about me. Each time He heard a car motor, He was thinking it would be me. At one point He sent Pappu and Pathi Ji out to the road for an hour to wait for me. He was very loving. He told me that He had received my letter from America just that day, and that my penmanship was very good, and my Hindi was easy to read. The letter made Him feel like taking wings and flying directly to us, but He could not because He would have had to carry Pappu and Pathi Ji!

I related the saga of the long route I had taken to arrive at His Feet, laughing at the craziness of it all. Still needing some reassurance, I asked if my trip had been useless. He said that Master had meant for Dennis Huntington to have that service of assisting with the visas, and that the *seva* of the others was not wasted. Later He added that I was supposed to be here, which did relieve me. He said that the delay of the Tour (from July to August) was not the fault of the people at Sant Bani, but that He had gotten sick from the injection required for immunization. He suggested that in the future someone should be in India to help with the preparations, now that we knew what was required. Such arrangements could be made when either Russell or I were there. It was a very sweet session – yet I left knowing that something inside of me was just not clicking.

After seeing Sant Ji, I went into the living room and immediately felt the love flowing from the Bagga family. They greeted me so warmly and plied me with delicious food and the inevitable cup of *chai*, the sweet and delicious Indian tea. Pappu's mother, Chai Ji, said that she also had been so worried about me. Needless to say I was very happy to have arrived. I went to bed at 11:30 Thursday evening and woke up at 2:00 a.m. for meditation. Thinking of the requisite visits to downtown Delhi for final ticket arrangements, as well as the trip to the airport for my now found baggage, I was fairly certain that a long day stretched ahead of me.

The Third Day – Friday, August 13th, 1976

Our first trip to the airline offices went smoothly, and we were anxious to get back for a meeting with Sant Ji at 1:30 p.m. We entered His room, accompanied by Pappu's father, Papa Ji, and sat on the floor. I was shocked to find that my mind was like a stallion. Here I was, sitting in front of the One I loved, and I was not feeling at home in His august presence.

I had been so happy to see Sant Ji when I arrived the afternoon before, even though I had realized that I was not completely in sync. The only thing that occurred to me was that I had taken too much for granted. I came assuming a level of relationship that was not appropriate for me to adopt. While He was acting as if I were an old friend, treating me with infinite care and love, I felt out of place, and it was quite painful. My mind, without enough physical or inner contact with the Master, had really come back into its own. My thoughts reared and bucked like wild horses. While Sant Ji was looking and talking to me, everything was racing around like crazy. Thoughts went through it like, "Why don't you just get up and walk out now?" It was very strange and difficult to bear. It was not at all that I did not love Him or believe Him to be real – it was just that I was twisting knives into myself.

Sant Ji understood this. He turned His attention to Papa Ji, and at that point it was just what my soul needed – a relaxation from His intent gaze, and from the tremendous guilt and torment that I was feeling because I was not responding to Him the way I wished. As I watched Him, the waves of His love began to flow over me, and I began to feel much, much better. After a while, Sant Ji turned back to me.

Although I had said nothing about being confused, I obviously looked it, because He proceeded to talk to me at length about <u>not</u> being confused. He said, "Don't be confused and don't be worried; it is the Master's plan working behind everything. The Master Power is working behind the curtain, and therefore it is really wrong to be confused and worried when you are doing service." He repeated that I was supposed to come to India, adding that it had been written in my fate to eat and drink in those particular places with those very people. It was all part of the Master's plan from behind the veil.

Next we spent about half an hour going over the map of Sant Bani Ashram in great detail. Something had inspired me to bring a copy (perhaps His earlier questions like how far the houses were from the

Satsang Hall). I pointed out everything and He asked me a lot more. I indicated everyone's house by name, as well as the School and the gardens. I told Him that recently there have been bears spotted in the woods. I had forgotten the Shannon's house, so He asked me where Susan Shannon lived. He wondered what we cultivated in the gardens. When He asked if there were any fruit trees, I said that we had planted about forty this year. He commented, "They will develop soon." He asked who had drawn the map and when I said that I had, He said I was "competent."

We got into a discussion about *seva* (selfless service) and the Ashram and guests. He told me that it would be good to have a daily schedule for meditation as well as a period of organized *seva* for the guests. If the latter could not meditate, and instead used the time of *seva* for conversation, then they should be asked to leave. A *seva* period for about an hour after lunch was suggested.[6] At the close of this first Friday session I indicated my thankfulness to Him, and He said it was all Master's Grace. We left Him alone on His bed.

Pappu and I had to return to the offices of both the travel agent and the airlines to attempt, once again, to finalize the itinerary. The group planned to fly on Air India, and the travel agent thought he could switch my return from British Air to Air India. As we left the house to locate a three-wheeled scooter for the trip to Connaught Circle, the busy central complex where the airlines had offices, we caught the briefest glimpse of Sant Ji. I told Pappu that all I needed was just a glimpse – I did not always have to be in His presence. On the surface this seemed like a good statement – one that showed the respectful kind of love that the Masters appreciate. After all, Sant Ji had told Pappu that he and I should just go about our business. As soon as it came out of my mouth, however, I realized it was only pride speaking. I could not help but wonder where my overflowing love had gone? I felt different from the April trip in some way, and I really wanted it to clear up. Seated in the back of the scooter I told Pappu that although I was feeling better, there still seemed to be something else – something that was holding me back from Sant Ji's Love. I wondered again if I had taken way too much for granted.

Sitting in the Air India office and trying to unravel all of the knots, I caught myself thinking, yet again, "Oh God, this is all so confusing."

---

[6] Pappu later told me that when he went to 77 RB to bring Sant Ji to Delhi, Sant Ji, in work clothes, was working with the villagers in preparing the land for the new Satsang Hall.

Immediately His words came back to me, "Don't be confused," and I felt better. We haggled some more, seemed to get everything settled, and headed back through the frantic Delhi traffic. By the time we arrived home I was very tired. I lay down on the bed and was about to fall asleep, when Pappu came in and asked for the letters I had brought for Sant Ji. Despite my prideful thought that I only needed a glimpse of Him from time to time, I suddenly had a great urge to accompany Pappu when he took the letters to Sant Ji. It felt like the right thing to do, so I went.

Pappu read all of the letters to Sant Ji. After the letter from an older Sanbornton woman was read, Sant Ji wanted to know if there was a picture of her in the magazine. I told Him how devoted she was, and added that while she said that she was not a good satsangi, she cried on first hearing His name. She really loved Him and had worked very hard beautifying the Ashram grounds. There were letters from other devotees, including one from Colombia.

Sant Ji explained that He was suffering from fever as a result of the immunization shot. He indicated that He did this for our sake, so that He could come on the Tour. As I listened my eyes were as dry as could be, and I wondered where were my tears? I understood that I had had only two and a half hours of sleep, so I was definitely exhausted, but I wondered if my heart was too hard for these things to pierce. And yet I was starting to feel more happy in His presence.

Sant Ji had indicated that the illness had caused the delay in plans. Now, however, He let us know in no uncertain terms that all of the "politics of Successorship" that He was undergoing in Delhi was very unpleasant for Him. He downplayed much of it, and talked about it politely – cushioning everything with smiles and laughter. It did not take much reading between the lines to figure out that it had been an awful thing to have happen to Him. I was sorry for any role we may have had in it. It became clear to me that we should not bring Sant Ji anywhere where disputes of Successorship were going to come up. Further, it would be a great mistake to take Him anywhere where people did not really love Him. Pappu told me that Sant Ji said He would be very happy just to stay at Sant Bani the whole time. He had said that He would feel badly about not going to other places only if it meant that, as a result, the people there could not see Him.

Sant Ji explained that most of the Westerners who came over to see Him had a question in their hearts as to whether the "Successor" they were following was competent or not. Sant Ji wondered why they would come to ask Him if they were certain in their convictions. Why wouldn't they just have stayed at the other places and enjoyed? He said that when the Westerners first came to see the various Successors, they were full of love, not critical of anyone. Then the people around the so-called Successors began to work on the Westerners, so the latter came over here and wanted to get a written statement proving Sant Ji's authority.

As an example He mentioned the case of one couple who were both disciples of Master Kirpal. When they came to Sant Ji, they explained that in America their meditations had been good, but since they had come to India to visit one of the Successors (not Sant Ji), their meditations had gone downhill. They asked what should they do. Sant Ji told them, "Go back to America. Don't even wait to get your shoes on! Go back!" A Western disciple, the same one who had accompanied the Delhi group to see Sant Ji in April (see Chapter One) had come over and, taking out *Sant Bani Magazine*, pointed out how Russell had distorted various events and facts. Another Western disciple of Master Kirpal had asked to see any letters exchanged between Sant Ji and Master.

Pappu had read every word of the first issue of *Sant Bani Magazine* to Sant Ji as soon as it was received in Delhi. And then the Western disciples of other Gurus had come and torn apart underlined passages of the magazine in front of Him. They had explained to Sant Ji that Russell Perkins was a journalist, and therefore prone to exaggeration. They would make comments such as, "Master Kirpal wrote that Saints have three physical signs of Sainthood: 1) special lines on the forehead; 2) a beautiful mole on the cheek and 3) a lotus mark on the foot. We only see the first two on you, so can you show us the third?" Sant Ji had responded, "I am not here to display myself." He told me that they came wanting certificates of proof for His Guruship. They asked the same questions over and over and over again. Sant Ji quietly observed that the "visits" from such Westerners had been very painful for Him.

At that point I was so exhausted that I caught myself silently wondering, "Oh gosh, Sant Ji, why are you telling me all this stuff? I am so tired. Why do I have to know all this?" Thoughts like that were going through my head when the truth hit me. If I were uncomfortable having to listen to a five-minute synopsis of what He had been going through, He Himself had been sitting in Delhi for the past month dealing directly with these events daily. Imagining what it must have been like for Him, I saw how little my faith and strength was, and this began to penetrate. Such sympathetic resonance caused more of the old love in my heart to start welling up. At that point I handed Sant Ji an apple that Wendy and

Robert had given me to bring Him. He had me cut it up, and then He distributed the pieces as parshad to everyone. He observed, "You and Robert and Wendy have so much love for me that you have sent me this apple."

In reference to the need for various proofs and letters of authority some had asked for, Sant Ji explained, "If you know someone, then you do not need to go and ask others about that person. If I know you, Principal Sahib, and you are my friend, do I need to go to someone else and say, 'Is Principal Sahib an all right guy? Is he this? Is he that?' No, I would not have to go and get confirmation that you were a good person – I like you; you are my friend." At that instant, instead of absorbing the reality of what He was giving me, I stupidly wondered if He ever referred to me as "Kent" or did He always call me "Principal Sahib?" The desire to have Him say my name welled up, and I was suddenly sick of myself. I tried to undo my wish, saying mentally, "No, *koi bat nahi* – it doesn't matter" and within five seconds He was saying my name loud and clear, and then a second time He said it, "Kent and Russell Sahib."

Pappu translated that there had been an angry fellow from the West who came to see Sant Ji. The man told Sant Ji that he was getting the inner confirmation that someone other than Sant Ji was the Successor, but that "Kent and Russell" were saying that Sant Ji was the next Guru. The fellow asked what he should do. He was literally filled with rage as he spoke. Sant Ji chuckled as He related how the fellow's angry demeanor finally caught up with him, for at the end of all his questions he asked, "And what do I do about anger?"

Sant Ji told me that Sardar Rattan Singh and Khushi Ram were remembering me, and I was able to say in Hindi, "I am also remembering Sardar Rattan Singh and Khushi Ram." He really laughed when I said anything in Hindi – He seemed to enjoy it. He asked me how many dear ones were learning Punjabi or Hindi. He also asked if Eric Perkins and I were singing the bhajans, and Pappu explained how we had provided copies of several songs for the Sangat to learn. I delighted in the news that Pathi Ji's cow had given birth unexpectedly, and that his crops were doing very well. Catching up on the village "gossip" was much more soothing than hearing more about various efforts to "work out" all of the problems of the divided Sangat – and again I realized that He was teaching me something. Could that be exactly how He felt? During the last trip Sant Ji had explained a great deal, through His words and His actions, about how to use the power of love to deal with adversity. He showed us how to behave then – but by bringing Him to Delhi we, unwittingly, had placed Him in the midst of it once again. And I was feeling "uninterested?" "Wow," I thought, "He is completely uninterested as well, but, because He loves us, He is here having to face it every day!"

With the Master's Grace manifesting through Sant Ji's overwhelming love and patience with me, it turned into a beautiful session that offered me a great opportunity to grow. I remembered how I had been flying as high as a kite on my last trip – except for the brief bump that came at the end when we had to stay in Delhi four extra days. And this trip started with a crash – I could not even enter India. I had spent half the day in scooters, and was so drained that I was falling asleep over and over again in the scooter on the way home – right in the middle of the exhaust-laden rush hour traffic! And here I was sitting at His Feet again, weary and tired, but beginning to warm up to Him at last.[7]

---

[7] After this session with Sant Ji, Pappu explained more about what had been happening since Sant Ji had come to Delhi a few weeks before my arrival. On a very positive note, Mr. Oberoi, the devoted initiate of Baba Sawan Singh, who had been serving Master Kirpal since childhood, had come to see Sant Ji and was now visiting Him daily. Mr. Oberoi was intimately connected with (and distantly related to) the physical son of Master Kirpal, Sardar Darshan Singh. As Mr. Oberoi recently explained, "When I first met Sant Ji, I was looking for someone who could be somewhat similar to Hazur Kirpal in all vital aspects. On meeting Sant Ji, I found that the power of Hazur Kirpal was working in and through Him. At that time I was feeling very upset and guilty about what was happening between various groups and wished deeply that the situation should improve. I broached the subject with Sant Ji, but He did not want to involve Himself in that, as He felt that matters relating to property, possessions and position are not usually solved peacefully." (personal correspondence with the author, April 7, 2001). Mr. Oberoi was immediately very devoted to Sant Ji and expressed a desire to serve wherever he could, but Sant Ji would accept nothing from him at that time. Mr. and Mrs. Oberoi's visits lasted for hours at a time (see also A. S. Oberoi, *Support for the Shaken Sangat*, pp. 201 ff).

Representatives from the "would-be" Successors came to see Sant Ji, including those representing the man who was sitting on the dais at Sawan Ashram as well as those backing Master Kirpal's physical son, Sardar Darshan Singh. A long-time disciple of Baba Sawan Singh Ji, the same woman who had visited Sant Ji with the Delhi Group in April (see Chapter One) sent Sant Ji a note saying that she was on death's bed. He went to see her and, instantly better, she used a phone to arrange a visit with Sardar Darshan Singh. Sant Ji met

The Fourth Day – Saturday, August 14th, 1976

We went to see Him again on Saturday and we discussed a number of ideas about the upcoming tour. Based on some of the things He had told me, I began to think that maybe there should be some kind of screening process for the questions when Sant Ji visited the West. I did not want Him to be subjected to all kinds of political questions, as had been happening there in Delhi. Perhaps it would be a good idea to have announcements made each time that only questions having to do with Sant Mat would be allowed. I also had some ideas as to how the Satsang ought to be conducted.

As far as the format for Satsang, we all (Sant Ji, Pappu, and I) felt that Pappu should translate as Sant Ji gave the Satsang, rather than waiting until the end. We thought it would work for Pappu to translate after every two to three minutes. Sant Ji told Pappu to have a notebook and to jot things down, so nothing would be lost. It evolved that Sant Ji would pick the bhajan the day before He used it, and then Pappu could have a translation ready. This would introduce the Satsang and give it cohesiveness.

I should have thought more about how it would appear if we tried to protect Sant Ji from non-spiritual questions. He commented that if He refused to allow people to ask questions, they would go away dissatisfied. He would tell them Himself whether or not their questions pertained to Sant Mat. He did not think that that type of question would come up at Sant Bani. Besides, either Russell or I would be there to handle anyone if they were very difficult. With complete humility He then asked me if this approach seemed all right?

Sant Ji went on to say that some people were involved with religion as a business. For them, if a competitor opened up shop, the object was to try to undermine the competition through such means as slander. He said that He had been in Sant Mat since He was a child, and that Spirituality was His only interest. He explained that other groups were afraid of Sant Bani Ashram in America, not of Him. He was sitting in a

---

Darshan Singh, and assured him that when Sant Ji went to the West, He would not talk against anyone, much less against Darshan Singh.

Master Kirpal's devoted disciple, Bibi Hardevi (known affectionately as "Tai Ji") came to the Bagga's house to see Sant Ji a few times. She requested that Sant Ji come to Sawan Ashram, but again, He politely refused in a most gentle manner (see A. S. Oberoi, *Support for the Shaken Sangat*, pp. 280 ff).

corner a million miles from everywhere, so why should they fear Him?
"Isn't that so?" He asked me. I drew a blank, and Pappu had to say, "He
is asking you a question – answer Him." I was still unable to get hold of
it all, so I just said that He was Sant Bani. Then I added that people were
afraid of Russell's influence. Sant Ji went on to tell me that not everyone
coming had abused and criticized Russell, that many had praised him. I
told Him that in New Hampshire many new people were coming to the
Satsang and to the classes for prospective initiates that Russell was holding.

My insensitivity to the consequences of protecting Him from questions, coupled with my confusion over my role, led me to ask something
that Pappu could make no sense of. It was a subtle, profound question,
and was pivotal to the lessons I was being given, but I could not state it
clearly. It had to do with the fact that although the Master is in control of
all, isn't it also in the disciple's power to please or displease the Master –
and therefore to cause the Master to suffer? Enough of the question was
successfully communicated that He answered that we all must do our
best, and that we should forget the past. Sant Ji repeated that Master
Kirpal wished for Dennis Huntington to do the seva of assisting with the
visas, but that the love and seva of others such as Anne Wiggins would
not be wasted. It would also be rewarded. He continued, saying that had
He known it would require visas to come to the United States, He would
have had us arrange it. He had thought it was like a train – one simply
bought the ticket and got on. I remembered how He had told us in April
that He knew nothing about this kind of thing, and therefore it had been
completely up to us to arrange it. Wendy's remark on the way to the
airport rang ever more true: "It ought to teach us that we can no longer
be children – just sitting back and waiting for the Master Power to do our
work. If His Will calls for action, then we must do it to the best of our
ability." Sant Ji said again that in the future either Russell or I should
come to India during these times of arranging things. I apologized once
more for my own failure, and promised to do better next time.

I showed Sant Ji a picture of my family – Karen, Chris (age six), and
Nick (age one) outside our house with snow on the ground. He looked at
the photo for a long time with much delight. He asked many questions
about my education, and how I had earned my living. Very sweetly He
requested a photo album of all the families at Sant Bani Ashram, so that
He could remember us when we were not with Him. I showed Him the
Sant Bani Ashram publicity file, and He was very interested, noting the
newspaper photos of Robert Schongalla and Eric Perkins.

Sant Ji appeared quite intrigued with the photo of Russell shaking hands with the President of India in 1974. He requested a copy for the Ashram at 77 RB saying simply, "It will help." And then He really shocked me. He began to read the caption under the picture, "Russell Perkins of Sanbornton NH meets the President of India . . ." I wish that I had a photo of the diameter of my eyes – I was so very surprised that He could read English. We all roared with laughter when He finished and I thought, "Why, You sly old fox, You." He read aloud the title for my article on the school at Manav Kendra, "Kent Bicknell, Principal of Sant Bani Ashram School, reports on the . . ." He had to read the word "human" several times, with the assistance of Pappu and me.

Pappu left the room for a moment and Sant Ji told me in Hindi that He wanted a picture of my family that had me in it. When Pappu returned, Sant Ji said how He was very pleased by the way we showed so much love for our family, and that in India a man would be embarrassed to talk about his love for his wife and children so openly. He was delighted with the photos of Wendy and her family – and of the wedding of Robert and Wendy. He was glad to see that I had so much love for my family. He said that in April He had been very happy at Khushi Ram's house when we had thought of taking the rock candy back to our families. He added that He had chided the Indians because they dared not speak of their love for their families in the manner we did.

At this point Sant Ji commented that there were hippies wandering all around India, and that they seemed to have no love for their families. Speaking of their wild hair and sloppy dress, He stated that hippies now had a bad name in India. He mentioned that when Dennis Huntington went to the U.S. Embassy, he was all dressed up. Dennis had been well received, while the hippies were ignored – and then Sant Ji imitated a hippy taking a big drag on a cigarette. He stated, "Dennis was a lion among sheep."

Again He said how it was too bad that there were no movies of Master Kirpal and Him. He related that the people in Rajasthan did not like photos, but that He was now encouraging them to keep them for remembrance. I pointed out to Him that if I lived with Him there would be no need to have my photo. He said, "We will see," and then asked, "What about the School?" I laughed and said the Master Power would take care of it, and He said, "No, you have to do your duties." I talked then about some future time, say in a few years, when I might do some work for my doctorate on the system of education in India. Could I come

for a few months? He was guarded, saying, "What about your family —
how will they live?" I suggested that they could come also.

Sant Ji noticed that I was quite tired and asked Pathi Ji to give me a
rub down, which he did. Later that evening I went up to the roof of the
Bagga house for some time of quiet reflection. I still felt that something
was absent, that something was wrong inside. Last time when I had
come, I had opened my heart right away to Sant Ji – I had told Him all
my problems. Being so honest with Him was really wonderful. This time
I sensed that I was holding something back, but I puzzled over what. I
tried to figure it out, but could make little headway (other than to realize
I was physically drained and that a lot of things might have contributed
to my state).

The Fifth Day – Sunday, August 15th, 1976

I awoke early and sat for meditation, but the distress was still with
me. By early afternoon I was downright grumpy. Contrary to my
statement about only needing a glimpse of Sant Ji now and then, I was
feeling like I really wanted to be around Him as much as possible. Yet I
knew He was sick and needed to rest, as the afternoon before He had
cancelled the Satsang. As I sat watching people come and go from His
room, I wished more and more to see Him. When Pappu brought tea for
Sant Ji, he did not come out for a while. Feeling sorry for myself, I
became angry. I wanted to be in there, and that was all there was to it.

Somewhat bored and wondering what to do next, I unpacked the
movie camera. Using blades of grass on a white cloth with an em-
broidered blue background, Pappu's brother Jawahar and I set up the
movie title and filmed it: "The First World Tour – Sant Ajaib Singh –
Delhi – August 16, 1976." We were working on the front porch, right
next to Sant Ji's room. Suddenly the door to His room flew wide open
and He was standing there. He looked at me, and then closed the door
really quickly. Bang! That was it. A pang of something shot through me
and I was not sure what to make of it. After I had finished shooting the
movie title, I sat down in a chair directly across from His door.

Still upset, I had plans to say things to Pappu like, "Look, put
yourself in my shoes. Let's say I were in there all the time and you were
on the outside – how would you feel?" Pappu emerged finally and asked
me if I wanted some tea, but I told him that I had just had two cups of
black coffee, as I was tired of being drowsy and sluggish at mid-day

while most everyone napped. Pappu politely suggested that I go ahead and have the tea, so I did. Sitting there drinking the sweet chai, my mind churned with ingratiating ego-thoughts of self-pity.

Then Sant Ji coughed and I heard it. It reached me, through and through. I sat in the chair, staring at His door, and the closed box inside me began to open. As I continued sitting, the muse seemed to speak, and I picked up my journal and wrote the following with no effort, no forethought:

Now I am seeing a Saint suffer close-up. I know Saints suffer, but now I am seeing; hearing the dry cough; seeing the lines on the radiant face increase. And I know that I have contributed to this suffering. I have not done my best, and doing our best is what is required so that He does not live in pain.

Last time He was active and I was passive – He filled me with happiness. This time I am/have been expected to act; He is waiting. Who has not been remiss? Recall the words of Hazur Kirpal after his operation requesting us to introspect and change so that it may not happen again – and He left fourteen years early.[8]

He gives ONLY LOVE. This is SANT MAT, and as He told me yesterday, Sant Mat is a Path of Love, which He has been on since childhood. He asks for Love in return. Instead He gets old disciples of Master Kirpal coming to tear apart His magazine in front of Him. He gets me, coming with thoughts of sorrow for self, self-importance, and ego-need demands. Why in God's

---

[8] Master Kirpal, after undergoing a serious operation in June of 1971, asked all of His disciples to put in more time for meditation and to put the Spiritual Teachings into practice on a daily basis – and yet, owing at least in part to our shortcomings, Sant Ji had confirmed that He left His physical body fourteen years early. See *Sat Sandesh*, September 1971, "The Story of Master's Illness." In His first talk to the Sangat after the operation Master Kirpal stated, "The sickness which was there has now been cured, and I thank Dr. Mahajan for his help . . . The remaining one percent adjustment is being made. My Hazur (Baba Sawan Singh Ji) has accomplished a good deal of service through me up to now, and I can tell you there is much more yet to be done in the future. I request you all to lead a good life from now on – a chaste life – especially those of you who live in our ashrams. I know you try – but now really DO IT! I have great love for you. I know you also have love for me, but perhaps you do not realize the extent of my love for you." (p. 8)

Name can I not just LOVE HIM? Love knows service and sacrifice – love knows giving – GIVE, GIVE & GIVE. It is better that I go away and never see Him again if I continue on my path of take, take, take.

He is Satguru. He needs nothing. His love for/and from Kirpal is enough for all time. And the same may be said for Christ, Mansur,[9] etc. But who among us would nail the nails and strip off the skin? This is the mystery in my heart, the paradox of paradoxes which I tried to ask Him about but did not succeed; and it is also the central theme of my trip: The All-Powerful, All-Knowing, timeless Satguru is dependent on the love of His disciples. Shardik.[10] There are so many ways we can drag Him through hell – either through conscious or unconscious actions, or even by simply doing less than our best. He waits; He smiles; He laughs; He utters words of consolation and encouragement; and He suffers. Oh God, Kirpal, and Sant Ji, may I never forget this lesson you have given me.

That is what I was learning on this trip. I had been close to the Guru and had seen Him suffering, and that made it very different from my last trip. In April I had been a receptacle to be filled with all sorts of happiness from the Satguru, Who kept pouring it in. On this occasion, however, something more had been demanded of me – more trust and compassion – and I wondered where these were. My prayer became that we would not cause the Guru to suffer. Finally, after writing the above in my journal, my eyes began to mist. In my heart I really wanted to understand what I could do. I closed my eyes and prayed deeply to God and Master Kirpal to please lift Sant Ji's suffering. I realized that the best action I could perform would be to do more Simran. I prayed as hard as I could that any benefit of the Simran I did would not go to me, but that it would go to help Sant Ji. In retrospect, I see that my desire was impertinent, but that is what was in my heart.

---

[9] Mansur al-Hallaj (858-922 A.D.) was a Sufi mystic who was tortured and executed as a heretic, in part for His God-intoxicated statement, "I am Truth!" which could be interpreted as, "I am God!"

[10] *Shardik* is a 1974 novel by Richard Adams in which the God Power incarnates in a Bear, Shardik. Those who initially save, then worship Shardik, later come close to destroying the Bear.

Later, as I sat across from His door, every time I heard Him cough it would go into my heart like an arrow. Then the thought came to me, "Oh God, what if He's so sick that He says He can't go?" Then I thought would we all say, "Oh, You must go, we've bought the tickets. Everyone will be expecting You. Oh, You'll get better." When I realized that we might respond like that to Him, I immediately remembered the story of the king's servant who, unlike the wise ministers, was so willing to follow the orders of his king that he smashed the priceless treasure, a cup of gold, when ordered to do so. I thought, "No! If Sant Ji said that He could not go, then we, Pappu, Pathi Ji, and I, would definitely say, 'All right, You can't go. Whatever You wish.' "

I wondered if I should secretly go and cable or telephone Russell. I thought, "Without telling Sant Ji or Pappu, perhaps I should sneak away and send a message to Sant Bani that Sant Ji is really sick and that the whole Sangat needs to pray." It was all quite painful, especially seeing into the dark corners of myself so clearly, but it inspired me to want to be able to give Him that which He asks. I did want to change my path of taking to one of giving. I began to feel that a sense of purpose had come into my trip.

After a while some Indian people arrived to visit Sant Ji. Pappu asked me to socialize with them while they were waiting to see Him, which I did very easily. They went into Sant Ji's room and remained in there for quite some time. It occurred to me that a few black and white photos might be nice for *Sant Bani Magazine*, so I went for my camera. When I came back the guests were all on their way out. I had reached the point where I was not expecting anything – I did not want Sant Ji to feel He should do anything on my behalf. But when the door to Sant Ji's room opened, Pappu said, "Come on in."

One of the first things Sant Ji did was to ask about my arms. I had woken up on Saturday morning simply covered with spots on my arms, hands, feet and chest. They really itched. Everyone suggested that they were bug bites. Sant Ji, during a brief walk that morning, had said He thought they were from the heat. He was sitting on the bed, and I was on the floor in front of Him. He took my left arm and gently bent it back so He could see it. He slowly rubbed two fingers along the worst area. Then He took my right arm and did the same. I looked at Him, feeling joyful, but inside that joy there was a sense of what can only be described as total awe for this Celestial Being sitting in front of me, looking exactly like Master Kirpal in the well-known photo reproduced in the book, *The*

Wheel of Life. I said to Him, "You aren't taking my suffering from me are You?" and the answer came back, very gently and low, "You should have told me that before I touched you."

From my heart I told Him that I was very low, and had caused Him to suffer. He said, "Oh no, don't ever feel that I am taking on your suffering. I am serving you with love." So He was saying that indeed He was taking on my suffering, because that is what He had come on earth to do. Out of love for us He had come to serve. I wondered, how could we treat Him like we had been doing – even if inadvertantly?

Sant Ji proceeded to tell me that He felt better at that moment, commenting that the arrangements had not been good. He had been in Delhi for a month, and it would have been much better if He had come down from Rajasthan and gotten on the plane the same day. He repeated that twice, adding that such would have been the ideal schedule. He explained why His health had deteriorated. He had not had a proper schedule, because visitors had come all the time. He had been kept up very late at night talking to many different people. He was used to having two meals a day at the right time, or else He would get sick. He had not been able to get enough exercise (and I recalled that He had been working the land at 77 RB when Pappu went to get Him). On top of that, He had been taking quinine for His illness, and had reacted to the immunization shot. For all those reasons, He got sick. I felt that there was no denying the reality that we could have made much better arrangements. I asked myself if we should be dragging Him around on a Tour that was going to mean constant changes in schedule and other disruptions – and I decided it was something we really needed to think about.

He further stated that when I, Kent, had come with a confused and worried heart, it confused and worried Him. He really felt badly for me, because I had had to go all over and spend money on tickets and travel. Most definitely my mind had been confused. I referred to its wild horse quality, but the other factor was that I had not been able to be completely honest with Him – to tell Him exactly about my state. At that point I opened up and leveled with Him. I told Him how low my mind had been when I came, and that my heart felt like stone. Referring to that afternoon when He opened the door and then shut it quickly, He remarked, "When I opened the door and looked out at you, I wanted to talk to you." He added that He had felt confused and had closed it again. I thought, "Gosh, He remembers that. He remembers looking at me." After that He was feeling so ill that He was afraid He simply would not be able to go on the Tour. But the sickness lifted, and He said that as of the present He felt good and would be able to go.

My mind was boggling at all of this. Did my prayer to God and Master Kirpal help ease His suffering? Even though I knew He knew it, I asked, "Do You want me to tell You what was going through my mind when I saw You open the door?" He kindly responded, "You can if you like." So I told Him everything. I explained how I had been upset at Pappu and feeling quite sorry for myself, thinking that Pappu was in with Sant Ji drinking tea. I told Him how when He opened and closed the door I thought He was displeased with me. Next I related that when I heard Him cough, I began to see how selfish I had been. I told Him that I prayed to God and Master Kirpal to lift His suffering, and that I prayed that my Simran should be His. I said that the thought had even crossed my mind that He might be too sick to go on the Tour – and how I had remembered the story of the faithful servant who obeyed the orders of his king and smashed the priceless treasure. I laid my heart bare, holding back only that I had thought of sneaking away to phone or cable Sant Bani.

Sant Ji responded, "You know this day I didn't give Pappu any tea. Every other day he drinks out of my cup; but this day I didn't give him any. I didn't even invite Pathi Ji for tea." And then He told me how He had been feeling so stuffy in His room. He had tried to open the windows but could not, so He opened the door. He saw me, but closed the door again, because, He explained, His mind felt confused. Right then I understood that I had been given an extraordinary gift. At some level beyond my daily consciousness, He had made me in tune with Him. I thought, "Wow! That is what was happening to You? It was so parallel to what was happening to me!" And I did not need further confirmation, as I knew that He knew.

I reiterated that my heart had been stone when I had come. I had had to hear His coughing and suffering, and that this was the way He had had to crack the rock, so that I could begin to love Him again. I felt terrible, but at least I had come clean. He accepted it all. He told me that when He is not sick, He loves to see everyone and serve everyone, but when He is sick it is not good. He said how earlier when He looked out the window and saw me, He had a mind to call me in and talk Hindi with me, but He was not feeling well. He said His heart was really looking forward to the day when we could converse face-to-face in Hindi. And then He said how there was pain in His heart, because I was suffering.

He told me that my worries were His worries, adding that Soami Ji Maharaj had said that also: "Your burden, your worries are mine." He said that I should not worry about anything – that I had nothing to worry about. I asked how I could help His suffering and He told me, "Bhajan." It was a profoundly moving and intoxicating session and as we left the room, Pappu, very aware of my recent spiritual and mental angst, turned to me and asked, "Happy?"

Later I asked Sant Ji if I could take a picture of Him when His long hair was flowing freely about His shoulders and down His back. He wondered why I would like a photo of Him without His turban. When I told Him that these were for my own enjoyment and remembrance – not for publication – He graciously agreed to my request. I snapped three extraordinary photographs of Sant Ji alone – from the front and side – and with Pathi Ji and Pappu seated at His feet.[11]

After the evening meal, Sant Ji, Pathi Ji, Pappu, and I went out for a half-hour walk that, following the earlier events, seemed really beautiful. Pathi Ji and I communicated a little in my broken Hindi, and he taught me the chorus of a new bhajan: "Your love has given sight to my eyes, Oh Satguru." At one point as we were walking along, a stranger called out to us, "Baba Ji."[12] The man came closer and started talking excitedly and gesturing towards a nearby canal. Pathi Ji went over to see. As we approached, I initially thought there was a body in the canal, since it was dark and I saw the man was holding something fleshy and slick. I thought, "Oh my goodness, am I now going to see a scene of raising the dead?" But no, the man was supporting the head of a calf that had fallen

---

[11] Most disciples who saw the photos requested that I make copies for them – but I was careful to comply with what I had said to Sant Ji. Eventually a good friend prevailed upon me to loan him a photo for an artistic project – and I agreed, with the condition that it be for his use only. The friend forgot my concern and made up cards of the photo for general distribution. I was upset – and asked that he stop passing those out – which he did. Fifteen years later, as I stood outside Sant Ji's house at Subachoque, the spiritual retreat center near Bogotá, Colombia, a disciple arrived for an interview wearing a T-shirt with a large version of my "private" photo of Sant Ji reproduced on the front. I was reminded again of how I had let such a simple agreement slip through my fingers, silently asked for forgiveness, and shook my head to clear away the mist of shame that enveloped me.

[12] While Western disciples called Sant Ajaib Singh "Sant Ji," His devotees in India called Him "Baba Ji."

in a narrow deep ditch. The calf was very frightened. I went and helped, and the three of us pulled it out.

We enjoyed the rest of our walk. Everyone, including Sant Ji, was in the best of spirits when we got back to the house. After Sant Ji retired, Pathi Ji, Pappu, and I were so excited that we laughed and talked, and even played some *"ragas"* on makeshift tablas! I went to bed very happy. My heart had melted again, and I felt ready to accompany the Saint to the West at last.

The Sixth and Final Day – Monday, August 16th, 1976

During August in Delhi, with the absence of air conditioning, one slept outside whenever possible. At some point during the night it began to drizzle slightly and I pulled my bed right over next to Sant Ji's door – which was open. I woke up at 2:00 a.m. and meditated a couple hours, and then went back to sleep for a while. Pappu brought me chai at 4:45 and I got back into my meditation. I was determined to sit without moving, either until the clock struck six, or Sant Ji came out and cleared His throat. I kept sitting and it was good, even though I was dealing with things like flies crawling all over my face. Over tea I had thought – because my heart was singing – that if I stopped meditating before He came out, then I would sing a bhajan under His window.

I heard Him cough a couple of times and it bothered me. It did not go straight to my heart but it started to. Suddenly I heard Him cough really hard, and then came the sounds of vomiting – which went on a couple of times. Pappu and Pathi Ji began to run in and out of the room. I tried very hard to think that Sant Ji would feel better now – that this was simply a last ridding of the burdens He carried for us in preparation for the trip.

I attempted to keep on with my meditation, but after a while I started singing softly to myself. In a moment it all just overwhelmed me and I buried my head in my arms and wept deeply. Pappu came almost immediately and said, "Sant Ji wants to see you." I went into His room. He had a pillow brought for me and told me to sit really close to Him. He went on to tell me how He was very sick. He said that what He needed was rest. He was thinking maybe it would be better if He did not make the trip. I agreed at once, no doubt thanks to everything that had happened the day before. Someone (not Pappu or Pathi Ji) came in the room, and that person really wanted to bring a doctor. In my heart all I could think of was: "Doctor! What Sant Ji needs is to get out of Delhi, and for the Sangat to do Bhajan and Simran – more, more, more Bhajan and Simran." Sant Ji said He did not need a doctor. I said (and He may already have been saying it) that I thought He should go to Rajasthan and rest for a few days. He said yes – with ten days in Rajasthan with the right food, He would probably be all right.

At that point I knew that I was supposed to go back that night, because I felt I should be communicating all of these events to the Sangat. Someone suggested that I did not have to go right away, pointing out that waiting for my return date on the British Airways ticket could save $850.[13] Sant Ji said it would be fine for me to wait – whatever I wished. I told Him I felt I was supposed to go back, but that I wanted to do His Will. I added that while I would love to return with Him to Rajasthan, something inside told me I should go back to America. Pappu translated, and Sant Ji was very emphatic that I should fly out that evening. He said it was so important to do the Will of the Master, and that it was my duty to go back and explain the situation to the Sangat so that no one would be worried. At that point He dictated a letter to Russell, giving details of the whole situation. That took quite a while as He really put a lot of attention into it. Sant Ji sat with His Eyes closed and His head in His hands, and it was apparent that He was receiving the contents of the letter from within.

The sorrow in my heart at that point was not that He was not coming, but that He was suffering and that I had contributed to it – that I had failed to do my best. He began talking again about how He had come to Delhi and had spent such a long time there. Ever so gently, He went over it all again. In Delhi the atmosphere had not been right, the food was not served on schedule, people were coming at all hours, and that is why He had got sick. He said that it was the Master's Will that He was not going today – and that He did not want to do anything against the Will of the Master.

At that point I started crying and crying. He reached out His hand and placed it on my arm and said, "Kent, Kent, don't leave me crying. Don't leave me like this. I want you to be happy when you leave – not crying. Don't trouble me more." And I just cried – I was so upset that I

---

[13] My return ticket on British Airways was not valid until several days hence. If I wished to return immediately I had to use the Air India ticket, rather than cashing it in for a refund.

had caused Him to suffer – and still was – and I could not control it. He continued with His tender, loving and sweet message not to cause Him more suffering. As I could not help myself, He again helped me. He took on my sorrow. Suddenly I felt all my suffering go into Him through His Hand on my arm – there was a physical sensation of traveling energy – like a sponge soaking up water.

After a time I was able to talk again. I told Sant Ji that my heart was clear, and that I had many things to tell the Sangat. He told me to have a strong heart – that I should not be confused or worried. It is necessary to have a strong heart as it takes strength to do the Master's Will. He told me not to be failing. He asked, "If you fail, then what are others going to do?" He told me that He really had a lot of love for me.

He indicated that it would be better to communicate everything to the Sangat in person rather than trying to tell it all over the telephone. Lacking the courage to fly in alone to an airport full of expectant Satsangis, I asked if it would be all right if I at least conveyed the news that the Tour was cancelled. He said, "yes," and suggested that I read the letter to Russell over the phone. He asked me about my finances for getting back, and offered me money if I needed it.[14] I thanked Him and said that it would be fine.

There was a new phone in a neighbor's house, but after sitting through several false alarms I could not get through. At 4:15 p.m. Sant Ji called me to His room again. I had to leave for the airport at 7:30. He was lying on His back looking very ill. He told me that He had just vomited again, and asked me to feel how cold His wrists were. He told me that when He sat up and talked, it felt like fire was going up through His head, and that His hearing was blocked and His voice was low.[15] Again He told me that when I took leave of Him I must not be in a down state, as that would affect Him. He had been so worried about me when I had had to go to Katmandu, and that had affected His heart. He told me

---

[14] This was when I first came to know that Sant Ji had money set aside from His days as a land holding farmer.

[15] On the outer level of the physical plane it is obvious that Sant Ji was suffering a bout with malaria – thus the cyclical nature of the episodes of sickness and recovery. He was to suffer again from this illness during His stay at Sant Bani in 1977.

that Sadhus have Weak Hearts, that they are easily affected, and that it is not good for Them.[16]

I was biting my lip – trying to control that which had been flowing all day and continued to flow. In my whole life I had never been weeping so much, and Sant Ji proceeded to tell me not to leave Him in a sad state. It had to be one of the hardest things I would ever have to do, but I said I would try, because He really wanted me to do it. At that moment a false call to the phone interrupted me and I went to sit in the neighbor's house, trying to pull myself together.

I decided to ask Sant Ji one question: how was I not to feel sad? When I came back I did ask Him that, and He told me to write down His answer. He said it was a message for Russell and me.

> *Truth is always opposed. Don't succumb to any pressure, but carry out the Master's duties. Meditate, and tell others to meditate also. The duty of giving Initiation has been given to you (Russell) and you have to carry that out.*
>
> *My health went wrong only because of Delhi. My body was made weaker, and the fever and vomiting has not decreased. Because of my weak state, and the need to rest, I find that I should not go to the States now. And all this is in Satguru Kirpal's Will. If Master will wish, He will give me the strength to serve you.*

I asked Sant Ji if it was all right for me to keep a little space in my heart to be sad. He said He hoped I would have a sadness soon because my sins had separated from me. I also asked Him if I could cry some on the plane. He said that would be all right, as He would not be with me on the plane. I responded, "But You are always with me!" and He really laughed. He was patting my arm and shoulder all the time. He told me not to make haste to come back to India because I was worried about

---

[16] When this statement of Sant Ji, that "Sadhus have Weak Hearts," was originally published in the second issue of *Sant Bani Magazine* (Vol. I, No. 2), a long-time disciple of Master Kirpal wrote to Russell Perkins (the editor) objecting to it. Twenty-five years later Russell commented, "Saints are very vulnerable. This world is not Their Home, and when They take on a Body to come here to save us, that Body suffers. The behavior of the disciples can and does affect the Master. The Gospels are full of such-like stories." (Conversation with the author, March 1st, 2001).

Him. He advised me to carry out my duties, including Bhajan and Simran. I said, "You don't trust me now because I have a return ticket," and He really laughed, and said I could do what I liked as far as returning. He told me to write Him immediately upon arrival in the States and tell Him what I had said to the Sangat.

He sent His love to everyone at the Ashram. He told Pappu to go get something, and I could figure out that it was the picture of my family. When Pappu came back with it, we spent a long time talking about the snow, how the houses are heated in the cold season, electricity, winter apparel, and other things. He told me He had hoped to be meeting my family when He came, but for now He would take this photo to Rajasthan so He could remember them. I told Him that I was feeling stronger, and that I would try my best to leave in a happy state. He told me that if I left Him in a sad state it would take Him longer to get well.

Finally the call went through – shortly before I was to leave for the airport. I spoke with Karen and asked her to convey that I was coming alone because Sant Ji was ill and needed to rest. I said that the Sangat must be happy and not confused or worried, and that everyone should do more Bhajan and Simran. Finally, I asked her to tell everyone that we should pray that the Will of the Master be done, rather than praying that Sant Ji come on Tour. Russell had been working in the Ashram garden when the call went through to my house, so I had given the gist to Karen while someone went to get Russell. By the time he got to the phone, the connection had deteriorated so much that he could hear little of what I said, although I could hear him. I hung up the phone, thanked the neighbors, and went back to Sant Ji's room. I marveled that He had given me that call to make, and in so doing had turned my thoughts away from myself.

I sat back down at His Feet and related to Him what I had said to Karen. I added, "You have made me so strong, that now I'm telling them to be strong and happy!" He sat up and said emphatically, "On hearing this from you, I will recover very quickly." He noticed my tape recorder, and asked Pappu to bring a tape of bhajans. It was the Sangat at 77 RB, singing, *Dhan Dhan Satguru* [Hail, Hail to my Satguru, Who reunites the separated ones!] And so we left Him, sitting on His bed, smiling as He listened to the villagers singing the songs of devotion.

I left about three quarters of an hour later. I said goodbye quickly. He was standing at His window watching me go, and I said, "*Sat Sri Akaal*" and drove off in the taxi. On the plane I wrote and wrote and slept and wrote. I arrived home and did not feel confused or worried. What I felt instead was simply overwhelmed at the profoundness and realness of the Satguru. The "box" of understanding that had been closed to me had opened, and as much as I could comprehend had been given to me. By myself I had not been able to grasp the truth about His illness – nor had I been able to make the best of my failures. I prayed that my heart might never again be so stone-like that it took His suffering to awaken the love in it, and I thanked God for Him and the Reality of the Saints.

*   *   *

When I arrived back in America I tried to do what Sant Ji had asked of me. He had said to communicate everything to the Sangat, so that there would be no confusion or doubt or worry in anyone's mind. We read from His letter to Russell and I shared my notes. People understood that His message was that we should be strong and happy, and that we should have full faith in the Will and Protection of the Master. To worry is not to trust. Sant Ji had indicated that His suffering would be eased if we could maintain the mental states of being strong, happy, and trusting in the Will of the Master. The way to achieve this was through more and more meditation. He had said very clearly that what was required was the seva of meditation.

Sant Ji had asked me to write to Him immediately and tell Him what I had conveyed to the Sangat. On the plane I had dashed off a quick note that I mailed from London. Once home I sent Him a copy of my notes, which were later edited and published as an article in the second issue of *Sant Bani Magazine*.[17] In my packet to Sant Ji I included two photographs of the Sangat, and a covering letter in Hindi that said:

August 19, 1976

Beloved Sant Ji,

I am strong. I am happy. I am not confused. I am seeing Light. I am hearing Sound. All the Sangat is happy. We love You. I love You. You are my dear father. You see the picture of the Sangat. All are happy. No one is crying. Love. Kent.

---

[17] See the August 1976, issue of *Sant Bani Magazine*, Vol. I, No. 2.

Sant Ji responded with a letter on the third of September 1976:

My Most Beloved,
Kent Principal Sahib,

Much love to you and your family. I was happy to read the letter which you wrote in London and also received a registered letter along with your photo, Sangat's photo, and a child's photo.

My dear Principal, do Bhajan and Simran daily with love. From the 27th of August I am free from fever, but have a little weakness. Rest all is fine with Master's Grace.

I understand you as more dear than my life. I truly appreciate your love and true devotion. I pray to Master Kirpal to give you inner strength for Bhajan and Simran. Never miss your meditation. As food is required to run the pranas (vital airs), similarly, meditation, the food of the Soul, is also essential.

Convey my Namaste to all the lovers in Sant Bani Ashram.
With much love to you,
Dass Ajaib Singh

There was some more discussion of the Tour happening in the fall, but it was not to be. Instead, Sant Ji came to us the following spring. In the meantime I kept up a vigorous correspondence with Him, receiving two more letters from Him in September of 1976. These letters were sent directly from 77 RB, having first been translated into quaint but charming English by Babu Ji, a sevadar who lived in the village.[18]

Letter #1

13th September, 1976

My Satguru Kirpal's Beloved Kent Bicknell Principal Sahib,

The loving letter written in Hindi on the 24th of August by you received here. I am very much glad after reading it. Let me know if you can read Hindi written like this as written in this

---

[18] In both letters I have added a few words in square brackets "[ ]" for clarification.

letter, so that I may be able to write you letters in Hindi. You wrote that you have seen sphere and heard bells inside. My dear if you will try more like this continuously then you will see very much within. The Simran is the cleaner broom of heart's House. Simran by tongue is the word devotion of the tongue. Sound [Current] is the devotion of God's Tongue. The soul and mind are captivated and controlled by the Sound Word. The True Word is coming from Kirpal Shah's Mouth. If someone hears he gets rid of both the [lower] worlds and he becomes the owner of a Treasure. All the world has been dyed in doing the word's devotion. Someone remembers God as Sohang, someone as Allah, someone [remembers] God as Bhagwan, someone as Wahi Guru. They could not get God or He did not appear to them. Compared to the Simran this other word devotion is nothing. The Sound of God (Dhun) is knowledge, remembrance, and devotion. Real knowledge and remembrance is to get the Sound of God (Dhun). It is earned – does not come through saying. Unlimited Sound of God (Dhun) is always coming which connects with God. This is the real devotion to God. It comes in mind according to luck.

This Sound of God (Dhun) wealth is not found in scriptures. In scriptures there is suggestion. Simran tongue's remembrance is the broom to clean the heart . . . This Sound of God (Dhun) is within the Human, and the righteous man [the Guru] can tell about it. We can get it according to His kindness. We can hear Sound of God (Dhun) by the Grace of the Saints. Due to this we should catch the Holy Feet of Kirpal Shah in our hearts. All worries of Negative Power will be removed. When we catch the Holy Feet of the Saints the Negative Power cannot eat us. The Negative Power is very strong and cannot be removed. When we hear the Sound of God (Dhun), it [the Negative Power] goes away.

Naam Dhun, which is not moveable, is coming day and night in our hearts. We have this gift inside, but we are blank. This wealth supports within us and will go with us. People sleep, but the lovers awake in the remembrance of their Satguru and mix themselves with Him. This power is meant for those who love Kirpal Shah . . .

My health is now OK. Only there is weakness. Fever left me on 27-8-76 and never came back after that day. Give my much

love to the lovers of Sant Bani Ashram. Please read this letter at the time of Satsang, so that all of the lovers may give more and more time for Bhajan and Simran. To all the lovers of Sant Bani Ashram and your family I send more and more love.
Dass Ajaib Singh

Note: This is translated by Babu Ji. Let me know if it is clear so that I may send the letters direct to you.

Letter #2

20th September, 1976

My Satguru Kirpal's Beloved and Pure Hearted Kent Principal Sahib,[19]
The letter written by you is received to Pappu in Delhi. He has written many talks about you. As you have asked for coming to India, you may come very happily. I am very much glad upon you. You have also asked about how many devotees should come in the group. My dear, my mind wants to call all of you to me. But as per worldly concern as you know about me, I can manage twelve or fifteen devotees at a time. I am a poor mendicant sevadar (servant). Sat Guru Kirpal has given me the duty to serve the lovers like you. The lovers coming here should bring their bedding with them.
I wrote you a letter before this, might have been reached. If you like translation of Babu Ji please send the letters direct to 77 RB so that there should be no delay for sending first to Delhi

---

[19] As will be noted at length in another chapter, Sant Ji made it clear to me that when He used terms like "Pure Hearted" or "Ruby of Rubies" in reference to me, He was speaking to my potential – to what He saw I might become – not to what I was on a day-to-day level. As Henry David Thoreau (1817-1862) wrote in his first book, *A Week on the Concord and Merrimack Rivers* (1849), "We are sometimes made aware of a kindness long passed, and realize that there have been times when our Friends' thoughts of us were of so pure and lofty a character that they passed over us like the winds of heaven unnoticed; **when they treated us not as what we were, but as what we aspired to be.**" (from the Wednesday Chapter, p. 208-209 in the 1998 Penguin Classic Edition – emphasis is my own).

and then from Delhi to 77 RB. The lovers of the group will reach here easily if you accompany them.

Do not allow pride inside. We should act according to Sat Guru Kirpal's Words. Sat Guru Kirpal helps every Satsangi from inside. But only the Satsangi who goes within is benefited. Without reaching within, the mind always deceives. It is necessary to escape from the deceptions of the mind. One can escape by going above the stage of the mind.

Now my health is OK. There is only weakness – no fever. I am ready to serve if you come. If some of the people coming here want to get Holy Naam [receive Initiation], please arrange to bring from Russell a copy of the words which are taught to the Western people, so that there may not be some difficulty to make them understand. All the Western people should be told the same words.[20] The work is to be done by the attention of a Sant. But it is necessary that the words from outside should be the same.

The wire sent by you is received here. With much love to you, your family, and all the lovers of Sant Bani Ashram.

Dass Ajaib Singh

Thus commenced the wondrous era of regular pilgrimages to the Holy Feet of Sant Ajaib Singh. Group after group of eager devotees made the long trek over to that Blessed Spiritual Oasis in the desert of Rajasthan. Whether in India or the States, we were all busy preparing for a First World Tour that would actually come to pass.

---

[20] Sant Ji here refers to the Initiation instructions in English as used by Master Kirpal and His representatives.

CHAPTER THREE

Going to Receive Sant Ji
for the First Tour in 1977

In the fall of 1976 I began to receive thin blue air letters from India, sacred missives from the Master. Some were in English, others in Hindi. The latter carried a type of prolonged blessing in that I had to spend a good deal of time, dictionary in hand, simply to understand the contents. The monthly groups heading to Rajasthan also carried correspondence, and brought back much anticipated replies to the growing number of devotees anxious to be in touch with Sant Ji.

I sent Sant Ji a packet of drawings and messages from the students at the Sant Bani School via a group of disciples heading over to visit Him in October. Sant Ji responded, with what was to be the first of many written messages to the students at the School:

17ᵗʰ Oct. 1976

My Dear Children of Sant Bani Ashram School,

I send His Love and Greetings to you. I appreciate your love, which I have received through your drawings. Dear Children of Light, be obedient to your teachers and faithful to your parents.

The initiated children are advised to put more love in their practices, and keep close to Him. Non-initiated are advised to have Godly thoughts. Love all. Remember, Love is God, and God is Love. I love you all.

With All His Love,

> *Yours affectionately,*
> *Ajaib Singh*

The groups continued to travel to India each month. Disciples spent ten days with Sant Ji at the extremely simple but gloriously charged setting of the desert village, 77 RB. Sant Ji named His place, "Sant Bani Ashram" – so now there were two – East and West. My family looked forward with much excitement to our proposed visit to see Sant Ji that March. Karen, son Christopher, and I had been to see Master Kirpal Singh twice (in 1970 and in 1974) but now, with the addition of Nicholas in 1975, we were four. Master Kirpal Singh used to say that life is a series of interruptions, and happiness consists of adjusting to these. In January our family was thrown a big one.

One way to enjoy the cold winters of New Hampshire is to get out and play in the elements. At the School, this meant flooding an area of the parking lot to create a small skating rink. Our technology was not the greatest (viz. a garden hose at 10 below zero on a winter's night), and the ice often had cracks in places. Skating backward during a School recess, Karen hit a patch of rough ice and fell, shattering both her wrists[1] in the process of breaking her fall. The doctors, in an act of "kindness," put only one arm in a full cast from the hand to her bicep. The other they allowed to stop below her elbow, so that she might have some mobility as her wrists healed over the next several weeks. In the twinkling of an eye, we went from complete independence to needing all of the help we could get.

The Ashram community was wonderful as friends and neighbors stepped in to help out with what needed to be done. Evelyn Sanborn, a student at Sant Bani, moved in with us and provided critical care that was much appreciated. Of course we let Sant Ji know about the accident, and the group that went in January brought back this letter from Him:

18-1-77

My Satguru Kirpal's Beloved Jewel
Dear Kent (Principal Sahib)

   Pappu has told me about Karen's accident, that her bones in both the arms were broken. My dear, as you already know, happiness and sufferings are the reaction of past karmas. Everything is in Hazur's Will. Hazur will shower Grace and she will recover soon. Do not be sad in pains or sufferings. Sufferings lead to Eternal Happiness.
   Tell Karen to do more Simran. She will get strength for her

---

[1] Actually she fractured the ends of both bones, the radius and the ulna, in both arms.

soul and, come what may in His Will, it is our duty to bear that.
Keep me posted when the next groups come. To be in His Will is
His Devotion. Do not worry. Be brave.
  Convey my love to Karen, Chris, and Nicky
              With All His Love
              Dass Ajaib Singh

It never occurred to us that we should rethink our travel plans in
March. By that time, almost all of the people living at Sant Bani Ashram
had been to India to see Sant Ji except Karen, and we were quite intent
on making the journey. A couple of weeks before we were to leave, however, Sant Ji sent us the following letter:

                          18-2-77

My Satguru Kirpal's beloved
My dear jewel among jewels, Kent, Principal Sahib

  Received your letter full of love dated 8ᵗʰ Feb. and noted its
contents. It was all His Grace and His Will that Karen had to
undergo sufferings. Whoever has helped you in this time are
good people. He is the friend who helps in need.
  Karen had to pay a very hard karma, but with Master's
Grace it was reduced to a little suffering. Hazur changed that
from a gallows to a pinprick. He is very much Gracious on you. I
hope that she will recover very soon. But she should (must) not
work with her hands until she recovers fully, because it is the
matter of joints of bones. If she will use her hands, that will be
not good for her. She should not make hurry in doing any work.
She should not come to Rajasthan in March, because she needs
much rest now. I will be happy to see her there in Sant Bani. She
should wait till then. I hope to visit her in May.
  As far as I think, you should come in May to take all of us.
Pappu will write more about this to you. I am happy that Karen
has done more Simran. Master is very much gracious on you.
Convey my love to her.
  Much much love to you and Chris and Nick and Karen
              With all His Love
              Dass Ajaib Singh

Although we immediately understood the wisdom of Sant Ji's counsel, we did have to adjust. Karen, Chris, and Nick would not be going to meet the One Who was becoming so important to all of our lives – yet it was requested that I come in May to accompany Sant Ji and the party back to the States. Karen was most gracious, and shifted gear with amazing aplomb. In mid-March, she received an extraordinary letter from Sant Ji:

17th March '77

Dear Daughter Karen,

Received your loving letter. I am very much grateful to Hazur Kirpal, for He has cured you very soon. I am writing this in His Love – that you still need a lot of rest. You should not work hard with your hands. Happiness and sorrow are coming and going. The time spent in pain is the most precious time, as God is very much remembered then. Thank Hazur Kirpal who reduced your pains, from gallows to pin-pricks.

Your coming to Rajasthan will happen only with His Orders. With His Grace, I hope to reach Sant Bani Ashram in the first week of May. Sant Bani Ashram is my home. The lovers at the Ashram are dear to me more than the parts of my body. If you are suffering, I am experiencing its pain. Your happiness is my happiness. Your pain is my pain.

Our True Lord Hazur is very much gracious on you. Spend your each and every breath in His Sweet Simran. Pains and happiness are like the clothes which the body wears one day and removes on another day. In any case one should be devoted to Master. Devotion gives strength to bear the pain. Soul gets strength by constant Simran. One doesn't feel the length of time in pain.

I send much much love to you and Chris and Nick
With All His Love
Dass Ajaib Singh

I prepared to travel to India again. Someone returning from the March visit to 77 RB told me that one night Sant Ji spoke briefly about Karen's arms, and finished by saying that He would come to the United States "only when Kent comes to get me." What a mystery! I was thrilled to be asked, as well as honored, but as to why, I had no idea. My thought was that the invitation was Sant Ji's sweet way of forgiving all of my missteps when I went to receive Him the previous August, for the Tour that wasn't. Having learned my lesson the year before, I obtained a visa and was set to fly to His Feet once again.

Groups were going monthly, through April (later suspended as being too hot a month for visiting Rajasthan). The plan was for me to leave for India mid-way through the group's stay, arrange for the tickets in Delhi, and travel up to Rajasthan via train. Pappu and I would then accompany the group back to Delhi, staying in the city long enough for everyone to depart for their homes. We would return to 77 RB, and accompany Sant Ji and Pathi Ji back down to Delhi – and, after a day of rest, head for points west.

The First Day in India – Thursday, April 14th, 1977

I decided to fly with everything I needed stuffed into a large backpack. Given the difficulties I had had entering India the previous August, I felt that the last thing I needed to worry about was "checked baggage." As the plane departed on Tuesday evening, the twelfth, I sensed a profound calm that only got deeper as I went. I hurried off at Rome to make a tight connection, but my Alitalia flight had been canceled. I did Simran – without worrying – and within an hour I was on an Air India flight that got me to Delhi at 2:00 a.m. The airlines personnel would not have permitted me to transfer if I had not had everything with me – so I felt well taken care of. We landed in Delhi and, much to my relief, my passport was stamped and I was whisked along toward the crowd of taxi and rickshaw drivers awaiting the passengers who streamed out of the main terminal.

I arranged a cab and settled down in the back seat for the long drive through the maze of Delhi roadways, dotted with many small curbside fires in those pre-dawn hours. Each fire was surrounded by two or three shawl-draped figures, squatting to warm themselves – and each fire offered incense to the earth-like smells of "Mother India," and smoke to the haze of modern Delhi. I arrived at the Bagga household at 3:15 in the morning. I visited with the family until 4:00 a.m. (Pappu was with the group in Rajasthan), slept for two hours, and woke to sit for meditation. After breakfast, Jawahar and I headed for town for a day of hassling with the travel arrangements for the Tour. The roadblocks were seemingly endless. It was explained to me that, as an American, I could not buy

tickets for Indian nationals, and, again, that I would not be permitted to
fly with the Indians! But all of these obstacles fell quickly and quietly
with no effort on my part, except a smile and silent Simran with, as
Master Kirpal used to say, "the tongue of thought."

While I had hoped to bring the actual airline tickets up to Rajasthan
with me, there was one requirement that did not gracefully disappear.
New forms were required from the Reserve Bank of India, and these had
to be signed in triplicate by Sant Ji, Pathi Ji, and Pappu. It was clear that
I would have to take those forms to Rajasthan for the signatures – but as
that was only a formality and everything seemed in order, I booked a
ticket for the overnight train to Sri Ganganagar for that evening,
Thursday the 14th of April.

Friday, April 15th, 1977

I was met in the busy city of Sri Ganganagar by a Jeep, and we rode
two hours through the dusty roads and sleepy villages to my physical
goal, Sant Bani Ashram at Village 77 RB. We drove in through the
arched double doorways in the adobe walls, and I got out and collected
my backpack. As I walked inside the dining area I heard someone say,
"Kent . . . Kent." I went back out into the courtyard, and there was Sant
Ji with Pappu, looking down from above. They were both laughing. Sant
Ji motioned me to come up, so I did. He really was gorgeous to behold,
all resplendent in white and smiling so hugely, with His Twinkling Eyes
shining so brightly. I touched His Feet, and He gave me a big hug, then
threw His Arm around my shoulders and squeezed me. We went in and
sat down for ten or fifteen minutes. He told me that He and Pappu had
just been talking about me – about when I would come. That morning
some Indian Satsangis had been heading back to Sri Ganganagar and
Sant Ji had told them to wait for my Jeep – but the Satsangis were not
sure I was coming, so they did not want to wait. Then they heard the
Jeep's motor in the distance. Sant Ji related that He heard the sevadars
running around saying, "Kent has come, Kent has come!"

He asked about Karen's wrists immediately – were they getting
stronger? I said that they were still a little weak. He asked if she could
use them – do her hands work? And I said, "Oh yes." Then He said that
He was feeling very much pain in our pain – that there was a lot of pain
for Him. But the karma was there to be paid off. He jumped up and
grabbed the picture of all the people living at Sant Bani Ashram in New

Hampshire, and brought it down in front of Him. He stuck His Thumb directly on Karen right away, and looked up and asked, "Here?" And I said, "Yes, that is her – and You see that the photo of Master Kirpal is looking over her shoulder giving her protection."[2]

He told me how He was very happy to see me. I told Him that I was very happy being there, and I was so grateful that He loved me. I said that I did not understand why He loved me, but that I was really glad He did. He responded that when a Saint loves, it is because of the past connection. And then He said that if a person understood why a Saint loves him or her, that soul would have reached the goal. He went on to say that it was up to me to maintain the love that was given to me. The whole thing was beautiful. I told Him in Hindi that I was very low – that I was His low dog. He responded that the Master would make me strong like a wrestler. He then asked if everyone was happy at Sant Bani Ashram – "How are all the dear ones?" and I answered, "*Bahot aacha*! – Very good."

He asked me if I had finished my work of getting the tickets, and I explained that we needed new signatures on the forms. He confirmed that Pappu and I should go down with the group, finish the arrangements, and come back up as soon as we could.

I told Him that I could read His Hindi letters to me very well – but that it took me about an hour to read, as I had to look up so many words. He really laughed, and said that my handwriting was so simple that He could read my letters in one minute. At one point I commented, "If I don't come back with You this time, I think the Sangat is going to kill me." And He said, "No, Master will not let that happen." Then He said that He was remembering the trouble that I had gone to last August, and added, "It was out of my mouth that the idea came that you should come over and accompany me back!" It was really sweet. Several times He mentioned how happy He was that I was there. While I could not understand it, I certainly did feel warm all over from head to toe.

Sant Ji, concerned as always for everybody else's welfare, sent me downstairs to have *khanna* [food]. I obediently went to the dining area, but I immediately sensed that the whole eating "scene" with the Western disciples seemed confused and sad. People were complaining about the

---

[2] Just about every person in that village – young, old, male, female – asked me about Karen's arms. I even heard Bant, Pathi Ji's daughter, explain to another girl <u>how</u> Karen broke them, with an elaborate description of skating backwards, hitting a rough patch, and shooting out both arms to "break" the fall.

food – thinking that there was too much sugar, too much grease, too many spices, etc. There was a great deal of chitchat taking place on a variety of subjects. As someone remarked, there was too much conversation and not enough meditation and remembrance. Several people were ill, and blamed it on the food being served. My uncharitable (and personal) reaction was, "Wow, this is a big drag!"

In the early days the vast majority of searchers coming to see Sant Ji were initiates of Master Kirpal Singh, and many felt a need to "test" Sant Ji to see if He was, in their minds, the True Successor. I was present when a Colombian woman said ever so sweetly to Sant Ji that, while she liked His Eyes, she did not see her Master, Kirpal Singh, in Those Eyes. Sant Ji responded very lovingly that He felt sorry for her, because He saw His Master everywhere that He looked, including in her eyes. In my case Sant Ji had quite simply fallen me madly in love with Him from the moment we met. But some disciples of Master Kirpal chose to address Sant Ji as "brother," and felt quite fine in asking probing, searching questions that, from my perspective, felt as if He were being treated as a mere human being. On the other hand, as all of the Great Masters have emphasized how important it is to test the validity of a Master before one gives oneself to Her or Him, I tried to suspend my judgmental attitude toward them. An incident of what might be called "doubting Thomas's" had occurred right before my arrival.

In the morning meditation the day I came, someone had complained about a machine noise during the sitting. Sant Ji had responded that no machine had been running. Some people got upset, and said that they had definitely heard a noise. I thought it must have been the call of a particular bird – which sounds a good deal like a rhythmic machine to the unaccustomed ear. One fellow told me that Sant Ji had seemed "a bit angry" during the discussion.

That afternoon when we went out for a walk, Sant Ji mentioned the sound of a distant machine, drawing a distinction between that and the morning sound. A couple of people muttered that, in fact, the machine was what they had heard in the morning. My heart panged, and I felt like turning to them and saying, "Gee, let's get the cross and the nails." Sant Ji proceeded to tell stories about how the Saints never mind when the people disrespect them. He said that in a Saint's heart there is not any place for anger – and when a Saint does show anger there is Grace coming through – that the anger is for a reason. So if the Saint is angry at you then there is a Grace that is coming through. At one point He turned and looked at me and said, "We should not be proud of our *seva*. We should not think, 'Oh, we are being important in the Master's eyes.' Sometimes we do *seva* and we expect to be rewarded by the Master." Then He talked about the true *seva* being meditation.

Mildly put, the group seemed at loose ends. There was a lot of disharmony – a lot of sickness – and the big room was like a hospital, with ten to twelve people sleeping through the early hours due to sickness. There was lots of irrelevant chatter all the time in the room, and I moved over to the Indian sevadar's section for the rest of the time. It seemed to me like the mind was wreaking absolute havoc on some people. More than one person said to me, "Sant Ji has got Master Kirpal's Eyes, but my mind has doubts." My arrival at that time seemed like no mistake, as several people used me as a sounding board for their concerns. Sant Ji continued to work His Magic, and the atmosphere began to change. By the last day (and for many, only on the last day) the doubts had vanished, and everyone was experiencing great love.

At one point during the day I was sitting in the shade of the manger, and a tall, imposing figure walked around the corner. He saw me and asked, "Kent Bicknell – what on earth are you doing here?" I replied, "Neil Wolf – what are you doing here?" and we laughed at the seeming absurdity of it all. Neil and I had attended the same private secondary school in central New Hampshire a dozen years before, and had not seen each other since. Neither knew that the other was "on the Path" – although I recalled that Neil, a year ahead of me, had had a keen interest in the writings of Henry David Thoreau. Less flatteringly, Neil remembered that, at the time, I had struck him as a "preppie" through and through. We were happy to get reacquainted in the desert of Rajasthan.

Later that evening, we all attended the Satsang, lit as it was by two powerful kerosene lanterns that needed to be adjusted continuously. I felt delight when Sant Ji began by asking me to sing a bhajan – and then He called on others who wished to sing. At the end He asked me to sing once again. I was sated and tired when I lay down on the simple rope bed set up for me, and drifted off at once.

Interview in Sant Ji's Room – Saturday, April 16th, 1977
Broken Arms and Doctoral Degrees

The following morning Sant Ji called me for a long interview. At that time we all meditated in a room that served as Sant Ji's living quarters – at the top of a flight of stairs. Interviews and group darshans took place there as well. When Pappu and I went up to talk to Him, I spotted a thumbtack right in the place where a friend from New Hampshire had been sitting at the early morning meditation. I picked it up and gave it to Sant Ji, and I said that particular disciple was sitting on it because he was an ascetic. I laughed and Pappu translated, explaining that I was making a joke, as the tack was there quite by accident.

Later on, when everyone came up to meditate, the first ones to enter the room were that same disciple and I. As we were sitting there, Sant Ji picked the thumbtack off a windowsill and held it out to the fellow. So I related to my friend what I had told Sant Ji. He laughed and took the thumbtack from Sant Ji and stuck it under his blanket – and Sant Ji said, "No, no – don't do that." And then we had a really beautiful meditation session where Sant Ji said many things including that we should not be lazy – and that it was "illegal" to rest. As we were getting up to leave, He said to my friend, "Don't sit on nails any more." And we all laughed most heartily.

In my interview we had a funny discussion about the sleeping bag I had brought for His use at the Ashram. He wondered if I had used my own funds to buy it, or had I used the account that Sant Bani had started to provide things for the set-up at 77 RB? If it were the former then He really wanted to be sure that He paid me for it.

I showed Him my Hindi lesson book, a drawing from my son, Chris, and photos of the family. He commented that when the Bicknell family could not come to India in March, especially after the pain and suffering we were going through, His Heart was broken. I asked if I could talk more about that after turning on the tape recorder, because I wanted to send a detailed letter to Karen. He graciously consented, and I recorded the following:

Kent: . . . She asked me to write a letter all about what is happening and send it back with the group. What is happening with her is that she is very, very strong – she is very independent. She doesn't like to have any-one serve her or wait on her. And this was difficult for her to accept all of the service. But she had no choice – so in some ways, I think this was good for her – to be put in a position of having to receive service. But still every day we thought that now the time is getting closer to go to Rajasthan – and now only two weeks are left – and now we will be going. And then Your letter came that we should not come – so we accepted this immediately as Your Will. But I think she felt like she could not count on anything outer, so in many ways she felt that all she had left was her Simran. So this has been very good for her and her Simran has become stronger, and she is putting in more time each day. But she also worried, I think, that maybe she has done something wrong – or that perhaps the Master does not love her. And I cannot say to her, "Oh, as soon as you see Sant Ji, He will pour love onto you and everything will be wonderful" because I don't know what is written in her fate. But I thought if I could write her some words of reassurance . . . like she is wondering if she will ever be able to come to Rajasthan?

Sant Ji: The advice which I gave her to do Simran, that was from Hazur. Because by doing Simran the soul gets strength to tolerate the pain. The letter which I wrote about not coming – that was also in the orders of Hazur. Because at that time her arms were too weak to come here. If we climb any bus or any train it may happen that it again gets hurt. So whatever I have done is all for her benefit. Only his welfare is done to whom One has full love. I have done her welfare because I love her. And that you accepted the letter I wrote – that was very good for you – that was very good for your welfare. If we understand the things of the Saints then nothing is difficult in this world. And I hope that when we meet her, her love will become even more. [there is a pause – I start to say something – but Sant Ji interrupts me]

Sant Ji: And when I heard about her arms – that both the arms were broken – I was very much worried about how she would do all of the things one needs to take care of oneself. I was worried more than for my own body. And my request to Hazur was to send anyone – any girl or any lady – so that you may get help. When you wrote me in the letter that one girl from the high school [Evelyn Sanborn] has come to help you, then I had very much good feeling because Hazur had accepted my request.

Kent: And now that girl has taken Naam.

Sant Ji: *Aacha!* – Good. To serve a Satsangi is the best thing. She has got the fruit of that. If any other part of the body is hurt at least a man can do his daily work – washing, wearing pants, wearing shirts – like that. But when the hands are broken you cannot think of doing anything.

Kent: No, she couldn't. We had to dress her and help her with all of that stuff. She couldn't brush her teeth.

Sant Ji: Whenever I was sitting alone and thinking of her I was also feeling how she would have been doing at that time. Because you cannot even eat.

Kent: We had to feed her.

Sant Ji: I was understanding her each and every problem. That is why my heart was worried. If she had tried to come to Rajasthan and if again she had hurt herself, how could I bear that?

Kent: The day that Your letter came – she had had her casts off on Friday, and her hands were much weaker than she thought they were going to be. But on Tuesday, when the group arrived back, that day she had been working very hard – washing dishes and things like that. And when we read the letter then her hands began to ache very much. And we understood that she was trying to work too soon. And we also understood immediately that we should not come. On one level our hearts were broken, but on another level we did not want to do anything that was not in the Will of the Master. So we didn't want to come to Rajasthan.

Sant Ji: Now Russell has mentioned that she will ride with me in the car, and I am happy about that. He has written me a letter.

Kent: Russell is taking good care of her.

Sant Ji: I had told Russell to do that *[Sant Ji laughs]*.

Kent: When he came back he stopped at our house first, and for two hours he told all of the news to Karen and me.

Sant Ji: Because I love you truly, your pain is my pain. In this world I have learned only to love and nothing else. And I got love from Hazur. Whatever I am speaking from outside, that is coming from my within. And when I heard that she will ride in the car I was very much happy. And at once it came in my mind that she will get the same benefit as if she has come in Rajasthan.

Kent: I think, from being down there in that big room, I can see how it would have been difficult. My two year old is very noisy – and he wakes up several times during the night – many times – five or six times – and I think it is better that we didn't come.

Sant Ji: It is a lack of accommodation. The time will come when that will also become all right. I plan to make some small rooms in which individuals or couples or three people can stay.

Kent: It would be very good for my Hindi to stay. Now I only go once a week for three hours – and then now and then during the week I study some – but it is hard to learn enough when you are not hearing it all day.

Sant Ji: It is all right. When the time will come everything will become all right. Now there is a lack of accommodation here, and we also feel that lack of room here.

At this point I asked a personal question that was very much on my mind. I had been struggling to juggle the responsibilities in my life and hoped that He would advise me to leave a task or two behind. His response, as often happened, surprised me. Not only is it a strong statement as to how Sant Ji felt about higher education, but both the content and the manner in which it unfolded served as an anchor in my long (and ultimately successful) quest for a doctorate.

Kent: Do we have time for me to ask one more personal question?

Pappu: Yes, yes.

Kent: I don't like to bother you with non-spiritual questions on the one hand, but on the other hand You are my Father – so sometimes I need help. There is one thing. I really love having time for my family. I love to have time to meditate. I love learning my Hindi. And I love my job. And that takes my day – sleeping four or five hours a night. But also I am getting my doctorate in education. And I don't know whether I should finish that or not. Sometimes I think it would be a good idea for the Sant Bani School for me to finish – it would be good for me to finish that doctoral program I am in. And at other times I think that it is not necessary – that it is useless. Especially if it takes away from my meditation time. I don't want that to happen.

Sant Ji: To get a degree is good.

Kent: I already have two. [Pappu explains in his translation that I have a B.A. and an M.A.]

Sant Ji: It is not bad to study more. That is a good thing in this world – it is necessary. I am in favor of that.

Kent: *Teek hai!* [okay] But my idea . . . *[Sant Ji laughs, and then interrupts]*

Sant Ji: You should get that degree of doctor, even at the cost of studying Hindi.

Kent: But you told me that one day I would be an expert in Hindi. So my idea is that it would be very good for me to do a study of Indian education – for my dissertation – my thesis. And I could pick a simple Indian village school – 77RB – and write one thesis. Because I think that in the West they would be very interested. Not many people know Hindi, so very little has been done on Indian education for Westerners.

Sant Ji: It will be seen according to the Will.

Kent: Right now the Hindi course that I am taking at Boston University is counting toward my doctorate degree.

Sant Ji: Your Hindi is good. I can read it very easily. And I have heard the bhajans which you have sung and your pronunciation is also good.

Kent: Balwant [Pathi Ji's daughter, Bant] has written out *Mere Sataguru Pritam* and if Sant Ji likes, tonight I will sing that. Because now I know the words to sing in Hindi.

Sant Ji: Yes, yes. Tomorrow, from three to four. I will call you again if there will be time.

I left the room in the happy state of spiritual intoxication I had often experienced in the presence of Master Kirpal, and now, with God's Grace, with Sant Ji. That night I did sing *Mere Sataguru Pritam Pyara* [O my dearly Beloved Satguru, I have forgotten Your Name], but I mispronounced a word. Sant Ji stopped me and had me sing it again. I made the same mistake – so He had to correct me once more. After meditation He asked me to sing, *Apana Koi Nahin* [No one in this world belongs to us except our dearly Beloved Satguru]. I struggled with the last verse, however, and Sant Ji had to help me with the words. I bent down and touched His Feet and said, "*Mere Pita Ji*" [My Respected Father].

Sunday, April 17th, 1977

On Sunday the seventeenth, I wrote the first words of each verse of *Dhan Dhan Satguru* [Hail, Hail to my Satguru, Who reunites the separated ones] on my hand in case Sant Ji asked me to sing after meditation. He sang first, and then asked, "Which of you is prepared to sing?" Someone sang a beautiful song, and then someone else sang – which I was happy about, as at that moment I did not feel like singing.[3] And then I remembered, "Oh, He asked, 'Which of you is <u>prepared</u> to sing?' and here I am prepared to sing and I am not saying anything." Before volunteering I glanced at my hand – and could barely see any ink at all! I had been sweating so much during the meditation that all the words were almost totally gone. I explained to Him exactly what had happened – that I did prepare myself in such a way that He would not have to outwardly help me as He had earlier – but that the writing had all

---

[3] In those days there were only a few Western disciples who knew how to sing bhajans.

but disappeared. He said that He was aware of my preparation, but that I was reserved for the evening – that I would sing this evening. On the way out the door, I was the last one, and I tried to tell Him I was like one of those *chipkalis* [chameleons] that wanted to live in His room. I repeated the line from the bhajan, "Please do not throw me from Your Door." He observed that those words came when the soul is really longing – when it understood what the Master was and really longed for Him. That is where that song came from.

The next two days passed in a loving blur, and suddenly the group's time was up. With everyone in a jolly mood, as we knew He would soon be traveling to America, we left to catch the night train from Sri Ganganagar to New Delhi. We traveled via Second Class sleeping cars. The click-clack of the rails merged with my sleepy Simran and even the wooden slats of the "sleeper" felt comfortable. We arrived in Delhi on Wednesday morning.

Several of the Westerners needed help arranging various things in Connaught Circle (a prime business district in downtown Delhi). By the time I got to the bank with the new forms and obtained what I needed, and then rushed over to the Alitalia Office, they said it was too late to do anything that day, and that it might take a couple of days to issue the tickets. There was a possibility it could be done the next day, so we got train tickets for going back up on Thursday night. As I was dying to return to Sant Ji, I came up with a variety of schemes to allow Pappu and me to leave, even without the tickets. If they were not ready, I thought, then perhaps Pappu's brother Jawahar could come in and pick them up. If there were any trouble he could cable Sham Sunder (a Satsangi from Sri Ganganagar), and Sham Sunder could travel to the Ashram in a Jeep and tell us what was happening. Finally Pappu stated simply that we should not go up to Rajasthan without the tickets, and I agreed immediately.

I dashed off a letter to Karen and gave it to someone in the group to bring back to her:

> *. . . Pappu and I took the forms in today and there should be*
> *no problem. Sant Ji told us to spend the night. We will go out to*
> *the airport at 2:00 or 3:00 am with the group, and come back to*
> *Rajasthan when we have the tickets, hopefully tomorrow night.*
> *So as you read this, I'll probably be on the train back up, or else*
> *just arriving in Sri Ganganagar.*

So that will be on Friday that we arrive in the Ashram (God Willing). On Monday, Sant Ji, Pathi Ji, Pappu, Sardar Rattan Singh and his son (the one who used the Master Power to drive the tractor), and Sham Sundar, and I will be coming down Second Class – to Delhi. Sant Ji told Pappu that if I didn't like Second Class, then He and I would ride down in First Class while the others rode in Second Class. Can you imagine?

After I said I was fine with Second Class, Sant Ji confided to me that His real fear was that the others – who were about to be separated from Him for three months – would feel compelled to buy First Class tickets to be with Him, and that worried Him since they could not afford that! Second Class is fine. I have been taking scooters and riding Second Class to save the Sangat's money.

We will get [back] to Delhi on Tuesday and fly out that evening, arriving [in Boston] on Wednesday the 27th. As our only long stop is Bombay, I am not going to call from anywhere, unless something is wrong. So assume that things are correct and on schedule unless you hear otherwise.

One thing: Pappu has requested that there be some wheat flour and vegetables and milk and vessels for preparing things in Master's house when they arrive. We don't plan to eat food on the plane, but to take chapattis, etc.

The whole trip has been extremely positive for me – He is absolutely Magnificent. You will see how much love will be coming.

Love,
Kent, Principal Sahib

Here is the itinerary, Alitalia all of the way:
26th April, Delhi to Bombay—Depart 9 pm
#IC 184— Arrive 10:45 pm
27th April, Bombay to Rome—Depart 1:25 am
#763
27th April, Rome to Boston—Depart 10:30 am
#686—Arrive 3:40 pm

I have learned much about serving here. I have been allowed to serve in both the Ashram and the Bagga house. I have seen my own selfishness. Our job (as Sant Bani Ashram sevadars) is to

GIVE GIVE GIVE to each and every person with LOVE LOVE LOVE. These are definitely His orders for us! Otherwise we are not serving.

As it turned out, not everything was ready on Thursday, so we canceled our train reservations and waited another day. I had been going in and out of Delhi twice a day (using the famous three-wheeled scooter), so when we finally did get the sacred plane tickets for America, it was such a relief that I was very happy. I thought, "Now I can go to Rajasthan and just be in heaven." We took the train up that night, Friday, but by Saturday morning I had begun to feel sick. When the train pulled into Sri Ganganagar, I really did not feel well. Pappu kept asking me, "What is wrong? You look sad. You are not smiling." I could not answer. I was not certain what I had, but it was some kind of stomach problem that began to affect everything.

We arrived at the Ashram, and it just wasn't my picture of how it was going to be. My projection was shattered. I had thought I would be in heaven, and I arrived there almost grumpy – very aware of my body, and really depressed because I was like that. Sant Ji was incredibly beautiful, but I felt "off" because I had wanted to be hale and healthy. When Sant Ji asked me, "*Raji khushi?*" [Hale and healthy] I said, "*Sab*" which means "all" [completely]. "Are you hale and healthy?" and I said, "Yes – all!" For some reason I did not touch His Feet when He came down. Pappu did – but I didn't. And I wondered about that.

Sant Ji talked about how He had this problem with His back, and He pulled up His shirt to show it to Pappu. And Babu Ji and I looked too. It was a big, red sore, covered by a white ointment. All I could think about was how much my back had been hurting in those scooters that I took everywhere instead of taxis – and how so many of the Westerners in the group had been uncomfortable due to the aches and pains in their backs. I groaned as I wondered how much He carries for all of us.

Sant Ji asked Pappu to write a letter back to Sham Sunder to arrange the program for our coming to Sri Ganganagar to get the train – and then we just sat there and chatted. In the end I was told to rest.

Later on I wanted a little water, but I was worried that the water was not boiled enough. Someone in the Western group had remarked that he was not sure how well the water was boiled, and I had begun to think about that. I went on to tell a few other people that the water may not have been boiled sufficiently, My secret, I proclaimed, was to drink tea, which had been well cooked, adding that was why I did not get sick. I decided to ask Pappu about the water before taking any.

Babu Ji was in the room and he said, "Yes, it was boiled and boiled!" I felt good about it, but when Pappu indicated I should take the water from the brown ceramic pot, I wondered if perhaps it was left over from the group. Pappu said that, indeed, that was the case. He went into the kitchen and asked the sevadars how fresh was the boiled water, and they all, including Sant Ji, roared with laughter. They had been expecting us to come Friday instead of Saturday. Sardar Rattan Singh had come over on his tractor and spent the night, hoping to see us when we arrived. And then he had left just a little while before we did come on Saturday. They laughed so much because Babu Ji had not boiled water the night before like he usually does – he had boiled it in the morning of the day they thought we were going to come – Friday – and then he spent a long time trying to cool it. Babu Ji poured it from pot to pot to have it all ready for us. So it was very fresh. Sant Ji came over to tell me all of that, adding, "I take great care of the water. I make very sure that the water you all get is safe."

When Sant Ji approached me to tell me that, I felt as if I were a fly that should be stepped on – almost as if I really did not belong there. Then I felt the tears overflowing, and I bent to touch His Feet. After that, I felt better. He advised me to sit for meditation, but not any longer than my body could take. And then I should rest. I meditated for a brief time after He left, and then lay down and slept.

Pappu woke me to ask if I wanted to go for a walk with Sant Ji, and I said, "Yes." He felt my forehead and said, "You have a fever." He went and asked Sant Ji if I should go, and Sant Ji came back to see me. Sant Ji felt my wrist and remarked, "I told you to take care of your health." I answered, "I meditated for fifteen minutes, and then I lay down to rest." He answered, "Your each and every breath while you are here is counted to your Bhajan."

Later I asked Pappu what He meant by that, and he said that Sant Ji meant my seva was being counted as meditation – that it was okay for me to rest. Not surprisingly, Sant Ji told me to rest, rather than go on the walk. He asked me if I wanted my bed outside, and I said, "Yes, that would be a good idea." He had it taken outside for me. As I sat on my bed, Sant Ji put His hand on my shoulder and said that Darshan Singh, Pathi Ji's brother, would give me a massage in the evening after Satsang. Pappu kept telling me, "You can't get sick. If you get sick we will be delayed. Be strong!"

I didn't take any food at that time. I had a little water, and some tea without milk or sugar, and I missed the walk. I was lying on my bed, and they went out, and then they came back – and I felt like that walk was not in my fate – that was all.

It was important to think like that; otherwise I would have spun rapidly into that space of last August, mentally whining, "Here I am sitting here all by myself while Pappu is in the room visiting with Him." With God's Grace that did not happen, and my mind remained more tranquil – not always wishing it were getting something it was not (or vice versa!). No doubt it was all Grace, just as when I had really wanted to tell Sant Ji that, in fact, I was not really "*sab raji khushi*" [all right]. Without my saying a word, He had come over, and talked to me about the boiled water. I had bowed down, touched His Feet, and immediately felt lighter.

Pappu told me that they gathered 3500 pounds of wheat when they reaped the crop planted for the village. He mentioned that in helping to pack Sant Ji's items for the Tour, he had come across a letter from Master Kirpal to Sant Ji, dated February 1974. The letter was in Punjabi.

Evening Satsang was due to begin at 8:15 p.m., and, as my cot was still outside and at the back of the place for Satsang, I reclined and gazed upon the timeless scene. I had wished to record the village girls singing the devotional songs, but it turned out that Sant Ji had already done that in our absence. He had written specific bhajans into a notebook, and they sang from that while He used my tape recorder to capture the sounds. Weeks later, when He was alone in His room at Sant Bani Ashram in New Hampshire, He would play those tapes to Himself. As I sat or slept in the living room I would sometimes hear those wonderful village girls' voices – whom I fondly called "the Electric Tin Duet" – coming through the thin door of His bedroom.

During the Satsang I moved to a chair in back, and, even though I was sick, it felt extraordinary. I was getting more feverish, but I was sitting there watching Sant Ji and He was radiant. The sight of the Master surrounded by disciples, coupled with the sound of those girls singing, left me floating in the ether.

The Satsang was really jolly – that is, there seemed to be a lot of humor. Sant Ji told many stories that sent ripples of laughter through the villagers. I asked Pappu about some of the subjects discussed, and found that Sant Ji had asked what do the devotees get from pouring thousands of gallons of oil for the gods to drink? Who drinks that oil? And what do people get from worshipping Mother Kali – from making the sacrifices in her name? The Sangat was really laughing, and so was Sant Ji. It was a very special time for me to just be sitting in the back, watching Him among His children at the second-to-last evening Satsang.

Afterwards they passed out parshad, than Sant Ji told Darshan Singh to give me a massage. I heard Him saying, "feet, legs, head, every-thing –" And I did get a massage for 45 minutes. About two-thirds of the way through my "session," Sant Ji, in a very loud voice, started making humorous comments directed to the sevadars working on me. He spoke through the wall separating His room from ours, and the men were laughing and answering back.

Sunday Morning, April 24th

The next morning as I lay on my cot under the mosquito netting, Babu Ji, the very friendly villager who had translated Sant Ji's early letters to me, came to see me with words of caution for the upcoming Tour. He advised me as follows:

Babu Ji: . . . and ah, He [Sant Ji] is going there [to the States]. I am happy. Those people who do not know – they are somewhat sad.

Kent: I remember last year when we were over at 16 PS and Sant Ji told the story that some of the villagers had gone to the Satsang of someone else, and the people there had been abusing and criticizing Sant Ji. So the villagers made a joke that "the dogs are barking."

Babu Ji: Yes, our Pathi Ji told them . . .

Kent: And the villagers said that the dogs should go to America and bark – because then we would not want Sant Ji to come.

Babu Ji: The thing which I told you yesterday – Please . . .

Kent: To watch out for Sant Ji. Yes, we will be careful.

Babu Ji: Yes. Let the people see. But the people who are quarreling with each other – you see how these people are quarreling with each other.

Kent: Yes.

Babu Ji: They cannot do good things. They cannot do good things. They give many difficulties to Master also. You should remember all these things and be careful. Only this is my request.

Kent: We will be careful.

Babu Ji: And just now when Sant Ji called me inside and gave me these books, I also told Him. But He does not know English, and also Pathi Ji is not knowing any language except this Punjabi. And Pappu will be very busy. And if somebody is talking in their presence but they cannot understand what these people are telling – then you people should be very careful for this. Nowadays you know how the parties are doing. These parties are quarreling with each other.

Kent: Right.

Babu Ji: And He is going, but these parties are not happy that Sant Ji is going to the States. These people are not happy, and the public of Delhi is very clever. The kingdom also can be changed by these people. You know – these are very clever people . . . so please care for us. Only this is my request.

Kent: Right.

Babu Ji: I also talked to Sant Ji to be careful – but He is very simple. He does not care for such things. We should care. We should care.

Kent: My wife gave me the same advice. She said to me, "If you are in Delhi and you should meet anyone from these two parties, then be very careful. Don't say anything."

Babu Ji: This is the thing which I am telling you. And because they could not do some good things for the Master [Kirpal], then how can they do good things now? They want wealth. They are quarreling with each other. They have put cases upon one another in the courts. They are quarreling. But there is no truth. According to my idea there is no truth when these people are quarreling with each other for the wealth. But all other things will be okay. Everything will be okay. The question is that Sant Ji does not know the language. At this place there is some difficulty of accommodation – we are trying our best to make rooms. When the rooms will be prepared – after that the people can come in numbers as they like. At present, you know, our position is this – we can accommodate only twenty – not more than this. And only this small hall is there. After that – when the rooms will be prepared – then everyone will be allowed. And many of the Western people are coming – they are asking Sant Ji to stay here for some time. But we are telling them that we have no accommodations.

Kent: Right.

Babu Ji: And if there will be accommodation they can sit here in the presence of Sant Ji and they can get more benefit. If they will like to stay here – no matter. But at present due to the accommodation we cannot allow these people. This difficulty will be removed, but it is removed when its time comes. We tried our best, but the bricks were not available. The work was stopped. And now what will you eat? You will eat something?

Kent: Yes, Pappu is fixing something . . . *keeri?*

Babu Ji: Oh yes, *kheer* – rice and milk. Only *kheer*? Some vegetable?

Kent: Yes. I am having a little *sabji* [vegetables] Thank you Babu Ji.

Babu Ji: Ah yes. We have prepared some *khichri* – rice and lentil mixed – for Sant Ji also. If you like that can I bring that?

Kent: Maybe a little later I could have that.

Babu Ji: All right.

I was served the *khichri* – a very cooked dish that is a standard Indian home remedy for ailing stomachs. As I lay back on my cot, I realized that once again my plans had gone awry. My visions of returning to 77 RB and sitting for hours in meditation were not to be. The warm food soon began to have the proper effect, however, and I really did feel better. Later, after my fever broke, the delicious rice pudding Bant had prepared was just what I felt like having. With my focus deflected away from my "aching flesh," I began to eagerly anticipate the upcoming session with Sant Ji scheduled for the early afternoon.

Interview in Sant Ji's Room – Sunday, April 24th, 1977

I spent a glorious, instructive hour and a half with Sant Ji. When I arrived at His door He had His shirt up, exposing His back to the air. One of the first things I told Him was that when I had arrived the day before and He had asked if I were *raji khushi* [hale and healthy], my answer that I was fine had not been true at all. I explained that I had wanted to feel hale and healthy, and I did not want to upset anyone. When we had bought the tickets in Delhi, I had felt really happy and thought, "Now we can just go up and enjoy." But on the train I had begun to feel sick – which was not going along with my idea. I felt sad, but I had not wished to make anyone worry for me, so I was not truthful. Sant Ji looked kindly upon me, and answered quietly that He could see from my face that I was sick. He accepted my apology, and I was grateful.

I asked Him if I could turn on the tape recorder and He chuckled, saying, "Last time you left and you took the tape recording – but now you are going to take me. So why do you need it? Now you will be taking all six feet of me!" We all laughed.

I brought up a personal issue. In April 1976, at our first meeting, I had felt such a deep connection with Sant Ji the instant I met Him. Among the many subjects we discussed, He had given me advice about being chaste. I went over with Him how I had not really followed that counsel very well. And when I came in August, and He got so sick – at least then I should have learned to love Him and follow His command-ments. Yet I continued to entertain thoughts and act in such a way that the goal of a pure, chaste, married life seemed, if not remote, then certainly not just around the corner. In October I had written Him about it, and He had responded:

17ᵗʰ Oct. 1976

My Satguru Kirpal's Beloved
Dear Kent "Principal Sahib"

Received your loving letter and came to know its contents. Now I am well with Satguru Kirpal's Grace. You have written that you are not improving. So, my dear, time is passing so fast as the airplane flys. Dwell Master Kirpal in your heart with each and every breath. Leave the worldly pleasures. That is all Kal Power's. You are Satguru Sat Purush Kirpal's son. You have to become good. Hazur Baba Ji is waiting for you in Sach Khand.

Nobody keeps the dirty rag with him. So, if you will be dirty, He will not be pleased. And if He is displeased, nobody except Him can forgive you. For pleasing the Master, refuse your mind, telling it that, "I will not obey you. I will be a true disciple."

I send love to you and your family,

In His Sweet Holy Name,
Dass Ajaib Singh

The notion of being likened to a "dirty rag" that would, basically, be cast aside had given me enough impetus that I wrote again, suggesting I would put in more effort. Sant Ji, with ultimate humility and deep kind-ness, answered:

18ᵗʰ Nov. '76

My Most Beloved Ruby of Rubies
Kent "Principal Sahib"

Received your two letters; one in Hindi and another came with the group. You are fortunate, for you are trying to protect yourself from lust. Lust is that very bad disease which cuts the roots of life. There is only one way to keep oneself protected from it. Dwell Satguru Kirpal very deep in your heart, and in your thoughts, understand yourself as a soldier of Master Kirpal.

Tell your mind that now you'll obey Master's, Satguru's, Orders, and not mind's. Always do "Kirpal, Kirpal." While sleeping do "Kirpal, Kirpal." In the back is Kirpal. In the front is Kirpal. While you are awake do "Kirpal, Kirpal." Even in dream say "Kirpal, Kirpal." Where Satguru Kirpal is dwelt, lust will find no place there. Dwell Him within. This is the best remedy to cure lust.

I send much much love to you and your family
With All His Love
Dass Ajaib Singh

Sitting at His Feet once again, I told Him how worried I had become when He wrote me that no one likes to keep the dirty rag, and I apologized for my behavior. Sant Ji's response was simple and direct. He told me, "There is no need to tell a Saint everything, as the Saint is already aware of everything. I knew about all of this. Saints are never displeased inside, but outwardly, they advise a person how to change." He continued, "Enjoyment of lust stops the love from the side of the woman. Not many women desire to be unchaste, but most men do. It is the organ of lust that wants that thing, and then, for just a few minutes of enjoyment, a person goes through so much pain and suffering and sorrow. *Bhramcharya* [a life of chastity] will help you in everything. It will make your home life happier." He concluded, "Now you have enjoyed lust – so you can leave that thing. As much lust as you want in your life – that you can have. And as much as you want to decrease lust – you can do that."

I mentioned that my meditations seemed useless – that I had not been able to do anything by myself. He told me to concentrate. I brought up Simran, explaining that working on Simran is what I really wanted to focus on now, but I felt badly about the fact that I wanted His help. When I asked Him what He recommended, He answered, "Prayer – prayer is a good thing."

I went on to say that sometimes it seemed to be good that I realized I could not do anything by myself – that He was the Doer. Yet at other times it seemed like I was not trying hard enough. Sant Ji said that it was important to try – that we had to make the effort. And if we weren't succeeding after making the effort, then pray. He gave the example of the schoolboy whose job it was to get to the school in order to be taught. What would it be like, Sant Ji asked me, if the boy sat down in the road on the way to school and prayed to the schoolmaster to please teach him?

He mentioned that Hazur would give us strength [for the Tour]. He said that I had gotten sick from so much traveling, but I had more traveling to do. He told me to get more rest. He added that He had hoped to rest today, but people had been coming to see Him at every moment.

We talked about who would ride in the car [from Boston to Sant Bani] and that was really nice. Pappu was listing out all the names, and instead of saying "Karen," he said "*bibi*" [wife]. Sant Ji asked, "What is her name?" and Pappu answered, "Karen," and Sant Ji repeated, "Karen, Karen." He asked my children's names, so Pappu said, "Christopher or Chris, and Nicholas or Nicky." And Sant Ji said, "Christopher, Nicholas – Chris, Nicky" – and added that "*nikee*" means "small" in Punjabi.

He asked about the physical layout of the Ashram in New Hampshire, and I told Him about many aspects of the set-up. He wondered about the water down at the Master's house where He and the party would be staying – what was the situation with that?[4] I didn't think that Master Kirpal had had the water boiled – that the water there came from deep underground and was pretty clean. Sant Ji commented that Master Kirpal never had to have the water boiled here in Rajasthan either. He asked how many houses were on the Ashram – and then asked by name whose was whose. He would say, "Larry . . . Fletcher . . . Randy . . . Wendy," wondering where those people lived. He asked how far my house was from His house, and I said it was about as far as from His room to the little meditation hut down the dirt road (the simple place where He had meditated at 77 RB). I added that the Bicknell house was

---

[4] Western sevadars had built a separate house for Master Kirpal to reside in when He visited Sant Bani Ashram for five days in October of 1972. The dwelling, known as "Master's house," and greatly expanded over time, has been maintained and reserved for the use of the Masters ever since.

the first house He would see on coming into the Ashram. He really laughed and said that that made Him very happy, as now I would not need to say to Him, "There's my house!"

Sant Ji asked many questions about traveling on the plane. I told Him about it, and mentioned that the airline people come around to sell alcohol and cigarettes. He responded that that kind of thing would not bother Him, so I should not worry about it. He said that He does not hate anyone – He hates the sin of smoking cigarettes and drinking alcohol – but He doesn't hate anyone who is doing it. He is not affected by it.

Sant Ji continued asking questions: what about the food on the plane; how long would the journey take; how far was it; how long was the daylight in Sant Bani; when did the sun rise; how long was it from Boston to Sant Bani Ashram? He asked how the School would run. What hours? He wondered when it would get out for holidays. I told Him that I was still not certain how we would arrange the whole schedule for the School. As the conversation went on, my excitement grew, as it seemed like the Tour really would happen this time.

I mentioned that Karen and I had been talking, and we were hoping to be able to accompany Him to Colombia, South America – but that we were not sure our current financial situation would permit travel to California and Vancouver, for instance. His response was really nice. He said, "We will see what Hazur will bring" and then He added, "That place which you go is by Hazur's Will, and that is for your benefit. And that place which you do not go, that also is Hazur's Will and that is for your benefit."

I left His room certain that if we were meant to go, we would go – the money would come. And if we were not meant to go, we wouldn't. The way He phrased it made it much easier to be happy no matter how it turned out.[5]

Toward the end of the session I remembered the thumbtack, and I asked to have it so that I could deliver it to my friend when I saw him again in New Hampshire. Sant Ji's Face lit up, and He offered the tack so graciously, adding that He would give it for my friend, but for remembrance and love only – not for sitting on! He added that I should not sit

---

[5] As a general rule, Sant Ji asked Karen and me to remain at the Ashram in New Hampshire to maintain it during the various world Tours so other Sant Bani sevadars had the opportunity to travel to see Him. The exception to this was when He visited countries in South and Central America and asked me to come, because I knew the language.

on things like that either. I commented that I had sat on something sharp, but not nails. We all laughed and I backed out of the room, folding my hands as I bowed at His golden form.

That afternoon there was a good-bye Satsang, and in the evening again there was a session for the devotees. Many were bereft at the thought of Sant Ji's imminent departure for three and a half months, but He comforted them with sweet words, loving glances, and gentle touches. Long after the sun had set, the desert was still throwing off heat, and it was most refreshing to sleep out in the courtyard, under the stars.

Leaving 77 RB for Delhi – Monday, April 25th, 1977

The next morning we arose and made the final preparations to leave for Sri Ganganagar to catch the overnight train to Delhi. I was still not well, and anything I consumed seemed to leave my system moments after it entered. It is always hard to lose control of bodily functions – and to do so while traveling in a Jeep in India with the Master was a thought that filled me with a certain amount of terror. I did not eat much and hoped for the best.

By the time we were to leave 77 RB, the Sangat was even more anxious, and many weeping souls surrounded the Jeep that was to take Him to Sri Ganganagar. The vehicle proceeded slowly through the crowd, and then we were gone.

Our first stop was at the remote village of Netewala, where followers of the Master had begged Him to stop and give a Satsang on His way to the station. I was told that this was a village that had not seen a white person in decades, so there was much interest in who I was as well. Sant Ji gave a beautiful discourse, seated on a low platform, with Pathi Ji beside Him chanting, and a small fan attempting to keep away the heat and flies. The crowd was a sea of red cloth, as many of the women were of the sect that completely covered their faces from public view. Later, at Sant Bani Ashram in New Hampshire, Sant Ji made us all laugh as the slides of this event inspired Him to tell stories of the place.[6]

It was at Netewala that I first saw the remarkable photo of Sant Ji in His late thirties – a formal portrait taken in the early 1960's where He looks so handsome and strong. I photographed it for publication back in the States, but when the owner became aware of my desire, he graciously

---

[6] See Chapter Four below.

loaned it to me. It was published in *Sant Bani Magazine* (Sept. 1981), and subsequently in the pamphlet, *Sant Ajaib Singh Ji: A Brief Life Sketch*.

After a small group darshan and a short rest, we left the village and proceeded on to the train station in Sri Ganganagar, accompanied by even more disciples now. While the steam engine slowly chugged out of the station, Sant Ji, with folded hands, kept looking out the window as people ran alongside on the platform, trying desperately not to let Him disappear from their view.

We settled in, but I was still sick – quite sick in fact. My stomach was very uneasy. Sant Ji, noting my state, directed that I should be given a pill. This was a large, crudely shaped, homemade remedy of some sort, and there was nothing to take it with. Not surprisingly, it got completely lodged in my throat. I did not want to make a scene, but I was getting pretty uncomfortable trying to get it down. I looked over at Sant Ji and He looked at me – and then I saw Him make a big gulping movement with His throat – enough so that His adam's apple bobbed up and down. The pill shot down my esophagus, and it was fine. Sant Ji smiled and said nothing.

I began to feel somewhat better, and lay down to rest on one of the benches in the Second Class compartment. I drifted off – until a strange pressure on my abdomen awakened me. When I opened my eyes, Sant Ji was standing over me with His Hand pressed gently on my stomach. Again He smiled, and I experienced no more sickness for the rest of the trip.

As we passed into the night, I climbed to my upper berth and gazed down at the reclining form of my Beloved Master on a wooden "bed" beneath. It really did feel like we were on our way to the West at last.

Leaving Delhi for America – Tuesday, April 26th, 1977

When we arrived in Delhi, the Bagga Family again opened their house – not only to Sant Ji and the party, but also to the many disciples who came to have a last darshan and to say good-bye. That evening we headed off to the airport for our first flight to Bombay, and then, after a wait of a couple of hours, it was on to Boston via Rome.

Sant Ji, Pathi Ji, Pappu, and I were traveling in Economy Class, seated together, four in a row. Immediately after take-off, I was mortified when a passenger just in front of us lit up a cigarette and blew the smoke back over her shoulder in our direction. We were, after all, in the non-smoking section – and so was she! I was all set to make a fuss, when Sant Ji put His hand on my arm and gently wagged His finger at me. I relaxed, and everything was fine.

The flight was not exceptional, except for Sant Ji's humility and seeming simplicity. Near Tel Aviv, He wondered if He could get tea, and I asked the stewardess. She brought a Styrofoam cup with a tea bag floating in a swirling mix of tepid warm water and milk. Sant Ji took one look and quietly turned His head away to gaze out the window. I felt useless and berated myself for how ill prepared we were. It does not take deep reflection to see our naïveté. We learned, and on later trips we booked First Class and brought food and drink that worked for Sant Ji. Still, He often seemed to be thrown upon the mercy of the moment, even by people who loved Him.

The airline had a bad movie scheduled for the transatlantic leg of the flight. Just before the film began, I located a row of seats that allowed Sant Ji to stretch out. I spread my meditation robe over Him, and then squatted in a nearby seat to keep "guard." As I watched over His reclined Form, I was afraid that He would decide to sit up before the movie ended – and, having already dragged Him through so much, I did not want Him to have to be exposed to that. With the Grace of God, Sant Ji kept resting until the film was done, and I was happy to see the credits rolling up the screen.

We landed in Boston on schedule, and cleared US Immigration and Customs with relatively no problem. As we approached the last exit, I saw the automatic doors swing open several times for other departing passengers. Each time they framed an excited crowd of disciples, eagerly straining for a glimpse of the Divine Form. As Sant Ji, Pathi Ji, and Pappu passed through those doors and into the care of Russell and Judith Perkins, I slumped against the wall and gave an enormous sigh of relief and gratitude that He had arrived. After a moment Karen found me, and we hurried after the group, very happy to be passengers in Sant Ji's car, as Russell drove from Boston to our sylvan home: Sant Bani Ashram, Sanbornton, New Hampshire.

CHAPTER FOUR

The First Tour–Sant Ji in America–1977

We had a delightful journey north to Sanbornton. Sant Ji was very sweet to Karen, and as I watched Him talking to her, I recalled His comment at 77 RB, *"And when I heard that she will ride in the car I was very much happy. And at once it came in my mind that she will get the same benefit as if she has come in Rajasthan."* Judith had made a thermos of real tea (*chai*) for Sant Ji, and we served it to Him in a very special cup that Karen and I were lucky enough to have.

When Karen, Chris, and I had spent six weeks with Master Kirpal Singh Ji in New Delhi in 1974, on our last night we attended a dinner with Master and the many other disciples who were departing that evening. *Chai* was served to all, and both Karen and I noticed that Master Kirpal kept rubbing His finger round and round the rim of the cup He was using. Later, Edna Shinerock, a Canadian devotee who lived and served at Sawan Ashram for many years, asked us if we would like that cup. We were astounded and thrilled – and eagerly packed it away in our carry-on as a treasured possession.

That is the cup that was used to serve *chai* to Sant Ji. I mentioned that Master Kirpal had drunk from that very same cup. Sant Ji paused for a moment, contemplated the cup, and then said in a very matter-of-fact manner (but with twinkling eyes), "Different horse – same Rider."

It was the twenty-seventh of April when Sant Ji arrived at Sant Bani, and I wrote in my journal for that day, "Arrival of God!" The next few weeks were so full that I cannot render an accurate account of what was happening on a daily basis. Rather, the story jumps from event to event, and it is in that spirit that this narrative continues.

Reflections on the First Week of May 1977

A week after Sant Ji arrived at Sant Bani, I realized that so much was happening that it was very difficult to remember each and every thing. A regular program of meditations, interviews, and Satsangs was beginning to unfold, and the Ashram grounds were filling up with many guests. On top of all of that the Sant Bani School was still in session, and classes were running "as usual."

For a couple of days running I saw Him only briefly. I just darted into His bedroom to say "*Namaste*" [Hello]. When that had happened on Monday, I touched His feet and He laughed and laughed, and kept patting me on the back. I told Him that because I had been taking care of our two sons, I had not been down around His house much, but I still felt I was in His Will. He answered, "You are never far from me. I am always with you."

He proceeded to say that Karen needed it – that it was good for her. He added that I should never feel sad because Karen was there at the meditation and I was not. I said no, that I was very happy, and she was also very happy. He said that I was always most welcome to visit His house – I was always invited to come. I laughed, and as I got up to leave, He again said, "You are always welcome."

On Tuesday the third when I saw Him to say, "Good morning!" Pappu mentioned that I could not stay long as I had to get up to School before it opened. Sant Ji said that was good – that I should go attend to the School. Later that day He saw my homemade bhajan books. He asked me what they were, and I told Him. I said I was learning a new bhajan and that I would probably sing it that evening at Satsang. I mentioned to Him that when the Hindi and Punjabi bhajans were sung, I really loved them, but that when the songs in English were sung, I did not always sing along.[1] I felt that I would rather gaze at Him and do Simran. At Satsang two nights before, He had talked about singing along when the bhajans were sung so as to help the mind become intoxicated, and I wondered if I was doing something wrong by not singing along with the English songs. Sant Ji said that it was, "*Teek hai*" [Okay]. In a very animated response using both His voice and His hands, He emphasized that the bhajans in Punjabi and Hindi are those written by the Saints, and are very full of the love of God. He concluded, "They are better!"

After evening Satsang on the third of May, Karen and I were invited in to see Sant Ji. It had been a very long day for Him, however, and we did not want to keep Him from retiring. During the Satsang, Sant Ji had

---

[1] In the early days the bhajans were not yet published, and people enjoyed singing devotional songs in English.

been talking about the rain-bird, telling how the rain-bird can only survive on pure rain, and will die of thirst rather than take any other form of water. I told Him that Karen was like the rain-bird – that she was going to die of thirst unless she had a drink. He asked me how everything at School was going, and I responded that it was going very well. I mentioned that both teachers and students were very anxious to have Him come visit, and He said, "We'll see."

He mentioned that people were always outside – always waiting to come in to see Him – and when they saw Him, they wanted it to be for a long time. Further He said that seeing Him in the big room (the living room) was not enough. The people wanted to see Him alone, in the small room (the bedroom). Then the others waiting outside thought that those inside were talking about very important things with Sant Ji – but that was not the case. The people in the room did not even have any questions to ask. They just wanted to look at Him. I remarked that I felt like that also, and added, "I am very naughty." I said that just coming in for ten seconds once a day was enough for me – that I did not need an hour. And Sant Ji really laughed.

Karen and I were awed at the sight of Him. He did not have His turban on. Instead, He had a simple cloth wrapped about His head. But there was also that bittersweet feeling that He was really tired, and we were not sure we should be there, as we did not wish to impose. Pappu mentioned that to avoid interruptions after Satsang, everyone had been told that they were working on correspondence. Sant Ji laughed and said, "For your sake, we have said we were doing the correspondence." As we sat there at His feet, He laughed again and, indicating our presence at His feet, said, "This is writing a letter – this is what we have told everyone!"

I explained to Sant Ji that in 1972, when Master Kirpal Singh Ji had stayed at Sant Bani, I had felt really desperate to get into the house and see the Master. I was very grateful that I did not feel like that with Sant Ji. He said, "It is Hazur's Grace." He proceeded to ask how long Master had been in residence at Sant Bani, and at what other places had He stayed for a long time on the '72 Tour.

At the end of the short session He mentioned that He was very happy to see my son, Nicky, on the bicycle with me (as He had walked by Nick and Chris and me in the morning, He had looked at Nick and said, "Nickeee!"). He stated again that it was very good for Karen that I was taking care of the children, so she could go to the meditations with Him. We said good night, and quietly walked back by the pond and up to our house.

I wondered to myself, "How much do I want to take from Him before I begin to earn what He is giving me?" and I had no good answer. Could I really "earn" anything? He was allowing me to be close, and I did not know why – but I resolved to try not to violate that gift. Seeing Him for ten seconds felt like enough. And every day the Satsangs were getting more extraordinary.

On Monday evening (the second) the Satsang had consisted primarily of devotional songs sung by the devotees. Sant Ji had stared into Donna Pollard's eyes as she had tried to sing. Somehow she had been able to continue, and it had been a beautiful experience to witness. On Tuesday there was a lot of singing as well, and my mental frame of consciousness began to alter. It became like a meditation as I stilled my body and just focused on Him. At one point I again became aware that He was giving a discourse. He spoke of how the owner of the animal takes care of each and every thing. He feeds and cares for the animal so much that if it is sunny, he moves the creature into the shade. Everything is taken care of so that the animal has no worries. And then Sant Ji said another short line in Punjabi – and He glanced at me while He was saying it. The translation was that God is taking care of each and every need for us, so we don't have to worry about anything. All the little things are being taken care of. And that is how I felt. I felt that He was absolutely aware of everything and that He was taking care of it all. And, as I said to Karen, He kept showing me that this was what was happening. I felt very happy, and only wished that I were meditating more.

On Wednesday morning I had some details to discuss with Pappu, so I went running down to Sant Ji's house before School started. Just as I approached, Pappu came from around back, saw me, and laughed. Sant Ji, Who was in the house, called out, and Pappu said, "It's Kent!" And Sant Ji really laughed. When I walked in He said, "I have been waiting for you. It is your time to come. I have been looking at my watch wondering when you are going to come." And I just laughed like anything.

I told Pappu that I could work on the correspondence during the day because I thought it would be better to get to sleep at night. I asked if Pathi Ji could help me with the bhajans, and Sant Ji said that he could go from 4:00 p.m. to 6:00 p.m. every day. He said that we could start at 3:00, if we were really going to work on the bhajans. Sant Ji was laughing and very jolly the whole time, then He looked at me ever so sweetly, and said, "Now you go back and run the School."

On the evening of the fourth, Sant Ji asked to see all of the *sevadars* at the Ashram. It took some time for everyone to gather, as we were not expecting this invitation and some people had already dispersed. In the meantime, Sant Ji looked at a whole stack of recent black and white photos that Jonas Gerard had brought, commenting that Jonas has the great power to make everyone laugh. He paused at one of me taken in the School, observing that it looked like I had a *tilak* mark on my forehead.[2] I looked at the photo and noticed a reflection on my forehead and, as I was also grinning from ear to ear, I appeared pretty intoxicated in the shot. When we had all assembled in the living room Sant Ji laughed as He pointed out that Dick Shannon's son Matthew was sitting on Dick, and that Nicky was straddling my shoulders.

Sant Ji explained that He wished to speak to all of us. He began by saying that when you first meet a man, you don't know everything about him, and then as you get to know him more, you know more about him (implying, I think, that He now was aware that we needed to hear something as a group). He said that very few were the people who had gotten Naam, and rarer still were those dear ones who were allowed to do *seva*. He added that we were extremely fortunate. He said that it was really important that we not be disunited – that we love each other. He repeated that we have to develop love for each other. He explained that the Kal Power would play tricks – would come in and create disunion. After five to seven days the Satguru Power would take over again, but we needed to be on guard about the Negative Power. He said that Kal was thrown out of the Court of the Lord for creating disunion There.

It was a powerful session with Sant Ji – especially His emphasis on our needing to learn to forgive each other. Living in community was not always easy, as none of us had risen above our individual personalities. Serving the Master and His party, as well as hundreds of guests, was challenging for all of us – and some jobs seemed more desirable than others. I had only to look at myself to sense exactly what Sant Ji was talking about (e.g. my envy of Pappu as expressed in Chapter Two above). As Master Kirpal pointed out, it is all too easy to grumble about the things we do not have, rather than being grateful for all that is given to us. We left the house, sobered by His Words to us.[3]

The fifth of May was a busy day for Sant Ji, as He gave Initiation to

---

[2] The *tilak* is the dot placed in the center of the forehead by devout Hindus.

[3] A few weeks later, Sant Ji elaborated on this theme in a more lengthy (and stronger) talk to us. See "The Enemy Within" in *The Ambrosial Hour*, p. 87 ff.

many dear ones in a sitting that lasted several hours. He then traveled to nearby Plymouth College to visit an Oriental Philosophy class in which Susan Dyment, Ashram sevadar, and a local satsangi, Kim Illowit, were enrolled. Sant Ji addressed the class, and answered questions from the students.

In the early evening, Karen stayed with the children and I went to the Hall for meditation – although Sant Ji was not there. After some time I began to cough, and took it as a sign that I should leave. When I stepped out of the door, there was Pappu, who had come to look for me. We went down to the house to work on the correspondence. A little before 7:00 p.m., Sant Ji's door opened and He called me in. He was sitting on a small foam pad on the floor. He talked about the program at Sant Bani, saying that He had planned to visit the sevadars' houses in the afternoon, but then He had needed to rest. I said that it was all right, adding that the daily cleaning of His house, postponed because He was resting, could happen during Satsang. He laughed.

He explained that at the evening Satsang, He was not going to talk, and therefore I should be prepared to do a lot of singing, or to arrange that a lot of singing happen. I told Him whom I would ask to sing, and He said, "That is okay. It does not matter who sings – just be prepared to fill up the hour until nine o'clock."[4] I mentioned that over the weekend I planned to make copies of the bhajans that had both the translation and transliteration ready, so that people could begin to learn them. He said that would be good, as it developed the love within them.

At that point Pappu asked me if I were following Sant Ji's words directly, or should he still be translating? I responded that sometimes I did not even listen to the translation, what to speak of the Punjabi! I commented that I was like a Western disciple from France, who had become so divinely intoxicated at 77 RB that he could barely function – and Sant Ji laughed heartily.

Sant Ji looked at my School notebook and asked me what it was – and I told Him. I said that I had some questions about the School, adding that they could certainly wait. He answered simply, "Tomorrow." I wondered if I should leave, so that He could continue resting, but He said, "No. I am about to take food." Pappu gently added, "That does not mean you can stay with Him while He eats," and I said, "Yes, I know," and we left Sant Ji sitting alone in His room. That evening the entire Satsang consisted of devotional songs.

---

[4] The evening Satsang was from 8:00 to 9:00 p.m. at that time.

On Friday the sixth of May, I got up at 3:30 a.m., showered, and sat for meditation in my home. I was struggling with the process, feeling especially tired and grumpy – to the point that all I could think of was how delicious it would be to go back to sleep. I continued the mental wrestling for a couple of hours, until twenty-six month old Nicky woke up and needed me. Karen had already left for meditation in the Hall, as she did every morning. My routine was to get Chris (age seven and one-half) and Nick up and dressed, and then the three of us would go down to see Sant Ji as He came up from His house on the way to the Hall at 7:00 a.m. I lay down beside Nick and was trying to do Simran. He went back to sleep and so did I.

The next thing I knew, I awoke in the midst of an unchaste dream. I looked at the clock and it was ten after seven. We had missed the darshan when He arrived at the Hall, but we could still catch a glimpse when He left at 8 a.m. At that point, however, I felt so down on myself that my heart sank. How come I was supposed to be meditating, in the presence of a living Godman, and instead I was sleeping and having bad dreams? I wondered, "Will I even get to see Him this morning? Should I go down?" I felt embarrassed to stand in front of Him. And then I thought, "Well, I have to go. Who can forgive me other than Him?"

I hurried everything together. Chris decided to stay and clean his room, because Sant Ji might be visiting later in the day, but Nick was ready to go. A day or two before, Karen had begun to make fresh yogurt for Sant Ji, so I put the new batch, still at room temperature, in its ceramic pot. I put Nick in the backpack, grabbed the pot, and headed off toward the Ashram complex. Just as I rounded the corner of the Big House, I saw His Turban going across the field. We had arrived too late to see Him leaving the Hall.

Nick and I continued on towards His house, since I needed to bring the yogurt to them. Sant Ji had paused on the porch to talk with Judith and Russell. I thought, "At least I will get to see Him and perhaps He will say hello to me." But that did not happen. In fact, He did not even look at me. He went inside, and I lingered to deliver the yogurt to Pappu. And then I heard Sant Ji's Voice calling me from inside the house, "Kent! – Come in!" I yelled for Karen, who was standing at the bridge, and the three of us went in. I was sorry that Chris had chosen to stay at home, until I recalled that these things unfold as He wished.

We sat down on the floor of the living room. Sant Ji came out, and was really interested in the backpack and how it worked. He looked at it, handled it, saw the two holes, and asked if those were for the legs? He took it in front of Him, and called Nicky over to get in it – at which point Nick was very shy. I told Nick to sing *Apana Koi Nahin* and he said, "No!" I translated the "no" and Sant Ji really laughed. He took the yogurt from me. I had attached a label that said "*Dhai*" [Yogurt] in Hindi. Sant Ji read my sign, and commented that this yogurt we were making was very good. He liked yogurt, but the store bought kind provided initially had been really cold, and thus they had not been eating it. He asked who had made this yogurt, and Pappu said, "Karen." He took the lid off, looked inside, and then handed it to Pappu, who took it to the kitchen.

He asked Karen how her meditations were, and she answered. He told her, "Keep doing the practices that Master has taught you. That would be good." I mentioned that since I had been back, I had struggled with sleep and laziness – all of which seemed connected to lingering stomach problems. Sant Ji observed that in India I had become sick because I had drunk the water (not the water at 77 RB – but elsewhere), but now I was back home. Why, He wondered, should I still be having difficulties? I suggested that there was something in my system that still had not cleared up, and He said it would become all right.

I chose that moment to mention to Sant Ji that, while I had heard Him call other devotees "good meditators," He had (understandably) never said that about me. I hoped that one day He would also call me a "good meditator." His response was swift and strong: "You should never think that! It will not be good for you." He proceeded to tell a story about a fellow who was very strong in his meditations. His name was Sheeli, and everyone praised him for his meditations, calling him a "good meditator." When Sheeli came to see his Master, that Guru rebuked him, called him a "low dog," and threw him out of the ashram. Sant Ji commented that the roots of that disciple's spirituality were being cut by the sword of praise. The Master explained that He had to use the shield of insult in order to save Sheeli's spiritual roots from that sword – from that praise. Sant Ji added that those who are called "good meditators" by the Master get lazy and they stop. So, it is better to be rebuked by the Master.[5]

I said, "Oh, please rebuke me then" which, of course, He had just done by telling me to never think that I wanted Him to call me a good

---

[5] Alas, I did not remember this advice enough to follow it, and in the spring of 1978 Sant Ji needed to save my meager roots of spirituality with the shield of rebuke. See below, Chapters Seven and Eight.

meditator. He quoted someone as saying that every day he prayed to maintain that which he had been given. He looked at me and said, "Your one prayer should be this – to maintain what you have been given." He observed that since I was living at the Ashram, and having a chance to meditate and to serve, it would be very good for me. He indicated that everything would be all right. He pointed out that when you are in your own home, then things do come up, like the children, and other responsibilities, – and that can make you lazy for meditation. Sant Ji said that He Himself used to pray to Master Kirpal, "Oh, don't kick me from Your door."

Sant Ji wondered what time I had to get to School. I told Him that it would begin soon, and that I still had to eat. He then asked what time I ate – and I answered, "Just after this!" He was looking very intently at me – and I knew that He knew all about my current state, including my dream that morning. All I had told Him was that I had meditated two hours, and then fallen asleep when I lay down next to Nicky to get him back to sleep. But He clearly knew it all, and was so gracious and forgiving.

He asked if we wanted the yogurt pot back, and we said no, that it was all right – they could keep it. Pappu brought it to us anyway, remarking on how tasty the yogurt was. We talked some more about the backpack. In India, said Sant Ji, the mothers have to carry the child (and here He imitated a mother wrapping both arms around a child) – but with this, both hands are free and the child is free. I explained that I had to use it, as I was bringing the yogurt down. Sant Ji leaned over and said, "NICK—EEE" and flicked Him on the cheek – and Nick turned around and said, "Hi!" in a really loud voice. And Sant Ji roared with laughter. At that point He said that it was time for us to go – and we giggled our way back home, eagerly awaiting our "family interview" later that same day.

May 6th, 1977 – Family Interview with Discussion of the Sant Bani School

In the afternoon Chris, Nick, and Karen, walked by the Big House and wound their way down the dirt road – over the bridge and by the pond – to Sant Ji's house, where I joined them via my bicycle. When we entered, the first thing He said, in English, was, "Bicknell family." And when we left, the last thing He said, again in English, was, "Bicknell family – good family." We sat down and He talked to us. He told us that the yogurt was very good for His heart. It made Him feel good, as it was like what He got in Rajasthan. We said that we would bring it every day. He asked if Pappu should come and get it, but I said that I could bring it down when I came with the children to see Him.

Sant Ji looked around and said, "You forgot the backpack." I responded that I had come on the bicycle. I said we just wanted to see Him as a whole family, as Chris had missed out in the morning. He said, with a really sweet smile, "I am understanding all of that." Sant Ji asked Chris what his name was, and Pappu said, "Chris." I mentioned that Chris was good at singing bhajans, and so He asked him to sing – but Chris was too shy. Sant Ji said that He would visit our house the next day, Saturday the seventh. We talked about the houses on the Ashram. Sant Ji observed that the Gerard house was very big – and I said that our house is small. He asked if it worked for us – were we comfortable in it – and we said we were.

Sant Ji spoke to Nicky a bit, and then I asked if we could discuss the School. He said that would be fine, but mentioned that when He had seen my journal, He thought that it was a whole book of questions. We laughed, and I proceeded.

I explained that since we were a Satsangi School, supported by Satsang funds, we wanted to be able to take every child from a Satsangi family. While we felt this way, the reality was that some children were difficult. They had trouble staying within the bounds of School behavior, and they created problems for other students as well. I mentioned that I did not know how it was in India, but in the States some students required a lot more support than others – and the teachers felt concerned if they could not help a child as much as was needed. The staff wondered if the School should accept every child, or were there some whose emotional needs were too great for us to serve them properly.

Sant Ji closed His Eyes and thought about it for a while. When He opened His Eyes, He said that in India and America the children were the same – the same problems existed. He said that teaching was a hard job; it did not matter if one were in the East or West. It was difficult and a lot of work. At this age the children were mischievous – that there were only a few who were not so.

He talked about the parents – how sometimes when it was a bad home situation, the children followed that example. If the children were misbehaving, then they were reflecting the fact that their parents did not understand the Path so well. He said that when a child came into a new

situation, the child, not knowing any better, would reflect the surroundings of the home life. He said that we should continue teaching all of the
children with love.

He indicated that we should try to serve every Satsangi child, stating
that if the School asks them to leave it will break their hearts. It is not
their fault – the problem lies with their parents. We should work with the
students. I said that we wanted to keep every child in the School – that
we did not like to ask anyone to leave – but we had had to ask one girl to
leave this year because she was polluting the atmosphere.[6] It made us all
very sad to tell her that she could not continue, but she would not change
her ways. He said that if we had to do that, then we should go ahead with
it, but we should be sure to give the students fair warning. If we gave
them a warning, and explained to them what they were doing wrong –
and they still did not behave, then, if they were polluting the atmosphere,
we might have to ask them to leave.

I mentioned that sometimes I had difficulties with parents, and Sant
Ji laughed and asked what would life be without these kinds of problems.
He observed that the world did not work in such a way that everyone
would always be coming to me and folding their hands – bowing down
quietly. We all laughed a lot as He imitated such a gesture. He asked if
the parents were allowed to come in and visit the School. I said, "Yes,
they have always been invited to come." He told me to go on teaching
with love. I mentioned that sometimes I had gotten angry with certain
parents and their attitude, but that now I was learning. He advised me not
to become angry, saying that I should have a cool heart. He observed that
if someone came in with anger, and that person was met with *shanti*
[peace], that would take away the anger. He said I should be strong, and
continue to teach with love.

He asked about corporal punishment at Sant Bani – as He was going
to suggest that we not use it. We explained that no one was punished in
that way in the School. This evolved into a very interesting discussion as
to whether parents in America were legally allowed to punish their
children physically – in the family. I explained that even within a family,
the police could become involved. He asked if the children could go to

---

[6] "Polluting the atmosphere" is a phrase I had learned from Miss Sati, the
principal of Master Kirpal Singh's School at Manav Kendra in India. She used it
in relation to a particular student who had been expelled because, even after
repeated warnings, he would not stop being verbally abusive toward other
students.

the police themselves, and if children were aware that they had the right to do this. I responded that sometimes teenagers did that – but most often only if the child were injured. He wondered if one could bribe the police here like one could in India? I said, "No, it is not so easy to bribe here in America." He observed that in India you could bribe some policemen with just a cup of tea!

I got the feeling that we should try our best – in a loving way – to meet every child's needs – unless that child were really "polluting the atmosphere." I told Him that owing to all of the children who were moving into the area, we would be constructing another building, and that a local Satsangi would be helping us with a generous contribution. While a new building seemed like a good idea to me, the staff wanted me to check with Sant Ji before proceeding. He said that it was a good idea, and that it was good for that Satsangi to do that service. He stated that even more children would be coming into the area, and that the School would get bigger, so we should construct a new building. I said that we would construct the building in such a way that during the tours it could be used as a dormitory, and He said that would be good.

I told Him that we planned to hire Shipp Webb, and He said that Shipp had already related that to Him, and that it was fine. When I mentioned our plans to hire Jon Engle as well, Sant Ji said that while Jon had not told Him that yet, it was a good thing to do.

Saturday, May 7th – Visiting the Homes on the Ashram

Sant Ji visited our house on the morning of the seventh, and it was very nice indeed. Pappu had told me to come down at nine for correspondence, which I did. Sant Ji came out from His bedroom at 9:30, all ready for the walk, scheduled for 10:00. As we stood around outside His house, Sant Ji felt my nylon jacket, and asked if it were the same material as the sleeping bag I had brought Him. I said it was.

Sant Ji walked all around visiting the various places, and when He arrived at our house He came in and sat down in our back room. He gave us a long talk on how we try to make ourselves comfortable in this world, but it is just a temporary stay. If we could only get one glimpse of the comfort in Sach Khand, the comforts of this world would mean nothing to us. I said, "Well, it is still very nice to have You here in our house," and He said, "These houses are very good." He observed how good it was that the houses in America were very neat, and that everything was in order. You could actually find a needle and thread if you wanted it. In India it was not like that. He added that you could tell a person's wisdom by seeing how well he kept his house. Sant Ji looked around and said that the books were in order, the clothes were in order, and everything was where you could locate it.

Of course we were thinking, "Thank goodness we tidied up!" But it was nice. When we showed Him the meditation room, He looked into my eyes very deeply and said, "*Aur bhajan karo!*" [Do more meditation]. I mentioned something about the walls in the room – how we had painted them so it would look like Rajasthan (using a sandy textured reddish paint) and He said that our walls were better than the walls in Rajasthan because ours were inside. There it rains, and then they have to do the walls over again. In a flash, Sant Ji was gone.[7]

Later in the day I went down to the house to get Pathi Ji for working on the bhajans. Pappu was nowhere to be found. Sant Ji was in His room by Himself, and I knocked on the door and stuck my head in. He saw me and said, "*Aao, aao*" [Come in, come in], and threw His arms around me. With one arm still around my back, He told me in really clear, slow Hindi, that He was very happy that day, because He had visited our house, and that the house was full of love – that He was feeling that love. I responded that it wasn't my house but His house. I told Him that after He had visited, my meditations were better. I left, but saw Him again later when Pathi Ji and I returned. The Satsang that evening was very powerful. Sant Ji told many stories – including the tale of the man who got so angry when he could not start a fire that he burned down the whole cantonment.[8]

After the Satsang Russell and I were in His living room when He came out of His bedroom dressed casually without His turban – His hair tied up in a topknot. He asked me what was the meaning of "Bicknell?" and "Perkins?" I said that I knew of no meanings. Russell explained that the meanings for many English names were lost long ago.

Monday, May 9th – A Challenging Interview

I had to attend a state-level educational meeting off the Ashram on the ninth, so I went down at 8:30 a.m., and asked Pappu if I could say goodbye to Sant Ji. Pappu told me to just go right in – that at that

---

[7] At another point during the tour, Sant Ji and Pappu visited our home when we were not there. They left a signed note, saying simply, "We were here."

[8] Published as "The Fire of Anger" in *Sant Bani Magazine*, May 1977, p.3*ff.*

moment I did not need to knock. Sant Ji was standing there with His hair down, as He had just washed it. I told Him that I was going to Concord, the state capital, and Pappu added that I had to go to a meeting all day. He told me to go. Later that day I was telling Karen how I went into Sant Ji's room without even knocking – and at the sound of those words tumbling from my own mouth, I realized how involved my ego was. I prayed for Grace.

When I got back from Concord, Russell told me that Sant Ji had requested our presence at an upcoming meeting with a Satsangi who meant well, but who had a tendency to be headstrong and difficult. We went for the interview, and, sure enough, the fellow became argumentative. Sant Ji had asked him not to advertise the tour and Satsang through posters and such, but he had gone ahead and done that anyway. As Sant Ji attempted to offer gentle guidance, the man's voice got louder and louder, and took on a strident, belligerent tone. When Sant Ji said, "I never gave you permission for this – I told you not to do any work in my name!" – the fellow angrily proclaimed that Sant Ji had given His permission. And that is where Russell stopped him. Russell spoke in a firm voice, saying, "Listen. You call Him 'Master' and you call Him 'Saint' – but you won't listen to a word He says. Now this is His house – this is His place – and when you come here you listen to Him and treat Him with respect. You are sitting in the presence of God!" This was delivered with a great deal of strength. The man became quiet, and was respectful and polite for the remainder of the interview.

After the fellow left, Russell asked Sant Ji if what he had done was appropriate, and Sant Ji said that it was a good thing. In fact, Sant Ji added, if Russell had not spoken to him like that, then he would have just kept going on and on. Sant Ji then asked, "What is the point of coming to a Fakir and trying to make Him understand things? You should listen to what the Fakir says. He will help you understand." And then He repeated, "You should listen to what the Saint has to say. He will help you."

Sant Ji asked Russell to publish a statement in *Sant Bani Magazine* that everything regarding Sant Ji's work should be coordinated through Russell – that everything should come through Sant Bani Ashram, in New Hampshire. Hopefully that would help everyone to avoid situations like the above – where the fellow went off and did things on his own. Sant Ji added that, later on, if it were necessary, He would also write a letter for publication stating that everything should be coordinated through the Ashram.

Sant Ji told us that the day before, a follower of another guru had come to challenge Him, demanding to see the mark of the lotus on His foot.[9] The man said that he could see the other two signs, but he wanted to see the third. Sant Ji had responded, "Well, you can see two signs – so what is the use of seeing the third? What are those signs good for anyway?" Sant Ji told us that if a Man goes to Sach Khand, then what is the need of seeing "signs" on Him? Russell commented that he had been initiated for eleven years before he saw the lotus mark on Master Kirpal's foot. And then it was just because Master had His shoes off when they were going somewhere in a car. Russell added that he had never had any desire for that – he took Him as a Master without seeing those signs.

I had not thought of looking for those signs before – on either Master Kirpal or Sant Ji. The mind, being what it is, suddenly gave birth to a little desire that astounded me. Completely unannounced, the thought popped up, "Gee, maybe it would be nice to see those signs." I thought, "Oh, come on!" and then, "Well, if He showed them . . . I mean I wouldn't ask for it – ever – but . . ."

Sant Ji, sitting on His bed, started to pull His sock down – and my heart jumped a tiny bit. I instantly recalled that Master Kirpal had removed His sock to show a friend of mine the mark of the lotus when the friend expressed the desire to see It. Taking off His sock completely, Sant Ji began to rub His ankle. I looked down, and there was a round scab there. I thought, "Oh Kent, how can you be such an idiot – there it is – there is my lotus mark!" I decided that Sant Ji's scab and the assumed karma it represented were sure enough signs for me. Right at that moment, Sant Ji told us that He used to give Master Kirpal massages, but He never thought about seeing those things. He did not bother with those outer signs.

Sant Ji explained that He was never allowed to do much seva around Master Kirpal, but that He had tried to serve whenever He could. He mentioned that He had become a good actor; that is, He was good at imitating, and He would pretend to cry and be very unhappy if Master Kirpal would not let Him come near. He would say to the Master things like, "Oh, I am young and you are older, so I should be allowed to serve You!"

Sant Ji closed by stating that He had never again received love like

---

[9] The mark of the lotus flower is one of the sacred signs on the physical body of a Master.

that from Such a One. Throughout the session, Sant Ji was wiping His Eyes a lot with a handkerchief. Russell and I took our leave and backed out of the house, folding our hands to Him.

May 10ᵗʰ – Breakfast with a Saint

Tuesday May tenth was a very special morning for me. Karen woke me up at 4:00 a.m., but since I had been working on correspondence and gone to bed after midnight, I just wasn't ready to get up. I told her that if she didn't mind staying around for another half an hour, she could wake me up at 4:30 – which she did. I got up and took a shower, and started sitting at five. I had a pretty good meditation considering how tired I was – and although I fell asleep some, I dreamt that I was with Sant Ji. When I awoke I was still sitting in the upright position without a backrest.

It was raining, so I decided that I would just let Chris and Nick sleep, and wait until Karen came home to take the yogurt down. Then I realized that bringing it down at eight might mean that it would not be available for their breakfast. It was hardly useful to bring fresh yogurt after they needed it. I left the house with it at 7:30. I met Karen on the path and told her what was happening – how I had left Chris and Nick sound asleep.

When I got down to the house Sant Ji greeted me, but since He was talking with Judith and Russell, I continued on to the kitchen to exchange the new container for the old. Pathi Ji asked me if I wanted a *chapatti* [the staple flat bread of India], and I hesitated as I had not been eating much grain. At that moment Sant Ji came through, and stated quite simply that I should eat there. He held up His finger and said, "*Eyk roti*" [one *roti*, another name for a *chapatti*]. I thought, "Okay, I will eat here. Fine." After Judith and Russell left, Pappu and I sat out on the floor of the living room, and our breakfast was really sweet. I also had some yogurt. Sant Ji came into the room and said that I should have some fruit as well. Pappu ran into the kitchen and brought me a banana – which I ate. Sant Ji was walking around and around the living room while we ate. He looked at the map of the United States, and then, seeing my boots on the porch, He asked if they were mine.

Pappu had to go up to the "Big House," the Ashram guesthouse. Sant Ji disappeared, and I sat with Pathi Ji, who told me to bring only half a container of yogurt the next day, as two thirds was too much. I said okay. Sant Ji came into the room – so quietly that I did not hear Him. Suddenly the lights flicked on – first one set, and then another as He flipped the switches. I said, "*Roshni data*" [light giver] and He chuckled. He thought about it some more, and He really laughed and was joined by Pathi Ji. He began to speak to me in Hindi. I was sitting on the floor and He was looking down at me – standing up and towering over me.

When Sant Ji talked to me in Hindi, He tended to use a strong voice. He would begin slowly, and then pick up the pace. I could not get everything, but when He acted out some of what He was saying, I understood more. He was very happy to find that at the Sant Bani School we did not strike the children – that we did not use corporal punishment. He said that in India it is a real problem, as there the children are hit a lot.

I looked at my watch and it was eight o'clock and I thought, "This is really nice – I can hang around until 8:15 and then whip up to School." Immediately Sant Ji asked me what time School began, and I said at 8:15. He looked at His watch and added, "Well, when should you go?" I said, *"Jaldi"* [soon], as I had just finished my breakfast. He said, "Go then." As He watched me put on my coat, I told Him that Karen had made it – and He said, *"Aachaaa!"* [Good].

As I rushed back home, I realized what a great honor I had been granted; to eat in His house. I was happy that I had not delayed bringing the fresh yogurt, as it was served the moment I came in with it. I laughed, and thought of saying to Him, "Don't You think my wife should go with You on the tour – because who will make the fresh yogurt?" What a great blessing! Under my arm I carried the leftover yogurt – and Pappu had given me some other *sabji* [cooked vegetables] from the kitchen. When I got home we all ate the blessed parshad.

During these first weeks I was really busy. I ran the School (teaching several classes), spent hours on the phone arranging things, meditated, ate, went to town for errands, made trips to Concord and Boston, worked with Pathi Ji on the bhajans, went to Satsang, attended various meetings, and helped with the correspondence until late at night. I was exhausted, but in an exhilarated way – and very happy to flow with the intense rhythm.

In the afternoon Karen went for a private interview with Sant Ji. She seemed very happy when she returned to our house, so I asked her if there were anything she wished to share. She mentioned that she had asked Sant Ji if it were true that one could perfect the Simran in seven days. I anxiously questioned her as to what He had said. She was still rather *mast* [intoxicated] from the experience, so she just giggled and answered, "He said that a pure soul can perfect it in seven minutes – what to speak of seven days!" and we both began to laugh.

After the evening Satsang on the tenth, Sant Ji again asked to see all of the sevadars who lived at Sant Bani. As we were arriving, Sant Ji asked specifically for Gerald Boyce, and just then Gerald came in the door. Jonas Gerard said, "Ah, Gerald will have a long life." And Sant Ji said that yes, there is that proverb in India where it is said that if you are thinking of someone, and then they appear, it means that they will have a long life. I remembered that recently He had told me that He had been thinking about me and wondering where I was, when I appeared. He had been looking at His Watch and thinking, "Well, it is time for Kent to come" – and outwardly it had not been a time I was scheduled to come to His house.

When we all had gathered, He told us a story. In India there was going to be a wedding, but one of the two parties involved declared that they did not want any elderly people present. They wished that only young people would be permitted to attend. The groom's party, however, wanted to bring one elderly man, so they hid him in a trunk. Explaining that the trunk had all their clothing, they carried it with them in the procession. Whenever any question or test came from the bride's party, the groom's people would secretly consult that old man for the correct answer. Sant Ji was laughing so much throughout Pappu's translation, that it was difficult to concentrate on the words. Sant Ji concluded that wherever we go as a group, we also should take our *buddha* [elderly wise one], Gerald, with us. Everyone, including Gerald, laughed and laughed and laughed.

He said that He would give us more time later, adding that what He was saying then was not worth recording. He decided to see us again on Sunday night, because there was no evening Satsang that day. He told us that out of millions of people, only six or seven get opportunities to serve like we have – to serve directly. Many people go to serve the *gurdwaras* or churches – but we were serving the people who love God. He added that the people who came here would be inspired by our service to do more meditation. He related that Sardar Rattan Singh used to serve the temples and bring the devotees to the holy places to bathe – and how his donations of grain were sold by the priests for purchasing meat and wine. The first thing Sant Ji told Rattan Singh, after he came to Him, was to leave off eating meat and drinking wine himself – which he did. Then he began to bring the grain over to 77 RB, and in that way he began to help bring the people to the pilgrimage of Naam, rather than the pilgrimage of the "holy" river.

Sant Ji told us that if we lived up to the Path, the Ashram would grow into a fragrant bloom. He said that more people would move into the area, and that many of the people around – because of our example – would take Naam. And then He mentioned the School. He said that just as the School was growing – people were hearing about it and they wanted that education for their children – so the Ashram would grow. He added that the schoolchildren themselves would bring this thing home – that they were seeing a Saint and that they were being affected by their good teachers. They would bring that home and some of their parents would become interested.[10]

Those were breathtaking statements as to the future of both the Ashram and the School. Sant Ji said that we should continue to do our seva. We should live together harmoniously – that would be good for us. We should all love each other. In times of sickness we should all help each other – just as when Karen's wrists were broken in the accident, and everyone served her with love. That made her accident so much easier to bear, He added, that now she had almost forgotten about it. Then He said that seva was a very good thing, and we should consider our seva first. At the end He mentioned that it would be very easy, because of our seva, to loot the Bhajan of the people who came here to meditate. And He and we all laughed heartily.

May 11th, 1977 – Visit to the School

On Wednesday the eleventh of May, Sant Ji came to visit the Sant Bani School. He walked through the original Stone Building and the addition added in 1975. He visited every class. In one, pausing at a globe, He spoke about the need to have someone who has already traveled to a country in order to understand what the country is like – that books and maps are not enough. In the same way we should have some adept of the spiritual planes to guide us within.[11]

Students, staff, and a few parents assembled in the space reserved for our daily Morning Session (the community gathering that begins each day), and the children sang some devotional songs for Sant Ji.[12] Seated on a wooden bench, Sant Ji commented that when I had gone to see Him

---

[10] It did come to pass that several students and School parents became interested in the Path and became initiates.

[11] Aspects of the visit were captured on 8mm film.

[12] At present this space is the Third Grade classroom.

in Rajasthan a year ago, the first thing I had requested was that He visit
the School. And, by the Grace of Master Kirpal, it was happening. He
added that He was very happy to be there. His talk, captured on tape, was
sweet, funny, and powerful:

*The building of our life is starting, and childhood is the center
stone for the foundation of the life of man. If we are wholeheartedly studying the studies which we are being taught here,
and if we make our life pure, that will help us very much in our
future because when we go up for further studies, the effect of
this time will be on our hearts. That will not allow any bad
thoughts to come into us, and that will prove very good for us, to
make our future. We can get the qualities of our teachers if we
respect and obey them; because if a student is obeying and respecting his teacher, the teacher gives that student much of his
attention, and he helps him, and he loves him very much. That
proves very good for his studies. We are studying for our own
selves, and that's why we should not be angry or displeased with
our teachers.*

*In the future you will realize how much these teachings
would have been helpful if you had obeyed them. Master Sawan
Singh Ji used to tell about His childhood—when He was studying
in school. He was living in a village named Mehmah Singh
Wala, and he was going to Nanangwal, another place, for study.
And when he was going there to study, first of all he would go to
the teachers' home and clean the house and wash the vessels,
and in that way he was respecting and doing service to his
teacher very well. Even when he was getting the Engineering
education in Roorkee College he was respecting and obeying his
professors very much. After getting the degree, his teachers
greeted him with very much respect and said, "Now there is no
difference between you and us, because you also have become
like us."*

*Very often he would talk about a fellow student whose name
was Kartar Singh, who didn't like to study at any time. What was
he doing? First of all, he was not ready to start from home to
come to school, and he would always cry and make excuses.
Sometimes he would lie down on the floor and in that way he
was not coming to school. But if anybody took him to school,
with any pressure or something like that, when he came he would
not obey his teachers; he never was doing his homework, making
excuses, and he never was respecting the teacher. Once he
(Kartar Singh) saw that one dead man was carried in a coffin by*

*four people, and there were many other people who were
following them. And because he knew that he was always carried
by some people to school (because by his own self he would not
come to school), so he thought that this man is also not ready to
go to school, that's why they're carrying him. So he asked them
—because he had that quality, that's why he thought that everybody was like that.*

*We should obey our teachers and respect them because
whatever they are teaching us, that is for our own good. It is said
that in Rajasthan once a man was carrying four bushels of wheat
on one side of his horse, and four bushels of sand on the other
side, and in that way he was carrying a lot of weight on the
horse. One wise man was coming from the other direction and he
asked the man, "What are you carrying on the horse?" He
replied that, "On one side there are four bushels of wheat, but to
equalize the weight I have put four bushels of sand on the other
side." So the wise man told him, "Oh fool, what have you done?
You should have put two bushels of wheat on either side. Why
are you carrying the dust here?" But instead of accepting the
wise man's advice, he became angry with him. We should not do
that, because whatever wise people—whatever teachers—are
telling us, that is for our own welfare.*

*So we are studying for making our own success; we are not
doing any favor to our teachers. So if our teachers start telling
us to do anything, we should do one extra thing for them. If they
are telling us to solve one question, we should solve one more
question, because whatever we are doing, that is for our good.
We are not doing any favor for our teachers. So we should
always respect our teachers and obey whatever they tell us to do.*

*In our days in India there weren't any very good arrange-
ments of school and education, but then also we were three who
were sent to school. One was the son of a weaver from the
village, and two of us were farmer's sons. So when we went to
school, our teacher gave us some lessons to learn, and then he
went away for some other work. So out of the other two boys
only one joined me, and we both learned that lesson very well.
But the other one, he sat on the wall of the school, and he was
enjoying the cool breeze coming from the other side. So when the
teacher came back, he asked whether we had learned our lesson
or not. We both had learned that, so he was very much pleased
with us. But the other one, he said. "No. I was enjoying the cool
breeze while sitting on the wall. It's very good to sit there. Why
should I learn the lesson? If I want to learn the lesson, I will*

learn by my own self. Why are you worried about me?" I have seen him when he was grown up, and he was suffering a lot, and repenting that he hadn't obeyed his teacher.

In America it is not the usual thing to give punishment to the children, but in India it is exactly the opposite. Children are given a very good beating if they are not obeying the teacher. So when that son of the weaver didn't obey the teacher, and he didn't learn the lesson, the teacher gave him punishment. He told him, "You catch your ears." (In India, to catch one's own ears is a sign of repentance.) And when he told him to do that, instead of catching his own ears, he came to the teacher and caught the ears of the teacher. So that poor teacher was very much upset, and at last he told him to leave the school, and in that way he was thrown out from the school.

So with love we should study wholeheartedly, and we should respect our teachers, because whatever they are teaching us, that is for our good, and if we will obey them, it will make our future bright.

After the talk Sant Ji asked Pathi Ji to sing a bhajan, and then He took His leave of the group. Sant Ji, Pathi Ji, Pappu, Russell, Karen (with Nick on her back) and I walked out via the small office, and He pointed to the chair at the desk and asked me if I did not get upset when someone else was sitting in my chair. I laughed, and said that I did not really use that office much. Sant Ji said, "Well, you know what I mean." He explained to us that it is human nature to become upset when someone else seems to be doing the work or seva that has been given to us. He went on to say that the service of the Sant Bani School, the education of the children, was very important. We needed to make the School good.

Friday, May 13th – My Thirtieth Birthday
Advice for Talking with Parents Who Have School Issues

Friday the thirteenth, my thirtieth birthday, was a very interesting day. In the morning we only had darshan – I did not talk to Him at any length. Chris, Nick, and I took the yogurt down at 7:30 a.m. Nick found a ball near the dais, the platform where Sant Ji sat to give Satsang. It was located in the small field just outside of the house, facing the pond. When Nick saw Sant Ji coming, he yelled, "See my ball Sant Ji?" I prudishly observed, "Nick, that is not really your ball." As Sant Ji got closer, however, Nick held out the ball and said, "This is my ball Sant Ji." Sant

Ji came by and said "Chrissy . . . Nicky" and laughed and went on.

I returned to my house with a certain dread that I needed to call a particular Satsangi parent who often challenged School policy as it related to his child. He had already called me, but said that he would call back at 10:00 a.m. As he did not call right at ten, I stepped outside – and suddenly got a strong urge to see Sant Ji. It occurred to me that I ought to consult Sant Ji before I made that phone call, so I went down to the house and was graciously allowed to sit before Him. I explained what I thought the issue was going to be. Recently the School had set up a study hall for students who had not done their homework, or who were fooling around in class. This took place during the second recess in a designated room, monitored by a teacher. This fellow's son had been assigned to that, as often the boy had a difficult time taking care of himself in class.

The pattern in the past had been that when something like this happened, the father would call me up and say that we were being unfair, and would demand a change. I explained that I had trouble dealing with that man with a cool heart – as Sant Ji had advised me to do. I thus felt that it was important that I talk to Sant Ji about it before I called him back. And I explained that I was only guessing what the phone call was going to be about.

Sant Ji laughed a lot and said, "Well, you call . . ." and I got the feeling that He was saying, "What am I supposed to do – make that call for you?" So I began to laugh as well. I commented that maybe I should not have come down there – that perhaps it was something I needed to do myself – and I should not have bothered Sant Ji with it. But I said that I had had a strong feeling in my heart that I should come to see Him before I called.

He said, "What can I tell you? Some people have the habit to argue, and they will go on arguing. If you meet him with a humble heart, he won't listen to your humility." Then He told me that He had had long talks with a few families who were not getting along with the Ashram and the School, and that they knew that when they were not getting along with the Ashram, it was not the fault of the sevadars there. In their hearts they knew it was due to their own faults and failings.

He explained that in India the parents had nothing to do with the school. They did not have any say in how the schools were run. The school officials could beat children, and the parents could not do anything about it. He added that in America not even the parents could reprove their children – so how did I expect the School to run? In India the students thought that the teachers were like Yama – the Angel of Death – because the teachers limited the children's independence.

Then He told me not to be nervous when I made that return call. He said, "First you meet him with love – and then whatever comes up will be taken care of by Hazur [Master Kirpal] sitting within you." He talked about that parent as a devotee, and again instructed me not to be nervous. Sant Ji left the room briefly and Pappu served me some juice. When Sant Ji returned, He commented that people were devoted, but anger could steal that devotion – anger got in the way of devotion. People understood that the problems were their own fault, but it was very difficult to change one's nature.

I was left with the clear impression that we were supposed to go ahead and run the School, always doing the best job we could, and that we should continue to work with the children – but perhaps not worry so much about the problems of the parents.

Before I left, Pappu mentioned that it was my birthday. Sant Ji said in English, "Oh, oh ho ho . . . Haappy Barthday to you!" which He said several times. Pappu corrected Him because He was saying "Varth" instead of "Birth." He got it, and we were all laughing and laughing. I said to Him, "Next week is my spiritual birthday.[13] I have been nine years on the Path and I have not done anything." And He said, "*Koi bat nahi* [it does not matter] – now you are doing something!" And I said, "Yes." He said that I was doing very good seva at the School and that I had a good chance for seva at the Ashram as well, and all of that was good for me. I was glowing when I walked back to my home.

Sant Ji asked that we come down and show slides of India that evening. It was just Karen and I, and Sant Ji was so intimate. He really seemed to enjoy the slides (quite likely He had never – or rarely – seen slides before). He said that they were really good color, and that they were just like real life. When the figure of Babu Ji, with a mattress slung over his shoulder, came on the screen, Sant Ji called to the image, "Babu Ji . . . *Kya hal hai? Sab raji khushi hai?*" [How are you – is everything okay?]. Later, when Bant's picture came, He told her to come, "*Aaja, aaja!*" He asked another image, "Why are you just standing there? Come on out here!" He laughed a lot throughout the whole series, and said that the slides were very good indeed. At the end of the show He examined the projector.

Then He said "Happy Birthday" to me again. He asked Karen what

---

[13] Karen and I were initiated on May 20th, 1968.

she had made for me, and she described it to Him – a cherry-o cream cheese pie. He said, "*Now* you should go home and eat it!" Yes, sireee, it was a very fine birthday for me in every way.

May 14th – A Day of Reckoning

A lot happened on Saturday the fourteenth of May. The saga actually began the day before when a woman had a breakdown of some kind. She had been sitting outside Sant Ji's house near the pond and suddenly jumped up and dove into the water. Hardly anyone was around, but when we realized what had happened, Robert Schongalla used his excellent swimming skills to search the pond. As she was not found in the water, a group of sevadars was organized to go into the woods to look for her. In the meantime, as we left the house for the woods beyond, Sant Ji called Fletcher Lokey back, and told him to take a blanket with him, in case she needed it when found. As we went further into the trees, we began to see articles of her clothing along the way – shirt, shorts, and then undergarments. Fletcher was the one who found her, and she was naked. She came back quietly, and, as she seemed to have gathered herself together, she left the Ashram in her own vehicle.

The next day, the fourteenth, she returned and created more of a scene. When a second person acted in such a manner that was upsetting to others, a chain of events unfolded that forced us to begin to understand how to deal with guests who were mentally unbalanced to the point that they disturbed others. It was a difficult and painful time for everyone involved.

At 7:45 a.m. on the fourteenth I was just getting ready to take the yogurt down, when Karen came back and told me that there had been a major disturbance during the meditation. At Sant Ji's request, we had a set time for the meditation sitting, and if you arrived after the doors were closed, then you had to wait until the sitting was over. The alternative had been the constant shuffle of people coming at all times – so we began the "closed sittings." In the middle of the meditation hour, the woman involved in the pond incident the day before had thundered up to the back door of the Satsang Hall and demanded to be let in. The door sevadar stopped her, and Russell, hearing the noise from inside the Hall, went out to see what was happening. She claimed that she was the "Virgin Mother," and, wrapped only in a blanket, she wished Sant Ji to see her in her original form. Although she did not succeed, there was quite a loud commotion.

I was in a hurry to bring the yogurt to Sant Ji's house, but I swung by the Perkins house on my way, as Judith had asked me to come in. I caught part of a conversation indicating that the woman had just left the Ashram, driving so fast in her car that people were concerned someone might get hurt. I assumed she had left the premises.

I continued on to the house, and Sant Ji, Pathi Ji, and Pappu asked me if I had heard about the incident. I said I had, and that I thought she had left. Sant Ji went over and looked out the window. He commented that He did not believe she had gone. He was right; as the truth was that she was sitting on the back porch of the Satsang Hall at that time.

Sant Ji asked me to sit down. My plan had been to drop off the yogurt and run – as I had only meditated for fifteen minutes, and I wanted to sit for another hour at least – but Sant Ji said, "*Betho!*" [sit]. The card-table was brought into the living room for Him. Pathi Ji brought in chapattis, and Sant Ji gave me one from His container. He handed me the butter and then the butter knife. He had me drink some chai. I ate my chapatti and drank my tea.

Judith came in and mentioned that the woman was still here. We developed a plan, which was to have her go to my house, and the Sanbornton Chief of Police would meet her there and take her wherever she needed to go. I suggested I could invite her for tea at my house, and Sant Ji said that was a good plan.

I went up and asked her, but she did not want to go. I said that Sant Ji has said it would be good – at which point she asked why I had not mentioned that at first. So she came with me. She came to the house and had tea, and then the Chief came. We all talked quietly, and finally she agreed that she needed help. The Chief took her to a facility where she could be treated.

The second person who was acting in a strange way was an eccentric disciple of Master Kirpal whose behavior started out as odd, but harmless. While several guests had expressed concern about him, no one had been bothered to any degree. That is, he initially remained wrapped up in himself. Still, we checked with Sant Ji, and, based on what we presented, He said that as long as the fellow did not disturb others, he could stay. Unfortunately, the harmlessness did not continue. The man began to say more and more bizarre things, and other guests became upset. He claimed that he was at the Tour to control the weather; further, he needed to be there to "protect" all of the women from dark forces present, as he was the *Avatar*.[14] When I heard these developments, I spoke to Judith and Russell, and we all agreed that it would be best if the man did not continue attending the program. I offered to take care of the situation.

Dick Shannon, Robert Schongalla, David Teed, and I found the fellow and talked to him. He informed us that he was actually Jesus Christ, and that we were all agents of the Negative Power. He explained that in this Aquarian Age, man is dog and woman is cat, and that he was the Supreme Cat who had come down to liberate all women. He added that he needed to stay at the Ashram to protect people from Sant Ji! I returned, and reported to Russell and Judith that he really was unbalanced, and that his talk certainly disturbed the four of us. We all felt he needed to leave, and that it would be just as well not to involve Sant Ji.

I went back to tell the fellow that it was time for him to go, but he began to plead for at least one more glimpse of Sant Ji before he left. He promised that he would do anything Sant Ji asked of him. He continued, "Isn't that only fair? Am I just a street punk that you should be throwing me off the Ashram?"

I wavered. I thought that maybe this disciple of Master Kirpal did have a right to see Sant Ji. Who were we to decide his fate? And, in a real breach of the trust given to me by Sant Ji, I decided it would be much easier – for everyone – if he heard directly from Sant Ji that he should leave. He was, after all, saying that he would do anything Sant Ji wanted. After checking with others, I headed off to speak with Sant Ji.

Down at the house I told everything to Pappu. Sant Ji was bathing, but in a few minutes He finished, and Pappu went in and related it all to Sant Ji. From where I was sitting, I could hear the conversation. And from the tone of Sant Ji's voice as He answered Pappu, I knew that something was wrong. Pappu came out, looking like a cat dragged out of water. He said, "This is bad. You should handle this yourself. Sant Ji is upset with me for bringing Him your question. He said I should have told you to handle it, and sent you away." Pappu did not know what to do at that point. I felt terrible, and said that I would go and handle it immediately. I asked Pappu to tell Sant Ji that I was sorry I had bothered Him, and Pappu answered that he could not go back into Sant Ji's bedroom right then. I said, "Not now – but please tell Him, sometime during the day, that I am sorry that I blew it."

---

[14] An *Avatar* is a chosen vehicle of God whose role is to bring order back into a world gone awry.

Right then Pathi Ji came out of Sant Ji's room and said, "Kent, *aao!*" [come in]. I said, "Okay" and started to go in, but Pappu told me that he could not go back in there – that I should go ahead by myself. I told him he had to come, as he had to translate. So we went in.

Sant Ji asked me to sit down. He told me that we had to learn how to handle these kinds of situations without involving Him. It was confusing for the Indians, as they were guests here in America, and did not know our customs. When we came to India, He did not come to us with these types of problems. We knew all of the laws here – we knew whom to call – and He did not know the laws or whom to contact. Just as He had advised me when I came to talk to Him before I made the phone call to the difficult parent, it was up to us to be strong, and to learn to handle those kinds of thing. We should be strong in our seva and <u>trust</u> the Master.[15]

Sant Ji said that it was not good for the mentally disturbed people to come in the private interviews. If any guests were causing trouble and disturbing others, they should not be permitted to stay at the Ashram. Sant Ji explained that they should be asked to leave in such a way that they hardly even knew they were going. He added that it would be good to get the help of professionals who had training in handling people with mental problems. He was quite specific that sending such people to see Him was not appropriate, and He asked me to inform the other sevadars of that. One way or another, it was our job to be certain that the other dear ones who were here for the spiritual benefit were not being disturbed by a few who badly needed professional help.

I apologized many times for causing Him any pain or hardship or confusion. He never said, "Oh, that's okay," or anything like that. He just kept saying, "This is not my country – and you have to handle these things because this is your place, your country." At one point, He even said that if we could not handle these things, then we should take Him down to the airplane and send Him back to India!

Sant Ji was very stern and powerful in a manner I had never experienced. While He was not angry, He was certainly speaking strongly to someone who had made a big mistake (me). It was clear that I was being rebuked – outwardly and inwardly. When Sant Ji said finally, "I am here

---

[15] In two Satsangs right after these incidents, Sant Ji made the point quite clearly that we needed to trust the Master inside, and, having faith in the Master, we should go ahead and do the seva.

for your meditations and to give Satsang," I knew I had really let Him down.

At that point Sant Ji asked that tea be prepared. When it arrived, He poured me a cup out of His own container. He handed me the cup, and when it was empty He refilled it for me. When I stood up to leave I had this feeling that He was going to put His Arm around me, and He did. He told me again to go and do what I had to do – not to be nervous. And then He commented, "What would the Satsang be like without these difficulties? What would it be like if everyone came folding their hands and being very nice? It does not work like that." I understood that He was saying both that these problems were going to arise – there was no ducking that – and that it was necessary for us to learn how to deal with them effectively, without involving Him in an outward manner. They came up for us to learn – not so that we might come running to Him every time. I headed off to "do my best and leave the rest to Master."

I immediately found the man, and, as gently as I could, told him that he did have to leave the Ashram right away. When he resisted, I explained that I did have the authority to tell him that – that it had been given to me by Sant Ji, by Master Kirpal, and by Russell, and he responded that the sin would be on my head. I said that was okay. Someone was willing to drive him back to Boston, so he packed his things and left, quietly and peacefully.

In the evening Satsang Sant Ji told the story of the two devotees who wished to see God. They were both meditating, and wondered how long before they could see Him face-to-face. Narada was a servant of God who saw Him every day. The devotees thought it would be a good idea to ask Narada to bring their questions to God, which he did. God responded that Narada should tell one fellow that it would be after six more years. The other devotee would get to see God only after as many years as there were leaves on the pipal tree under which the devotee was sitting for meditation. So the second man should count the leaves on the tree to know how many years it would be.

Narada went to the first man, thinking that he would like the message that he only had six years to wait. But that fellow became angry, and yelled, "Six years! Why so long?" Then he gave Narada a beating with a stick. Narada thought, "Gee – what on earth is going to happen when I give the message to the second man, telling him that he has to count all of the leaves on the pipal tree?" So, Sant Ji said, Narada was afraid to deliver God's message.

Narada finally got up the courage to go, and the second devotee served him tea, and was really polite, and did not ask anything. In the end, Narada gave him God's message: count the leaves on the pipal tree and you will see God in that many years. That man became ecstatic that God had promised that one day the devotee really would see God's Face. It did not matter how many years it took, the reality was that God had promised that one day God would show Himself. The devotee jumped up and danced with so much joy that at once he was united with God and saw Him directly. As I sat and listened to the story, one line jumped out at me – that the servant of God was "afraid to deliver God's message." And I realized, "When God gives us something to do, then we need to do it!"[16]

The next morning I had such a strong desire to sit for meditation that I sat much longer than usual. In the end I fell asleep, however, and did not wake up until 7:45 a.m. when Karen came in the door. I had missed the chance for the early morning glimpse of Sant Ji going to and fro from the house to the Hall, and I felt pretty down. Later in the day, Eric Perkins and I were seated in the Satsang Hall singing a bhajan when He arrived, and at the end of the song He asked me to sing another. Then, as He told the following story, He seemed to cast many long love-filled glances directly into my heart via my eyes.

Mastana Ji was the very devoted disciple of Baba Sawan Singh. Baba Sawan Singh gave Mastana Ji a cave to meditate in. One day Mastana Ji decided to have some tea upstairs. He fixed himself tea, and sat down at a table and chair upstairs from the cave. Suddenly he saw Sawan Singh's two sons coming, and he got scared that they would see that he was not in the cave – that he was not sitting in meditation. He worried as to what they would tell Master Sawan Singh.

Then Mastana Ji remembered, "Who am I to be afraid of anyone? My Master is Sawan Singh. The Lord of All Creation is sitting inside of me. So why should I be afraid?" He threw away the table and chair and went back down and sat in the cave. At that point Sant Ji asked why

---

[16] There were many disciples who were certain that all that was required to heal a troubled soul would be a glance of the Master. Thus the idea of dismissing someone from the Ashram – without the Master's specific order to do so – was perceived as cruel. Further, it was not seen as within the realm of a decision that sevadars should be making on their own. But that was precisely what was being asked of us. All of those factors combined to make such situations quite challenging.

should a man who is an initiate of a perfect Master be afraid of anyone in the world? Saying this, He looked right at me, and I prayed that I had really received the counsel.

I ruminated more over the reasons behind His rebuking me. Outwardly, I did have to learn to be stronger, clearly, in that kind of a seva. After Sant Ji had talked to me and given me tea, He had sent Pathi Ji to find me with a further message.[17] Pathi Ji said that Sant Ji was not displeased with me – He wasn't angry with me – but I had to be stronger in my service. Pathi Ji demonstrated how sometimes in the Ashram at 77 RB they had to physically remove troublemakers. He grabbed my arm and pulled me, and said strongly, "*CHELO! CHELO!*" [Go! Go!] And Pathi Ji made threatening motions with his fist to really get the point across.

I recalled Sant Ji telling me that Pathi Ji and Babu Ji took care of all of those situations at 77 RB – that they never bothered Him with that kind of thing. I thought, "Yes, I must get stronger." Then I remembered something else. Just a week and a half earlier, when He said that it is better to be rebuked by the Saint than to be praised as a good meditator, I had asked Him to please rebuke me.[18] The lessons were coming hard and fast, but always with the gentle hand of love.

May 15th – Malaria

At that point I had not yet attended a morning meditation with Sant Ji in the Hall, as I had been baby-sitting so that Karen could go. I really wanted to sit with Him, so I asked Karen if I could go the next morning and she agreed. However, today was the day that the signs of Sant Ji's intense bout with what we later learned was malaria began to manifest. In the evening, although He did not feel well, He gave a beautiful Satsang. The announcement was made that much of the daily schedule including the interviews and the morning meditation with Him would have to be suspended until Sant Ji's health improved.

In order to ensure that Sant Ji would not be bothered at all hours, we set up a system of sevadars to "guard" the house and grounds. I was scheduled to be a door guard from 6:00 to 9:00 p.m., so I headed down

---

[17] Pathi Ji was very patient with my so-called Hindi – and, given enough time, we were able to communicate quite well together.

[18] See above, May 6th.

and parked myself on the porch. At eight Richard Hamilton came and did some body work on Sant Ji until nine. Russell came at that point, and Sant Ji called both of us to see Him in the bedroom. We sat on the floor. At first I said nothing, but after a while He looked at me and said, "*Aur*?" ["and" or "more" but here, "Yes, anything?"].

I mentioned that I had one joke for Him, and He asked what it was. I explained that tomorrow I was planning to go to the morning meditation with Him for the first time – but that now He was not going because He did not wish to sit with me – I was such a low one. Russell and Pappu were both cracking up, and when Pappu translated, Sant Ji really laughed. He had His hands cupped in His lap – and He lifted up one hand and slapped the back of it down into the palm of the other. He said, "I told you that you have been in India three times, so it is good for Karen to have these sessions. Don't be greedy!" I said, "She can go all the other times, but tomorrow when I go, You won't be there." And He laughed and said, "Yes, go tomorrow!" He looked at me with great love as He smiled.

On Monday the sixteenth, all activities with Sant Ji were canceled. I went down in the evening to help Pappu with the letters, and Sant Ji called for me when He found out I was there. He asked how I was doing, and I laughingly told Him that I had a very good time in the Hall this morning – a very good meditation. He responded, "And now your turn is done!" and really laughed. I said, "Yes, now it is over."

He asked me when School was getting out, and I said Friday the tenth of June. He wondered if we were going to come to Vermont (His next stop on the Tour), and I said that perhaps on the weekend we could come. He turned and asked Pappu if they could come back through Sant Bani on the way down to Boston, but Pappu said that they would go directly to Boston. I told Him that we would meet them at the airport in Boston before they departed for points west. Sant Ji asked why I could not come to the Boston program. I answered that at this time the Boston sangat was asking people not to attend their short program, as the facilities at Millie Prendergast's house were extremely limited. He responded that I should come to Boston. He ordered me, "*Aao*!" [Come]. He said it would not be any problem – that I could stay in Millie's house. If I had any trouble getting permission, I could talk to Pappu. He suggested that I sleep on the floor in Pappu's room. He added, "After all, you are one of the party. You have become a third Indian [along with Pappu and Pathi Ji] as a member of the official party. Certainly you should come to Boston." All the while He was laughing and very kind to me.

Further Developments with Malaria & an Amazing Session
Wherein Sant Ji Asked Me Many, Many Questions

So much happened on the eighteenth and nineteenth of May, that it all became somewhat of a blur. Sant Ji's condition became worse, and He went through cycles of being very uncomfortable no matter what we did for Him. A local doctor was brought in to see Him, but could find nothing to speak of. Richard Cardozo, a satsangi physician from Hanover, NH, was consulted, and he suspected malaria, given the cyclical nature of the attacks. He said that the only way to know was through tests at the hospital. Sant Ji requested to be taken for testing right away. Some thought it wiser to wait, but Pappu, Pathi Ji, and I all remembered the story of the king who was so pleased with the minister who was willing to smash a valuable bejeweled cup — because he understood the orders of his king as worth more than any material thing.[19] The decision was made to go to Hanover right away.

We drove to the hospital and, with the help of Dr. Cardozo's skilled colleagues, a sample of blood was drawn and the malaria infection identified. While the whole ordeal was very tiring for Sant Ji's already exhausted body, it was good to know the specific nature of the outer illness. It was a time of intense Simran for all of us — but there was a feeling of peace on the long car ride back to the Ashram. Pathi Ji and I, squeezed into the back section of the full station wagon, held hands most of the way, watching over the reclined form of Sant Ji in the seat in front of us. It was decided that I should stay in the house with them that night.[20]

On the evening of the nineteenth I again slept in Sant Ji's house. He had to take His malaria medicine at 1:30 a.m. and it was requested that I be available should any unexpected needs arise. The next morning, Friday the twentieth, Karen reminded me that it was our ninth spiritual "birthday," as well as the tenth anniversary of when we had met in Denver in 1967. I walked to the house and saw Him briefly before I went off to School. I returned to the house in the afternoon, to work on bhajans with Pathi Ji. Sant Ji had told Pappu that when I came, He wished to see me — but Pappu forgot. At 4:00 p.m. he remembered, and we went in to

---

[19] See above, Chapter Two.

[20] Cf. Russell Perkins in *Sant Bani Magazine*, July/August, 1977, "The First World Tour of Ajaib Singh, Part I: In New England," pp. 39-42, for a more full account of Sant Ji's illness from a different perspective.

Sant Ji's bedroom where we stayed until 5:30. Sant Ji engaged me in a wide-ranging conversation that, as there was no tape recorder, I tried hard to recall as soon as I left. It was so free flowing, however, that I could not retain everything. Among the subjects we "covered":

- We looked up "malaria" in the encyclopedia volume I had brought, and I told Him that at the hospital I had seen the parasite through the microscope.

- Seeing a map in the "M" encyclopedia, He took out the map of the United States, and we looked at all the places that they were going to visit. I mentioned that I would fly from Boston to Miami, and join them there for the South American Tour. He asked Pappu, "He is not coming here – or here – or here?" as He pointed to places on the map. Pappu said I was not. I said, "I will come if You want?" and I laughed. He answered, "If it is a question of money, I have $200 that could be used. It is seva." I mentioned that just this morning Russell was telling me that he had this fear that Sant Ji would ask me to go on all the Tour, and then who would be left behind to do all of the responsibilities here at the Ashram? At the end of the conversation Sant Ji said, "Well, Russell will be out here, and here, and here – so you will have to be at the Ashram."

- The conversation changed to a discussion of America. Sant Ji asked me many questions. How long ago did we get our independence? Did we fight like India did? How long were the English here? Why did the U.S. join England in the Second World War?

- Sant Ji talked a lot about Hitler. I told Him that I had heard that an early representative of Master Kirpal used to include Hitler on a list of prominent vegetarians. Sant Ji asked how many people Hitler had killed, and I told Him. He said that in India people were very frightened of Hitler, and that now it is like a proverb that when someone is becoming very bossy, they say he is becoming like a Hitler. He asked why the U.S. fought against Japan as well as Germany. And why did the U.S. drop that big bomb? When I explained that the U.S. thought it would make the war end sooner and save lives, He said, "*Teek hai*! [as if to say "I understand" – not necessarily "That is okay"]" He said that when someone like Hitler comes into this world, the Negative Power gives them a lot of power and surrounds them with powerful people. He talked a lot about that. He asked how one could call someone a vegetarian who had killed seven million people.

- He talked about drugs and smoking tobacco. He asked me if I had ever smoked. I told Him that when I was growing up all the young people were taught – not by our parents but by those around us – that smoking and drinking were all good things. When that was translated, He hit His forehead with the palm of His hand and said, "Oooh, ooh, ooh . . ." and closed His eyes and pursed His lips, with a very concerned look. Then He asked again if I had ever smoked, and I said, "Yes, once." And He asked, "One time?" And I said, "No, for a short period in my life." I explained that when I got out of the polluted air of New York City into the clean air of Colorado, I decided that I should not smoke anymore. He asked if that was before, or after I came to the Path, and I explained that it was before. He observed, "Now Master has found you. He brought you to Him, and you were lifted up out of all these things." I said, "Yes, without the Master I would have sunk in the sea of the world."

- We talked about marijuana. I mentioned the possibility that it might be legalized in this country, and He said, "That would be very bad for the country. It would be like putting stones into the boats of the coming generation."

- He asked me what the difference was between tea and coffee. I told Him that tea did not affect me as much as coffee. I understood that they both had a common bad ingredient (caffeine) but tea has a second one, and coffee another. I added that coffee made me more jittery. He said that coffee is more *tamsic* [of a lower nature – something that causes the lower passions to arise]. He said that in India, the cheap tea is safe for the Indians – the exquisite fine quality tea is exported for foreigners – and that is why the tea in India is better for you. It is cheaper tea, and does not affect the body and mind as much. Then He asked me how many times a day I drank tea – but I never really answered, as we got onto other things.

- He wished to better understand how it could be that children here can report to the authorities if they are beaten, as this was so different from the situation in India. I explained that it was a question of protecting children from harm. Sometimes children needed to be saved from parents who were strange or misguided, and abused their own children. When Pappu translated how some parents really mistreat their children by giving them physical beatings, and that is why police protection is brought in, again Sant Ji hit His forehead with His hand and said, "Oooh, ooh, ooh . . ." He added that He thought it must have been something like that.

- We talked about why people immigrated to America. I mentioned that all four of Karen's grandparents were from Sweden.

- He asked me if New York were the biggest city in the world. And then He asked about elections in America and how they worked – whether there was corruption and bribery or not.

- In the midst of the conversation, Karen came down with the fresh orange juice and an extension cord for Pathi Ji. Even though Sant Ji was in His pajamas, when He found out it was Karen, He asked for her to come in. He said hello to her, and mentioned that He liked the clothes that she had washed by hand. Sant Ji asked if she would mind doing more washing. She said she would be delighted to, and I later brought the clothes home.

- He asked me about the bhajan book – how many bhajans were going to be included. I said fifteen or twenty. He mentioned that another bhajan should be in there, *Char Padarath* ["If anyone wants the four boons – *artha, dharma, kama, moksha* – he should do the seva of the Sadhu."].

- He talked about getting close to the Guru and seva. He explained the difference between seva and meditation: in meditation no one sees you, but in seva people see you, and your ego swells up. When people start singing your praises and holding you in awe, then it is very hard. This is what happened to the people around Master Kirpal. They begin to think that they could control the Master – that they owned the Master and could make Him do this or that. He told me that one sevadar in Delhi would keep Master waiting for hours sometimes, sitting in the car while that person ran errands. He said that the seva of only one person in thousands goes with them, as most lose the benefit by becoming too attached. Sant Ji told me that seva counts for the Satguru's *bhakti* [devotion]. I told Him that I did not think seva and meditation were the same, even though some people had been telling me that. I had missed being able to meditate a normal amount while He was here. I mentioned that I had not been seeing much Light and I had not been able to meditate that much – that I was often tired and sleepy as I was up very late with the seva. He asked me why I could not get to bed early, and I told Him. I asked if I should be able to get in four hours of meditation while He was here, and He said, "You have many duties while I am here." I told Him that I did not want to become like the people who had been around Master Kirpal, and that I was afraid that we could become like that. He said, "No, you should not become like that. You should take their lives as a lesson and you should learn from how they behaved."

• Sant Ji talked about how the ego enjoys, and I said that sometimes when I go here or there my ego thinks, "Ah, I am a big sevadar." Sant Ji laughed, and said that I should say that I am doing nothing, but Satguru is doing it all. He mentioned that this is what Hazur Sawan Singh used to say about Baba Jaimal Singh, and what Master used to say about Sawan Singh, and now Sant Ji was saying, "I am nothing. I am a man like you. It is all Hazur's Grace."

Pappu and I staggered out of Sant Ji's bedroom and sat on the rug in the living room. We were both very happy that the medication seemed to be effective, and that the malaria was lifting from Sant Ji. We laughed about the session – certainly a unique one in my experience.

On Saturday (May 21ˢᵗ) Sant Ji called me in to His room and explained that when He returned to Sant Bani in August, He wanted to discourse four hours a day on the *Anurag Sagar [The Ocean of Love]* of Kabir. He mentioned that He had already talked to Russell about this.[21] In the evening I went down after Satsang, but the door to the house was locked. I sat on the porch for fifteen or twenty minutes until Judith and Russell were finished seeing Him. Then I went in to do bhajans with Pappu. Before I left, Sant Ji called me in and served warm milk to Pathi Ji, Pappu, and me. As I walked home I marveled over His very kind treatment of me.

---

[21] The work on the great spiritual volume of Sant Kabir (1398-1518), the *Anurag Sagar*, did not begin until 1979. See below, Chapter Nine.

Sunday, May 22nd – Mango Shakes

Karen and I had been invited down to Sant Ji's house for mango shakes, late Sunday afternoon, May 22nd. We joined a few other devotees sitting in the living room. After a short time, Sant Ji emerged from His room, spoke briefly to the group, said good-bye, and returned to His room, closing the door behind Him. Everyone else left. Sant Ji came right out again, threw Himself in His chair, let out a sigh, and looked at us and smiled. He told Karen to come closer, and then asked that she be served a mango shake. The Satsang that afternoon had been outside in the blazing sun, and Sant Ji said He had been glad to see we were wearing our hats, so that our faces were shaded from the sun. We had been sitting quite far apart from each other, yet still He noticed such small details. We floated back home together, with the sweet taste of the mango shakes lingering in every cell.

Andy Prokopis, Alejandro Correal, and I went to Boston on Monday the twenty-third, to buy various foodstuffs at an Indian grocery store. We also picked up some recent newspapers in Hindi and Punjabi. When I got back, Judith said, "He is not seeing anyone for the rest of the day, but He asked that you come when you returned." I hurried down to the house. I had purchased some mosquito netting for Him, and we had a delightful interchange about it. The mosquitoes were copious around His house, and, as malaria is transmitted through mosquitoes, we were doing everything we could to lessen the risk. When I brought in the netting, He asked me how much it had cost. "It was only a couple of dollars; well, closer to three." He asked, "*Saacha?*" [Really – Is that true?], and I said, "Well, it was four . . ." and He asked again, "*Saacha?*" He was stretched out on His cot, and I was standing towards the end. I reached down and grabbed His foot, and answered, "*SAACHA!*" and He roared with laughter. He used that netting for the remainder of His stay at Sant Bani.

On Tuesday at noon Pappu and I worked for an hour on the bhajans, preparing them for publication, and then I went back at 2:45 p.m. I translated a letter from English to Spanish that Sant Ji had written to the Satsangis in Bucamaranga, Colombia. I saw Sant Ji briefly. Karen and I returned at 7:20 p.m. to get my bhajan books, for singing in the Hall before Satsang, and Sant Ji invited us in. He asked what time it was, and I remarked that we could stay a little while. He said, "Okay, five minutes," so we sat down.

I wondered if I could ask a question, and He said that I could. I mentioned that I still had trouble with dreams – with bad thoughts coming up in the dreams. He responded, "Every man is a reservoir of bad thoughts – and those will come up in the dreams. But now you are replacing those with good thoughts. So do not be worried about the dreams. At some point the balance of good thoughts will outweigh the bad, because you are putting in good thoughts now. The reservoir is filling with good thoughts and good thoughts will flow out in the dreams."

He asked where Nicky and Chris were, and we said they were home with a babysitter. Again, it was amazing to sit in front of God while He made it seem so casual, willing to engage with us in conversations about the little things in our lives. The warm, sweetened, milk kept flowing, spiritually and literally, from His inexhaustible cup to my tiny container. I realized that in less than a week He would be leaving the Ashram, and it all seemed like a dream to me. On the evening of the twenty-fifth, standing in the living room just prior to walking up to the Satsang Hall, Sant Ji looked exceptionally radiant and powerful. It was as if He were making it clear that the ravaging effects of the malaria were being left behind, and He was ready for the rest of the Tour. His long glances filled me right up, and I felt such a relief to see Him standing in Glory rather than suffering in the throes of a mighty fever.

After Satsang, I again went down to assist with the correspondence, but Sant Ji wished to see slides. He added that there was no need to go get slides, as it was late, but if some were available it would be nice. When, with a big twinkle in His Eye, He asked us, "Well, do you love sleep more than you love slides?" we took the hint. Pappu and I laughingly piled out the door and rushed off to borrow slides from Larry Matty. Sant Ji, Pappu and Pathi Ji enjoyed the show immensely, as it brought back the feel of being in India as effectively as anything could have done.

Thursday the Twenty-sixth of May – Sant Ji and My Parents

The next day, Thursday, I continued to work on correspondence at Sant Ji's house, including translating into Spanish more of His responses to letters from South Americans. I was excited. This was the day that I was to bring my parents to meet Sant Ji, face-to-face. Both my mother and father, who lived in a near-by town, had met Master Kirpal Singh when He visited in 1972, and they were eager to meet Sant Ji as well.

When my mom and dad entered the living room and saw Sant Ji, they folded their hands and said, *"Namaste."* Sant Ji welcomed them heartily, smiling and chuckling all the while. He proceeded to tell my parents that their son was competent. He explained that, since they were both teachers, it was due to them that I was a good teacher. He shared with them that He was very pleased with my seva, and then invited them to attend the Satsang that evening. He gave them both parshad – just as Master Kirpal had done five years before. My mother and father again folded their hands, said, *"Namaste,"* and left. I turned back and He was gazing with such intensity – at the same time that an enormous smile played across the universe that is His face.

In the Satsang He told a great story about the mind. He explained that the mind always tells you that tomorrow is a holiday, so you can go to bed tonight without meditating, and then get up early in the morning to sit. You have all day. Plus, the mind adds, you have the afternoon, so there is no need to meditate before sleeping. And if you do begin to sit, the mind requests that you just lie down for a few minutes. The next thing you know, you wake up and it is morning. Everyone roared with laughter. Sant Ji told a story of a baby goat who came to a tiger for protection. The tiger really liked the goat, so much so that he arranged for the goat to be able to ride around on an elephant. My parents really enjoyed these stories.

Sant Ji also said that we should do our Simran, and that in a few days we would see what a change there was. He said that by completing the work of Simran, a Satsangi could acquire many supernatural powers – but that those must be used for inner work. If one displayed those powers, they would be taken away.

After the Satsang, Dr. Cardozo visited Sant Ji to see how He was doing with regard to the malaria. We were all pleased at the progress. I returned to the house at 10:00 p.m., and Sant Ji, dressed in boxer shorts and a tee-shirt, with a thin cloth wrapped around His Upper Body, came out from His bedroom to say, "Good night."

On Sunday evening, the twenty-ninth, Sant Ji invited Karen and me to see newly developed movies of the stay at Sant Bani, which were quite enjoyable. The quality of the film was good, and Sant Ji made many complimentary comments as we watched. When He heard Eric Perkins and me singing bhajans together on the soundtrack, He noted that we had very good voices. At another point when we were singing, He looked over at me for a long time, and broke into a smile. The movie captured a sequence of sevadars pushing a stuck tractor, which reminded me of a story Sant Ji had told Russell and me earlier. A Western disciple had come to India on his own, and found his way to 77 RB. In the short time he stayed, that fellow attempted to help with physical tasks, always beginning by saying, "One, Two, Three, Lift!" or, "One, Two, Three, Push!" So I called out to the people on the screen, "One, Two, Three – Push!" and Sant Ji laughed a lot.

After the film, Sant Ji said that the following evening – the last night of His stay at Sant Bani prior to returning in August – I should be prepared to sing bhajans for an hour. He added that I could get my friends to help me, and that Pathi Ji could sing as well. At any rate, He explained, He was not planning to give a discourse.

At that point it was decided that I should begin to stay overnight in Sant Ji's house – rather than always coming and going – if that would be acceptable to my family. It was, and as I curled up on the living room rug that night, my "tummy" full of warm milk, I again marveled over how much He had made me feel at home in His house.[22]

Monday, May 30th – The Saint and a Bicycle, the Last Satsang in May, and the Women of Netewala

Sant Ji had told Pappu that when they returned to Sant Bani in August, I should teach Pappu how to drive my car. Sant Ji's thought was that they could take the car down to the golf course – what Sant Ji called, "the open area." At that place, they could walk around together while Sant Ji discoursed to Pappu about Kabir's *Anurag Sagar [The Ocean of Love]*. Sant Ji explained that at the Ashram, it was so closed in, that the air was not good. He added, "Here we breathe in mosquitoes!" He felt that the open fields of the golf course would be much better.[23]

I was enjoying some minor successes with translating small things from Hindi to English and back. Sant Ji was talking to Russell and me, when Pappu had to rush into the kitchen to stir the vegetables. Sant Ji

---

[22] It was my extraordinarily good fortune to be invited to stay in His house shortly thereafter. I was a guest in His home during subsequent visits to Sant Bani, as well as when I accompanied Him to South and Central America.

[23] Each tour, the sevadars of the Ashram seemed to better understand what a Saint needed to be at all comfortable in this world – and we did provide more open physical area for Sant Ji as time went on. The trips to the golf course in August did not occur, and the *Anurag Sagar* was not published until 1982.

commented, "*Doe Pappu – iddar, uddar,*" and I translated, "There should be two Pappus – one for here and one for there." Sant Ji told me to practice speaking in Hindi more – but Pathi Ji was my only real "victim."

Sant Ji graciously granted another interview to the fellow who had been belligerent towards Him, but He requested that Russell and I attend once again. This time there was no need to interrupt, as it was short and sweet. After he left, Sant Ji reminded Russell and me that it was very bad to come to a Sadhu and then try to tell the Sadhu what to do. One should listen to what the Sadhu has to say, and learn from it.

At this time, Sant Ji also spoke again about the bhajans in Punjabi and Hindi, referring to how good they were for people's devotion. Russell mentioned that he loved the bhajans, but he also loved the discourses at Satsang – perhaps a hint that he thought it would be nice to hear a discourse that evening – the last before Sant Ji left for Vermont the next morning. Sant Ji commented, "Well, you have a language barrier. You do not understand the Hindi. But the bhajans are very powerful, and a lot of charging comes through them. They are very much a part of the Satsang." And Russell said that he really did love the bhajans – but he loved the talks as well.

A short while after Russell left, Sant Ji went outside while Pappu and I remained in the living room, working on correspondence. Pausing to glance out the sliding glass doors, I did not see Him. He was neither out front by the pond, nor out back. My bicycle was behind the dais, and I wondered if He might be over near it. I was quite proud of my bike – a top-of-the line 15 speed French racing model with high-end components. Thanks to the generosity of parents, I had been able to buy it over time. As an Ashram resident living a somewhat ascetic (or at least not extravagant) lifestyle, I had not been at all loose with my tongue regarding the cost of that exquisite machine.

When Sant Ji came back in, however, the first thing He asked was, "How much did your bicycle cost?" I rolled around on the floor in agony, laughing and covering my face as I thought, "Oh no! I can't believe He is asking me this!" Sant Ji said, "No, no. Just tell me a rough amount." So I told Him that it had cost several hundred dollars. Next I was asked, "How many hundreds?" When I answered, "Five," Pappu's eyes got really big and white. He repeated in disbelief, "Five hundred dollars?" and I said, "Yes, five hundred dollars."

When Pappu translated that for Sant Ji, He said, "Five hundred dollars – why you could buy a car for that much." I felt flustered, and tried to explain myself, saying that it was really a good bike with parts imported from everywhere. Then I said, "Wait until Karen finds out that You asked me that question." Sant Ji responded, "Oh, I won't tell her!" and I said, "Yes, but I will!" And then He went outside again.

When Pappu and I stepped out soon after, Sant Ji was over by my bicycle, squeezing the brake lever. When He saw us, He quickly took a step back, and put His hands behind His back. He looked exactly like a small boy who had been caught handling something in a department store. He asked to see all of the features, so I showed Him each and every aspect of the bicycle.

I explained how the gears worked. He pointed at the brakes and said, "Brakes?" and I said, "Yes" and pulled on them. I explained why the handlebars were in that position – so that you had less wind resistance. Pappu asked if it were a racing bike, and I said it was. Pappu translated for Sant Ji, Who kept nodding and saying, "*Teek hai. Aacha, aacha!*" [Okay. Good, good]. He pointed to the toe clips and asked what they were, so I told Him. Then He asked for a demonstration.

I rode the bike around in a circle, and came back. I said that it was very light in weight, and He lifted it up to see. When I pointed out which components were from France, Italy, and Japan, He remarked, "So, the Americans import things too," and I said, "Oh yes, lots of things." In the end I mentioned that I understood that Master Kirpal had also ridden a bike, and that I had heard He said it was the cheapest form of transportation. Sant Ji said, "*Aacha!*" and returned to the house. In all my experiences with the two Masters, many features of the "bicycle interview" stand out as unique. In what was no doubt a case of very wishful thinking, I rode away feeling that Sant Ji had graciously blessed my extravaganza.

That evening Sant Ji did give a discourse, and it was very powerful. Among other things He told the story of Surdas – how Surdas had put out his own eyes because he had had an unchaste thought. He told a second story about a man who walked by the house of an impure lady every day. One day, as his Master's stove had lost its fire, the man was sent to that woman's house for a light. She told him he could have the light if he put out his eyes; which he did right away. The next day the Master used a common expression like, "Eyes have come" – which ordinarily meant that a person had something in his/her eyes. But when the fellow took off his bandage, his eyes had been restored.

Then He told the story of Gunga – who was on track to become an officer in the army until he killed some policemen. One day he had observed some policemen beating a few innocent people, and they would not stop when Gunga pleaded with them. He met force with force, and killed the policemen in the process. After that, Gunga became an outlaw and a *dacoit* [thief]. Later he was initiated by Baba Sawan Singh. As a disciple of a True Master, Gunga turned himself in, was tried and found guilty, and ultimately hanged for his crimes. But, Sant Ji said, Gunga was very happy when they hanged him, as he was remembering his Master. These powerful stories, so far removed from our usual Western context, seemed to float through the charged atmosphere of that final Satsang, taking root in the Ashram soil.

After Satsang we returned to the house. Sant Ji invited Russell, Karen, and me to see the slides of the trip to 77 RB in April (when I had gone to receive the party), so I ran up to my house to get the carousels. After we set up the projector in the living room, Sant Ji came in and sat in a chair, dressed for the evening in His casual clothes.

Sant Ji became very animated when we reached a particular group of slides. They were shots of the women at the Satsang in Netewala – the ones who covered their faces completely with red veils.[24] He said, "Some of these women cover their faces all of the time, and from all angles. And they come up to me and they say, 'Do You remember me?' " Sant Ji imitated the women's voices. We all roared with laughter.

After the slides were over and the lights were on, He elaborated. He took off the cloth that had been loosely wrapped around His head, and draped it over His face, and imitated the women again. He mimicked, "Do You remember me?" He explained that He had been associated with some of those women for twenty years, and, even though He had never seen their faces, they always asked if He remembered them. And He concluded, "So I tell them, 'Yes!' " and again we all laughed and laughed. With the grace of an artisan, Sant Ji quickly spun the cloth around His head, threw the loose end over His shoulder, and strode into His bedroom after saying good night to us. We looked at each other, grinned, figuratively pinched ourselves, and found the dream to be real.

Tuesday the Thirty-first of May, 1977 – The Last Morning

On Tuesday morning, May thirty-first, there was a final darshan for all. Sant Ji had asked that packets of sweets be prepared for distribution,

---

[24] See Chapter Three above.

and then He came and sat on the dais. After blessing all of the packets, He sang His "Song to Kirpal" in a most melodious and haunting manner, while the parshad was being handed out to all the devotees. At the end, He bowed to His Master and to the God within each of us, stepped down from the dais, and got into the car for the trip northwest to Kirpal Ashram in Vermont.[25] As people got up to head for their cars, I tore off to our house with Nicky in my arms, and beat the caravan to the bottom of our driveway. We stood with hands folded as His car drove slowly by. He looked at both of us, folded His hands, nodded His immense head, smiled, and then laughed. We watched the car disappear as it came to the end of Ashram Road and made the left turn onto Osgood Road.

Saturday, June 4th, 1977 in Vermont

Sant Ji had asked Karen and me to stay at the Ashram and maintain the daily schedule of Satsangs and meditation for those devotees who could not travel to Vermont. He also gave us permission to visit if we could. As the Sant Bani School was in session until June tenth, we had plenty to occupy us in Sanbornton. Still, it was very hard to go from daily contact with the physical presence to none. I was not able to drive up to Vermont until Saturday morning, the fourth of June, although Karen, Chris, and Nick had gone the day before.

The spirit of my visit is perhaps best captured through the following notes, dictated into my small Sony recorder:

So here I am, Saturday, June 4th, I think that is right, at Kirpal Ashram. It is ten o'clock and I am sitting down on Nina's lovely little flat rocks, and the fireflies are flickering around, and the water is trickling in the background. It has been a very beautiful day. When I came here I did not expect to see Him at once. Judith saw I was here, and called me into the room. It was a group darshan. He saw me standing at the back and smiled and raised His folded hands at me. The people left after fifteen minutes, and I went with them. Sant Ji came out and saw the people who had been waiting outside for Him. When He walked by me, He asked that I come back in. I went in and sat down, and it was really sweet.

I had an idea to ask Him one question. I wanted to say,

---

[25] Kirpal Ashram is now called "Wawasiki."

"Sant Ji, this is a bad question and I am naughty for asking it – and it is a very selfish question – but I really want to know if I, Kent Bicknell, can really perfect my Simran? I find it so hard. And in Rajasthan, You told me to pray, but I even forget to pray. Will it really be possible for me – say in the next year – to perfect my Simran?" But I did not ask this.

His eyes were magnificent as I sat in front of His bed. Judith asked if the Wiggins family could come in? Sant Ji said, "Bring them." So they came in and sat for ten minutes. David discussed with Him whether he should go on the Tour or not, and then they left. Sant Ji had tea brought in and He served me. He poured it Himself into a cup, and gave it to me. And then I had more tea from His container. He poured it. What a blessing! What an incredible blessing! Now to live up to it.

He lay back on His bed, looking like Baba Sawan Singh the whole time He was talking. It was magnificent – I just kept sitting and looking at Baba Sawan Singh. And His eyes were these orbs of light. I won't say that it wasn't outer – or it wasn't inner – I won't say. I don't know. They were just these beams of light, and He was Baba Sawan Singh reclining there. The three of them – Sant Ji, Pathi Ji, and Pappu – were talking, and I was just sitting there observing.

He asked me something about the Ananda Marga people and I said that I did not know, but that I thought Ananda Marga was a path of service. In the group darshan, some Ananda Marga people had been there and asked Sant Ji for help. They wondered if Sant Ji could do something to help get their leader out of jail. Sant Ji said at the end of the conversation that their leader would be released soon.

Anyway it was just magnificent – and I decided not to ask my question about perfecting the Simran, as it did not feel right. Sant Ji asked me if I were staying through Satsang on the next day, and I said that I would if I could, but I needed to get back to Sant Bani in time to do the Satsang there.

The hour of the evening Satsang approached, but Sant Ji got up and went for a walk. I watched Him from a distance, and then went to my room to drop my things. I stepped out onto the porch, and there He was, walking up towards me with Pappu. Everyone else had stayed behind. He asked me what the program was. I said that I was not sure. He asked me about singing bhajans, and I responded that we had started at 6:00 p.m. at Sant Bani. He answered, "That is when the Satsang begins here," and I said, "Well I think that someone is over there singing now." His kind

*response was, "You can walk over with us and sing one bhajan."
I said, "Teek hai."*

*Sant Ji walked out back onto Nina's porch, and knocked the
wind chimes so that they would ring. He picked up a maul, and
Pappu told Him it was an "axe." And Sant Ji said in English,
"Akk-ss!" and repeated it a few times. He asked what the snow-
shoes were, and we talked about those. He asked if they were
skis, and I explained that they were different from skis.*

*A really beautiful thing happened just before we walked over
to the house across the way where the Satsang was to be held.
We had all gone back into the main house, and Sant Ji went into
His room for a moment. Earlier that day, He had been looking at
the decorative objects placed artfully around the room – feathers, pieces of colored glass, stones, etc. There was a trinket of
purple glass that He had picked up and twirled around. Nina has
a prism in her window in the main room that really throws a nice
six or eight inch long color rainbow on the screens that were set
up for the kitchen. And I noticed it, and I thought, "Oh, Sant Ji
would like to see that." I since learned that the day before it had
been well pointed out to Him, so there was no need, but I
thought, "Hmmm . . ."*

*When Sant Ji came out, Russell said, "Pappu – latrine," and
pointed toward the door to the bathroom area. Sant Ji nodded
and said, "Betho" [Sit down]. I went over and sat down behind
Russell. I looked over at the screen, but I could not see the prism
colors any more. It had been a big patch of color, but I figured
that maybe the sun had shifted in that short a time. Then Sant Ji
looked at me, and smiled and laughed, and motioned towards
me. I heard Him say "ranga" which is "color," so I looked
down. Right on my heart, covering my heart, was that whole
rainbow which I had been so anxious for Him to see on the
screen. And I said, "Mere hirde – mere dil me" [in my heart]
and He laughed. I had looked for it on the big screen, and there
it was, cast right over my heart! That moment felt so sweet it was
unbelievable.*

*We walked down the road and over to the Satsang. On the
way, Nina told me that she was to learn "Apana Koi Nahi." She
also mentioned that it had been so nice to have Karen there.*

*When we arrived at the Satsang, I remembered how He had
told Pathi Ji to chant Sant Kabir's bhajan on Simran – and the
whole Satsang was about doing Simran. It was the answer to that
unasked question that had been burning in me when I came. I
tried to listen very carefully. The discourse was on the same*

*bhajan that Master Kirpal commented on, with the examples of
the village girls and their pots and the cow always thinking of its
calf even when it is away. We all do simran or remembrance of
worldly things anyway – so we have the skill to remember. Why
not begin to replace the remembrance of the world with the
Simran of God?*

*Sant Ji made an observation that really struck home. He
pointed out that the unchaste man is always ready to stay up all
night. He is never troubled by laziness to be with his wife – to do
unchaste things with his wife. In the same way we should be
doing Simran.*

*He told a really nice story of when He was in the army and
His squad had been surrounded by enemy troops. Prior to that
time His fellow soldiers had teased Him because He did not eat
meat or drink wine. When they were going off to the front in
Kashmir in 1947, everyone teased Him more, saying, "Now we
will see how strong you are." But at this moment, when they
were surrounded by the enemy, the commanding officer had
given up hope. He ordered Sant Ji, who was the troop signal
man, to flash to the others that they were done for – that there
was no hope. Then the officer came to Sant Ji and asked Him to
pray. But Sant Ji said, "Why should I pray now? Now you are
ready to pray because you are in trouble," and the fellow made
a promise to give up meat and wine if he could be helped this
one time. The enemy withdrew, and Sant Ji's troops were saved.
Sant Ji added, "That man became a good man."*

*Sant Ji told many more stories of doing Simran – of not
forgetting your Simran even in the world – in your business –
you must do it. You must remember it.*

*After Satsang we walked back over to the main house with
Sant Ji. As we passed by my car, parked in the lot quite far from
the house, Sant Ji asked why it was so far away. Pappu
explained that only the two cars involved in seva were allowed to
come close to the house – to keep the noise of traffic at a mini-
mum. Sant Ji asked Pappu to make a special request of Nina for
a third car to be able to come close to His house as well. Sant Ji
went into the house and I did not see Him again. Again I say, it
has been a very sweet day. Good night!*

I spent the night, and early the next morning headed back to Sant
Bani. As might be expected, the Satsang Hall at the Ashram was nearly
deserted, as most everyone had been able to go to Vermont. There were

two or three local disciples who could not make the trip, however, so we sat together and remembered God.

June, 1977 – A Few Days Later in Boston

Sant Ji and the party left Vermont on June seventh, and traveled to Millie Prendergast's house in Brookline, Massachusetts. As Sant Ji had invited me to come there, I did. One evening He spoke to a small group of Sant Bani sevadars. He said that as a child He had never believed in the caste system, and He had always mixed with all kinds of people, and not been afraid to drink from a common source of water that low caste persons used. His father used to get upset at that, and hired various priests and pundits to "purify" Sant Ji.

As Sant Ji was speaking, He turned to one couple and asked if they really had to drive back that evening. Addressing the husband, a man licensed to perform marriages, He asked, "Is there any important work you must do there – Is there any wedding?" Then He said that they could stay with Andy and Diane Prokopis. Or, He went on, "You can sleep under any bed in this house. Now the nights are short. You get up at three and the day starts at four. Take some blanket and go and sit in anybody's room, and say that you are meditating. Nobody will kick you out!"

Sant Ji spoke at length of the relationship between Baba Jaimal Singh and Baba Sawan Singh. He mentioned that when Baba Sawan Singh first came to Baba Jaimal Singh, Baba Sawan did not want to use the word "*Radhasoami*." Then Sant Ji referred to how Baba Sawan Singh had read the *Anurag Sagar [The Ocean of Love]* at Baba Jaimal Singh's suggestion. Sant Ji concluded by stating that only those whom the Master wished would get the Initiation – would receive the Naam. He said Baba Sawan Singh had an orderly who served Him for years, but that fellow never got initiated, as it was not written in his fate. Saints come into this world, He concluded, only to spread the "disease" of Naam.

After a delightful couple of days in Boston, we saw Sant Ji off at the airport. I drove back to Sant Bani to wind things up at School. Sant Ji, Pathi Ji, Pappu, Judith and Russell headed out west for a series of stays in California, Vancouver, and other places. Karen and I stayed at the Ashram so that other sevadars could travel, and we prepared to join the party in Miami en route to Bogotá, Colombia, in mid-July.

While we waited in New Hampshire, a couple of very sweet things happened. One day I had to call the Perkins in California. As I was talking to Judith, she exclaimed, "Oh, Sant Ji just walked into the room." I asked her to tell Him that we sent our love. A minute later she said that He sent His Love. A few days later I again had to call – this time to Debbie Asbeck at Don and Charlotte Macken's house in Sebastapol. I spoke with Debbie, and after a while Pappu got on the phone. He asked if I wanted to speak to Sant Ji, and I said, "Yes, sure!"

When Sant Ji started talking to me, it was just incredible. It was unlike any other experience I had ever had in my life. He said hardly anything other than, *"Kya hal hai?"* [How are you?] and *"Teek hai"* and *"Aur bhajan simran"* [Do more meditation]. And I answered, *"Hunh!"* [Yes], and told Him in Hindi that I was doing three or four hours daily. There were all these long silences – and either He would start laughing, or I would. Pappu was on the phone too, and I called for Karen to get on the phone as well. At one point He asked, "Chrissy?" and I said, *"Teek!"* [Fine] and then "Nicky?" and I repeated, *"Teek!"* There was a pause and I asked, *"Meri bibi? . . .* Karen Ji?" [my wife], and He said, *"Hunh, hunh!"* [Yes, yes]" And I said, *"Teek hai!"* At the end I said, *"Sat Sri Akal"* and He answered, *"Beek-a-nell Parivar ko, Sat Sri Akal!"* [Sat Sri Akal to the Bicknell family]"

Pappu and I resumed talking. After a while I asked, "Pappu, is Sant Ji still on the line?" Pappu spoke His name, "Baba Ji?" and there was no answer, so Pappu repeated, "Baba Ji?" and we heard Him say, *"Hunh! Hunh!"*[26] Pappu asked Him if He were still on the line, and He said, "Yes, I am just listening to your conversation." I asked Pappu to tell Him that in my case there was nothing to hear but the barking of a very low dog. When Pappu translated, Sant Ji responded by saying, "No, no – Kent is a very good lover." We just kept laughing and laughing, and finally I said goodbye, and Sant Ji said, "Bye, bye!" Karen and I were ecstatic after we hung up from our cosmic call – as the experience had been breathtakingly beautiful.[27]

---

[26] Sant Ji was almost always called "Baba Ji" by His Indian disciples, not "Sant Ji" as in the West.

[27] Over time I was to have more extraordinary phone experiences with Sant Ji. Once when He was visiting Australia, Pappu called me at 2:00 a.m. my time. I answered the phone from deepest sleep – and Pappu told me that Sant Ji needed the phone number for an Indian disciple living in the States. I said I did not have it, but Pappu responded that Sant Ji said I did. I paused a second, put

Robert and Wendy Schongalla arrived back from the California stay on the twelfth of July, and they came to the house and told me that Sant Ji had been trying and trying to telephone me. The afternoon they returned from the Shamaz Retreat Center to Sebastapol, Pappu was on the phone a lot – and the next morning also. They noticed that Sant Ji would keep picking up the phone and saying, "Hello hello" – and they assumed that He was trying to call the Bagga family in Delhi. And then they found out that it was me He wanted to talk to. I had no idea why – and never found out. Truly, only God knows.

Along those lines, Pappu had told me that Sant Ji was counting the days until we were together again, often asking, "How many days until we see Kent?" Every day Sant Ji would ask, "How many days now until we see Kent?" And then He would say, "Don't count today, because today is already almost through – and don't count the day we will see him." Robert told me that Sant Ji had added a new twist: "Well we won't count today, because today is already gone – and we won't count the day we see him – because we will see him on that day. But also we won't count tomorrow – just because . . . well, just because we won't count tomorrow!" Sant Ji had reduced the time to six days until we would meet again in the Miami airport, and fly off to the warm hospitality of the hundreds of devotees gathered in the foothills of the spectacular Andes Mountains.

---

down the phone, stumbled into another room, and opened a flat topped desk that I rarely used. I reached into a small cubbyhole, and pulled out a piece of paper – on which I had written the name and number!

On a later Tour, in His house at Sant Bani Ashram, I was part of a four way phone hook-up that allowed Spanish speaking prisoners – satsangis and seekers who had been drawn to Sant Ji through the prison program – to have an interview with Sant Ji. The beauty of that experience – laced with the compassion of the Saint for His imprisoned disciples – was extraordinary.

CHAPTER FIVE

Sant Ji in South America – 1977

Interlude

The reader should know that the personal notes, journals, and tapes which I accessed to write about Sant Ji's first trip to South America had been maintained in a less regular manner. I was so busy in South America that it was very hard to find any time to record what was happening. The third day after our arrival in Bogotá, I began to recount the trip thus far, introducing my notes with:

> *And now I will begin my hundreds of feet of recording which up 'til now I haven't had any inclination to do. It is the twentieth of July – today is something like Wednesday – in Bogotá. I am lying up in the little room in Sant Ji's house where I sleep. It has been an absolutely incredible stay in which I suppose I should be noting things down. But up until this point I just haven't been able to talk. I don't have any time for even one thing.*

For guidance on how much to say about the meeting of Sant Ji with the hungry souls of South America, I relied on a discussion I had with Sant Ji right after the stay there. On August first, we flew back to Sant Bani, but the full program in New Hampshire did not start for a couple of days. That gave Sant Ji and the party a chance to "rest" – to catch up on correspondence and other necessary tasks. To help fill in the time, on the evening of August third, I was asked to speak in the Satsang Hall about the South American journey.

Prior to the talk, Sant Ji asked me how I was going to begin. I said, "When we met You in Miami." He continued, "Tell me what you are going to say." I told Him a few things I had been thinking of, and He said that all those were good to mention. I had a question for Him. I had sat in on all of the interviews as a translator and heard some wonderful answers to people's questions – but those were, after all, private interviews. I asked Him if it would be all right to share some of what had been said, in a general way, and He was very strong when He said that, yes, that was fine to do that. Then He added a few suggestions as to what I should say as well. All of this is incorporated in the account below.

Monday July 18th, 1977 – Miami to Bogotá

Karen, Chris, Nick, and I arrived in Miami and were very happy to see Sant Ji once again. For some reason I was assuming that I could fulfill both my role as a family man, traveling with two children, and as the liaison for Sant Ji and the party with regard to the Spanish language. From the moment I got on the plane – actually beginning in the airport in Miami – Sant Ji pointed out that I needed to be with Pathi Ji, Pappu, and Him at every moment in order to explain details as they arose.[1] This was not easy on my family, and I felt as if I had been torn in half at first, but, with His Grace, it all worked out.

When Sant Ji arrived at the airport in Bogotá, the waiting crowds were so anxious to meet Him that the scene bordered on pandemonium. I was doing the translating – working to get the party through customs, and gather the luggage, etc.; all the while looking over my shoulder to see how Karen and the boys were doing. At one point, carrying Nick in my arms, I ran out to the car we were to ride in, and saw that a huge crowd had begun to surround Sant Ji. I dashed back into the airport, thrust Nick into Karen's arms, and ran back out again. I jumped into the car and we were on our way to the Ashram. I could only trust that Karen and the children would make it – which, of course, they did. I was able to check in on them later that evening, and, while things had been hectic, everyone was fine. They were staying in a Satsangi's house near the Ashram complex.

The Ashram itself was situated on a very small, steep plot of land in a residential neighborhood – with several of the near-by houses owned by disciples of Master Kirpal and Sant Ji. It was not possible to drive all the way up to Sant Ji's house, and when we parked at the bottom of a

---

[1] Cf. Russell Perkins in *Sant Bani Magazine*, January, 1978, "The First World Tour of Ajaib Singh, Part IV: In South America," p. 20: "Up to this point, my orders had been to stay with Sant Ji and Pappu no matter what. But in South America . . . it was Kent, whose knowledge of Spanish is excellent, who was ordered to stay with Sant Ji no matter what . . ."

long flight of stairs winding up steeply through beautiful gardens, we emerged into a throng of devotees. It seemed as if every person was trying, gently, to touch Sant Ji – and all were calling out, *"Maestro, Maestro."* As we slowly made our way up to His house by the lovely thatched-roof Satsang Hall and flickering torch lights, it truly felt as if we were all floating. I do not remember moving my feet – as the experience was much more akin to being suspended in a wave – in this case, a wave of immense love. Russell Perkins, who arrived before we did and watched this event from above, remarked:

> *I went part way down the mountainside and then I saw: It looked like an ocean of people moving slowly along the path, way down the mountain. From my viewpoint, it seemed like a gigantic organism creeping slowly along, heading up the hill. I understood at once that Sant Ji was somewhere in the middle of it. I waited, and as they came closer I began to make out individuals shouting with joy, some crying, all dancing and running about and moving slowly forward just to be as close to Him as possible – the sheer happiness of that crowd was incomparable. As the ocean approached, at last I saw Him; Light was just flowing from His face and He was beaming. When He saw me, He stopped and said, "Russell, you have brought me to the home of love." Then I was very happy. That was a preview of the whole stay in Colombia.*[2]

Thus we reached the small dwelling constructed for Sant Ji. Like the Satsang Hall, the cottage was thatched-roof over white stucco walls. Within was a bedroom and bathroom for Sant Ji, a small sitting room for interviews and darshans, a tiny kitchen, and a loft perched at the top of a steep ladder. Pathi Ji cooked a meal for Sant Ji and the rest of us, after which Sant Ji retired for the evening. Pathi Ji, Pappu, and I carefully climbed up the ladder and stretched out on our mattresses, made up with much loving care.

The days and nights were so full in Bogotá that it seemed there was hardly a moment to catch one's breath. And, given the altitude of the city (8768 feet – closer to 9000 at the Ashram), as Sant Ji put it, "If you turn over in bed here, you run out of breath." Sant Ji spent ten days in Bogotá, and then flew to an Ashram on the outskirts of the small city of Buca-

---

[2] *Ibid.* pp. 20-21.

ramanga, for three more days in Colombia. Wherever He turned, the multitudes were there, expressing the love of the Saints so emotionally, that Sant Ji commented often on how He was reminded of the devotees in India. One of the first things Sant Ji said was that there was really only one language – the language of love. He added that the Negative Power had created all these different languages to give us a feeling of separateness.

Working among four languages (Punjabi, Hindi, Spanish, and English) led to inevitable misunderstandings and tensions, and, as these arose I would think, "Well, here's the Negative Power at work." It struck me that one way around that was to learn the language of love, and another way was to work on being able to speak different languages. The latter was the approach Master Kirpal emphasized in His plan for a language school at Manav Kendra precisely for that reason – to break down barriers between people.

"*Te amo*" means "I love you" in Spanish, and it was one of the phrases that Sant Ji learned. A few Colombians learned the Hindi or Punjabi equivalent. They would say 'I love you' to Him in Hindi, and He would say, "*Te amo*," and everyone loved it. It was, indeed, the language of love, and Sant Ji would laugh with much apparent delight.

There were many lessons in flexibility – including reminders not to impose our will on the Master's. It took me an embarrassingly long time to act upon Sant Ji's simple request to be with Him at all times. For instance, if someone wished for me to translate, I would assume that I should do that seva, until Sant Ji told the person to find another translator saying, "Kent is not available." One evening, for just a moment, I stayed behind at the Satsang Hall to help Dr. Molina navigate the dark path, as he did not have a flashlight. I then hurried up the path to unlock the door of Master's house. In those few seconds, someone had stopped Sant Ji, and begun to speak in Spanish, and Sant Ji had asked Pappu, "Where is Kent? He should always be with us!" In a subsequent Satsang, He stated that if you are given a duty to do, if you are assigned a seva, then that is the only seva that counts. To quit the duty assigned to you in order to do another is not seva.

As a student in high school I had become quite taken with the Spanish language. As I became more proficient, I delved into the literature of Spain and South America, and really loved it. I pursued these studies in college as well. The trip to Colombia was my first experience in a Spanish speaking country, and I felt right at home. From the abundance of literature I had read, I was more than ready for the emotional blood that runs at the surface and deep within, the intense honesty, the gaiety, the rich mix of Catholicism overlaid on indigenous worship, and the reality of dreams as carriers of truths and visions. The collective soul of the Colombians, Venezuelans, Ecuadorians, and Mexicans felt deep to me, and the expressed love flowed, even gushed at times, as if from a fountain.

Initially I translated for the private interviews, while Alicia Gomez, a Colombian devotee who lived right next to the Ashram, did the Satsangs. The interviews went very slowly – in part because my Spanish was not good enough to zip along. I would ask a person for clarification on something I did not understand. Some sessions would go smoothly – while others would take a long time. I felt badly when Sant Ji expressed concern that, "time was being lost," adding that in the time He saw two or three people He had been able to see twenty or twenty-five in the States. He suggested that it would help if people wrote their questions out in advance.[3]

Sant Ji said and did so many beautiful, direct things at those interviews. An eight-year-old girl came into the sitting room all by herself, and Sant Ji at once called her over close to Him. He put His hand on her head, and was pouring out love. She had written out her question, and I translated it into English:

Dearly Beloved Sant Ji – My name is Maria Consuela[4], and I am eight years old, and I am sending you this letter because I want the full Initiation into Light and Sound. I know, Master, that you are going to say, "No" because of my age, but I will keep on insisting until you say, "Yes." I promise that I won't ever again try meat or eggs, but initiate me, please initiate me. I asked for this interview so that I could ask you this in private. I know what Naam is, and I, Maria Consuela Gomez, have been going to Satsang for the last three years.

Throughout the translations (Spanish to English – English to Hindi),

---

[3] After a few days, Silvia Molina began to translate the interviews, with my assistance. This worked much better – except that Sant Ji would tease us both, as we would become too involved in the emotional aspect of the interview, and begin to weep ourselves. See below for a further incident regarding the translating efforts for the interviews.

[4] The name has been changed.

Sant Ji simply loved her. After the letter was read, He told her, "You will get the Initiation, but you have to wait for three years, until you are eleven." He said a few more very sweet things to her, placed His hand on her head again, and she left. Outside the door, someone asked her what Sant Ji had said, and, with great joy and a touch of disappointment, she answered, "He said that I could get Naam – but in three years." I watched her walk away – a very determined little girl.

One woman brought her husband so that Sant Ji could "convince" him of the benefits of the vegetarian diet. Sant Ji, while very polite, did not hold back, and the man's initial laughter subtly changed to quiet listening. To a young man who seemed overly interested in developing supernatural powers, Sant Ji related a cautionary tale of one yogi that He had known in His days as a seeker of Truth. That yogi knew how to project himself from his body, and as he aged, he used to go into the bodies of animals if he needed to travel a great distance. But, Sant Ji pointed out, the yogi could not rise above his body into the higher planes.

The supernatural was a fairly common subject in the interviews. People would make reference, for example, to going to a medium and receiving a message from a husband who had been dead for years, or to dreaming about having a picnic with Lord Krishna and wondering if that meant Krishna was the person's guru in a previous life. Another person spoke of a friend's ability to bi-locate – to be in two places at the same time – while someone else wondered if it was acceptable, with regard to karma, to perform exorcisms as a means of livelihood.

In almost every case, Sant Ji explained that those events came from the mind, and were not occurring at any level beyond the mental one. Thus performing exorcisms and seeking out mediums had nothing to do with the Reality of the Inner Planes. People were disappointed to hear this – and, in some cases, they protested, but Sant Ji was firm and clear: the thoughts we have during the day get converted into the dreams we have at night. Again, however, this was the response to most questions of that nature, not to every one.

A very intellectual couple from Quito, Ecuador, came to ask Sant Ji some probing questions. The husband, an attorney, asked, "We read once that Master Kirpal called you to Sawan Ashram and you did not come. Why didn't you obey Him?" Sant Ji explained that this was a mistranslation. He always obeyed the wishes of His Beloved Master Kirpal. After Sant Ji had answered all the other questions, the man said, in a manner that I found very strange, "I don't see my Master's eyes in your eyes."

Sant Ji very politely told him that He respected the honesty of his questions. Then He said, "But the thing is, you haven't looked in my eyes; you've been looking at the translator the whole time" (which was true). And then He turned to the wife and said, "And you haven't looked at my eyes, either. You've been staring down at the ground" (also true). He proceeded to talk to them, and while He did so, He looked into their eyes and they looked into His. This went on for five minutes. The next day, the fellow returned for a group darshan, and I asked him, "How are the Eyes today?" and he just smiled and answered, "Marvelous!"

When people found out that Sant Ji was willing to say aloud the *Simran* – the Five Sacred Names – in a private interview (provided that only initiates were present), almost everyone asked Him to do that. Family groups would come in, and at the end, after photographs, the non-initiates would leave and Sant Ji would go over the Simran with the disciples. Sant Ji was very clear about non-initiates not being present – even infants and young children. It often fell to me to step out with a baby in my arms, or a child's hand in each of mine, so that the parents could stay behind and hear Sant Ji say the Charged Words.

One couple mentioned that when they were driving they would sometimes say the Five Names aloud – as their children were still small. They wondered at what age would the children be old enough to understand – so that they should then stop that practice. Sant Ji informed them very clearly that they must stop at once, as repeating those Names in front of any non-initiate, no matter how young, meant that they were giving out the charging of the Names – which was not theirs to give.

Wednesday, the Twentieth of July – Bogotá

In the evening, just prior to the special darshan for children held before the big Satsang, I looked out the sitting room window and saw my older son, Christopher. I invited him into the house, and, much to his delight, gave him some milk from the kitchen. As we stood there, Sant Ji came out of His room, but Chris had his back to Him. He came up behind Chris and grabbed him by the shoulders, swinging him around like a father playing with his child. Chris looked up and saw Who it was, and broke into an enormous grin. As Sant Ji chatted with Chris, I mentioned that he was a very shy boy – to which Sant Ji remarked, "Chris is a very good lover!"

I dashed down the hill to use the bathroom, and when I got back it was time to head out the door for children's darshan and Satsang. The whole tour felt like that – we were always on the move, and I never stopped running. In the Satsang that evening, Sant Ji talked about how it is really easy to say, "I am in the Will of God," but how it is very difficult to actually <u>be</u> there. As He explained, we have our own will, and what we wish often conflicts with God's Will.

After Satsang, the house guards told me that there was a man from Caracas, Venezuela, who was very anxious to see Sant Ji right then, as he had to return home very early the next morning. He played the violin, but recently a severe injury had damaged his hand. His only desire was to touch Sant Ji's hand. I went in to inquire of Pappu, but Sant Ji was on the verge of retiring. On hearing of the situation, however, Sant Ji said, "Yes, bring him up," so I sprinted down to get him. As we approached the house, the man explained that, although he was not initiated, he believed in Sant Ji, and simply wished to be healed. I said, "But Saints don't perform miracles," and he responded, "Well, then I just want to see Him!"

Sant Ji welcomed him, and then talked for a short while, saying that He was glad to see him and happy that he had been able to come to the Ashram. The man demonstrated his profession by slowly elevating his hands into the position of holding a violin – and then mimed a short piece. He held out his hand to show that it was hurt. As the scene played out, I was struck with wonder and admiration for the Latino ability to show deep feelings. Above all, I was overwhelmed by the sheer majesty of Grace in action. Sant Ji touched the fellow's hand and told him, "God will shower blessings on you."

Twenty-first of July, 1977 – Bogotá

On Thursday the twenty-first, Chris again came to the house to visit. He arrived at a time when nothing official was scheduled, and Pappu and I were in the loft working on correspondence. Sant Ji was alone in His bedroom. Suddenly, the tip of Sant Ji's head appeared at the top of the ladder, and up He came into the loft. Dressed in His casual clothes, with a white cloth wound around His head, He sat down and went over some of the letters we were working on. After a bit He called Chris over, and then He reached up and gently eased Chris down into His lap. I got my camera, and Sant Ji turned to Chris and softly squeezed his cheeks so that Chris would be smiling. When I snapped a photo, Sant Ji burst out laughing, saying He "wasn't ready," – and I took another.[5]

Sant Ji really laughed with Chris. He turned to me and asked if Chris ever got upset – did he have any anger in him? I answered, "No, he is really a good boy. He is a very sensitive boy. He feels things deeply." And then Sant Ji asked about Nicky, and I said, "Ohhh, Nicky . . ." and both Chris and I laughed. I said that Nicky could be a real wild one. Sant Ji pointed out that Nicky was still a little child, and then He commented that Chris was a serious boy – grown up. This interchange inspired seven year-old Chris to ask if he could accompany us on the walks we took – which he did from then on.

This gave Chris an opportunity for useful seva as well. At one point we returned from a walk to find that we were locked out of the house. As Sant Ji and the party stood on the porch, Chris and I realized that he was small enough to fit in a window that had been left open. We hoisted him up and in, and he quickly popped the door open – much to Sant Ji's delight,

The interviews went a little bit better for a day, as I made an effort to read people's questions before the doors opened. We saw more people than we had been able to see before. Silvia Molina had begun to assist – and that was a great help. At a group darshan in the afternoon, Sant Ji explained that on our way to reach the Naam, we needed to do more Simran – and in order to be able to do more Simran we needed to make our lives more pure. He mentioned that the glances of the Master – when the Master looked at the disciple lovingly – helped to purify the soul. As I sat there I realized, yet again, that I had no real idea of Who He was or how He operated.

He talked frequently about how any initiate of a true Master could be liberated in this lifetime. And He said that in many different ways and forms. At one point He even added a statement to the effect that He had made up His mind that His disciples should be liberated in this lifetime.

He told the story of a man who was doing seva in the Court of Guru Gobind Singh. The fellow was handing out parshad one day, and a couple of men who were soiled from working in the fields came. The two disciples were so anxious to have parshad that they did not clean up first. The sevadar said, "Why are you dancing around like a bear?" and he made them wait. When they said they were in a hurry, the sevadar

---

[5] These slides of a child seated in the Lap of His Father have always been among my favorite images of Sant Ji.

told them, "There, you take that parshad that has fallen on the floor." The two were upset, and they cursed him, telling him that he should take birth as a bear. When that sevadar died, he did come back as a bear.

That man, now a bear, had had a son who was growing up while the bear also grew. The son went to serve the Guru in His Court as well. At some point, the bear was captured and trained to be a dancing bear – a performing animal that travelled with the man who captured him.

One time that bear came to the Guru's Court, and, after starting to dance, suddenly began to stare at his own son. The Guru, after a while, laughed and told the boy, "You have some relationship with this bear," at which the boy was very surprised. By that time he was a young man, and he said that as far as he knew, he had never seen the bear before. And then the Guru told the whole story to him. That young man, that disciple, became upset, and asked, "Is this the fruit of seva for the Guru? I'm going to leave Your service if this will happen to me – if I will come back as an animal." Guru Gobind Singh explained, "No, this had to happen in order for him to pay off that karma; but he will be liberated." And, when the bear left the body, he was liberated.

When some of the South American devotees heard that Sant Ji had told this story, they wondered how this account fit with the assurance of the Saints that, once a person took the true Initiation – got the Gift of Naam – then, if it should be necessary to come back into this world, it would never be below the human body. How could this disciple of Guru Gobind Singh go into a bear's body? Sant Ji explained that the fact that we might be liberated in this lifetime had another side to the coin. At the time the disciple left the body, it was up to the Guru to decide where that soul went. The Guru could do anything with the disciple that was necessary for growth. The promise was that the disciple's soul was in the hands of the Guru and no longer in the hands of the Lord of Judgment (the Negative Power, Lord Kal). The Guru would give us whatever we needed. If we needed birth as a bear, we would get it. Sant Ji gently pointed out that the story came from the Sikh scriptures, and that it had happened to a disciple of Guru Gobind Singh, not of Master Kirpal or Sant Ji. He added that if a disciple loved the Master and was doing his/her best at the moment of death, that soul would be liberated. Even those people who were not having stupendous meditations at that time would be freed.

Some times when Sant Ji spoke, the whole concept of Indian mythology began to turn into Indian history for me – and the sheer power and immensity of the Guru came through. Sant Ji, seated on the

Previous Page
Sant Ajaib Singh
Ji walks through
the gardens in the
Ashram of
Bogotá, Colombia
in July 1977.

"Sant Ji turned to
Chris and softly
squeezed his
cheeks so that
Chris would be
smiling."
(see p. 176)

"When I snapped
a photo, Sant Ji
burst out laughing,
saying He 'wasn't
ready', – and I took
another."
(see p. 177)

Sant Ji, Pathi Ji, Chris Bicknell, Russell Perkins, and Kent Bicknell enjoy a pause on an extraordinary walk (see pp. 192-194).

". . . a little child shall lead them" Nicholas Bicknell leads the group back to the Ashram in Bucaramanga, Colombia (see p. 193).

Following Page "In Bogotá, Sant Ji had said that the places where the Saints have walked give off benefits for more than thousands and thousands of years – in fact, until the end of the physical world." (see p. 186)

dais in front of us said simply that the Guru had the liberty from God –
the permission from God – to do whatever He wanted. The Guru, in fact,
could liberate the whole world in one Glance if He wished to. I felt that I
was seeing the truth of those statements – and those moments filled me
with awe.

At one session, Sant Ji told a story I had never heard before.
Speaking of the days after Baba Sawan Singh had left His body (on April
2nd, 1948), Sant Ji explained that Master Kirpal Singh went to Rishikesh
to meditate, and sat on the banks of the River Ganges. I had heard that
before, but Sant Ji elaborated, telling us how the goddess of the River
Ganges would embody herself in the form of a beautiful woman, and
then come to pay homage to Master Kirpal. Many times, said Sant Ji, the
goddess came and thanked Master for purifying her waters. She told
Master Kirpal that her waters had become dirty from the millions of
sinners who had been washing their sins in her, but that He had made the
waters pure again. She thanked Master Kirpal over and over again for
that.

Hearing that episode, my Western mind wondered, "Gee, river
goddesses were really there, coming to see Master Kirpal?" I asked
Russell if he had ever heard that story, and he said he had. A devoted
sevadar of Sawan Ashram in Delhi, Princess Narendra (fondly known as
"Khuku"), had told it to him. Only Khuku added that Tai Ji (another
sevadar who accompanied Master Kirpal to Rishikesh) could also see
that lady. As Tai Ji assumed that the woman was bothering Master
Kirpal, she threw stones at her, until Master informed her, "No, this is
the goddess of the Ganges."

A Western disciple of Master Kirpal once referred to Him – with
respect and love – as "Mr. Snatchbottom," because every time you
thought you had Him figured out, He pulled the bottom out from under
you. At times it seemed to be that way with Sant Ji as well. One could
only try one's best to do the task given – knowing that at any moment
the job, as envisioned through mental limitations, might be undone from
Above. More than once I stood outside the door of Sant Ji's house after
the time of interviews had ended, and told a weeping soul or family, "I
am sorry, but there is absolutely no way you can see Sant Ji now. He has
already retired – gone to bed. You will just have to wait until tomorrow."
Suddenly the door would open behind me, and Pappu, or even Sant Ji
Himself, would say, "Yes?" I would explain, "Well, these people are
waiting to see You." And the response would be, "Come in, come in." At

such moments I would just chuckle, and feel very happy for the fortunate disciples.

In another interview, a woman physician asked a question as to how could she avoid karmas in connection with her patients? Sant Ji's first response was, "Never perform an abortion." As Sant Ji said more, neither Silvia nor I could understand what Pappu was translating. And Pappu had difficulty explaining it all. We kept asking questions, "What does Sant Ji mean that she shouldn't do any bad practices – she shouldn't accept money for bad practices?" We wanted more; we wanted to know what exactly was meant. This went on for a while, until Sant Ji finally said, "Look, just translate to her what I am telling you. She knows what I mean. She knows." And it was true. She did know what He meant.

A satsangi had brought her dying mother to the foot of the long stairs from the Satsang Hall to the house. As the woman could not get out of the car that brought her, Sant Ji descended the path to speak briefly to her, and to give her His loving glance. The woman died a few days later, after we had travelled to Bucaramanga. Her daughter came again to see Sant Ji, and informed Him that the death was very peaceful. Sant Ji comforted the daughter, explaining that she had done a very great service by bringing her mother to see Him – and that it was on account of that meeting that she had had a peaceful death.

When, on August third, Sant Ji had wondered what I would tell the Sangat about the stay in Colombia, He asked me to relate the story of the love of the people from South America. He laughed as He told me to be sure to mention "the kissing and weeping." It so often happened that the devotees, after coming in and falling at His feet, grabbed His hand and began to kiss it. This was usually accomplished through a veil of tears and smiling laughter combined. The other side of the coin of that love, expressed so emotionally, was a lack of discipline. People were so anxious to be close to Him, that they sometimes forgot boundaries and civility. The situation did improve, however, as Sant Ji requested the devotees to "remain in the discipline," often citing the North Americans as having been well-behaved. But the outpouring of love experienced on that first night, when we arrived at what Sant Ji called "the home of love," continued throughout the visit.

Asking Sant Ji to sign copies of His image was a phenomenon that began in Bogotá and grew dramatically. After a while, we "set up shop" in the private interviews. We kept a clipboard and pen at hand, because almost every person coming in had a handful of photos to be signed. While Sant Ji did not seem to mind, some of us were beginning to panic.

We thought that we ought to somehow stem the flow, if not stop the practice altogether. But the next person who came in would hand Sant Ji a number of photos, and He would smile, grasp the pen, lean over the clipboard, and – with great care – sign, "Dass [Servant] Ajaib Singh." Once again it seemed we knew so little about what would please Him.

At one point, as we were walking through the line of waiting devotees assembled outside the Satsang Hall, Sant Ji paused before a woman in a wheel chair. Clutched in her hand were several photos, awaiting His signature. The pen I provided did not take well to the glossy surface of the photos, and Sant Ji asked for another pen. Someone else provided a felt tip – which worked quite well. As we continued up the path, Sant Ji paused and said to me, "You are a principal. You should always have a variety of pens with you."[6]

Although Silvia had begun to do most of the translating for the interviews, we still moved too slowly to see everyone. One afternoon we had seen only fifteen people in about three hours. When, with five minutes left in the allotted time, I opened the outside door to the sitting room, I was surprised to find that a new group had appeared. A sevadar told me that all of those people were leaving the next morning, so they had to see Sant Ji then. I felt frustrated – why hadn't they been the first ones sent from below to see Sant Ji, instead of the last, I asked? It was hard to organize it all in such a way that it worked smoothly. And I worried about wasting Sant Ji's time.

At the end of the session, Sant Ji spoke to me. He said that in Colombia the people did not know how to ask questions. He mentioned the need for translations of the spiritual books into Spanish, so that they would be able to understand the elementary theories of Sant Mat. People asked for a prayer to say throughout the day, or wondered if it was acceptable to eat meat if one had not actually killed the animal – if one had bought the meat in a store instead? Sant Ji was giving out the most basic information over and over again.

He pointed out that in the States, He would have been able to see 100 people in the same time He had just seen fifteen. The people who spoke English, and knew how to ask their questions, were able to go right in and out, but here it was taking too long. The implication was that I needed to do something – but I had no idea what.

Sant Ji retired to His room for a tea break. After He left I just started

---

[6] A quarter of a century later, I may add that this is a commandment of the Master which I <u>have</u> been able to keep!

weeping. I felt like I had done my best in many ways, but I felt so upset – frustrated at being responsible for having misspent His precious time. I collapsed in the corner of the sitting room, with my head buried in my knees, sobbing like anything. Pappu had no idea what to do with me, so he went and told Pathi Ji what was happening. Pathi Ji was making chai for Sant Ji, and when it was ready, he carried it into Sant Ji's room. Pathi Ji proceeded to tell Him that I was out in the sitting room, weeping.

Sant Ji came out, and the first thing He said was that I had spoiled His tea! But this was actually very sweet, because He went on to explain that He became very sad when He heard I was upset. He asked me, "How can I sit in my room and enjoy my tea, when I know that you are out here weeping?" My first thought was, "Oh my God, I have a new title: 'Principal Sahib, He Who Spoils the Saint's Tea' – or, perhaps, 'Spoiler of the Holy Tea.' " Sant Ji then said that I had to be strong. He noted that this was only my second or third day of this, as I had joined them in Miami, but He and Pathi Ji and Pappu had been putting up with it for two or three months. In the end, He asked that tea be brought for me, and, sipping from that cup, the sweet chai definitely felt like an infusion of Grace. I felt much better, and resolved to keep trying my best to make things run more smoothly.[7]

Sant Ji went for a walk almost every day. Shortly after I had shed my tears, Dr. Molina, Russell, Chris, and a few others accompanied Sant Ji as He strode along up a rough road behind the Ashram. The terrain was mountainside jungle that was being developed into residential housing. The vistas out over Bogotá were fantastic. At a particularly lovely spot, Sant Ji paused and spoke briefly to the group, making a joke about both the food and me.

It had not been easy to acquire the proper flour for making the Indian staple, the flatbread known as chapattis or *rotis*. What we were provided was organic wheat flour – but it was far too coarse to create a chapatti that was similar to what the party was accustomed to eating. Debbie Asbeck looked hard for a finer flour, and eventually found one – but in the meantime the chapattis were so tough and gritty as to be almost inedible.

When we paused on the walk, Sant Ji laughed, and made the com-

---

[7] Among other things, I realized that it would be helpful to anticipate situations before they occur. For example, from then on I asked the sevadars helping with interviews to be certain that the people who had to leave that day were the <u>first</u> ones in the line.

ment that He had been hungry since He left India. He said that in Vancouver He had been able to get the right diet[8] – but that elsewhere,
especially in Colombia, there were problems with the food. And then He
said, "Our Principal Sahib is going hungry. He knows what the chapattis
are like." Sant Ji continued, "He was crying and weeping after only two
or three days, and we have been at it all this time." Everyone began to
laugh heartily, along with Sant Ji, Who was very animated as He spoke.
In closing He added, with an ever-so-sweet glance at me, "And after that
I caressed him like a child, and it was a beautiful sight to see!"

This incident of "Spoiling the Saint's Tea" ended up providing much
laughter in many forms over the ensuing years. Sant Ji referred to it
several times – always with gentle humor in His eyes and voice. Pathi Ji
was very fond of telling me that, *"America mai, Kent Bicknell bahot
barda admi hai – Eyk principal sahib hai – Lekin, Colombia mai, chotta
baacha hai!"* [In America, Kent Bicknell is a very important fellow – a
big wig – a principal; but in Colombia he is a little kid!]. The episode
also became the subject of a cartoon that I drew for Sant Ji – one of His
favorites.

While the story of how my ineptness at interviews evolved into a
cartoon for the Saint falls outside the chronological boundaries of this
book, it may be germane. Beginning in 1979 and throughout the 1980's,
I accompanied the Spanish-speaking group to Rajasthan for the Novem-
ber/December visit to Sant Ji's Ashram. I was often there on December
tenth, my wife Karen's birthday. During one of these early visits, I made
a birthday card for Karen, with a pen and ink sketch of 77 RB and
various features of the Ashram. I asked Sant Ji to sign the card – which
He did ("Love, Ajaib Singh"). This was, I felt, a nice way of making up
for not being present on her birthday.

The next year, Sant Ji asked me to make one of those "cartoons" for
Him – which I did most willingly. It featured various sevadars from 77
RB – all doing a variety of tasks (with humorous twists) – and Sant Ji
thoroughly enjoyed it. Over the years I produced more cartoons to share
with Him.

On one occasion I flew to Delhi a couple of days before Sant Ji was
to come down from Rajasthan. When He arrived, we flew together to
Bombay for a Satsang and meditation program there. The day before
Sant Ji came, Mr. Oberoi said to me, "You know, Kent Ji, I have just

---

[8] The presence of a large Indian population in Vancouver meant that basic
Indian staples were available.

come from the Ashram, and Sant Ji is very much looking forward to seeing you here in Delhi. He is very much looking forward to seeing the cartoon that you will have made for Him." I had not made a cartoon – but I certainly bent to the task that evening.

The cartoon I made featured the Colombian chapattis of 1977. I was in a corner, crying (of course). Pathi Ji was trying to cut the chapattis with a handsaw, and Pappu was banging them with a hammer. Debbie Asbeck was saving the day – as she drove an Army tank over a line of chapattis – thus making them soft and pliant. Sant Ji looked on with a smile, patiently waiting for His Food.

I showed the above cartoon to Sant Ji – explaining every detail – as we sat in the airport lounge in Delhi, awaiting our flight to Bombay. A few minutes later, Sant Ji turned to an Indian disciple who was traveling with us, and went over the cartoon, inch-by-inch, with her – with much laughter throughout. Later He told me, "You get enjoyment from making these cartoons and from showing them to me. But I get much more enjoyment than you from these. When I return to Rajasthan I will take this cartoon out and show it again and again to the dear ones who come to visit, and each time I will enjoy it." Again, I do not pretend to understand the Ways of a Saint.

Thursday, July 28th, 1977 – Bucaramanga

On Thursday the twenty-eighth of July, we flew to the city of Bucaramanga, located near the border between Colombia and Venezuela. The airport was a mountain whose summit had been sheared, and the landings and take-offs were, mildly put, exciting. When we arrived, we were much closer to the recently constructed Ashram than to the city itself. The latter was reached by descending tortuous mountain roads.

Bucaramanga was the most beautiful place I had ever been in the world. It resembled photos from a *National Geographic* – the Lost Valley of the Incas. It was a fairly sizable city, but we were at least forty minutes above it, surrounded by peaks and valleys. The city was always visible from the Ashram, however, and the evening lights of Bucaramanga looked like the Divali Festival in India – the Festival of Lights.

Sant Ji was very, very happy there. The only problem was that there was not any running water, so everything had to be brought in. Because of this scarcity of water, back in Bogotá the organizers had announced that not many devotees should travel to Bucaramanga. When Sant Ji came to know of this, He informed those sevadars that it was up to us to provide whatever the people needed, and that all of the dear ones who wished to come should be accommodated. He suggested that everyone use less water, which worked out very well.

For several months before Sant Ji came, a significant number of the Satsangis in Bucaramanga had been arising at midnight, sitting together in meditation until 5:00 a.m., and then holding Satsang before going off to work. Sant Ji told them that it was their love that had pulled Him there. Prior to His coming, however, some sort of friction had arisen among the group. In a very matter-of-fact manner, Sant Ji stated, "The Negative power saw how much love you were having, so it just planted some seeds of discord among you." He then told them that if you are given a seva, that is your seva. If you leave that seva to do something else that you want, then you are not doing seva.

Later in the session, with twinkling eyes and a big grin as He looked towards Russell, Pappu, and me, He explained that a son of Guru Nanak had become an *avatar* of Gorakh Nath. It was from this son that the path of just the first Two of the Five Sacred Names developed – and He added that His first Guru, Baba Bishan Dass, was of that line. The sevadars went back to serve everyone with huge smiles on their faces.

The food in Bucaramanga was very lovingly prepared, and artfully served, in beautiful surroundings. Most everything was cooked on a wood stove, using native earthenware pots. Simple gourds served as bowls and spoons, and Sant Ji remarked that Nina Gitana (who always kept everything gracefully simple at the Vermont Ashram) would have liked it very much there. As in other places on the tour, every day Sant Ji came and stood at the *langar* to watch the food being served to all of the devotees.

In Bogotá, Sant Ji had said that the places where the Saints have walked give off benefits for more than thousands and thousands of years – in fact, until the end of the physical world. That being true, the seeds of future benefits were amply scattered over the dusty red terrain of the Bucaramanga Ashram – seeds cast by the holy footsteps of Sant Ji as He walked all over the grounds.

The scheduled stop in Bucaramanga was only two full days, and Sant Ji wished to give as much as possible during that time. There was little time for interviews – and many who wished to see Him. This included initiates and seekers from Bucaramanga who had been unable to come to Bogotá. At the first session, on one of my trips out the door to get the next person, I was told that an elderly man, a plumber, had brought his fiddle to play some of his own compositions for Sant Ji. While not a Satsangi, he had helped to arrange the temporary pipes used for Sant Ji's house, and now he was inspired to see Him.

I was concerned that all of the Satsangis should be able to see Sant Ji, and I explained that to the sevadar pleading his case. She responded, "Yes, but he has come, and he has composed some songs out of love. He is an elderly man." I was still uncertain, and she observed, "But it is out of love." I recalled the saying in English that "the road to hell is paved with good intentions," and, while I wanted to help, I did not want to move the fellow ahead of any of the people who had been waiting so long. I suggested that he come back at 4:00 p.m. when the interviews were over, and we would see – but no promises. At 3:45 I heard the sounds of a violin being tuned, and the next time I opened the door, there he was, waiting patiently with his entire family.

As the hour drew to a close, I asked Sant Ji if the man could see Him, and He said, "Certainly. Bring him in now. I want to hear him play," so I did. Sant Ji was thus serenaded in the mountains by a fiddle-playing plumber. At the end of the concert, Sant Ji said, "*Bahot aacha*! [Very good]. "It is very good. Tell him that I don't know the language, but I understand him. Very good!" Then Sant Ji asked, "Do you want to take a picture" and they were all very happy – except that my camera was empty.[9] The plumber began to play again, and everyone laughed. The family mentioned that he was 75 years old, to which Sant Ji commented, "There is one old man in our village of 105 years old. He is working very hard. You are not very old – do not have this thought that you are very old." The man asked for Sant Ji's blessing, and Sant Ji laughed and said, "*Te amo, te amo*!"

Sant Ji had been so welcoming to the fiddler and his family, that I puzzled again over my role as to setting priorities for interviews. A little while later I said to Him, "Sant Ji, when I am in this position of perhaps deciding who can see You, and who can't, or who should see You first – sometimes my head makes all these reasons why someone should or shouldn't come in. And then my heart remembers the story of Harnaam,[10] and I realize that I don't know what people need. I don't know

---

[9] Although I was out of film, Steve Arky captured the session on an 8-mm movie camera.

[10] Sant Ji had often related the story of Harnaam, a laborer who saw Master Kirpal just one time. A few months later, Harnaam was working in the fields (at

who should see You or when – I don't know any of that." Sant Ji answered, "Those people who come in love to see a Saint – they get something, whether they are initiated or not. It makes no difference; it does not matter at all. It was very good that that man came to see me, and he will get a lot of benefit."

Sant Ji's answer was very sweet and strong, and that made my heart sing. Stepping back from my elation, I observed that my ego got very happy if it seemed like I had done the right thing in His Will, and very sad if I seemed to have erred. The truth was that I did not know what anyone "needed." Sometimes, sitting in an interview, I would think I knew – and Sant Ji would say just the opposite. Other times I would be close; and on occasion, one hundred percent right. Sometimes the advice seemed so hard, and I would think, "Ouch!" and the person would leave the interview in tears. By the next day, the operation would be over, however, the healing would have begun, and that same soul would be in heaven. I realized that He is the One who looked at their foreheads, read their fate, and gave them exactly what they needed.

Friday the Twenty-ninth of July – Initiation, a Visit to the City, and a Marvelous Walk

Friday the twenty-ninth was a day that unfolded like a miraculous dream. The few nightmarish moments that cropped up were directly related to my own shortcomings – as will be seen. The day began at two in the morning when I arose to assist with the Initiation. About twenty devotees from the area – young and old, and from all walks of life – quietly assembled outside the house, and came in to receive the Holy Naam when all was ready. Sant Ji sat in a chair, lit by the flickering flames of four candles, and the new initiates all had inner experiences of being connected with the Sacred Light and Sound. The atmosphere in that room was as ethereal as I had ever felt. [11]

Sant Ji's earlier place, Kunichuk Ashram), when he passed away. Before he died, he told Sant Ji that Master Kirpal had come to take his soul – even though he had only seen Him once, and was not initiated. Further, Harnaam informed Sant Ji that Master Kirpal would be coming to see Him at Kunichuk Ashram – which Master Kirpal did!

[11] Cf. Russell Perkins in *Sant Bani Magazine*, January 1978, "The First World Tour of Ajaib Singh, Part IV: In South America," p. 26: "There was one

After the Initiation, which was from 3:00 to 6:00 a.m., I was re-arranging the room to be ready for the interviews later that morning. Karen, sitting in the near-by Satsang Hall, told me that she heard Sant Ji call my "name," "Principal Sahib!" From His bedroom He had called to ask me, "*Kya kam karte hai?*" [What work are you doing?], and I responded, in my broken Hindi, that I was cleaning the room for the interviews. He then asked me if today, unlike the day before with the fiddler, I would have any film in my camera – and He really laughed.

We had taken a beautiful walk the day before, and again today we went out. The Andes were so special. At one point we rounded a crest in the road, and suddenly the view seemed to go on forever. My heart sang just being there – but the best walk – "The Colombian Hat Dance" – was yet to come.

At noon we drove down, down into the actual city of Bucaramanga. Sant Ji had been invited to visit the home of the Rosales Family, a very devoted, large, and lovely family wherein everyone was initiated. Sant Ji was given the grand tour of the house, visiting every room in turn. Sant Ji sat in a chair in the living room, surrounded by the family and quite a few guests. I sat at the back of the room and took a few photographs. After giving a brief talk, Sant Ji sang some bhajans that we had never heard before, and they were lovely – filled with the yearning and love of the disciple for the Master.[12] Parshad was liberally distributed to all, and then we were off to visit another home. On the way back to the Ashram, the caravan stopped briefly so that Sant Ji could bless the place where they hold Satsang.

---

day in Bucaramanga that was one of the most incredible days of the whole tour – Friday, July 29. It began with Initiation at 3:00 a.m. in the Master's house – a very beautiful candle-light event. The sight of Sant Ji sitting between the candles and being illuminated by that humble light was in itself worth the whole trip to South America. Twenty-one brothers and sisters were given Naam at this time."

[12] As Russell described it, "Later that morning we drove into the city of Bucaramanga as Sant Ji had been invited to visit several houses there. First we went to the Rosales family's house (Maria Victoria Rosales is the Bucaramanga group leader), and after going all through the house, Sant Ji held a very sweet Satsang and gave out a great deal of parshad. Here He sang a bhajan He had just written – or at least Pappu and Pathi Ji had never heard it before and could only sing the responses with great difficulty. After that, we went to other houses, including the regular Satsang meeting-place, and returned to the Ashram." [*Sant Bani Magazine*, January 1978].

There was a moment in Bucaramanga when Sant Ji spoke about the power of darshan. He explained that when Master Kirpal made Him sit up on the dais with Him, Sant Ji was so terrified of sitting next to that Great Power, that He would tremble. I thought how I was always hungry for darshan, and no doubt it was good for me – I knew that in my soul. But, sadly, I also realized that at times I simply forgot Who it was that sat in front of me. Some of that I attributed to what may be called, "drifting" – caused no doubt by the tremendous overload I experienced, rushing about almost every moment. More insidious, however, were the nightmarish periods of consciously not being content in the present, in the "here and now." I suffered an acute attack of such a spiritual malaise during our trip to the city.

The wave of "wishing & hoping" for something other than what was being given, had begun for me on the plane from Bogotá to Bucaramanga. I had hoped that my family would be able to sit up close to Sant Ji – where I needed to be. Instead, they were stuck all the way in the back of the plane. Although I did not say anything, I got upset, wondering why a couple of teenagers, who were supposed to be helping Karen with the children, were seated close to Him instead. I silently fumed, ruining the opportunity for constant darshan of Sant Ji, Who was right in front of me.

Two days later, when we drove down to visit the Rosales Family in Bucaramanga, I spent half the time wishing that Karen had been invited to come along. Once again I felt upset at what was not, rather than delighting in what was. When I spoke to Karen later, she said that missing the trip had not bothered her. Then she gently pointed out that we needed to learn to be thankful for where we were at every moment – to be glad we were there.

As I mulled it over, I wondered why I had fallen into such an unreasonable state. I recalled that once in India, Sant Ji had said something to the effect that, in order to live around a Saint, a disciple needed to have reached the third plane – to be quite advanced spiritually. Baba Sawan Singh used to liken the disciples who came from afar to see the Master, to the calf that came for milk. But those who lived near the Master were more like ticks, sucking the blood from the cow's udder. And who wanted to be seen as a tick?

I thought of all of those inspirational stories about the disciples who were asked to do seemingly impossible tasks by the Master, and the few, or often, just one, who would stay through until the end. One Master asked His disciples to continually build platforms – and then to unbuild them and put them elsewhere. Eventually the disciples went away, feeling that the Guru was old and had lost His faculties – but one disciple would not quit the Orders of His Master. I understood, perhaps for the first time, that whenever I heard those stories I did not wish to identify with the "quitters!" – quite the opposite. In childhood, when I read tales of the knights, I did not think of myself as the lazy, bad oaf – nor as the peasant bystander. I was on that stallion, sunlight glinting off my armor.

The more I reflected on my state, the more I understood that, as much as I felt God's embodied presence to be a fire that warmed and brought life, It could also burn. The world was a cold place, and attending Satsang and having darshan were opportunities to come, sit at the hearth, and get toasty warm. It made me feel so good all over. And then it would be time to head back out into the cold again. Somehow, however, living right next to Him, that same fire began to feel too hot for me. I stood too close for too long. What burned was not Him, however, it was me, as my own pettiness came crawling out of hiding again and again. Instead of idly wishing for opportunities to serve – to give and give – I was now being asked to live that givingness at every moment. At times, my ego balked, as I had not transcended my old self.

One evening Sant Ji talked about the sow that had a litter of many babies every time she gave birth – which happened three times a year. All of those piglets went off, and ate the mud and dirt of the world. But a tiger had only one child – and that child grew up to be the king of the jungle, the king of the forest. Sant Ji added that Master Kirpal had made all of us tigers, and that we should grow up to become emperors.

And that was it. When, for instance, I put off checking the latest arrangements for the upcoming interview session in order to grab a snack, I felt more like a pig than a tiger. Which was more important, being certain that the people were ready for Sant Ji when He was ready for them, or my desire for a slice of mango? In South America I was ordered to be with Sant Ji at every moment, and that was a tremendous, priceless blessing. But it was very painful to see my own weaknesses crop up, even (and especially) right in front of Him. And it was impossible to feel that I either merited, or had done any kind of justice to, all that He was giving. I was being served a heavily laden plate, overflowing with food for thought.

That afternoon, a seeker appeared at the interviews who had not been permitted to receive Initiation in those early morning hours. The day before, following the direction of Dr. Molina, I was designated to inform that man that he could not attend the Initiation, as he was not well enough prepared. He had not been studying the theory of *Sant Mat*, had not been attending the Satsangs, and had not been on the vegetarian diet for the requisite amount of time. He was very sad, and sought me out that evening. He explained that he knew about other yogic paths, so he felt that he was prepared – that he did have a background. He was familiar with the teachings in a general way. I said that I did not have the authority to change the decision, but suggested that he come for an interview the next afternoon.

The following afternoon, at Sant Ji's request, I checked to see how many people were still waiting as we neared the end of the time for interviews. I noticed that fellow at the end of the line, and I asked the sevadars to be sure he got an opportunity to come in. They said, "All right, he can come next." I closed the door, and reported to Sant Ji that the line was not that long. He said, "Okay, then that is all for today." But it was five minutes until four – the hour we were scheduled to stop. I groaned inwardly, screwed up my courage, and talked to Sant Ji about that man. Standing right beside me, Sant Ji grabbed my bicep firmly, and said, *"Leo!"* [Bring him!], and He gently guided me over to open the door.

When the man came in, he knelt down in front of Sant Ji, and presented Him a little bouquet of flowers with a stick of incense in the midst. As if in slow motion, Sant Ji took the flowers and carefully looked at them all. He proceeded to tell the man that he would get Initiation. He advised him to attend the Satsang, and to understand the theory. Sant Ji wrote, "To Alissa – Love, Ajaib Singh," on a photo for the fellow's mother, and then signed a picture for the man himself. The minute care that Sant Ji brought to this interchange, and the healing effect on that seeker's broken heart, were wonderful to behold. The man left, and Sant Ji suggested that we go for what turned into an amazing walk.

Sant Ji invited Russell to come along, and then sent me to gather "the Bicknell Family" to accompany the party as well.[13] When I returned with Karen, Chris, and Nick, Sant Ji asked me to wear "my" hat. This was a large straw *sombrero* hanging on a wall of the house, apparently for decorative purposes. The day before, Sant Ji had taken the hat off its

---

[13] I had not breathed a word to anyone (except Karen) about my distress over the family missing out on the trip into Bucaramanga earlier – but, as Baba Sawan Singh used to say, a Saint can tell just by looking at someone what his/her state is – just as you can tell if a glass jar is holding candies or pickles!

peg and placed it on my head at an angle, stepped back to observe, and we all had laughed heartily. He told me, "You should always wear a hat like that." I thought He was suggesting I always wear a sombrero, but Pappu explained what Sant Ji meant: when I did wear a hat, it looked good tipped at an angle. Debbie Asbeck commented that if I always wore my hats like that, one of my ears would get awfully cold in the winter!

I grabbed the sombrero, and we all headed out the door and down the steep Ashram entrance road. At the intersection with the "main" road – a slightly wider avenue of reddish-brown sand and dust – we turned right and headed for the hills. We walked for more than half an hour to a spot with a beautiful overlook of the mountains and valleys beyond. We paused, and Sant Ji suggested that Pappu try on the sombrero. We all laughed, and Sant Ji asked me to snap a photo of that. Then Pappu took a picture of me in the hat – and then of Russell wearing it – and finally of seven-year-old Chris in it. The sombrero moved from one head to another with a good deal of hilarity – and the series of photos generated was published in *Sant Bani Magazine* under the title, "The Colombian Hat Dance."[14]

Not in any particular hurry, we turned to come back. As we walked along, Sant Ji took one hand of two-year-old Nick and I grabbed the other. We began to count, "One – two – three – wheeeeeee!" and lifted Nick way up off his feet, much to his delight. After a bit, Nick went on ahead of everyone, creating a perfect "photo op" that Russell titled, "and a little child shall lead them" when it was published on the back cover of the September 1977, *Sant Bani Magazine*.

At that point, Sant Ji noticed that it was getting late – the hour of Satsang was fast approaching. He began to accelerate the pace, and it was a challenge to stay with Him. Clip-clip, clip-clip, clip-clip went His feet, and we all raced behind. Impossibly, we arrived back at the Ashram exactly at five o'clock – right on time. We entered the house and, with the exception of Sant Ji, we were all out of breath. He laughed, thanked us for coming, and went into His room to select the hymn for the upcoming Satsang.[15]

---

[14] *Sant Bani Magazine*, September 1977, p.20.

[15] Cf. Russell Perkins in *Sant Bani Magazine*, January 1978, "The First World Tour of Ajaib Singh, Part IV: In South America," pp. 26-27: "After a brief rest, Sant Ji told us He was going to take a walk. This was the walk during which the beautiful pictures of this place that appeared in the September issue were taken, and all of us who accompanied Him – Pappu, Pathi Ji, Kent, Karen,

It was the last evening in Bucaramanga, and the Satsang was powerful and moving. When we returned to the house, Sant Ji asked, "Shall we walk around to the tents?" The grounds of the Ashram were colorfully dotted with many tents – accommodations for the devotees from afar. We covered the short distance to the tents, and examined several, including the one used by my family. Pausing at another tent, Sant Ji observed, "You people are lucky. You have come to live in the tents due to devotion – your devotion to God – but I had to live in the tents in the army." We all laughed. And then He said, "Actually, this is an army – the Army of Hazur Kirpal!"

When Sant Ji descended the road and steps to the langar area, it was twilight. He was dressed all in white, and there was a darkening green sky behind Him. A full moon – as full as it could be – played in and out of the almost dense clouds. The latter were gray on the edges, but close to charcoal at the centers – and the full moon slid between them. Stretched out far below were the twinkling lights of the city. Sant Ji stood and stood – and only after a very long time did He ascend back to His lamp-lit Home. After Sant Ji had closed His Door, Russell turned to me and, with a huge, intoxicated smile on his face, said, "Quite a day!" and we both burst out laughing, completely caught in the Joy of the Divine.

As I lay in bed that final night, I realized that not only had the day

---

Christopher and Nicholas Bicknell, and myself – will surely remember it as long as we live. It began as one of the happiest times ever and developed into something much more, because all of a sudden we became aware that we weren't going to be back in time for Satsang at 5:00 p.m. Sant Ji doesn't like to be late, as He's told me many times. So He started walking faster, faster, and faster until He was not running, but – I once saw a cartoon of John Henry laying down rails and all I could think of watching Sant Ji's legs, was John Henry's arms competing with the machine that was laying down rails beside him. I was at my absolute physical end keeping up with Him. I was three or four feet behind Him, I couldn't get any closer than that. I was just going and going and going and going. And the closer we got to the Ashram, the faster He walked. It was like there was no end to it, we just kept on going faster. I was barely aware of Pathi Ji who was a couple of feet behind me. Pappu, Kent, Karen, Nick and Chris were somewhere in Never Never Land as far as I was concerned. All I wanted to do was just not drop behind. We came to the corner of the driveway – it's very steep – He didn't slow down one bit. He kept moving on up that steep hill. Satsangis were there to greet Him, and He greeted them, and just kept moving. We reached the Ashram at exactly five o'clock."

been magical, but everything, including my head, seemed transformed. Clearly, the walk had done its work. My only sorrow was that He had had to provide me with yet another dose of spiritual medicine. Earlier someone had asked Karen if I was attending the Initiation that morning, and when she answered that I was, the person commented, "Boy, Kent better improve after all he is getting." I was really glad that Karen passed that remark on to me. The truth was that I had not been nearly grateful enough for all that was being given to me. At times, it was true, I had felt like a patient under anesthesia, and although I had had a vague idea that the Doctor was operating, I had no idea of what He was doing or how. I was reminded that even just a look towards Him was not to be under-estimated. As He Himself had said in Bucaramanga, to gaze upon any part of a Saint's body provides a great blessing, since, truly speaking, every part of a Godman radiates.

I could not get to sleep, so I decided to go for a stroll by moonlight. I grabbed my tape recorder, and as I walked about, a monologue spilled forth:

Ahhh, the lights of Bucaramanga are now immense. I am just walking and walking. I am real spaced, but, you know, that sometimes happens. In fact I haven't felt this good in a long time. I don't want to go to sleep, that is the thing. I don't want to wake up tomorrow and "wake up" – I want to stay in this dream. It is very beautiful – very, very beautiful. Bucaramanga is unreal [and I start to sing, "Likhan Valya"]

I was just meditating for about half an hour – I don't know – fifteen minutes, ten minutes – five minutes it felt like – I don't know. I opened my eyes and was I surprised [laugh, laugh] to find myself sitting on a hill in the middle of the Andes, looking all around. I guess I had better walk back – wherever back is.

And now I am walking back and it seems very sad to think of going back and going to sleep. It is so beautiful here. I can't help but think little thoughts like, "Wouldn't it be nice to have a little house sitting on one of these little hills?" Meditating here is very nice. It is the nicest I can remember anywhere. I noticed that this morning when I sat down – before I ate.

You know, it is such an interesting eating schedule we have, that I am never sure when I am going to eat. But it seems like just when I am ready to meditate, then that is the time to eat. And

I am always told to eat, so I eat. And then I am full. So today I
didn't eat when food was ready. I just decided to meditate and I
did. And as soon as I started meditating it was a real meditation.
And the same thing just happened here. And I just think – I think
the place has it. And the Saint has it. Ahhhh. Okay.

The next morning we packed our bags and loaded them into the cars
waiting to take us to the small airport. A huge line assembled by the side
of the road, and Sant Ji's car drove slowly along so the hungry souls
could have a last glimpse of their Beloved. The tears flowed, and the
fragile discipline was shattered, as the devotees were desperate to see
Him, touch Him, speak to Him, kiss Him – anything to hold Him back
forever in their broken hearts. We made it to the end of the line, and
climbed the steep switchbacks to the airport. The small jet roared down
the short runway, and dropped off the edge of the mountain. We were on
our way back to Bogotá for our final night, as we were scheduled to fly
back to the States the following day.

Again and again, the sheer volume of what Sant Ji gave was
amazing. If it seemed like at one time He was sending out more than at
another time, it was really only a question of receptivity. The Grace was
always flowing in abundance. As Sant Ji used to say, quoting Baba
Sawan Singh, "There is no problem with the Giver – the problem lies
with the receiver."

On the last night in Bogotá, right before it was time to retire, Sant Ji
came out of His room and found me all alone. He invited me to go on a
walk with Him – just the two of us. We wandered around the Ashram
grounds, seeing many disciples going about their tasks, but no one saw
us. It was as if He had donned the fabled Cloak of Invisibility. We
descended the winding stairs, continuing on past the Satsang Hall, down
to the little house near the residence of Alicia Gomez. This was a place
where many North Americans were lodged.

As we stood and watched, more people came and went. We talked
quietly some, but mostly we were silent. The lights were blazing in the
house, so we could see clearly. In the kitchen, some were eating, while
others were just sitting and talking. One person was at the sink washing
dishes, and although he scrunched his eyes to look out the window, he
saw nothing but darkness. At one point, a voice floated up saying, "Gee
. . . It seems like I have hardly seen Sant Ji at all today." I translated for
Sant Ji, and He quietly chuckled as we turned and began the long climb
to His house. I pinched myself and thought, "Wow, what an allegory!

We may not see Him, but He is always there, looking at us."

On the last day, Sant Ji asked to meet with the Board of Directors of the Bogotá Satsang. He talked very positively about Colombia as a country with a spiritual future. He said that He loved the country, and that the South American people genuinely loved Him. He told the Board that He had been very happy to come and stay with them. He added that He had sown many seeds amongst the people who came to see Him.[16]

At one point in the meeting, a dedicated sevadar asked Sant Ji if it would be all right for him to resign from the presidency of the Board. He explained that he was feeling somewhat like a fifth wheel, as Dr. Molina was doing so much of the work as authorized by Sant Ji. He did not blame anyone – but he felt that the work might be better accomplished if someone else were in his place. He added that he would be happy to step aside. Sant Ji would not accept his resignation. With great love, He pointed out various aspects of the work that had been accomplished by that individual, making it very clear that He did not want anyone else to be president. The sevadar put his hands together and bowed to Sant Ji, accepting the Will of the Master.

As the Board was getting up to leave, Sant Ji asked Dr. Molina and Russell to remain. When the room had emptied, Sant Ji told some extraordinary stories of His own life – examples demonstrating that everyone needs to be recognized for the work that they are doing. As Sant Ji lovingly explained, until a soul reaches beyond the lower planes to Sach Khand, the ego is still vulnerable to attacks of "name and fame."

Sant Ji began with a story from His days as a soldier. At one point, His division was involved in fighting around Kashmir, and they won a significant victory. Later, the troops went to Amritsar to be honored for their valor. As they marched into town, joyful crowds lined both sides of the street, placing garlands of fresh flowers around the head of each soldier. Sant Ji was also garlanded, but, He told us, He got upset when He noticed that many soldiers were receiving multiple garlands – and He had only gotten one!

The second story was from the days at Kunichuk Ashram. Sant Ji and His good friend, Sunder Dass, were accustomed to giving Satsang once a month. One time a so-called guru came to the Ashram with his disciples, and, after visiting a while, asked to give the upcoming monthly Satsang. Sant Ji agreed. Soon after, however, Sunder Dass came to Sant

---

[16] It is a fact that the spiritual mission of Sant Ji in South America exploded during the next two decades.

Ji with an objection. Sunder Dass explained, "Look Baba Ji [Sant Ji], we are naked yogis who have given up everything. All we have left is our name and fame. Why should we let this fellow take one of our times to do the Satsang – with the result that we would have to wait another month before we can get up and sit in front of all the people?" Sant Ji agreed with Sunder Dass, so, He concluded, "Sunder Dass and I threw that so-called guru and his followers out of the Ashram!"

There was a great deal of laughter from all of us as Sant Ji told these remarkable stories that pre-dated His full enlightenment. At the end, Sant Ji reiterated the main point. Praise and recognition were essential for all who had not yet transcended to the highest plane. It was, Sant Ji concluded, the lifeblood of people, and those of us who had been given positions of responsibility needed to remember that. Dr. Molina, Russell, Silvia, Pappu, and I sat in quiet reflection after Sant Ji retired to His room.

The Masters have explained that although Saints come into this world fully realized They take on the garb of human identity in order to teach us. I have always remembered those stories, and the lessons He gave us through them. It struck me that when Sant Ji was residing at Kunichuk Ashram He had already realized the goal of the first Two Sacred Names, as given to Him by His first Guru, Baba Bishan Dass. And while He had mastered the first two planes, He had not yet met Master Kirpal Singh – the One Who was to bring Sant Ji fully back into the Lap of God. In effect then, Sant Ji was sharing with us how, even though He was quite spiritually advanced, still He had not been above the ego. I did not pretend to know what Sant Ji's true spiritual state really was – that hardly mattered. The point was that the compassion for the human condition that flowed through those stories, as well as the altered perspective they revealed, were to prove quite inspiring in the near future and beyond.

Later in the day we descended once more the stone steps – this time to the waiting caravan of automobiles. Extended darshan was given to a near-hysterical line of devotees that amorphously surged toward Sant Ji's car as it left the Ashram precincts. Over and over again, Sant Ji told the devotees, "Te amo . . . Te amo!" We continued on to the airport, driving through sections of Bogotá that were lined with shops on either side of the narrow streets. Again Sant Ji remarked that Colombia and her people reminded Him so much of India. At one point we passed a giant billboard advertising KENT cigarettes. Sant Ji saw it, read it aloud, and laughed heartily. He revealed that, as the party had been traveling in the

U.S., whenever they would spot an advertisement for KENT's, Sant Ji would laugh and say that they were doing my remembrance. Neither for the first nor the last time, I thought, "How mysterious are the ways of the Saints!"

We arrived at the airport, cleared customs, and with a final good-bye wave to the many Satsangis who had been allowed through, Sant Ji boarded the plane. At some point on the flight to Miami, Sant Ji spoke to me about how pleased He had been to visit Colombia. As He talked, He seemed to look me up and down. In the end – out of the blue – He said, "When we get back to Sant Bani, I want to have some pictures taken with you and your family. You should arrange that. Bring them down to the house some day and we can do that." Then He added, "And you should dress like a principal!" As I had worn a coat and tie when traveling with Him, I took it to mean that I should be dressed up to that extent, at least.

Approaching Miami, I asked Sant Ji if He wished for me to stay close to the party once we had landed. He laughed and said, "I told you to keep your mind with me, not your body!" We landed in Miami, and all went smoothly. Since my services as a translator were no longer needed, I sat with Karen, Nick, and Chris for the flight from Miami to Boston. It was August first, and we were "home" again – for three more glorious weeks.

CHAPTER SIX

Return to New Hampshire

As stated in the previous chapter, there was no formal program for the first couple of days after Sant Ji arrived back in New Hampshire on August first. I was asked to speak to the sangat about the just completed trip, which I did on the evening of August third. The next evening, Sant Ji gave Satsang, and on the following day, August fifth, the full program of meditations, private interviews, group darshans, and Satsangs began in earnest. We had luxuriated in the Physical Presence of a Saint for so long, that it seemed as if it would never end. Yet the chock-full days began to fly by, and, as the word of Sant Ji's greatness spread, and the opportunities to see Him shrank, people from all over the world began pouring into the Ashram. In the end, several hundred guests were attending the program on a daily basis.[1]

When we returned in August, Sant Ji asked if my family would allow me to stay in the house with Him on a full-time basis. School was no longer in session, I could work with Pappu on the correspondence and with Pathi Ji on the bhajans, and it was useful to have someone available to help handle the variety of situations that arose. My family graciously gave me permission. I joined Pathi Ji and Pappu, helping wherever I could during the day, and retiring at night on the thick pile carpet of the living room floor.

It was, again, a busy, busy time, and we all seemed to run everywhere in order to keep up with the demands of the schedule. Having Master Kirpal Singh in residence in October of 1972 had been glorious, but that divine stay seemed to have come and gone in the blink of an eye. For a five-day visit, the house had been adequate for Master and the two sevadars who accompanied Him. When Sant Ji came, He actually lived with us. Given our collective naiveté, we were always scrambling to

---

[1] Cf. Russell Perkins and Michael Raysson in *Sant Bani Magazine*, February 1978, "The First World Tour of Ajaib Singh, Part V: The Last Three Weeks," p. 25 *ff.* Their account gives a good sense of the day-to-day scope of the final leg of the tour.

figure out how to best make His physical body, trapped as it was in a foreign land, as comfortable as possible. The bout with malaria was very much on our minds, and we wanted to do everything in our feeble power to ensure a healthy living environment. Pathi Ji and Pappu worked harder than anyone, as they cooked, translated, chanted, talked with Sant Ji, attended to correspondence, interviews, Satsangs, held bhajan practice for devotees eager to learn the devotional songs – all the while putting their own needs on hold until they could get to them. We had not even provided them with adequate facilities for personal essentials. We had constructed an "outhouse" for them a short distance from the Master's house, and felt that was enough! Thank God we learned, and, as indicated in Chapter Four, each time Sant Ji came, we had renovated the house, which made it easier for Him, and for the sevadars traveling in His party.

The pace at which the days unfolded precluded much attention to the maintenance of my daily journal. Certain events burned into the memory, however and, after close to a quarter of a century, those scintillating moments still shine forth with abundant clarity.

The School faculty had been discussing our need for more physical space, and we were excited about the possibility of adding to our existing facilities. Robert Schongalla and I had been the point persons for talking with architects about a design, and one afternoon we were able to talk to Sant Ji about our plans.[2] A Satsangi architect from Boston had developed a very creative plan that would have incorporated the three basic shapes – circle, square, and triangle – into a revamped complex for the original Stone Building and its addition.[3]

Robert and I went into His bedroom and sat on the floor in front of Sant Ji, Who was sitting cross-legged on the bed. We showed Him the plans, explaining everything in detail. I told Him how Master Kirpal had advised us to construct gradually, basing it on necessity.[4] Sant Ji said that if we had the money, it would be good to build thinking of the long-range plan. He explained that this is what Master Kirpal meant when He said to build gradually based on what we needed. If we had the money to add more space, and we needed it, then it would not be good to move

---

[2] I did take extensive notes on this session.

[3] The Stone Building (1973-4) and the wooden addition (1975) are now called the "Upper Building.".

[4] Letter from Master Kirpal Singh to Russell and Judith Perkins, April 25th, 1973.

slowly. However, He advised us, do not build something that would be left undone. He paused, and added that, on the other hand, Grace might come. He suggested that Hazur Kirpal dwelling within people might inspire them to donate money. Still, we should only plan to build according to the amount of money we could be sure to have. It would not be right to plan on building something that we did not have the funds for. And then, with that unmistakable twinkle in His eye, he hinted, "Spiritual works are never left unfinished – your building will be done."[5]

Hearing this, I mentioned the idea of building by stages – of constructing in a modular fashion, step-by-step, based on the finances available to us. He said that would be good. He added that, as far as He was concerned, whatever plans we developed would be fine.

The time seemed right to bring up another School topic with Sant Ji. I mentioned that recently, perhaps due to the growing excitement over finding Sant Ji and His planned visit, a couple of non-satsangi families had expressed concern that the spiritual component of the School was being overly stressed. They sensed this as a change, and were not comfortable, because they had understood that would not happen in the School. They thought that we would not "push" the Path on anyone. One family had gone so far as to withdraw their child from Sant Bani. It was true that our teachers had been very excited about the upcoming visit, and their enthusiasm sometimes spilled over into the classroom. Non-satsangi children were caught up in the atmosphere, and encouraged by at least one adult, to be sure to come to Satsang and to see Sant Ji. Within this climate, I wondered how direct we could be as regards certain aspects of *Sant Mat*.

Sant Ji asked for specifics. I gave the example of how we spoke of the teachings of Jesus Christ. Whereas, in this country, it was believed that Jesus ate meat and drank wine, we presented it differently. We talked about the Essene Gospels, and how Jesus was committed to a reverence for all life. Sant Ji stated, "Truth is truth. Why throw dirt on the good name of that Pure Soul? People do this kind of thing – make this kind of so-called teaching – in order to hide their own faults."

Sant Ji leaned forward and continued with great power, "We really do not know what the original teachings of Jesus were. But Jesus never ate meat or drank wine, and neither did any of His followers. Saints know the truth – and that is true. But Saints do not like to argue or debate

---

[5] Over the years the School's physical plant has greatly expanded, although the design described above was never used.

with people, because the other people become argumentative. They are doing that, presenting those so-called teachings, to hide their own faults."

Sant Ji referred to a similar occurrence in the Sikh religion. He explained that the Sikhs, in order to justify their own eating of meat, say that Guru Gobind Singh ate meat. They give an example of how in one town, Guru Gobind Singh supposedly killed a goat and cooked it, and then He threw out the bones. Somebody saw Him doing this and complained – so in order to keep that person quiet, Guru Gobind Singh gave him some gold coins. And this was a story told to "prove" that Guru Gobind Singh was not a vegetarian.

Sant Ji shook His great head. Once, when a Sikh was telling Him that story, Sant Ji asked, "Do you think that Guru Gobind Singh was crazy? Would He just have thrown the bones around, even if He did eat the goat? And do you think that great Godman would have had to pay gold coins to someone, to bribe that person to keep quiet? What can you be thinking when you talk about a Guru behaving in that way?"

Sant Ji told us that sometimes the Negative Power took birth in the family of a Saint. And when that child grew up, he twisted the teachings of the Saint. He defamed the Saint, by writing his own book and story of that Saint – which was twisted.[6]

The above prompted Sant Ji to speak of the Virgin Birth of Jesus. He mentioned that people are very concerned as to whether Jesus was really born of a virgin mother or not. He said that no one knows the truth – no one really knows. Then He added that people say that Kabir Sahib also was born of a virgin mother – but that was not true. As Sant Ji said that, I recalled hearing that Kabir Sahib had emerged from a lotus flower – with no earthly mother or father. My mind began to fill in the silence, "Oh, so Kabir had a normal birth after all," when Sant Ji continued. "The real truth about Kabir Sahib is that He never took birth from any human," He stated, adding, "He always came down into this world without coming out of the womb of any woman."

With our minds swirling with building plans, virgin births, and Saints Who come down to earth by simply appearing, Robert and I rolled up the plans and took our leave. I went to visit my family, and the whole story of the interview spilled out. Karen said she would bet that that is also how Sant Ji came amongst us – by just appearing. I agreed, "Yes,

[6] Cf. *The Anurag Sagar* for more on the birth of the Negative Power in the family of a Saint, and the subsequent distortion of the teachings.

He is Sant Kabir. When He was telling me all of that, He would stare into my eyes and say, '*Saints know the truth*,' as He talked about Kabir Sahib. Karen added, "Whenever I sit in front of Him, and He talks about Kabir, it seems like He was and is Kabir." I added, "There is no doubt about it – He really loves Kabir!" and we both looked at each other and began to laugh as ones who were drunk on love.[7]

Sunday Satsang, August 14th

Two thirds of the way through Sant Ji's final three weeks, I had a unique experience. Sant Ji asked me to learn a particular bhajan, *Nach Re, Man Nach Re, Tu Satguru Age, Nach Re* [Dance, Oh Mind, Dance – Dance in Front of the Satguru] written ostensibly by the contemporary Saint, Mastana Ji, but actually of Sant Ji's own composition.[8] When I

---

[7] Neither Karen nor I had any sound basis for the thoughts expressed in the above paragraph.

[8] From a talk at SKA Retreat, Sampla, India, 12-13-95, published in the January/February 1996 issue of *Sant Bani Magazine*, under the title, "To Become the Child of the Master":

[Sant Ji relates] I met with Mastana Ji many times at the feet of Baba Sawan Singh. During the Satsangs I had many opportunities to spend time with Mastana Ji. He was my old friend; we had a lot of love for each other. He was a lover in the true sense. He used to call Master Sawan Singh as Sawan the Emperor, and he used to remember Him with his every single breath. In fact, the bhajans which you sing, written by Mastana Ji, are bhajans which were penned by me. But after Mastana Ji left, since He did not leave any successor, there was a person who started writing his own name at the end, saying that he had written those bhajans. But I did not feel comfortable, after Mastana Ji left, to delete his name and add my name. So that is why we wrote the name of Mastana Ji. But in fact, the bhajans which you sing which have the name of Mastana Ji, were written by me.

Mastana Ji used to have anklets with tiny bells on his feet, like dancers have, and he would dance in front of Master Baba Sawan Singh. I was also very fond of dancing in those days, and in that mood I had written this bhajan, "Dance, mind, dance; dance in front of the Satguru." In the presence of Master Sawan Singh I said, "Just as Ranja (a great lover in Indian folklore) said, 'Come with me all those who want to become a fakir — because I neither got married, nor will I get married, and there is no one in this world who will mourn my death.' So those who want to become a fakir should come and follow me."

had learned it well enough to sing in public, He added, He would like me to be the *pathi* for the upcoming Sunday Satsang. That is, He wished me to chant the verses of that bhajan so that He could discourse on them. I was astounded – completely flabbergasted – speechless. That Sant Ji wanted me to take Pathi Ji's place up on the dais – even if it were only for that one time – made absolutely no sense to me. But of course I agreed, and on August fourteenth, it happened.

As the day approached, I worked hard with Pathi Ji to learn the correct phrasing as well as the proper pronunciation for every word. I had a copy of the bhajan – seven long verses and the chorus – written out in Hindi, and we worked with that. In the meantime, on one of my trips to Concord, I had purchased a big box of rock candy, very similar to what Sant Ji had given to Robert, Wendy, and me as parshad, on our first trip to His feet. I offered the box to Sant Ji, explaining that I hoped it would remind them all of being home in Rajasthan. Sant Ji took the box, looked within, laughed, and observed that, "The rock candy is the same everywhere – it makes no difference East or West!"

Just as Master Kirpal Singh [later] made me sit in the underground room to do the meditation, in the same way, Master Sawan Singh had made an underground cave for Mastana Ji and had made him do the meditation. I also got the opportunity to be in that meditation cave and meditate there.

Dear Ones, when Mastana Ji gave the Initiation, He had a very large following, but still the love which He had for me was the same as it used to be in the court of Master Sawan Singh. Whenever I would visit Him, in front of His whole following, in front of His whole sangat He would call me and He would say, "Okay, now you tell people what Master Sawan Singh was like; how did He look?" So I would describe the glory and beauty of Master Sawan Singh to all Mastana Ji's sangat in exactly the way I had witnessed.

Master Sawan Singh was very beautiful; He was very handsome. In fact, He was the true gentleman Guru. He had a gold chain fitted to His watch, and He always used to wear very clean clothes. Nobody had seen any stain on the clothes of Master Sawan Singh.

When He would laugh it would feel as if His whole being was laughing, and as if flowers were pouring down from His mouth, when He laughed like that. He was so beautiful, so handsome, that even the fairies used to pay homage to Him, because even the fairies were not as beautiful as Master Sawan Singh was. His style was such that He would be talking to a person, but on the other side somebody else would be trembling there, realizing his sins.

On August thirteenth, the day before the Satsang, Sant Ji called me into His room. He handed the box of rock candy back to me, saying that I should distribute it to all of my friends. I must have looked puzzled, for Sant Ji, with a loving chuckle, explained, "In India we have this custom, you see. Whenever anyone gets a new job, then it is expected that they will buy the sweets and pass those out to the friends and family." While I was happy to have the box in my hands, I still did not understand what He meant. He leaned forward and said, "You have a new job. You are going to be the pathi at tomorrow's Satsang!" Finally I understood, and we all laughed most heartily. I left the house and passed out a good deal of the parshad to friends and family, but, as it was a large box, I saved a goodly portion as well. That rock candy would have its own role to play in my spiritual growth – as will be seen in the next two chapters.

When the time came to do my "new job," I felt nervous, but I had a very strong sense of support from Him. I reasoned that He would not have asked me unless it were for my own good, so I took a deep breath, did Simran, and began to sing when He looked at me and said, *"Bolo"* [Speak]. I worked hard to be alert as to when Sant Ji wished me to stop so that He could comment. Mostly He allowed me to sing an entire verse, and then spoke. The extraordinarily powerful Satsang flowed on, in spite of the few words I botched.

The discourse Sant Ji gave on *Nach Re, Man Nach Re* was published in the October/November issue of *Sant Bani Magazine* (1977), under the title, "Dance, Mind, Dance." The bhajan describes how we are all caught in the web of attachment, and we are all dancing to the tune of Maya. Even the great ones of the past like Brahma, Vishnu, and Shiva, as well as famed yogis such as Durvasa Muni and Shringi Rishi, fell to the wiles of the Negative Power through its servant, Dame Maya. In this dark Iron Age, only the True Power of the Satguru can defeat Maya – and thus the mind should, "Dance in front of the Satguru" so that it "May cut the sin of birth." We should, "Deal in the True Merchandise: Truth knows no fear!"

As the verses proceeded, Sant Ji told story after story of the fall of advanced souls – mostly to the call of lust. The tale of Shringi Rishi, which He had told in great detail at a Satsang two days before, was no exception:

Shringi Rishi lived in the forest for a long time and he had been doing meditation there. King Dasrath was childless, and the astrologers told him, "If Shringi Rishi comes into your home and performs the Yajna [a certain religious ritual], only then will you have children." But Shringi Rishi was not ready to come into any village, and it was very difficult to bring him into the world to make him perform the Yajna. So King Dasrath announced that he was offering a big prize to anyone who could bring Shringi Rishi into his village.

There was a woman who accepted that offer, and she said that she would be able to go and bring Shringi Rishi. She went to the forest where Shringi Rishi was living, and she disguised herself as a lady sadhu, and she watched what Shringi Rishi was doing. She came to know that he was not eating any food and was always remaining in meditation. But once a day he would come to a particular tree and touch that tree with his tongue; but he was not eating or drinking any other thing.

So at the place where Shringi Rishi was touching the tree with his tongue, that woman pasted some honey. And on the next day, when Shringi Rishi came and put his tongue on that part of the tree, he found the honey there; and it was very tasty. Before that Shringi Rishi had never tasted honey. So when it tasted very sweet, instead of touching his tongue once, he tasted it two times. On the next day, that woman pasted some nourishing food there. In that way, Shringi Rishi started eating the food which was pasted there, and, as his body got strength, desires were also awakened. He felt like enjoying lust, and the woman was there.

Eventually they produced some children, and the woman said to Shringi Rishi one day, "You see, once we were alone here, only the two of us were living. But now we have children and we should move to some place where other people are living, because this forest is not a good place to bring up our children."

So, at that time Shringi Rishi had three children, and it was decided that they would move into the city. So it was announced that Shringi Rishi was coming to the city where King Dasrath was living, and everybody gathered there to have the darshan of such a great Mahatma.

But people saw that Shringi Rishi was coming carrying one child on his shoulder; another in a backpack, like those in which the American people put their babies; another was holding his finger; and last, was the woman. So when people who were gathered to have the darshan of such a great Mahatma saw that he was coming with three children and a wife, they felt very badly and they said, "Who will call him as the Mahatma? This Mahatma's condition is worse than the worldly people." When they taunted Shringi Rishi, then he realized that he had been deceived by that woman; and leaving the children and the woman there, he went back into the jungle.[9]

When Sant Ji arrived at the mention of Shringi Rishi, He looked directly at me, and His shining face broke into a huge smile. Two days before, when He had told the above story and made reference to "a backpack, like those in which the American people put their babies," He had also spotted me in the crowd and nodded and smiled, motioning to His back as if He were wearing a backpack Himself. And when we walked down to the house afterward, He mentioned that when He saw the Americans with babies on their backs and holding the hands of other children, He was reminded of that story of Shringi Rishi.

I never have been able to figure out a good "reason" that Sant Ji asked me to be the pathi that Sunday. The most obvious one is that I really needed to hear the theme of the Satsang – to stay connected with the Truth, to not be afraid, and to know that even the great Mahatmas, who had advanced very far in the spiritual practices, fell victim to their desires. Another was the humorous, but no doubt deeper, connection Sant Ji enjoyed making between Shringi Rishi's state and my own. Finally, however, it was a gift He chose to give me – and what mattered more than why He gave it, was how I would appreciate and use, or, misuse the gift.

A sad, but understandable, consequence of the attention I received from Sant Ji at this time, was that more than one person told me how much they envied my position. A friend related that, when we all walked down from the Satsang Hall to the bridge near Master's house, and a guard asked everyone to stop, it was very hard to see me continue to walk over to the house with Sant Ji, Pathi Ji, Pappu, and Russell and Judith. Why should that be happening to me and not her, she wondered?

---

[9] As noted, on August fourteenth, Sant Ji said, "The day before yesterday I told the story of Shringi Rishi; maybe you people remember that." There is no doubt that we did. When *Sant Bani Magazine* published "Dance, Mind, Dance," the entire story of Shringi Rishi from the twelfth of August was printed as well. (See *Sant Bani Magazine*, October/November, 1977, pp. 15-16).

And then she said that, rather than experiencing joy for what I was receiving, she felt a burning resentment – a hatred even – toward me. I could find nothing to say that would help, except to know I could not judge my friend for something I had done. As described in Chapter Two, and again in Chapter Four, I also had fallen prey to similar feelings of wishing I (or my family) were receiving something other than what the Master was giving. And I recalled what Sant Ji had told me when we first met: that it was "luck" that brought me close to Him.

Towards the end of the stay, Sant Ji reminded my family to come down to sit with Him and be photographed. I, of course, did my best to "dress like a principal," donning an old tweed coat over my button-down shirt and tie. I made efforts to comb my long frizzy hair, but, as may be seen in the photos of that session, it remained mostly out of control. I can only plead that, at the time, I thought I looked like a principal. Sant Ji was very sweet to my family, and we enjoyed the house specialty, mango shakes. Sant Ji said that He was very pleased with us, and that He would be very happy to have those photographs to carry back to Rajasthan.

The strongest memory I have of those final days is of a public statement Sant Ji made, in a very matter of fact manner. He was speaking of Who the Guru really is in relation to the soul. He pointed out that, when we finally reached the goal – when we arrived at the other side – we would come to understand that it was actually the Meditation of the Master that had saved us – that had pulled us across the inner planes. We think that we are doing all of this meditation, but the reality is that, from the Master's perspective, the practices we have been given are similar to the dolls and playthings given to a child to keep it occupied. These have their place, no doubt. In the end, however, what will take us to Sach Khand is the Meditation of our Master.

Hearing this, it might have been easy to think, "Then what is the point?" Yet I have never understood this "fact" in that manner. The way Sant Ji said it, so casually, made it very clear that while our work was to meditate, we should never forget the reality: the Saint would accomplish the real work. It was the Master – not the great Mahatmas or Yogis of yesteryear, or us – Who really was able to deal in the "True Merchandise" and save our souls.

The pace continued to accelerate until hours were swallowed up like minutes. I cannot restore the lovely mosaic from the scattered pieces: final good-byes in the house, rushing to join the caravan of cars to Boston, second – and third – poignant, painful leave-takings in the airport.[10] In the end, as we walked slowly back to find our car – parked in a rush and frantic haze – we were left with an extraordinary combination of overflowing tears and joy, coupled with the hollowness that crept in when the doors at Logan Airport finally closed on Sant Ji's animated, waving form.

Although it was a long drive back to New Hampshire, we did have a treasure that had just been entrusted to us. There were many seeds to nurture, and we felt ready to re-enter "the world" once again. Three weeks after Sant Ji, Pathi Ji, and Pappu returned to India, we received the sweetest, simplest note from Sant Ji. Reading it, we could easily picture our Beloved, pen in hand, bent over the piece of white stationery, carefully signing His name, with His title, "Dass" or "Servant."

September 8, 1977

My very dear Kent Bicknell (Principal Sahib):

Whatever love and regards you and your family showed to me, I am thankful for all that to you and Karen.

Sant Kirpal's Love to you,
Dass Ajaib Singh

---

[10] Again, for further detail, see Russell Perkins and Michael Raysson in *Sant Bani Magazine*, February 1978, "The First World Tour of Ajaib Singh, Part V: The Last Three Weeks," pp. 28-29.

CHAPTER SEVEN

Spiritual Vanity

The letters to and from India continued to flow throughout the fall and winter of 1977. Sant Ji provided us with updates of happenings in the Ashram at 77 RB, including the good news that He was feeling fully recovered from the malaria and the physical demands of the Tour. In each letter, I would send kind regards to Sant Ji's Ashram sevadars, and, in His return letters to me, Sant Ji would name each one, writing that they sent their love to my family and me. He always asked about the School and the Ashram, sending His Love to everyone involved with both. On the eighteenth of September, He sent a second letter of thanks for our seva and help during the Tour. In each blue airmail letter, He spoke of the Bicknell family most lovingly, and called us His "dear children" – always reminding us to do our meditation daily. Sant Ji wrote in Punjabi, but I was learning Hindi – a totally different script. This meant that Sant Ji dictated the letters for someone else to write in Hindi, although He addressed most of them Himself, and, of course, signed them all.[1]

I was very busy – teaching full time at the School as well as directing it, and traveling to Boston each week to complete my doctoral courses, as instructed by Sant Ji. He often asked about my progress toward the degree, reminding me that both He and Hazur Kirpal would be pleased when I had reached that goal. Several times He wrote that He would be very happy when the day came that He could call me, "Doctor Kent Bicknell, Principal Sahib!" As I was able to include a second level Hindi course as part of my studies, I eagerly wrote to Sant Ji as often as I could – and He always wrote back. If a subject were complicated, subtle, or the answer critical to others, however, I wrote in English.

---

[1] Years later, Sant Ji mentioned that He had written one letter to me all by Himself – but it took Him a long time, as He was not accustomed to writing in Hindi. Then He apologized for the form of His characters.

Guidance for the Sant Bani School

We had initially intended the Sant Bani School to serve through grade eight only. Responding to community needs, we began to accept high school students in our third year (1975-1976). By the fall of 1977, we had four seniors – and we naturally had concerns about how they would fare beyond the rather protected walls of Sant Bani. A second question came from some parents who wished that we had less emphasis on academics, and more on vocational skills. We wondered if it would be appropriate to begin more practical training for students – to accompany the academic program. With these thoughts in mind, I wrote to Sant Ji, referring to Him affectionately as *"Pita Ji"* [Dear Father].

December 8, 1977

My most dearly Beloved Pita Ji,

I am sorry to bother you, but I have two questions about the School that I want to ask you. Karen will be coming next month and will bring a couple of other questions about the School at that time.

The first question is about the high school. At present we are preparing the students to go on to college and encouraging the ones that can go to college to do so. Some people however, feel that college is a waste of time and money, and that we should be preparing the students by training them in practical skills so they can get a job in the world. We will do both some day, but at present we are emphasizing the preparation for college through school studies of mathematics, science, history, etc. Is this in accordance with your wishes?

Also sometimes we worry about the students when they will be going off to college. Here they have a very protecting environment, and are supported by the Ashram. But in college they will be surrounded by worldly people involved in worldly pursuits, pleasures, etc. Some of the students and teachers worry that it will be hard for them to be strong on the Path and also to make new friends, etc. without being like the worldly people. What can the School do to help prepare the high school students for going out in the world, especially to college?

Sant Ji responded as follows:

December 17, 1977

My most Beloved Kent Bicknell Principal Sahib,

   Both the types of studies are good at their own places. I am pleased with that. But as you mentioned in the letter about giving practical training to students and preparing them for jobs, I will be much pleased if some day by Hazur's grace you will start giving them such training in your School.
   You should not worry about the future of students because everybody has his own karmas, his own fate. As long as they are under your guidance you should do your best. If the foundation of a building is strong, that building won't fall down easily. In the same way, if your studies and teachings will have much impression on them, they won't get spoiled easily. If a student, who has got good education in his childhood, goes in bad company, he will realize his mistake very soon. So please don't be worried for student's future. Do your best.

We took that advice to heart, and over the years there has been significant progress in giving students more practical training.[2] Although it falls outside the chronological range of this book, it may be appropriate to cite a further conversation I had with Sant Ji six years later. The School staff was concerned that we were trying very hard to be all things to all people. It began to feel as if there were situations where we were not meeting the needs of some students with learning disabilities. Further, as teachers attempted to focus on a student, or group of students, in a particular class, other students might not be getting what they needed. At the time, the obvious solution seemed to be to create some kind of dual track for students in the secondary school: those who were college bound, and those whose final degree would likely be a high school diploma. I brought this to Sant Ji in a private interview in Rajasthan, in November of 1983.

---

[2] These range from "shadowing a professional" opportunities in our Projects Periods to art blocks with practical skills; from a life-oriented high school course in economics to math classes that build simulated investment portfolios and track them over time.

Kent: Sant Ji, our "open admissions" policy presents problems when we are trying to be a solid college prep high school. The mix of backgrounds and abilities dilutes the quality of many classes, as teachers have to slow down, etc. The weaker ones are helped, but sometimes at great expense to the other students. Should we develop two or more tracks to the high school? One would be a program for those going on to higher education; and another for those going on to trade or technical schools – or not going on at all.

Sant Ji: You should not have this two-track system. You should have an examination or test-like thing before admitting the students. And you should take only the good students, or the students who can become good after some time.

Kent: Everyone always thinks that in the goodness of our heart we should try to serve everyone. So when we make deadlines, etc. people think we are not doing the seva – when we are firm like that. But I worry about the School's reputation falling.

Sant Ji: You can increase the standard of the School only if you will accept good students, and only if you make good students.

Kent: I'm talking about the high school. At the elementary level we can still work with the students.

Sant Ji: Yes, at the high school. And you should have a firm policy for this – for closing the applications. It will be difficult for you, as well as for the Satsangis – those whose habits are spoiled – to accept this for the first year only, but later on they will know that you have assumed this policy and they will improve their habits, and it will not be difficult for them. So you should definitely have this policy.

In the above letter to Sant Ji of December 8th, 1977, reference was made to "a couple of other questions about the School" that Karen would bring to Him when she came to India in January. Some parents had raised questions about the role of athletics and competitive sports in the Sant Bani curriculum. While such activities had seemed normal and healthy to me, my father had been an athletic director and coach (as well as a high school teacher), and I had been actively engaged in sports in high school, college, and beyond. Some Satsangi parents, however, wondered if the basic premise of competition was not in conflict with concepts like *ahimsa* [non-violence] and rising above the ego.

Accordingly, Karen brought the issue to Sant Ji on her first trip to 77 RB in January of 1978. He spoke to her of the positive value of athletics. He explained that He had learned the games in the army adding, "I myself have played them – it is very good to have them." He mentioned a number of reasons to include athletics in a school program. First, they provide exercise for the body. Next, the children benefit because they get some excitement; and finally, they learn to progress and have success. Seven years later (December 4th, 1984), I reviewed with Sant Ji those early statements He had made to Karen regarding the benefits of sports. He nodded, and said, "You can even add that it increases the enthusiasm and excitement of the students as well as of those who see it. It is very good for the health. It even glorifies the name of the nation!" As with all of the counsel from Master Kirpal and Sant Ji, we were grateful to have divine guidance on seemingly mundane issues.

Spiritual Vanity Takes Root

In the section that follows, it should be clear that, while other people may have had various roles to play, I alone was responsible for my actions. One of the major lessons I learned in this personal saga, as will be clear by the end of Chapter Eight, is that Sant Ji held me accountable for what I did with what He gave me. Thus, the account should not be read from the perspective that anyone, except me, acted in a thoughtless, inappropriate manner. Everyone did whatever s/he was supposed to do – and we all grew from it.

One afternoon in the late fall of 1977, I was sitting alone in my office in the Stone Building of the Sant Bani School. All the students and staff had departed for the day, and I was lingering to finish up a few tasks on the docket. A Satsangi parent and friend stopped by to say hello. In the course of the conversation – but completely out of the blue – she asked me, "Do you know who you are?" I answered that, yes, I was Kent Bicknell, Principal Sahib! She looked intently at me and said, "No, do you know who you _really_ are?" I was startled, and at that moment I felt a slight chill – literally – go through me from toe to tip. In retrospect, it would have been much better to have taken that "electrical" charge as a warning – but I had many lessons I needed to learn. So I asked, "Okay – who am I?"

The person proceeded to explain that, based on her observation of the way Sant Ji had treated me on the recent Tour, He was expecting much from me. She hoped that I was sincerely doing every aspect of the Path, and that I took His Words quite seriously. She offered a plea that I think about what I had been given, and that I do everything within my power to cultivate it. She departed gracefully, leaving me alone once again.

I thought and thought about her words. I had been practicing the Path for almost ten years, but I felt that I had made very little real spiritual progress. Master Kirpal Singh Ji used to say that if a student could complete one grade a year, then why should a devoted disciple not be able to do the work of one inner plane a year? We should, He indicated. I knew that, wherever I was, it was not on the tenth plane!

I recalled the tremendous love that Sant Ji had showered upon me ever since we first met, and how He had encouraged me, again and again, to be strong and to meditate. He had asked me to be the *pathi* for that Satsang, and He continued to write to me as "My Most Beloved – Ruby of Rubies – Kent Bicknell, Principal Sahib." He had allowed me to come so close to Him physically – even sleeping in His house – and He had fed me so many chapattis, cups of warm milk and chai. At the least, I thought, I must put more time into the devotional practices, and then let God take care of the rest. I was due to go to India in March, so I decided to work really hard, from that moment until I saw Him again – with the hope that I would actually bring some spiritual fruits to Him, rather than coming, yet again, as a dry, empty, weak vessel.

I began to meditate more and more, and to work on the mental repetition of the Five Sacred Names – the Simran. As I redoubled my efforts, I saw that in order to have any degree of success, I needed to exercise more control over those areas of my life that were within my reach. Diet, I reasoned, was critical – as food was the daily "medicine" we ingested to enable our physical frame to function. The more I focused on all of this, with the constant thought that I was finally doing what both the Masters had been asking of me since the day I was initiated, the easier it was to accomplish. I saw what was occurring to me as a direct result of the Grace of the Master flowing my way.

Before I knew it, I was sitting for six to eight hours a day of meditation. In the evening, after meditating for a couple of hours, I would lie down to sleep around 10:00 p.m. By midnight or 1:00 a.m., I would awaken – without an alarm of any kind – and begin to sit for the next four to six hours. During the day I worked hard to always be remembering the Master – most specifically through the practice of constant Simran and/or the singing of bhajans. All the while I went about my normal life of being with my family, teaching at School, and driving to Boston once a week for my doctoral courses.

I was delighted at the results of my efforts. I was sitting for long hours with real results. I was remembering the Master throughout the day – more than I had ever done before. My thoughts were much more in my control, and I was not at all troubled by those two *dacoits* [thieves], lust and anger. I was so extraordinarily focused that I felt "high" or "intoxicated" most of the time – but it was a very clear state of mind. Along the way I lost thirty pounds.

Throughout this period I continued to write to Sant Ji in Hindi – and He would send me such sweet letters in return. When I would tell Him that I was meditating much more, and that I was doing much better at maintaining more constant repetition of the Names of God – as well as a chaste life – He would write back, stating how pleased He was to read all that I wrote. He said He would be so happy to see me in March – that I was most welcome – that *"Rajasthan ashram aapka hi ashram hai"* [the Ashram in Rajasthan is your Ashram also]. I took all of His Words as further endorsement of my recent direction.

So intense did I become, that if I should forget the Simran any time, for example, on my two-hour drive to Boston, I would deny myself one of the two chapattis I was allowing myself per day. Two *roti* and a cupful of cooked brown rice were the extent of my daily sustenance – with bancha tea and water to fill in the gaps. I shunned mortal foodstuff such as cookies and cake. These, I felt, were beneath me, as it had become so evident that such tasty items did nothing more than enslave us to the passion of our tongues. Should I become sleepy in my meditations, I would grab some of the Lego blocks (building blocks with many bumps on them) that belonged to Chris and Nick, and place those under my ankles. The latter actually developed calluses from my sitting on the bare wood floor with no cushions – and, of course, I used no backrest.

On this spiritual Path we generally are prohibited from revealing our inner experiences. There are, no doubt, many reasons for this – spiritual and otherwise – but the Masters speak of two that involve basic human nature. If we talk about our experiences to others, we might become proud of them. On the other hand the listener, who may not have had such experiences, may become discouraged, depressed and jealous. If a disciple persists in revealing what is happening within, the Master may cease to send such experiences. In giving the following examples of the state I was in, I hope that I am not violating that order. These were outer experiences, rather than inner – but they were powerful and beyond my ordinary ken of day-to-day living.

My classes at Boston University were quite demanding. The expectation for each course was to attend class and take notes, read a ton of outside material, and write a paper synthesizing what I had gained from those two sources of information. The outside reading was onerous in terms of a time commitment – especially as I wished to spend my evenings and early mornings sitting in the sweet remembrance of the Lord. When I needed to write a paper for a class, I tended to flip through the books randomly, and read from whatever section happened to open. I often found great quotes that way – and my papers were quite successful. One professor even wrote that he was so impressed by my citations – they were the very ones he would have chosen. It did not occur to me that I was misusing the Master Power – not unlike the fellow in Chapter One who used It to drive his tractor. I reasoned that my method was a convenient way to give myself more time for meditation.[3]

One evening, while I was watching a slide show in the Satsang Hall at Sant Bani, a particularly beautiful slide of Sant Ji came on the screen. He was sitting up on a dais in front of the Indian Sangat. The slide had been shot from the side, and His profile was gorgeous to behold. The person showing the slides lingered on that particular one, to tell a story. As I steadily gazed upon the image, mentally repeating Simran, I was stunned when the projected form of Sant Ji turned His head in my direction and nodded at me. Surprised and delighted, I went home that evening on a cloud, and sat for many hours of meditation.

A final event was one that caused me concern – but I reasoned that it would all get sorted out when I was able to see Sant Ji in March. One winter evening during the height of this period, I was the only one awake in my house. It was close to ten o'clock. I stepped into the bathroom for a couple of minutes, prior to heading off to bed. While there, I caught a glimpse of my face in the mirror and, recalling the question that had begun my new phase, I asked my reflection, "Who are you?" Master Kirpal Singh once wrote of the self-induced, waking trance experienced by Alfred Lord Tennyson when, as a child, Tennyson had repeated his own name several times, silently.[4] I would love to be able to write that

---

[3] Years later, a Western disciple I hardly knew asked me if it were true – as he had heard – that I once used the Master Power to help me write my papers for graduate school. I felt ashamed, as not only had I done that, but I had obviously told people about it – at least to the extent that it "got out there."

[4] See Master Kirpal Singh, "Simran: The Sweet Remembrance of God" in *The Way of the Saints* [Second Edition, 1989], p. 131.

that is exactly what happened to me – that I entered some higher state of consciousness. The truth is, however, I seemed to disappear. When I suddenly snapped back, three hours had elapsed. I had no idea what had happened – where my consciousness had been – and still today I have no idea. That experience made me wonder if everything was right in my little heaven, and I was anxious to see Sant Ji in person – to be able to talk to Him about what was happening to me.

In all of this, did I ever think that I might become a Master? While I can honestly say I did not – the reality is that other things I thought were just as damaging. I made a fatal spiritual mistake. Looking at my brothers and sisters on the Way, I began to think that I, Kent Bicknell, was finally really and truly practicing the Path, and that, in some way, this would help Sant Ji with His burden. Of course, all the Masters have asked the disciples to do just that – to devote themselves to the spiritual practices that have been given to them and help make Their Work easier. But implicit in all of my observations, was a rampant judgment on the spiritual state of my neighbors. I began to see myself as belonging to a select group of disciples who really took the Path seriously. If we could begin to carry some of our own karmic debt, Sant Ji's burden would be lighter. In the words of another disciple who seemed very committed to spiritual growth, Sant Ji might be freed of enough of our karmic burdens to become "the first Master to be able to enjoy His incarnation here on earth." It all seemed so noble.

Within any group or organization the feeling sometimes comes up that some are on the inside, while others are not. While there may be rare souls who are not bothered by such feelings, it is only human for people to feel disenfranchised when others seem to be in power. Neither Sant Bani Ashram nor the School was above these dynamics.

In the first chapter, I made reference to a few disciples who wished to live at Sant Bani, feeling that the Ashram belonged to the Master, and therefore no mere human should be able to deny their wish. If it were not their "right" to make that choice, then at least the Master should decide, not the sevadars at the Ashram. In the same way, not all Satsangi parents agreed with the policies of the School – and often cited the Teachings of the Master to make a point. People are human. As we did our best to interpret divine direction, it was understandable that different perspectives arose – and disciples would disagree on certain particulars. This was not a new development on the Path, and Master Kirpal Singh had to issue more than one message to remind everyone of the need to work together in harmony for the Sacred Cause, rather than wrangling discordantly.

As I began to do my spiritual practices more and more intently, it seemed as if a number of those who had felt disenfranchised from the Ashram and/or the School were more inclined to communicate with me. To them, I suddenly seemed more "open" and "receptive" to how things really were and should be. The moniker "Mutual Admiration Society" might well have been coined for us, as we complemented ourselves on finally recognizing the "Truth" and as we devoted ourselves to the meditation practices. The concept of the *Khalsa* – a group of advanced disciples who were important in the mission of Guru Gobind Singh – was talked about – and we wondered if we could create such a circle around Sant Ji. Some people made reference to two kinds of followers of the Master – those who were merely disciples, and those who were more deeply committed.

When Master Kirpal Singh had told the story of Bibi Hardevi's (Tai Ji's) efforts to match His hours of daily meditation before going to meet Him, He concluded, "such-like competition is good!" We reasoned that, to inspire each other, it was acceptable to talk about the hours we were spending in meditation, the bhajans we knew by heart and what they meant to us – and, without revealing inner experiences – our general progress on the Way.

I still had some of the rock candy parshad that Sant Ji had handed to me when I was given the "new job" as the pathi for Satsang. He had told me to share that with my friends, so I took much pleasure in giving it out to the select few. As I began to identify more and more with this small circle of disciples, to exchange my old ways for new, the obvious occurred. I began to separate myself from former friends and colleagues at the School and Ashram – including Judith and Russell. While I never shirked my duties at School – after all (I thought) that was Divine Work, entrusted to me by both the Masters – people began to sense that I had become aloof. And I had. As I was teaching, sitting in meetings, or doing my duty on the playground, I understood that my main task was to maintain the constant, silent, mental repetition of the Names of God – and then everything would take care of itself.

One of the lowest points for me – which I considered a high point at the time – came at the School Valentine's Day party. I recall standing there, watching the students and faculty enjoying the shared love of the exchanged cards – topped off by cookies, cake, and punch. I smiled and made small talk, while I secretly and smugly cast judgment on all. I condemned adults and children alike as mere slaves to their tongues. I can only thank God that Sant Ji showed me the true value of food as an expression of love when I went to His feet the following month.

There were cracks in my Eden, however. I recall a long discussion with a very devoted disciple. We discussed the notion of the protective power of Simran. We wondered whether one could be led astray by the mind, or by the Negative Power, if one were engaged in constant repetition. The devotee thought not – but suddenly I recalled Sant Ji's instructive stories, told right before we left Bogotá. Sant Ji had told personal tales of His time in the army, and of His days at Kunichuk Ashram. In the latter, He had been quite advanced in the spiritual practices – having achieved the goal of the first two inner planes. Even so, He explained, He and Sunder Dass were not above "name and fame."[5] I told my fellow disciple that I did not feel that we were above the wiles of the mind and ego, even if we seemed to be in a state of continual Simran.

My desire to be in His Physical Presence again grew and grew, and it became harder to wait for my turn to come. The letters to and from Rajasthan continued, and with each group I sent a taped message to Sant Ji as well. I spoke in Hindi, and often Karen, Chris, Nick and I would sing a bhajan for Sant Ji. He patiently wrote back each time, commenting on how much He enjoyed hearing the sweet voices of "the Bicknell family" on the tape. Occasionally He sent a taped message back to us.

On one tape I recorded a variant bhajan – with an explanation of why I had done so.[6] There is a hymn of Guru Arjan Dev Ji Maharaj which states, "The hot wind does not blow over one who has the Guru's protection." This is a most appropriate line for the hot climate of India. We were right in the midst of a frigid New Hampshire winter, however, so I changed the word for hot, *tati*, to cold, *tandi*: *Tandi Vao na Lag di ji, Gurandi, Sharan Peya* [The cold wind does not blow over one who has the Guru's protection]. I recorded that for Sant Ji, and, in my broken Hindi, explained why.

---

[5] As explained previously, I am not suggesting that Sant Ji was caught by the ego. Rather, it was His way of telling us what we needed to know. See Chapter Five above.

[6] This was not the first time I had changed a lyric in a *bhajan*. One evening in May of 1977, when I was the only Westerner present at 77 RB, I added verses to a *bhajan* of Guru Nanak, *Naam Guru da Sacha Hor, Kur da Pasara* [The Name of the Guru is True – all else is false]. I simply contributed the names of more things that were false, and Sant Ji asked the villagers to repeat the verses after me.

When Karen went to Rajasthan in January, her rendition of Sant Ji's bhajan, *Dekhi Bahot Nirali Mehima, Satsang ki* [We have seen the unique greatness of Satsang] made an impression on Sant Ji and the villagers. She has a quiet voice, high and somewhat unique. In a letter to me that Karen brought back when she returned, Sant Ji wrote, "*Karen meri beti badi aachi hai. Usne bhajan bola, 'Dekhi Bahot Nirali Mehima, Satsang ki' jo bahut mitha tha.*" [Karen, my dear daughter, is very good. When she sang the bhajan, *Dekhi Bahot*, it was very sweet].

As February passed, I continued to spend a lot of time in the devotional practices – and the concern of old colleagues continued to grow. I received anonymous notes, wondering what was happening to me. One cited the Bible, making reference to the eagle that flew too high for its own good. A co-worker became desperate to understand the changing nature of my state of mind. Years later she told me that one evening, unable to stand it any longer, she stole into my office and searched through everything she could, trying to find some clue – some letter from Sant Ji – anything to help her understand the change that had come over me. When Russell wrote to Sant Ji and asked Him if it would be acceptable for me to help with the Initiations, Sant Ji answered positively. He told Russell, yes, that would be good. He added that I loved Russell and had appreciation for him in my heart.[7] This had to have been a confusing response, as I had quite withdrawn from the old days of camaraderie with Judith, Russell, and most of the other sevadars living at the Ashram.

March came at last, and, with much excitement I gathered everything I needed to travel once more to those desert sands of Rajasthan. Always in the past I had known that I did not deserve to be in the physical presence of God – but Grace or luck had allowed it to happen. This time, however, I wondered if I was finally "ready" to see Sant Ji. I was fairly confident that He would be pleased to see me, but I kept room in my heart for the possibility that my recent efforts would not be what He had been asking of me. On every level, however, I was certain that He would look deeply into my soul and let me know exactly what I should do next. When I walked out the front door, I did not yet know that I was a patient being wheeled to the intensive care unit of All Souls Hospital. The roots of spiritual vanity had grown quite deep, and their removal – a beautiful albeit painful process – required major surgery.

---

[7] Sant Ji referred to this same letter when I saw Him in March. See below, Chapter Eight.

CHAPTER EIGHT

Spiritual Surgery – India in March of 1978

With a full heart, and a bag stuffed with freshly made chapattis, I headed south from New Hampshire to begin the seemingly endless series of planes, trains, buses, and jeeps required to travel to Sant Bani Ashram, Village 77 RB, District Sri Ganganagar, Rajasthan, India. Several colleagues from the Ashram and the School were in the group that left Sanbornton, and along the way, devotees from various other locales joined us. My new-found strength manifested in a variety of ways, as I sat with eyes closed for hours on end, or nibbled at my "Simranized" food supply – all the while wondering how my neighbors could eat the airline fare midst chatting about such trivial things as news, sports, and weather. If my mind were not engaged in the mental repetition of the Sacred Names, then I was sure to be singing one bhajan or another. I quickly discovered one other disciple who seemed to be in my state – and we occasionally exchanged knowing glances during the long journey.

We arrived in Delhi, and were met at the airport by Pappu. He had arranged everything so well, and his family was most gracious to all of us again. I was very happy to see him, and he gave me all the news about Sant Ji and everyone else at 77 RB. After the group was settled in the Bagga's new house in the Delhi neighborhood known as Bali Nagar, Pappu headed out to complete the preparations for the trip, and I tagged along. There was a great deal of shopping to accomplish, for in those days Pappu carried most of the needed food supplies to Rajasthan with the group.

We stopped at the open market in Chandi Chowk to buy huge baskets of bananas, crates of oranges and apples, and tins full of raw cashews – half of which were then roasted by the Baggas when we returned home several hours later. As our three-wheeled scooter made its way through the incredibly narrow, crowded streets of Old Delhi, I breathed in deeply and felt that I was truly home once again. Watching Pappu wheel and deal with a competence that seemed far beyond his twenty-

225

one years, I thought how miraculous it was that anything got accomplished in the rich complexity that was Mother India. Our last stop was the railroad station. We picked up the tickets for the overnight train to Ganganagar leaving that evening, and returned to the Bagga house for a few quick hours of rest. I was bone tired, but ready to go.

There were more than the usual number of mishaps on our journey northwest to the Ashram. At one station, we were all asked to disembark. Several devotees grew anxious, but those of us who had traveled the route before recognized the routine, as some of the railway cars needed to be exchanged before proceeding. This time, however, the whole train, with all our belongings, departed from the platform and steamed out of sight. People became more agitated – but I just smiled smugly to myself and said, "Well, isn't this interesting? Let us see what the Will of God brings next!" Fifteen minutes later, the train returned, and we were on our way again.

The delay caused the train to miss a connection, and we arrived in Ganganagar much later than scheduled. Rather than a caravan of Jeeps, a bus had been hired for the final stage to the Ashram. We were all happy to see the familiar smiling face of our dear friend Pathi Ji, standing beside the colorfully decorated Indian tour bus. We boarded, and settled in for the two and one half hour ride over tarmac that got so narrow it eventually dwindled to nothing but fine, pure sand.

As we got close to the Ashram, we came upon Sant Ji's new Jeep, parked at a narrow bridge that marked an intersection of canals and roads. Sathi, the son of Sardar Rattan Singh, was standing beside it, waiting for us. Pappu got down from the bus, turned and called my name, and then headed for the Jeep. I was sitting in the back of the bus, and could not respond quickly enough, so we started off again, following the Jeep. I began to mull over how nice it would have been to arrive at the Ashram in the Jeep, when I thought, "No, what is really nice is to be in His Will. If I am supposed to be in the Jeep, I will be in the Jeep. The ride isn't over yet. And if I am not supposed to be in the Jeep, I do not want to be there." That lasted until the bus passed the Jeep – and suddenly I wanted to jump out the window and land in the Jeep. "Ahhh," I thought, "So much for letting go!"

The Jeep overtook the bus, and stopped ahead of us. I stuck my head out the window, Pappu called for me again, and this time I ran to join them. Babu Ji, who had been in the Jeep, took my place in the bus. I thought, "Wow, this is wonderful" and then realized, "Oh, the ride still isn't over yet." Less than five minutes from the Ashram, the bus broke down. We loaded more people into the Jeep, and began to ferry people to the compound at 77 RB.

When we swung through the open gates of the Ashram, Sant Ji was not in view. I tumbled out of the Jeep, and immediately caught sight of Him, flowing around the same corner where I had caught my first glimpse of Him in 1976. When I heard Him say my name to Pappu, I was at His feet in a flash. He pulled me up, and His eyes were dancing. Putting His arm around me, He asked, *"Kya hal hai?"* [How are you?] I responded very enthusiastically, *"Teek hai!"* [Great!] Sant Ji turned and spoke to the small group in front of Him. He said that while our delay was in the Master's Will, still, He had been worried about us. He invited us to come into the dining area and eat.

I was not hungry, so after a few moments I stepped back into the courtyard. Sant Ji and Pappu were sitting there, waiting for the next Jeepload to arrive. Sant Ji invited me to come and sit with them, and asked again how I was. I gleefully responded, *"Hunh, raji khushi, khushi!"* [Yes, very happy, happy], and He knew that I meant it this time. I felt as if His eyes were talking to mine – and it was wonderful.

Sant Ji sent Pappu off to eat, stating that I should be the translator. As each group arrived, He told them that He was very glad to see them, that it now was time to eat, and that afterwards they should rest – all of which I was able to translate. In between Jeeploads, Sant Ji and I talked. He asked me how the sevadars at Sant Bani were, and I was guarded in my response, suggesting that "health wise" they all seemed fine. When He inquired about a couple of people in particular, I indicated that they seemed to worry too much about how things were going or not going, adding that they got upset when things did not go as they wished.

Sant Ji asked how Karen was, and I said that she was very good, very strong. He mentioned that He had heard the tape of Chris and Nicky singing the bhajans, as well as my altered chorus for *"Tati Vao"* – exchanging a cold wind for a hot one. I told Him that it was true; the winds were cold in New Hampshire, and we both laughed.

Noting that one of the Western disciples in the group had stopped shaving since Sant Ji last saw him, I commented, "Now he is a *dardi vala*" [bearded man]. Sant Ji observed that in America we did not have the social pressures like in His country. In India, if someone had a beard and shaved – or vice versa – people put a lot of pressure on that person to return to how it had been. Growing or shaving a beard was done as a statement of something – not merely to be fashionable. Sitting there, engaged in informal conversation with Sant Ji, I began to feel so at home that I was sure I had the blood of India running in my veins.

In retrospect, it must have been difficult for some of my recently estranged colleagues to arrive at the Ashram and hear Sant Ji's greetings filtered through me. A while later, Sant Ji (through Pappu) comforted someone who had been visibly upset. When I overheard Him say, "It is okay – don't worry – Master will make everything better – everything will become all right," the proverbial prick of conscience made me wonder if the interchange had something to do with ripples caused by my current state.

For the first evening Satsang, I sat down at the back of the room. Until that point, I had always positioned myself as close to Sant Ji as I could, but I honestly thought I was being humble by plunking down behind everyone. Sant Ji immediately asked me to move up closer, indicating a spot next to Bant and Parmeshri (my favorite singers – the Electric Tin Duet). Sant Ji asked Bant for a bhajan that the Westerners had learned, and she sang, *Mera Sataguru Pritam Pyara* [Oh my dearly Beloved Satguru, I have forgotten Your Name]. Then He asked the Westerners to sing, and someone began with, *Tati Vao Na Laga Di Ji*. Parmeshri smiled knowingly, and substituted *"Tandi"* for *"Tati"* – so I did as well. The village children seated behind me started to lovingly tug ever-so-gently on my coat and, with a great sense of belonging, I melted into the Satsang. In the end, Sant Ji asked me to sing a bhajan while Darshan Singh distributed parshad to everyone, so I sang *Satguru Ke Guna Ga Le Bande* [Oh man, sing of the qualities of the Satguru, and wind up the births and deaths]. Back in the courtyard after Satsang, I attempted to meditate, but I kept nodding off. Finally, after Pappu kindly brought me a glass of warm milk, I stumbled to my rope bed, and sank deep into the night.

The next thing I heard was the long vigorous notes of the three o'clock bell that Sant Ji rang to help us arise and sit. The morning meditation with Sant Ji was quite powerful, and, again, I felt that I was finally doing what He had asked me to do. Beyond a slight tendency to review the past and rehearse the future, I was able to remain in the moment, repeating the Simran. It had been my experience that an inner voice would sometimes speak to me when my mind was quiet enough, and that morning it whispered, "Abandon everything but the Simran."[1]

---

[1] I have always understood this phenomenon as my mind speaking to me, not the Inner Master.

At the end of the sitting, Sant Ji began to ask people about their experiences, but He did not get to me. As I sat and stared at Him, I felt more and more intoxicated – just filled with delight. He said that while we were there, our work was to remain in the Stream of Simran. He added that, if one were doing Simran throughout the day, then the constant repetition needed for meditation would be much easier to attain. I went back to my room, and recorded in my journal that I should keep in that Stream, *"that River that runs deep, mysterious, dark, swift, and cool – cool water, protecting one from the heat of the world. Stay in that Stream now. And make all the nows add up to forever."* And then, thinking of my desire to abandon everything, I wrote, *"Definitely, definitely, definitely, friends are false. Love them and Simranize them."*

Standing behind the long wooden tables with cloth covered buckets in front of us, Pappu and I helped serve breakfast to the Westerners. From a constantly renewed source, we distributed two or three, warm, stuffed chapattis to each person, and then ladled hot cereal onto the tin trays presented to us. When everyone was fed, we retired to the semi-covered kitchen area to eat by ourselves. As we sat on low straw footstools, trimmed with recycled bicycle tires, we chatted quietly. Sant Ji appeared before us. Putting His hand on my shoulder, He commented:

Sant Ji: You can only eat with me!
Kent: Yes.
Sant Ji: In America too, you always ate with me.
Kent: Yes.
Sant Ji: The love that you had for me in America made me happy.
Kent: That love came from You.
Sant Ji: And the tears you cried in Bogotá made me happy.
And we all laughed.

After we finished, I went back to the dining room and picked up a stack of dishes. When I headed out to the washing area, Sant Ji was standing there, watching me as I approached. I squatted down and started to clean the trays, but Sant Ji told me not to. A sevadar quickly came over, and, shaking his finger gently at me, said, "It is my duty!" Sant Ji proceeded to tell me, in Hindi, that during my stay, my duty was to sit for meditation, not to wash the plates. Thinking that I was supposed to do what He asked, I went off to meditate more, disregarding my just completed breakfast.

At mealtimes I continued to be very careful of quantities – even though everything served was parshad. I stuck with my daily regime of two chapattis and a small helping of *sabji* [cooked vegetables], but allowed myself to drink as much chai as I could hold. I took Sant Ji's comments to me as endorsement for eating with Pappu and the other Indian sevadars, and that morning I moved my rope bed into Pappu's small room.

I was aloof from the other Westerners, but I did not care. I understood the self-imposed exile from my fellow disciples as a gift. As mentioned, Sant Ji told us that we should make every effort to "stay in the Stream of Simran," so I felt justified in limiting my communications to nods and smiles, over folded hands – even to old friends. Every single thing being sent my way, I reasoned, was an opportunity to practice being in the here and now – what Master Kirpal called, "the living present." And yet, I merged with the Indian Sangat as much as possible, speaking Hindi to anyone with the patience to listen. Intimations of hypocrisy were dwarfed by my joy, and by the sense that I was bathing in His Love – finally tasting the fruit of His Words to me, "the Rajasthan Ashram is your Ashram."

Parmeshri, Pathi Ji's niece, was one of my willing Hindi victims. She informed me that Sant Ji had played my tape for the villagers, and that she had enjoyed the bhajans of the Bicknell family very much. She said that everyone, including Sant Ji, had really laughed when they heard me singing of the Gurus' protection from the cold winds, instead of the hot ones. Sant Ji liked it, she said. She asked if there were snow in New Hampshire, and I said, yes, a lot! I added that when I sang about protection from the cold winds, I did not feel the frigid air quite so much. She laughed, and mentioned that Sant Ji told them all that in America I was a big man – a principal – but in Colombia I had become a little child, and cried. Finally she talked about Karen's bhajan, *Dekhi Bahot* – and left singing the song in an excellent imitation of Karen's unique style.

It came to me that it would be nice to stay and meditate a few days after the group left. When Pappu asked Sant Ji if I could remain for a few days, He wondered why. Pappu related my plan, and Sant Ji said, "*Karlo*" [Do it!] I was happy to get that news, but I was more anxious to have my private interview. At my request, Pappu informed Sant Ji that I hoped to have a long time with Him, as I had much to talk about. Sant Ji said, "Good."

As the first day for private interviews came, I was excited. At last I would be able to check with Him, face-to-face, to see if I were, so to speak, on the right track. When Pappu told me that he was scheduling me for the very first session in the morning (9:00 to 11:00), I remarked that I might need the whole time. I asked Pappu to change it to ten, at least, so that some others who were dying to see Him could go first. When Pappu checked with Sant Ji, He said, "No, no. Kent won't be first. I have much time for him. He will get much time." He added that my interview could come out of His own time – that I could see Him anytime – nine o'clock at night even. But, He said again, it should not come out of the interview time.

Although that left me without a scheduled time, I accepted it immediately. While I had been very eager to talk to Him, I also sensed that events were about to unfold graphically, and it might be just as well to let more time pass. The question kept gnawing at me, "Was He pleased with me?" At Satsang the night before, I had sat right in front of Him, until He asked me to move aside a bit. As the Satsang progressed I had become very intoxicated – hardly aware of my body at all – and at the end He asked me to sing, *Sachya Guru Meharbana* [Oh Benefactor, dye my garment in the saffron color (of the Name of the Lord)]. As I lay down to sleep, I thought, "Wow! He really wants me to do this thing and He really wants me to get strong."

At the same time, I began to wonder if I had cut myself off too much from things past. I recalled the simple round that Mildred Meeh had taught the Sant Bani students to sing: "*Make new friends – but keep the old. One is silver – and the other is gold!*" I had certainly made new friends, but, with some exceptions, how could I feel that I had sustained the old? And were all these thoughts racing through me just a ploy to distract me from remembering the Lord? When I awoke the next morning my hair was full of tiny pieces of *parshad patasa* [a thin sugar wafer]. I had used my hat as a receptacle for the parshad distributed at Satsang, and had apparently not removed it all before donning my hat as a nightcap.

The inner dialogue continued. I began to see that a by-product of my zeal had been criticism – trying and judging the behavior of others. I had invested so much in the past six months, however, that I desperately wished for His approval. I recorded in my journal that I now understood my role: "*to be strong, to support everyone, to not be worried and confused, to give out as much love as I can, to go on maintaining the inner strength, to develop that, in the darkness, in quiet.*" But the words, "worried and confused" began to enter into my journal more and more.

A friend asked how I was doing, and I responded that I was feeling excellent, but that I sensed Sant Ji might have been a bit concerned for me. I likened it to the worry a parent feels for a child that, in learning to walk, keeps stumbling. The father has to continue picking that child up – but is not really displeased. In the Satsang that evening, Sant Ji discoursed on a hymn of Sant Kabir. One of the verses spoke of the parent assisting the child who stumbles, and Sant Ji elaborated. He said that when children are learning to walk, the parent lifts them up again and again when they tumble down. In the same way, the Satguru uses Satsang to lift up the disciples when they fall. Through the entire process, the Satguru really loves the devotees – He has nothing but love for them. At the end, when Sant Ji left, I said, "*Gracias!*" and He tossed back over His shoulder, "*Te amo!*" [I love you!]

The following evening, on the way to Satsang, Sant Ji asked me how I was doing. All I could say was, "*Teek*" [Fine], as I felt there was no other answer allowed. How could I not be fine? I touched His feet, but He picked me up, put His arm around me, and hugged me. At Satsang He related that Master Kirpal never let Him touch His feet. The Master always picked Him up, and hugged Him. As Sant Ji left, this time, I said, "*Te amo!*" and He responded, "*Gracias!*"

The next day Sant Ji invited me to go for a walk outside the walled compound. We headed out the main gate, and He began to tell me about the neighboring land. They had been able to buy several parcels, He explained, and was about to say more when two Western disciples came around the corner. We had been told not to leave the compound, but these two had gone out for an extended walk. They were very excited to see Sant Ji, Who spoke briefly to them. That ended our walk, and I tried not to feel disappointment. How was I to know what the *Mauj* [Divine Will] was?

That night someone reminded me that the closer one came to a Saint, the harder the tests would be. The mind has a way of seducing us with noble, beautiful, subtle things – often disguised as the work of the Lord – done "in His Name." I thought deeply about that, and the desire to talk to Him became more acute. That wish was reinforced the next morning, when Sant Ji spoke about how powerful the mind was. During the Second World War, no one from His area dared go into the army, because the soldiers were sent into battle. When Sant Ji volunteered to go, everyone was surprised at how brave such a young boy was. But He didn't mind at all. Later, when it came time to fight His mind, He found out that it was much more difficult to do battle against the mind than to go to battle in war. He explained that He knew all about the mind, because for fifteen years He was an initiate of Baba Bishan Dass, Who made Him meditate underground. For all that time He had to battle with His mind. And when Master Kirpal initiated Him, He still had to battle with His mind. The mind is a very powerful and cunning foe.

Sant Ji talked to us about His childhood. He used to ride horses, and, like Baba Sawan Singh, was adept at mounting a horse that was already on the move. He was a skilled rider – with or without a saddle. He also loved to run. As a child, He felt that He had springs in His feet and, when He ran, He would repeat the Names of the Lord with every step. He told us that He never let anyone beat Him in a race. In the army He had been the champion runner for His outfit. At the army games, a champion from another unit – one of the mighty Pathans – came to see Sant Ji, as he had heard that Sant Ji was very fast. When this tall, strong, meat-eating soldier looked at Sant Ji, He laughed, and after teasing Him for being a weak vegetarian, said that he could win the race carrying Sant Ji in his arms. When the race began, Sant Ji lagged behind for the first portion – as was His style. His fellow comrades began to yell for Him so much, however, that He became inspired and took off with great speed. When he passed the Pathan champion, the latter was so surprised, that he suddenly stood still. After the race he congratulated Sant Ji, commenting that Sant Ji had gone by him so quickly that he thought he must have been standing still – so he stopped. These stories conveyed more of the strength and focus that had been Sant Ji's – right from His childhood.

Sant Ji continued to caution us about the mind, and to tell stories of how difficult it was to truly practice the Path. Those years were the era of the "walk-talks." Every afternoon, Sant Ji would lead us out the compound gate and down the sandy road, until we came to a little path that led to the tiny mud hut in which He had passed so much time in devotion. Sometimes seated on a rope bed there, at other times stopping along the way, Sant Ji would talk to us. On one of the first days, as we passed the fields of sugar cane stalks, He spoke of the plant metaphorically. The seed was planted, sprouted, and then bore heat, cold, wind, and rain as it grew. When it matured it was cut, then crushed, after which its juice was boiled and boiled. The result was a sweet fruit that everyone enjoyed. Just so was the process of reaching our True Home.

On another walk, Sant Ji explained that He had meditated for many, many years before coming to Master Kirpal. When He did meet the Master, He saw Master as His Liberator. Thus, when Master Kirpal told Him to meditate full time, Sant Ji resisted. He asked Master Kirpal why He needed to mediate full-time, since the Master was going to liberate Him. Sant Ji said He already knew what it was to battle the mind – that it was easier to open one's shirt standing in front of a cannon than to fight the powerful enemy called mind. Further, Sant Ji said, he explained to Master Kirpal that he, Sant Ji, was not going to be liberating anyone – that it was enough that Master would liberate him. At that, Sant Ji told us, Master Kirpal grabbed him by the ear, told him to meditate full-time, and added, "We will see if you are going to liberate anyone else."

The warnings kept on. After a morning meditation, someone asked how clean the soul really has to be, before the Guru would take it up to the higher planes. Sant Ji answered that it had to be very clean – as clean as snow, or as clean as a glass – and He added that those were just images. He spoke of how we might think that we have broken away, but that the cunning mind was waiting to trick us. We may appear to have escaped the five *dacoits* [thieves] of lust, anger, greed, attachment, and egoism in our outer behavior – but the mind was such a force that it simply lay low for a while and then attacked us in our meditations and other places. When He concluded that we did not understand what was required to say good-bye to our faults once and for all, the gnawing inside me began to sound like a roar. Did I really think that I had accomplished anything before I came?

I lost track of time. I was sure it was Wednesday – only to find out it was Thursday. On Friday, the seventeenth of March, as I struggled to convince myself that I was neither "confused or worried," I wrote, "A lot of surgery is happening all the time, and I guess I am such a baby that I still have to be under anesthesia." By this time it had become apparent that something was not right. Instead of being super alert at the evening Satsangs, I struggled to stay awake. Old friends seemed to be avoiding me – expanding the circle of personal space as we passed by in the court-yard. Salutations and smiles appeared frozen and forced to me.

One day a co-worker at Sant Bani School took me aside. He wondered if I were aware that some of the members of the group were talking to Sant Ji about me? Why? I asked. From what he had gathered, my old colleagues were telling Sant Ji that they were quite concerned for me, as I no longer seemed supportive of the Ashram or the School. I had become too independent – I was not my old, friendly, comfortable self. Sant Ji told them He would speak to me, indicating to them that I should not have been acting in the way people described. My desperation grew

– and still there was no time set for me to meet with Him. Crossing boundaries I should not have, I tried to wheedle information from Pappu. He, of course, would tell me nothing of what people were saying to Sant Ji. Still I bugged him, until at last, right before he fell asleep for the night, he gave me a hint: "Well, it is possible that Sant Ji is going to give you a little spanking." I asked him what he meant, but he would say no more – except to tell me not to worry, that I was certain to get exactly what I needed.

By then, six of our ten days had passed, and Sant Ji had not arranged a time to see me. Doubt and pain began to take the place of intoxicated joy, and I searched for the strength that had carried me through the last few months. As I began to feel heavier and heavier, I wondered where the lightness had gone. Was the former strength actually based on a deep-seated pride? Sant Ji said in Satsang, "For the true lovers, the pain never goes away even for one second." I thought, "Is this what I am experiencing? Is this pain just a by-product of the process of cutting, crushing, and boiling the sugar cane, in order to extract sweetness at the end?"

I began to wonder if Sant Ji would ever see me before I left. I imagined climbing aboard the plane in Delhi, still puzzling over when I would get my interview. I tried to tell myself that, even that would be "okay" – as long as it was in His Will, but such self-efforts to quell my rising panic were less than effective. My worries tumbled out in rapid succession. In the past, I had judged people for eating a special diet and keeping to a different meal schedule – was I not doing exactly the same thing now? Was I right to be aloof – especially on a selective basis. Had not Master Kirpal written in a circular on humility something to the effect that it was impossible to be humble if you were all the time thinking about how to be humble? Could I ever be a "Ruby of Rubies" if I was consciously striving to be one? Above all, I knew that I needed to talk to my Father.

Around noon, the message finally came that Sant Ji would be happy to see me, but only after Pappu and I had finished all of the correspondence. In those days, Pappu took all of the English letters to Sant Ji and translated them to Him, one-by-one. After each letter, Sant Ji would dictate a response in Punjabi into a tape recorder. Pappu would take the tape, and, on his own, write out the answer in English. At the end, the stack of letters would be taken to Sant Ji for His approval and signature. There was no typewriter (let alone a computer), so, whenever possible, I wrote while Pappu dictated – which made the process more efficient. I was so happy to hear that Sant Ji would see me, that I went off to get some chai.

Shortly after I returned, Sant Ji came out from His room, saw us both sitting there, and said that we should attend to the correspondence. We started up, but I decided I needed another cup of tea, and headed toward the *langar* [kitchen area] to get it. Sant Ji saw me again as I returned, and this time He said, "*Jaldi! Jaldi karo!*" [Come on, hurry up and do it!] So we hopped right to it, and completed fifteen of the sixty letters before we needed to help serve the lunch.

After we ate, while Pappu was otherwise occupied, I walked out to Sant Ji's hut and sat for meditation, which left me more at peace. In the afternoon we went for a walk and, again, I felt more alert – but I noticed that I had to force myself to do Simran – hardly the "sweet remembrance" described by the Masters. When we paused at the hut, Sant Ji talked about the climate of Rajasthan. He said that it became very hot at times, and that was hard to bear. In our country, He said, we had snow and cold, but in 77 RB the heat was the problem. I began to think He might mention how I had changed the words of the bhajan to describe protection from the cold winds. I was looking for Him to say my name to everyone – and that realization made me so sad. What had happened to not imposing my will over His? What had happened to my protective blanket of love? All at once I felt faint, and seemed to separate from my body. After that I became so tired, that I could have lain down in front of Him and slept. I barely made it back to my bed, where, upon realizing that I was now filled with worry and confusion, I fell into a deep sleep. My last thought was a silly wish that my mother was there to tuck me in with some milk and cookies.

When I awoke it was the hour for evening Satsang. I tried to sit up, but I felt some kind of cosmic weight, sitting on my chest and pinning me to the bed. While I saw nothing, it seemed real enough – all of which was very frightening. I had to force myself to my feet, swinging my upper body back and forth until I heaved it upright. Feeling numb all over, as if I had been given a sedative, I headed for the Satsang. No matter how I struggled, I could not stay awake. I noted the shining radiant faces of my friends and colleagues, but I could not keep my eyes open. At the end I was afraid He would ask me to sing a bhajan – for which I was completely unprepared. He did not, but when a Colombian devotee began to sing what was to become a beloved paean to the Master, He asked me to join with her: *San Yi, San Yi, San Yi – jubilosos Te esperamos* [Sant Ji, Sant Ji, Sant Ji – jubilantly we wait for You].

As we filed out of the place of Satsang, each of us passed by Sant Ji, Who stood at the door, lit by a powerful gas lantern. With His hands folded, He would look into our eyes – sometimes for an extended period of time – and then subtly wave us on. I was filled with shame as my turn approached. What had I to offer Him now, except a consciousness filled with fog? Barely acknowledging my presence as I paused in front of Him, He quickly motioned me on. I stood with the group outside, still eager for His glance to fall on me before He closed the double doors. When the last person had exited, Sant Ji looked once more at everyone but me. He turned to the person next to me, beamed, said "Good night," and disappeared.

My only goal was my bed, and I headed back to my room, feeling somewhat like a snail crawling back through its own trail of slime. I opened the door, stepped over the wooden threshold, and let gravity pull me into a prone position, limbs all askew. My eyelids started to sink when a thought struck with great force: *"Oh God! It is the letters that are standing between us. He said that we need to finish the letters before He will see me. We have to complete all of those letters tonight. We just have to."* But Pappu had stayed behind to talk with Sant Ji so, as I could do nothing alone, I continued to lie on the bed. I drifted off – awakening now and then to the voice of Babu Ji as he attempted to converse with me. When Pappu returned, I awoke once more, determined to do everything I could to remove any obstacle keeping me from time with Sant Ji.

It took all of my strength to sit up. I announced to Pappu that I was ready for more letters, adding that we absolutely had to finish them tonight. Pappu, who knew how tired and emotionally drained I was, looked at me in disbelief and said, "Get some sleep!" When I protested, he said, "I have a headache and cannot work now. I have to get a massage. You are ready – but I am not. It is not your fault. Now, go to bed!"

What a relief. Like Christian in *The Pilgrim's Progress*, I felt a burden drop from me. I had been ready to do what Sant Ji asked – even if it required an extraordinary effort. It may not have been much of a test – but for me it was enormous, and I lay back with an overwhelming feeling that, while things were not over, it was wonderful to think that there might be an end in sight.

At three the next morning I got up and stepped out to awaken Pathi Ji, so that he could begin to prepare the chai for the Westerners. My preferred spot for pre-dawn meditation was the *langar*, the partially covered kitchen area with simple clay ovens heated by open fires. I sat for a long time without moving, and the Simran was sweet once again. Now and then I would become aware of Sant Ji sitting in His room, as He cleared His throat, or coughed quietly. It came to me that the time would soon come when I would not have ready access to such divine reminders of His presence. The longer I sat there, the more I ached to be with Him. The day before He had said that nothing was more beautiful than the Radiant Form of the Master, and, while I prayed to remember that, I really wished to be sitting and talking with Him.

When Bant came over to make tea for Sant Ji, I could not stop myself from wishing for some of that elixir. I went to get my cup, all the while practicing clever things I could say to Bant in Hindi to let her know my desire. With God's Grace, I saw what I was doing and stopped. I thought, "Let Him take care of you, for God's sake! Let Him take care of you!" As I settled down to meditate once more, Parmeshri approached and stood in front of me. She held out a cup of chai – poured from the surplus prepared for Sant Ji – and I bowed my head and smiled. As I drank it I wondered, "How many times will Sant Ji have to send me yet another lesson of 'exactly what I need'?"

The more I thought about it, the more I understood that I was suffering from an acute case of spiritual vanity. I had never been above judging others – but since October I had allowed that "skill" to run wild. I judged people if they ate – I judged them if they didn't. I criticized what they ate – and what they did not. I saw who slept, and who stayed awake – and now it was all crashing in on me. He had said we should finish the letters before seeing Him, so I thought about what He wrote in one of them. He lovingly explained that the mind is a great trickster who generally does not allow the soul to get off the earth plane. And when mind does allow that, it comes up with a whole bunch more tricks to play on the soul – anything to keep it from reaching its True Home. Had much of what I had experienced been nothing more than the tricks of my mind – designed to trap me here more? Feeling bruised and shaken, I sat by myself, slowly dipping another glucose biscuit into my warm parshad chai. Today was the day – a day for letting go – a day for growth. I knew that He would have much to say to me. My first prayer was that I would have the strength to bear His Words. The second was that I could hear and accept Them.

My First Interview – Saturday, March 18th

Pappu was with Sant Ji, so I sat on my bed, waiting to be called. Feeling somewhat on trial – knowing that others had already "testified" against me – I asked myself, "Well, do you have any last words?" I made a decision not to tape the session, as, on more than one occasion when Sant Ji had spoken to me about deep personal matters, He had asked that the recorder be turned off. I did not want a whirring machine between us.[2]

Sant Ji was seated in a chair when I entered His room, and I immediately knelt down and placed my forehead on His feet. He lifted me up, so I was sitting on the floor, very close in front of Him. He welcomed me, "*Ji hunh – Swagat hai!*" – referring to me as "Kent Bicknell, Principal Sahib." I looked at Him, smiled, and said in Hindi, "Sant Ajaib Singh, God Himself!" No, no, He responded quickly, explaining that He was the servant of the Sadhus. I quoted a line from His bhajan: *Banda banke aaya, Rab banda banke aaya* [After becoming a man, God came] which He had written about Master Kirpal. My intent was to say that Sant Ji was God Himself. Choosing not to respond to this audacious outburst, He looked at me gently and said, "Yes, what do you have for me? Tell me everything."

For the next hour and a quarter – until Sant Ji stopped me – I opened my heart and told in great detail everything that had been happening to me. I talked and talked, pausing only long enough for Pappu to translate every five minutes or so. I reviewed my "progress" – telling much of what I have written above and in the previous chapter.

I began by saying that, after a decade on the Path, I had prayed that I might begin to live up to all that I had been given. I spoke about the hours I was sitting in daily meditation, the efforts to make the Simran constant, the successes in gaining control over my tongue – and in maintaining a chaste mode of life. I told Him how I sat on a wooden floor with no pillows – for hours at a time with no backrest. I mentioned how much I had enjoyed visiting other spiritual centers dedicated to Him

---

[2] The content of this interview and the two that follow was reconstructed from extensive notes taken immediately afterward. The notes were then reviewed with Pappu, who amplified some areas and added precision to others. The words in quotes are thus not transcribed from a tape – but are as accurate as the immediate recall of two who were present permitted. The content is very precise.

– and that it felt good to be coming close to other devotees who were very serious about the Path.

Sant Ji nodded His head affirmatively when I explained that I took references to me as, for example, a "Ruby of Rubies," as goals toward which I should strive. I understood that those were my orders from Him – that He wanted me to be strong, and not to be worried or confused. Again He nodded. And He got out a handkerchief and wiped His eyes, when I told Him that I was trying to develop a respectful love – such as the kind Master Kirpal Singh wrote about in a letter to His Master, Baba Sawan Singh.

I explained that I was tired of listening to person after person share how much they had gained from their trip to India – only to hear them talk about how they had lost or forgotten everything within months after their return. I wanted to be able to hold onto the spiritual seeds, and help them grow in His physical absence. Attempting to choose my words carefully, I criticized certain old friends and colleagues by "expressing concern" for them. I worried about how Sant Bani Ashram was being run, and mentioned that I had grown distant from Judith and Russell specifically. As an example, I mentioned that one day Russell had gotten quite upset at me because I was going to be visiting another center for the weekend, and I would not be available to do the Sunday Satsang for him when he needed to be away.

I even raised questions about some of the sevadars of 77 RB – wondering if they were able to meditate enough given their schedules. Referring to an older fellow, I mentioned that I was concerned when I heard Westerners singing his praises. They continually talked about what a great sevadar he was, to his face, and also when they spoke about their trips upon returning to America.

At that point, Sant Ji interrupted my monologue. He said, "All right, I have heard you. Now let me tell you some things. And I hope that you will not be too upset by these words, but will take them for your benefit." I sucked in my breath and said, "Well Baba Ji, You can give me a beating if You want, but please tell me what I need to hear."

He explained that even though He was very aware of everything I had told Him, still He had listened carefully to each word I had said. And, He added, He understood it all. He then said that while my understanding of what He expected of me had been correct, still He had some things to say to me. First of all, He wanted to tell me about the 77 RB sevadar to whom I had referred. In His own life, He always had the habit of just catching on to His Master. He caught Master Kirpal, and no one else. He neither praised nor blamed the people around Master Kirpal. He added that perhaps that was why Master had asked Him to live off by Himself – as then He only caught hold of Master Kirpal.

He spoke about those who praised the Indian sevadars for doing the work at the Ashram. If that is what the Western devotees saw, then that is all they took with them when they left. Who was it, He asked, Who was really doing all of the work? Right before the last group had left, the Westerners sang a song of praise written in honor of that elder sevadar. And, Sant Ji said, that poor man had been so pleased that he did not even try to stop them from singing. Then he had become puffed up – his ego got big – and he had fallen. Sant Ji added, "So if you hear people praising the sevadars, you should tell them that the sevadars are going to lose from that, as well as the ones who are praising. Tell them to just catch the Master and no one else."

He said that while He had love and respect for me, He loved and respected Russell and Judith as well. He pointed out that the Westerners owed something to Russell, as we all had come to Sant Ji through his efforts. He reminded me that He had given a talk about the Negative Power to all of the sevadars at Sant Bani Ashram in New Hampshire.[3] He reiterated: if people are living together in harmony, without interruption, then the Negative Power comes in and stirs things up. It disturbs the dear ones – that is the nature of things. But, with Grace, the devotees can get back together. He added that we should listen to that talk one hundred times.

I had told Him that there were some who thought the vegetarian diet at the Ashram was not conducive enough to real spiritual growth – that sugar, dairy products, and other kinds of foods should be drastically reduced, if not eliminated. He commented that the Ashram should not adopt a new diet, but should continue as it had been doing. If things had changed since He had left in August of 1977, then the Ashram should go back to its old ways. He advised us to sit together as a board of directors and to run the Ashram.

At that point He told me that, in some ways, my strength was causing the Ashram to fail. He affirmed that He expected me to be strong, and He reminded me that if I failed, hundreds would fail also. My strength was not taking the right form – what I needed, He said, was patience. He told me that I was wise, I had a cool heart, and I was strong.

---

[3] See "The Enemy Within" in *The Ambrosial Hour*, pp. 87-95, and Chapter Four above.

Therefore it was up to me to show leadership in the Ashram – not to pull away from people. And He repeated: I should be patient.

In the beginning I had tried to say that I was not really criticizing others – that I was simply observing, and trying to learn from the behavior of others. Sant Ji reminded me that in Colombia He told me to ignore the faults of others. If I had followed that good advice, He said, then none of this would have happened. If people have faults, and because of those faults they decide to leave the Ashram, then how will they ever learn to overcome those faults?

And, He added, suppose you replace those people with others whose faults are even greater? Sant Ji advised me that if, in the future, I felt I could not bear the faults of any of my colleagues, then I should pass those faults on to Him – He could bear them. Then He said something very powerful, and He repeated it several times: *If the Ashram were to fail, the worldly people would laugh. And only then would the mind realize what a terrible thing it had done.*

He observed that I already knew His condition: He was a *fakir*, and He would rather have had a different program for Himself. He would rather have spent the time underground, sitting all alone in the remembrance of Hazur Kirpal. Because of our love, however, He had become involved with us. At any moment, however, He could break that. He was very happy to be with Almighty Hazur Kirpal, as the Love of Master Kirpal was enough for Him. He did not need our love.

He reminded me that He had planned to begin the work of translating Kabir's *Anurag Sagar [The Ocean of Love]* when He got back from the Tour. He had not started that seva yet, because He knew that all of this turmoil was going on at the Ashram in New Hampshire. He would not begin that work, He added, until He got a letter from us saying that everything was back to the way it had been before. In both the Ashram and the School, He said, we should go back to the way we were doing things before He left in August. When I returned to Sant Bani, Sant Ji said, I should embrace Russell, ask for his forgiveness, and walk with him. I should also inform Russell that Sant Ji Himself had told me to do all of that. Sant Ji then asked me if I had read the letter that He wrote to Russell saying that I was a good soul and could assist with the Initiations? I said, "Yes. You wrote that I have love and appreciation for Russell in my heart." He laughed, and said, "Yes, and I will write that in the future too!" He added that people were upset by the fact that Pappu and I communicated so much, as they imagined I might be keeping information about Sant Ji to myself. In the future, He suggested, I could send messages to Pappu via Him – and that way no one would be bothered.

Sant Ji commented on visiting other places to meditate, again refer-ring to my need for patience. If you live at an Ashram, He asked, then why do you need to find another place to meditate? What would people think when they saw a responsible person from Sant Bani Ashram going away to another spiritual center? Master Kirpal had told Him that all He had to do was stay in one place and meditate, and the fragrance would come out and attract the devotees. I should continue with my medita-tions, He concluded, but I should also have patience. And, I should return to my old way of being involved at Sant Bani.

As we neared the end of the two hours, my mind was working overtime to process what had just been happening. At that point, I felt that He was neither displeased nor pleased with me. The image that entered my head was of a little kid who crawled behind the wheel of a powerful vehicle and began to drive in a wild manner – careening dangerously out of control. Sant Ji was the loving father who said, "Oh my God – he has got to be stopped or he is going to kill himself and others also!" and did something about it. What it felt like was love more than displeasure. At the same time, I was very close to plunging into a whirling vortex of total confusion, and the tears were streaming down my cheeks.

When we were done, I pulled myself up off the floor, and He stood up beside me and put His arm around me. He assured me that we would talk more, as He would give me time the following day. He added, "My heart is always with you." Then He looked deeply into my eyes and con-tinued, very quietly and with so much love, "You should tell people to catch hold of Kirpal only – just as I caught hold of Him." I grabbed hold of His sleeve and said, "Can I catch You?" He squeezed me very hard at that, laughed, and said, "Go jolly!"

I left His presence, and immediately returned to my quarters, determined to capture everything I could remember from the session. I lay on my bed, recording thought after thought as they tumbled out. Pap-pu had other work, but each time he came back to the room, I would verify the accuracy of another part of the interview. I spoke and reflected for a long time, and, when I was done, all I could think of was how much I wanted a glass of milk and a plateful of cookies. I got up from the bed and headed toward the langar to fulfill my desire. As I passed by the small mirror in our room, I glanced at the image looking back at me and stopped. I was struck – as never before – that rather than the grinning face of perpetual adolescence – what I saw was a man of thirty years.

I felt much better – much lighter – and I knew that He had begun to work His magic on me. I reasoned that Sant Ji did not tell me I was all wrong. Rather, He had indicated that I had gone about things in a way that was not correct. He had not told me to stop. I needed patience and I needed to be accessible – not distant. Sant Ji had analyzed it all for me. Clearly, it was not a loving thing to sit up in my house, feeling that I was strong in my meditation and strong in my Simran, judging and condemning everyone. While some people had tried to tell me that, apparently, it had taken Sant Ji's words for me to see. And not just His words, I thought. After all, I had been dying to see Him from the moment I arrived, but He had made me wait a week – until I felt that He had become distant and aloof from me. I concluded that I was "wrong in my rightness," in the way I had done it – which somehow felt better than just being wrong. I was very happy at the thought of seeing Him on the morrow. Little did I know that the spiritual surgery had just begun.

That afternoon we went on a walk that was out of this world. I felt a spring in my step, and every single person in the group seemed to be intoxicated – drunk on divine love. When we returned to the compound, Pappu and I were able to complete several more letters before it was time for the evening Satsang. And what a Satsang it was. Sant Ji sat and radiated, talking only through His eyes. My favorite singers, Bant and Parmeshri, sang several bhajans, including, *Mai to Kirpal se Vicherde ke, Roi Re* [Being separated from Kirpal, I wept], *Jiske Sir Upar Tu Swami* [One who has You over his head, O Lord, how can he suffer any pain?], and *Santa di Mehima Ji, Sun Le Mita, Sun Le Mita* [Listen, O friend, to the Glory of the Saints]. Everything about the Satsang, from beginning to end, was exquisitely beautiful, as it was permeated by such a strong sense of overflowing love. This was the fragrance that Master Kirpal said would come of its own from Sant Ji. At times I felt a pain in my heart so acute that I had to press my chest with my hand. The Tavern finally closed, and one-by-one we left – looking totally sated as we filed by, said "Good night," and floated back to our beds.

The Second Interview – Sunday, March 19th

The next morning, Sunday the nineteenth of March, I listened to the tape of my notes from the day before. While most of them made sense, I kept cringing at how arrogant I sounded. I had recorded that I was, "wrong in my rightness" – what on earth did that mean? Did my ego have no boundaries? Had I really heard what He was telling me? As I recalled how critical of others I had been in my opening diatribe, and as I chewed over the sheer pompous audacity of it all, I wanted to crawl back under the cotton quilt. I got the distinct feeling that there was more to come. I pondered what I would say when I went for a second interview, and knew that I had some deep apologizing to do. Not for the first time (nor the last, by any means) I took great comfort in the fact that, at the least, Sant Ji would be able to see whatever I brought in its real colors – and that He would know what to do with it, even if I did not.

I came into His room and dove down into the shrine of His feet. When I came up for air, He asked me if I felt better. I said that I did, and added that my stomach had been upset from eating too much *halvah* [a traditional Indian dessert – very sweet and laden with clarified butter]. Obviously He had meant more than my physical health.

I attempted to apologize to Him for all of my faults. In particular, I felt badly about being so critical of others. I began with the sevadars at 77 RB, expressing remorse that I had judged any of them. Sant Ji responded that those simple farmers came here for ten days only to serve us. They did not live at the Ashram, but left their homes and work in order to do the seva, so that the Westerners could come to meditate. After serving us all day, Sant Ji explained, they stayed up and had time with Him – and they needed to sleep in the early morning hours when we, who had retired early, could meditate.

He again remarked how important it was that we not bring gifts for the sevadars at the Ashram. He told me to announce that publicly. At present, He said, the villagers came to serve out of love. If they started to accept the gifts that people brought, then they might begin to look for bigger gifts, and that would affect their spirituality. In the end they would come to serve in order to receive the gifts – not out of love for the Master – and that would be very bad for them, for us, and for the Ashram.

At that moment I was sure I was going to burst into tears and collapse on His shoes, but I managed to nod and keep quiet. He leaned closer and, once again, began to speak, saying that He wished to tell me some things. First of all, He said, I had to be involved at the Ashram as I had been before. I had to relate to Russell as I had in the past. As far as the School went, it was the same. I should not hire a teacher without consulting everyone.[4] Then He repeated that powerful point from the day before, only this time He added the School as well: it would be very bad if the Ashram and the School should fail. In fact, He said, if the Ashram and the School should fail, *it would be the greatest trick Lord Kal could play*!

A friend had written a letter to Sant Ji, and asked me to personally deliver it to Him, but I had forgotten to bring it the day before. The devotee who wrote it had been very supportive of my increased spiritual zeal. I had been somewhat afraid the letter might praise my recent efforts – but, as I had no way to judge the contents, and I had accepted the charge of hand-delivering it to the Saint, I chose that moment to pass it to Him. Pappu started to translate aloud for Sant Ji, and I could follow enough to know that it did, indeed, have many flattering things to say about me.

After a page or so, Sant Ji turned to Pappu, held up His hand, and said, "Stop reading!" He turned back to me. I hung my head, mumbling that I had thought of throwing that letter into the fire, but had felt obligated to bring it to Him. He responded in a low voice, "It would have been better if you had thrown it in the fire." I sank further. And then He began.

"I don't love Kent," He stated, "I love My Master sitting inside you. That is what I love. That is the Ruby you have to become. I made you the Ruby of Rubies to become Master Kirpal's Ruby – not to become a ruby of the world. The ruby attracts flies. You should become the real Ruby, and not be down in the dust." He noted that in the letter I was being praised as if I were a god – and in the same way I had been praising my new friends. Then He remarked, "And you have not even talked to me about your family. You have not been telling me about Chrissy, and Nicky, and Karen." I thought it could not get worse, until He added, "I am giving you my love. Could you not at least have brought me some love from Karen, Chris, and Nick? Their love is the only love you need to bring me."

He told me not to be involved in either giving or receiving that kind of praise in the future. I should go on with my meditations and spiritual practices, but I should not be involved with people in such a worldly way, because in the end one gets nothing but kicked by it. After saying all of that, He combined a sigh and a soft chuckle, and asked, "Do you

---

[4] I cannot recall doing this, but apparently some of my colleagues, worried I might, had discussed this with Sant Ji.

have any more of those letters for me?" Through my shame and tears, I shook my head – No.

At last, words fled me. I was stunned and shaken. The arrogance and pride, thank God, were gone – crushed under the weight of my humiliation. I sat and wept before Him. Sant Ji did not rush to comfort me in an obvious manner. He did not say, "Oh, that is all right – just go on from here." Instead, He reminded me of the advice He had given me in May of 1977, when I told Him I longed for the day He would call me a "good meditator." He had ordered me not to think like that, He said, as it would not be good for me. And He had related the story of the disciple who was being praised by others as a good meditator. That man's Guru had been forced to use the shield of public insult and rebuke, in order to save the roots of the disciple's spirituality. Sant Ji repeated that it was far better to be rebuked by the Master than to be praised in public, as those who are praised tend to get lazy in their spiritual practices. [5]

A glimmer of hope came over me. No one could deny that He had just rebuked me – so perhaps there was a bottom to all of this. He continued to gaze at me, with great love and compassion flowing from His physical frame. No words were spoken for a short time. Then a new feeling entered the room. It felt as if a skilled surgeon had just completed a particularly difficult aspect of a delicate operation – and time was needed to see if the patient would accept or reject the results.

I recovered my voice, and apologized for what I called "my idiocy." He was gracious, and nodded His enormous head. I asked, "So, I should go on strong with my meditation – as I was before – only I should have patience and love, and not be separate from people?" He responded with a vigorous, "Yes!" And then, with an extraordinary blend of love, humor, compassion, and wisdom, He summed it up for me in the simplest terms imaginable: "I want you to go back to being the old Kent!"

Sant Ji hugged me again, and I left His room. I walked back in a dense fog – the thoughts piling down on me like hewn trees into a river logjam. How could I turn the tangled mess into an ordered pile of logs – to mill into lumber and rebuild the structure of my life? Had I really made a wreck of everything – including my relationship with Sant Ji – by becoming overzealous in the name of spirituality? That thought was terrifying to me – like a great abyss where I saw myself teetering on the edge. I looked at Pappu, and he, with much concern for my emotional state, suggested that perhaps I should not try to figure everything out

---

[5] See Chapter Four, above.

right then. He advised me to forget about it, saying it would become clear later on. My head sank back into my pillow, and I heard an unfamiliar sound. It may have been the call of an exotic bird from the courtyard wall, or perhaps the lowing of the newborn heifer in the nearby manger. Before I could put any meaning to it, however, I sank into a deep sleep.

Monday, the Twentieth of March

Sant Ji had made it clear to a few old friends and colleagues that He would say something to me before the trip was over – and people were aware that He saw me for a couple of long sessions toward the end. Several friends, with whom I had had very little recent communication, were anxious to talk with me – to find out how I was doing now that Sant Ji had addressed the problems at the Ashram. Perhaps because I was suddenly so very tender, it felt a little like "open season on Kent!" A co-worker and good friend shook her head as we talked and said, "You know, it is so amazing Kent. You are such a loving and devoted disciple – how could it happen? And who will the Kal Power get a hold of next?" It floored me a bit to realize that all of the recent stresses and strains at the Ashram were now understood to have resulted from the Negative Power manifesting within me. All I said was, "Yes. Spiritual vanity is a really big trap." My next interchange with another old friend was too much however.

This person approached me and said that she really wanted to talk to me. I said, "Of course," and we found a quiet, shady corner of the courtyard. The first thing she conveyed was that Sant Ji had told her that He had left such a wealth of spirituality behind at Sant Bani, that the Negative Power could not stand it. So that Kal Power came and manifested in the mind. I noted her use of the singular, "mind," but did not respond. She told me that I had not been myself for the last few months. She had felt that the person sitting in that office at School was no longer me – it wasn't the kind fellow that she had known for ten years. I did not disagree – how could I? But I did express some confusion as to how everything could have come to pass when I was trying so hard – when I was doing so much meditation. She had an answer.

"Well," she said, "I really hate to say this right now, as it might be much better for you to hear it directly on the tape of my interview, but when I asked Sant Ji about that very thing, He said that you were not really meditating! He explained that if you had been truly meditating, you would have been forgiving the faults of others, not criticizing them." I was completely shattered, and could find no response. She looked at me with a concern mixed with pity, smiled sweetly, patted my arm, and left me alone to reflect. I thought, "Sant Ji told her that all of those hours I sat for meditation were not really meditation? Does that mean what I thought was spiritual progress, was really only opening the door for Lord Kal to come in and destroy what Sant Ji had left us? How could that be? And if it is so, then what is the point? As Sant Ji had said to Master Kirpal, why sit for hours and hours when He is going to liberate us – especially since the fruits of my meditation appeared to be rotten?"

There were just too many unanswered questions ricocheting off the walls of my heart and my head, and I knew I needed one more private session with Him. I also felt very deeply – as deeply as ever – that He absolutely knew what He was doing with me – and that it would become clear at some point. With that as a guiding directive, I worked to remain open to whatever might come my way before I could see Him the next morning – the last of our stay in Rajasthan.

That evening in Satsang, Sant Ji discoursed on a hymn of Sant Kabir that was all about hypocrisy. He talked at length about the crane that tried to look like a beautiful swan. In the end, the crane's true nature came out when it ate the fish. Sant Ji told us not to think that others had any spiritual power, no matter what they did, unless it was the Saint Himself. That message went directly into my heart. At the end of the Satsang, Eric Perkins and I sang, *Asi Mele Satguru Ji, Oojal Karde, Oojal Karde* [We are dirty, O Satguru: clean us, clean us]. When we came to the line that says, "We are foolish – You are wise and clever," I could not help but break into a big smile. Sant Ji looked right at me, nodded His Head most lovingly, and smiled right back.

At some point during the Satsang, Sant Ji observed that there were two people who would criticize you. The first was the Saint. In a very loving and sweet way, He would point out your faults to you. The second person was your enemy. Your enemy would come to you right away and say your faults the very first thing. I was most appreciative when, after the Satsang, the friend who had been so anxious to share with me what Sant Ji had said, came and apologized for being so direct with me.

As I lay on my rope bed that last evening, I began to have second thoughts about my plan to stay an extra few days at 77 RB after the group left. I was anxious to see my family – and I wondered how Karen might feel if, days before I returned, she had to hear from others how the Kal Power had manifested in me. Besides, was I really ready to sit for long hours of meditation? I decided to ask Sant Ji for an update on my plan to stay.

Public Rebuke and the Needed Third Interview
Tuesday, March 21st, 1978

The morning meditation was the best one I experienced on the whole trip. A spontaneous silent prayer had arisen as soon as I closed my eyes: "Look Sant Ji, I really need your help. I cannot do this alone. I am not strong in anything without You. I am nothing without You." And Sant Ji was very helpful to me.

After the meditation, Sant Ji gave a very powerful talk. He likened all of the disciples to frogs. The Master spent time gathering all of the frogs and gently placing them in a basket – only to have them jump out again. The process then repeated. He also spoke of the process of attachment between two people. When you love someone, He said, you begin to eat with that person, and then to sleep with that person – basically to spend all of your time with that person. You feel pain when you have to part. But, such is the nature of attachment, that the day may come when you hate that person, and never want to see him/her again. Sant Ji advised that we should never develop such a love for someone that we feel pain at parting or at separation – except the Satguru. We should develop that kind of love for the Master.

Towards the end, Sant Ji went into detail as to how the Master prepared the disciple when He wished to give him something. The Master does not shower Grace on that dear one publicly – nor does He praise that disciple. Instead, He rebukes that soul in front of all the people. He prepares the vessel by publicly rebuking the disciple. That is how the Master makes the disciple ready to receive a gift of Grace.

At the end, Sant J asked that parshad be distributed to everyone. As Pappu was handing me a bag of *patasa* [thin sugar wafers], Sant Ji looked at me, laughed, and, for all to hear, asked, "Who are you going to give your parshad to, Principal Sahib?" Right away I called back, "My family!" He continued, "Oh, not to him who praises you?" and really laughed. I got it instantly – and laughed from my heart. I was amazed. I never told Him how I had reserved that box of rock candy to give to my new, "special" friends, but He knew. Given everything else I had been through, I felt most content to be receiving a very public rebuke from Sant Ji – my All Knowing *Pita Ji* [Beloved Father]. As soon as He left the room, a friend turned to me and commented, "Whoa! That was a surprise!" I flashed a Cheshire-cat smile, and said softly, "Nope, not to me."

Everyone left to finish packing for the return to Delhi, but I knew that Sant Ji would come back into the room, so I remained. He came in, saw me, and began to speak in Hindi. He told me that I should go finish getting ready, adding that, as He was coming down with us, we could talk again in Delhi. Instead of leaving, I began to cry. Pappu returned, and I tried to speak, but again the tears came. I knew what I had to do. I knew what the key was for unlocking my tongue.

Sometimes the Guru says that there is no need for us to tell Him everything that we have done – for He already knows it all. In this case, while I knew that He already knew, I also knew that I had to confess before Him.

Back at His house in New Hampshire I had taken something from His bedroom – something that I had no right to have. Filled with remorse, I withdrew a small plastic packet of cardamom seeds from my pocket, and held it out towards Sant Ji. I pleaded, "Please, Baba Ji – Let me take care of this first."

Just as I had explained everything to Pappu the night before, so Pappu told Sant Ji. That packet of *laichee* [cardamom] had been left by Sant Ji in His house at Sant Bani Ashram. Alongside the spice, He had kept a box of cassettes – the recordings of Bant and Parmeshri singing bhajans under the desert skies of Rajasthan. These were the very tapes He had recorded when He borrowed my machine the year before – the same ones He had played sitting all alone in the bedroom at Sant Bani. I had a key to the Master's house, and, I had taken His words – that His house was my house – way too deeply to heart. On occasion, I had slipped into the house and sat for meditation. As I was familiar with His bedroom and where things were kept, I had brought a small tape recorder a couple of times, and played the sweet tapes of the village girls singing. I had seen the packet of cardamom seeds, and, in a moment I had thought was complete remembrance, I took a few as parshad. The rationalization had come quickly. I thought that perhaps Sant Ji had left those there for me. I had had grave second thoughts, however, as I understood that I was caught up in complete forgetfulness – not remembrance. All I could think to do was to bring the rest of the seeds back to Him in Rajasthan, and tell Him how very sorry I was.

The three of us were still standing. Sant Ji did not take the cardamom, but left them in my hand. He said, "Well, I brought those with me from India for a purpose, and also I left those tapes of Bant in there for a purpose." He graciously added that I could listen to the tapes, "If you don't ruin them."

Finally I could talk. I told Him that I thought I should go back with the group rather than stay. I said that I was afraid Karen would have to hear how I was the cause of all of the problems – that I had been overtaken by the Negative Power. Sant Ji told me to go back with the group. The Kal Power does not just come in one person's mind, He explained, it comes in everyone's mind. That is how it gets manifested. The reason that the Negative Power had the opportunity to come in, was because the dear ones were not being strong in their devotion, in their Bhajan and Simran. He added that the blame for that is to be shared by everyone.

He leant toward me and said, "You have to do more meditation." I spluttered, "But I thought You said my meditation was not real. Someone told me that You said if I had been doing real meditation, then I would have been forgiving the faults of the other sevadars." I continued, "I did not know whether to believe that person or not, but it made me afraid. If the Kal Power can come when I am meditating . . ." and He stopped me.

"First of all," He began, "Keep on with your meditations." He added that it is difficult to understand what meditation really is. Then He looked at me more intently, and stated, "I said that to protect you. Because you are the principal, and you have a great responsibility to do with that School. Yes, you should definitely go back with the group, because who knows what might be said? But you go on with your meditation. Go on with your devotion."

He continued, "You have to become the Ruby of Kirpal, not the ruby of the worldly love. The people who were praising you were losing by it, and you were losing by it as well. If only the praise had been for the Satguru, then something would have been gained by it. When people come like that to praise you, don't accept their praise. Just love them. Love everybody."

I apologized again to Him for coming in such a state – so full of myself. I said that I was very sorry. He nodded and said, "Yes. Don't come again proud like you were – puffed up – feeling that you were something – like you talked to me the other day." He told me that I should not fast – that it was not good for me to go a day without eating anything. He smiled and added, "And it does not matter to me whether you sit on a wooden floor or use the pillows!" We both laughed.

It was time to go. Sant Ji beamed even more broadly, and asked "Will you give my love to Chrissy and Nicky and Karen?" And I said, "Oh, yes! Can I hug and kiss them for You?" He laughed and answered, "*Hunh, hunh!*" [Yes, yes!]. Then He grabbed me in a big bear hug and said, "If Karen were here I would be hugging her just like this." And He hugged me harder. Ever so sweetly, He suggested that I keep the cardamom seeds as parshad, adding that I should take them when I meditate.[6]

I stood wrapped in my gold meditation robe – the same one I had covered Him with on the plane from Bombay to Boston as we flew to America – on His first trip to the West. Bowing to Him, I took a step back, preparing to leave. Something snagged, however, to the point of stopping me. I looked down, and Sant Ji was standing on the corner of my robe. I smiled and said, "Ah-ha! Caught by the Guru!" and we all laughed. I was bursting with happiness. God had forgiven my enormous folly. As a last word I said, "Please don't let this frog jump out of your basket. I will try to stay in it." I floated out of the room and back to my quarters, lighter than I had felt the entire stay. I gathered my belongings and prepared to make the long trek back to the noise and confusion of Delhi.

Wednesday, the Twenty-second of March – Back in Delhi

We were given more opportunities to see Sant Ji in Delhi, as He did a program for satsangis in the city. A large number of Indian devotees came to the mid-morning Satsang. I sat down in the back of the room, happy to be able to gaze from afar and to have a wall to lean against. Sant Ji spotted me, however, and asked me to sing. I chose *Sachya Guru Meharbana* [O True Benefactor, dye my garment in the saffron color of the Name of the Lord]. The Satsang was in Punjabi, with no translation from Pappu. I paid close attention to see what I could gather, and surprised myself by being able to follow more than usual. Sant Ji used an

---

[6] I have never thought that the original "purpose" Sant Ji referred to in relation to the cardamom seeds was that He brought them for me. Far from it. I understand His gifting them to me as a concession He made – something sacrificed for my benefit – perhaps to save me from my own arrogance. While the cardamom incident was the most tempting thing to drop from this book – it cannot be deleted from my life.

image from field hockey that I could not get, so I asked Pappu about it afterwards. Sant Ji had said that one should be devoted in the same way that the player is in field hockey. No matter how fierce the opposition was, still the skilled and determined player took the ball to the other end and scored the goal. In the same way, we should do the devotion of the Lord.

Sant Ji held Satsang again in the afternoon, and that was very charged as well. Before He began the discourse, Sant Ji called upon Eric Perkins and me for a bhajan, so we sang *Dekhi Bahot Nirali Mehima* [We have seen the unique greatness of Satsang]. When Sant Ji asked me for another bhajan, I wondered if I should sing *Nach Re Man Nach Re:* "Dance, O mind, dance in front of the Satguru. Sing the praises of Satguru, so that you may cut the sin of birth – " the hymn which He had discoursed on at Sant Bani when I was the *pathi* [chanter]. He responded enthusiastically, *"Hunh! Hunh!"* [Yes! Yes!] When I sang that hymn, something further melted inside me. I felt the arrow of His love sink straight into my heart.

Throughout the remainder of the Satsang, Sant Ji looked so radiantly beautiful that the word that came to mind and stuck was, "Gorgeous!" He used many of the lines from *Nach Re Man Nach Re* to explain things in the talk, including how the great Yogis like Narada had fallen in just one second. The Indian devotees sat and listened to every word, every nuance. Sant Ji laughed and joked with them, gently admonishing everyone to leave off bad habits and cultivate good ones. As the waves of His love swept over us, the crowd seemed to ripple like stalks of wheat under a soft wind – only this field was a splash of bright silken colors. He ended by saying that when we are near the physical Master, we remember Him and think He is good – but as soon as we get away from His presence, we forget.

Wednesday Evening – The Final Night

That evening I experienced symptoms of the fast approaching "agony of separation" more than ever before in my life. At times I had trouble breathing, and the pain in my heart was enough that I had to apply pressure with my right hand. Yet it was beautiful. Sant Ji told us that when we went back to our homes, we would get caught up in our worldly lives again, and we would forget. All He had, however, was our remembrance – so imagine how much more He would be missing us! He observed that those devotees who really love and recognize the Guru are few. In the end, He commented on *Dhan Dhan Satguru Mera Jehda, Vicherdeya Nu Melada* [Hail, Hail to my Satguru, Who reunites the separated ones], and looked at me with a grand smile.

The physical *dénouement* was swift and sweet. Pappu's sister Bimla kindly stuffed my pockets with parshad for the long flight home. As we loaded up for the airport, Sant Ji stood by the bus door and gave each person *darshan* – love-filled transmissions from His eyes to ours. When my turn came, I could not stop myself from attempting to bend and touch His feet. Before I could get very far, Sant Ji grabbed my folded hands, and pulled me upright. In a quivering voice, I said, *"Te amo,"* and He answered, *"Gracias."* I climbed aboard and plunked in a seat next to the door. Sant Ji came up the steps and stood in the aisle for a last good-bye to all. He stopped right in front of me, and His feet were right below. No one could see – and the image of how I first touched the feet of Master Kirpal flashed before me.[7] I quickly bent and touched His feet. When I popped back up, He looked down at me, and broke into a big smile.

I was very sad to be leaving His presence, but I finally felt able to function. I felt like I could, "Go jolly," as He had ordered me to do. I realized that, to tell the truth, I did not know Him at all. I had absolutely no idea of Who He really was and What He could do. But I also understood that all He was asking of me was, that I do my best with what I had been given. Like Popeye, I felt, "I yam what I yam!" and that was acceptable. In terms of knowing who I "really" was, well, as He had told me: "Go back to being the old Kent."

A very important event occurred moments after I returned to Sant Bani Ashram. I walked across the field that separated Russell and Judith's house from mine, knocked on the door, went in, and embraced Russell. I apologized to him, and then we "walked and talked together." I told him that while Sant Ji had asked me to do that, it was coming straight from my heart as well. Russell was very kind and gracious to me. I also said that Sant Ji awaited a letter from us, stating that we were back on track, before He would begin working on the *Anurag Sagar [The Ocean of Love]*. Russell composed a letter in English, and, after I translated it into Hindi, we sent it off directly to Sant Ji on the twenty-seventh of March. Russell wrote:

---

[7] See Chapter One.

Beloved Sant Ji:

I lay my head in Your blessed lap. I bow down to the dust of Your Holy Feet. Kent is my true brother and friend. You have made everything better than it ever was. My gratitude knows no bounds. Kent and I will work for You together, as brothers, with the help and cooperation of everyone. Everything is perfect.

Please write The Anurag Sagar as quickly as is convenient for You, as the world is waiting for that blessed and holy book. Please, please do not delay on account of our foolishness. That is over and done with. We both promise. I will see You in October, God Willing.

> *Russell*

Sant Ji wrote directly back to us on the fourteenth of April, and I translated the letter for Russell:

My Beloved Kent, Karen, and Russell Perkins,

Your letter of 27 March came to me. I read it and came to know all the contents. I am happy that in Hazur's Love you will all be working together. It is my wish that Hazur will bless you, and the means for getting His Grace is meditation. With your work, you should always always meditate also. Soon I will begin the writing of The Anurag Sagar. I was waiting for your letter.

You should keep your promises to Beloved Kirpal. In this Kal Yuga, the Kirpal Power protects us from the suffering. Compared to Kirpal Power, everything else in this world is nothing. Hail Kirpal, Who in this Kal Yuga, protected His beloved Fakir, Ajaib, from the Negative Power. The Powerful Friend Kirpal showered Grace and Mercy.

Even though our souls have been separated from God for ages and ages, the Kirpal Power can save us from the claws of the Negative Power. So we should pray to this Kirpal Power. The Negative Power is always looking toward the satsangis like a hunter looking for his victim. After sitting in the minds of the satsangis, Kal, the cunning trickster, next separates the satsangis from each other. All satsangis should have the relation of brother and sister. Guru Nanak said that there is One Father – and we are all His children.

With much, much love to you and everyone,
And may best wishes be with you,
Ajaib Singh

When we received this letter, I had no idea how involved I was to become in the "work on the *Anurag Sagar*." Sant Ji and Pappu began to translate the epic poem of Sant Kabir shortly after He received the above letter from Russell, but the project stalled when the regular groups to India started up again. It was not until the last group had departed the following March that time was freed to continue in earnest. I stayed to help, and the story of that *seva*, coupled with the companionship of Chris, my eldest son, throughout, lies at the heart of the next chapter.

Epilogue for Chapter Eight

A night or two after we returned, members of the group spoke in the Satsang Hall at Sant Bani, sharing their tales of love and growth with eager listeners. I was present, but all I could say was that I had just had major surgery, and was now in intensive care to recover. It had taken half a year to build up my spiritual vanity to the point where I was, in Sant Ji's words, "all puffed up." It took another six months for me to unravel the experience in light of His guiding counsel. It seemed like almost every day, I woke up and, with groan and sighs, I understood more as to how wrong I had been. Finally, sometime in the fall, I reached bottom. Only then could I begin to build on what I had been given.

Many, many lessons came to me. I reflected on my attitude at the Valentine's Day party at School in February, and cringed. How could I have been so judgmental?

At some point during the visit to Rajasthan, Sant Ji had offered to have *halvah* [the Indian dessert loaded with sugar and clarified butter] cooked as parshad for us. When He humbly inquired if that would be acceptable, a Western devotee answered that no, it was too rich and too sweet. With even more humility, Sant Ji responded that He realized it was very rich, and that is why He did not make it very often. Other disciples chimed in, saying, "Well, we like it, so please make it!" Then someone asked, "How about if You gave us something as sweet for our within?" To that Sant Ji replied, "That will be coming, but this is an outer expression of my love for you." He added that in India it was the custom to make *halvah*, and it showed much love.

I thought about the Saint's perspective – delicious food as an outer expression of love – and shook my head at the new "truths" I had clung to in February.

I thought about how critical I had been of the 77 RB sevadar who had been praised by all of the Westerners. Was his story just a condensed version of mine? He served and was noticed. People praised his love and devotion, even composing a song about him. He took it all in, his ego grew, and then he lost from it. What I had done seemed far worse. I went back to the talk that Sant Ji had given to the Sant Bani sevadars in May of 1977. Listening to it again, it felt uncannily like a prediction:

> *If the satsangis are loving and respecting each other and doing their meditation, then if the Negative Power cannot do anything to the meditators, he goes to the sevadars. And sitting in the sevadars, he will pull their minds in different directions. He will tear the sevadars apart, and he will not allow them to make their seva successful . . .*
>
> *How does he dwell in the sevadars? He comes and sits in the minds of the sevadars, and that's why some of them think that they are very good sevadars, that they are doing very good seva, and that nobody else is competent like them. And some people think that they are very good at organizing.*
>
> *So sitting in their mind he creates this type of thing within the sevadars. Because if a few people start praising us and folding hands at us, then we do not want to stay on the ground; we start flying. We think, "We are also something."*
>
> *Now when the sevadars go in different directions and start fighting with one another, Master warns us and rebukes us, "What have you done? You should not do that." And then the satsangis realize and they repent. But they do not understand the tricks of the Negative Power.*
>
> *When the sevadars start fighting with each other and becoming angry with each other, Master rebukes us and tells us, "Your work is to do seva and you have to set an example for other people." When Master is telling us that, then our mind starts making excuses to the Master and people start arguing and explaining to the Master, "No, this is right," or "this is wrong."*
>
> *This is the Law of Nature: the soul which is affected by the tricks of the Negative Power, and who starts finding faults in*

Master, goes back into the cycle of eighty-four lakhs births and deaths.[8]

I heard new things each time I listened. Obviously the description of "not wanting to stay on the ground" and "flying" after people praised me fit. What about us "not understanding the tricks of the Negative Power" even after we had repented? And was there a chance that I might one day start finding fault with the Master, and go back into the cycle of births and deaths? Every word seemed in need of digestion.

I thought more about Master Kirpal Singh's circular on humility. The simple, eloquent words certainly held profound clues for what I had been through:

> *The truly humble person does not compare himself with others. He knows that none of us, however evolved, is perfect; none of us is complete in himself. The humble person does not regard one as better than the other; he believes in the divinity of each. If one says and asserts that he is better than others, then he is not perfect as yet . . .*
>
> *A man may strive to be humble, but for all his efforts, may become all the more proud. There is such a thing as the pride of humility; it is a very dangerous thing, for it is too subtle to be discerned by the inexperienced. There are some who will take great pains to be humble; they make humility impossible. How can a man be humble who is all the time thinking of how best he can be humble?*[9]

The new "spiritual" me had been constantly comparing myself to others. And even with ten years of practice on the Path, I obviously had been way too "inexperienced" to discern the dangerous pride of humility that engulfed me. I recalled Sant Ji's words at my first session in Rajasthan, when He reminded me that in Colombia He had advised me to ignore the faults of others. If I had followed that good advice, He stated, then none of what I had had to go through would have happened.

I thought of how the Masters work. They speak of the potter, who shapes the clay by beating it on the outside with one hand, all the time supporting the vessel on the inside with the other hand. I may have

---

[8] From "The Enemy Within" in *The Ambrosial Hour*, pp. 88-89.

[9] Master Kirpal Singh, "Humility" in *The Way of the Saints*, p. 345.

received a well deserved "beating" – but the more I thought about it, the more I felt that Sant Ji had given me only as much as I could take, knowing that the rest would unfold over the next few months. All the while, however, I felt the tremendous Grace of His loving hand within. I had not been "wrong in my rightness" – I had been wrong, plain and simple.

There were two areas that remained as puzzles. One I came to understand, but the other I never did. The Masters seem to interchange the words "Negative Power" and "Lord Kal" with "mind." Had the Negative Power really manifested in me and altered my consciousness? Had I been taken over by some exterior entity, like a B Grade horror film? Was that the weight I had felt sitting on my chest when I struggled to arise and go to Satsang? Or was all of that merely a quaint way of saying that my ego had run amuck? The latter I could comprehend and accept – the former was much harder, and far more frightening. I still do not know, and no longer think it matters. As will be seen in the next chapter, however, while our minds and egos may be convenient tools for the Negative Power, there is no doubt that that force is a very real entity in the universe described by the Masters. In the *Anurag Sagar [The Ocean of Love]* Sant Kabir graphically pens the power and nature of Lord Kal in frightening detail.

The second puzzle was how to reconcile, if only at a psychological level, Sant Ji's seemingly contradictory words. He told someone that my "meditation" was not really meditation – and then He told me that He had said that to protect my meditation. Which was right? It took me time to realize that both were absolutely correct. From the perspective of the person talking to Sant Ji, I had not been meditating. It was important for her to understand that. But from another point of view, I had been meditating. Otherwise, how could Sant Ji have encouraged me to do more? Sant Ji gave each of us exactly what we needed. A Saint is not limited like we are. God, working through the Human Pole, looks into our soul, reads us like "a jar of pickles," and gives us what is essential for our growth. These thoughts helped me put the whole experience in perspective. Above all, however, I understood that there were operational levels at play that I might never understand.

For years after this long "night of the soul," I would measure myself in terms of before and after my "fall." I felt like a cracked vessel that had been successfully repaired, but the fissure was always there – always apparent. Like a tongue running over a loose filling in a back molar, I constantly "worried" it. Initially I treaded much more lightly around Sant Ji – afraid to do anything spontaneous as when I had first met Him. I would be happy if a conversation, interview, or darshan glance felt like "the old days – before the fall." Of course it was me – not Him – who focused on this. All Sant Ji ever said – on numerous occasions – was that He was very happy I had returned to being "the old Kent."

Once a fellow initiate and I were traveling back from India together, and, on the long leg between Delhi and London, I told her much of this story. I was embarrassed, and added that it had been a very humbling experience. She looked at me when I was finished and said, "What a tremendous gift you have been given by our Beloved – what a gift!" As soon as she said that I thought, "Of course. She is absolutely right."

Towards the beginning of Chapter Seven, I wrote that I was the only one responsible for what happened to me during this time. I could not "blame" it on anyone else. The experience taught me much – perhaps more than any other *dharma* I have been through – and the lessons have not ended. My childhood and youth had consisted of a series of lucky opportunities that always seemed to fall right into place. I had no understanding that the fortunate circumstances of my life made it all too easy for me to judge those whose lives were a constant struggle. And so I was critical: of friends who struggled with their marital relations; of people who "left" the Path; of disciples who fell asleep during Satsangs and meditation sittings. None were above my scrutiny.

At last I remembered the Words of my Beloved Master Kirpal. He encouraged us to run toward the goal as if we were in a race – adding that we should not look to the right or left to see where others were. That seemed to lie at the heart of the lesson. And, I had allowed myself to think that my efforts had resulted in spiritual progress – that I had actually become something on my own. I knew, finally, that Sant Ji had saved me from myself. I also was aware that any chance for a successful recovery from such a profound and delicate operation lay in His Hands.

CHAPTER NINE

The Ocean of Love

"And the Healing Has Begun" is the title of a song by poet-songwriter Van Morrison, and for me, it had. The fact that I awoke each morning and understood more of my spiritual ailment and its effects was both healthy and hard. I threw myself back into my schoolwork and doctoral studies with a passion, anxious to reconnect at a human level. Spiritually speaking, however, I felt thin-skinned and somewhat vulnerable, and approached the practices with a certain amount of caution. Intellectually I knew what I should do – but at a profound level, I felt twice burned. That these burns were self-inflicted should have made the hurdle easier to clamber over, but an emotional gulf remained between "knowing" something and acting on it. I banked on time being a necessary part of any rehabilitation – and continued to trust that Master Kirpal and Sant Ji knew exactly what They were doing with me.

At the Sant Bani School we were approaching a milestone. As noted in Chapter Seven, the School had expanded to include a high school, and our four twelfth graders, Carolyn Hammond, Melissa Powers, Steven Rucker, and Evelyn Sanborn, were to be the first graduating class. I wrote to ask if Sant Ji would be kind enough to send a commencement message for them, which He graciously did.[1]

On a beautiful day in June, the seniors and their proud families, students, faculty, and guests assembled on the lawn in front of the Master's house. With the pond as a backdrop, the ceremony began. A couple of faculty spoke about the students, each senior shared thoughts

---

[1] Over the next twenty years, Sant Ji continued to send graduation messages to Sant Bani's senior classes. These have been collected, along with other inspiring words to the School from both Master Kirpal and Sant Ji, in a booklet entitled "Messages to the Graduating Classes of Sant Bani School" (2001). The mechanics of the School's simple commencement ceremony were established at that first graduation – and have carried through to the present.

with the audience, and diplomas were awarded. While every moment of that first graduation seemed like a highlight, none surpassed the simple beauty of the message of Sant Ajaib Singh Ji:

May 5, 1978

Dear Children,

On this occasion I send my congratulations to all the students who are going to step into the world after completing their high school studies.

The earlier days of school life are like the stepping stone to the building of man's career. You will be meeting many people in the world; will see many things in the world. Many ups and downs might come, but always remember your goal, which you have to accomplish.

The most important thing which every student must do is to respect the teacher and keep himself devoted to studies with full concentration. Our teacher or professor is a mine of knowledge. If we will respect him, he will give us the riches of knowledge, for which we go to college.

I pray to Almighty God to guide you and bless you with wisdom and right understanding in every aspect of life. My love and best wishes are always with all of you.

With all His love,
Ajaib Singh

Sant Ji's message was not just for the graduates. Even a cursory reading made it clear that He was speaking to all of us. In the School of Spirituality – His School – I had faced "ups and downs" and needed to remember my goal. And, there was no doubt that my Teacher was truly a "mine of knowledge," Who could give us the "riches of knowledge." Finally, I was very glad that Sant Ji was praying to Almighty God to guide us and bless us with "right understanding in every aspect of life." Summer breezes were now upon us, and there was time to reflect on how best to use the recently acquired "right understanding."

Sant Ji continued to write me letters, and most every one spelled out, in phonetic Hindi, the Spanish words. *"Te amo"* [I love you] and *"Gracias"* [Thanks]. Commenting on information in my letters to Him, He was pleased that the Perkins and I were "maintaining the love" as of old, and that I had succeeded in getting some control over my mind.[2] He was also happy that we were progressing with plans for a new school building.[3]

On the twenty-eighth of June, Sant Ji wrote that He was glad to receive love from Karen and me, and that He requested Master Kirpal that we may have even more love and understanding for each other. In a clear reference to my recent attempt to "remake" myself, He pointed out that, with the Grace of the Master, "householders" could reach the True Goal: to arrive at the Feet of Master Kirpal in Sach Khand. When He saw love in any woman or man, He wrote, He became happy, because humans come into this world for love. But, He cautioned, we may be misled, and leave aside the love we have for our companion. How can one expect to love God when one cannot even love one's own companion, He asked.

He went on to give news of 77 RB, and then reminded us to meditate every day. He closed by sending much much love and "*Te amo*'s" – but the central message of that letter shook me to the core. I loved my family – and had never felt distanced from them as I had from old friends and colleagues. But who can ever be sure of anything in this razor's edge of a world? Master Kirpal used to say that it is as if the soul had been placed on a plank in the middle of the ocean – and told not to get wet. Reflecting on Sant Ji's letter, I shuddered to think what direction my life might have taken if I had not gone under the knife of such a skilled surgeon.

As the summer progressed, our desire to see Sant Ji grew and grew. We had been spoiled by the sheer volume of His physical presence the summer before – and we missed Him so much. Karen had plans to go in January, and I the following month. The School had arranged its calendar to allow for teachers to go to India in late February and early March – and, as before, I was scheduled to be in that group. Chris, eight-and-a-half, began to express a strong desire to return to India once again.[4] Christopher's wish turned out to be deeper than a whim, so he wrote Sant Ji a letter requesting permission to come.

---

[2] Letter of May 5th, 1978.

[3] The particular building referred to never was constructed. In a relatively short space of time, the School acquired two neighboring properties, and converted the private homes on them to the needed classroom space.

[4] Chris had accompanied Karen and me to see Master Kirpal when he was eleven months old, and again when he was four years old.

July 24, 1978

Dear Sant Ji,

    Hi. How are you? I am fine. I did well in my school work this year. With God's Grace, Kent hopes to come to India this year. I would like to come with him. May I please come with him? Thank you for everything you have given me.
Love, Christopher

I enclosed this letter with one of my own, and sent them off to Rajasthan. We both received replies in mid-August. The letter to Chris was in English.

August 11, 1978

Dear Chris,

    I am fine. I am very glad to know that you did well in the school last year. I hope you continue this.
    You can come with Kent to Rajasthan when he comes. Be a good boy and obey your parents.
    I send much-much love to you.
With all love,
Ajaib Singh

The letter to me was in Hindi, and dated the seventh of August. Sant Ji included news of the Ashram at 77 RB. They were in the midst of a record-breaking heat wave. It was so hot that Bant could not record any new bhajans for me. Pathi Ji was still making tea, however. And everyone sent their love and remembrances to the Bicknell family. He was very happy to hear that Judith and Russell Perkins and "the Principal Sahib" were being old friends. He was pleased to know that Karen would be coming, and that I would be there in March. He said it would be fine if Chris came, but that He had some advice for us: we should not go into debt to buy the ticket. He sent us much *"Gracias"* and many *"Te amo's."*

In late September I received a unique letter from Sant Ji – one that He had written out entirely in His own hand. As He later explained, it took Him a long time to craft the Hindi script – as He was accustomed to writing in the Gurmukhi script of Punjabi – a different alphabet altogether. I was used to seeing His penmanship on the address panel – and enjoyed the variants of my name as He sounded out and wrote in English (a skill He had learned in the signal corps of the army): "Kant Beknal," "Kent Biknal," and, my favorite, "Cent Bicnal." But this letter was special. He wrote:

Sep 22-9-78

My dear Kent Bicknell –

Your loved filled telegram and letter arrived. With Master's Grace, one day the school building will surely be completed, and I will be very happy. You will have understood why the Saints love the souls – for what reason. The Saints have only one duty. The Saints grab the souls to take them to Sach Khand, after releasing them from the clutches of the five dacoits [lust, anger, greed, attachment, and egotism]. In Rajasthan it is now very hot. But, with Hazur Kirpal's Grace, all the work is getting accomplished well.

I send much love to Karen, Nicky, and Chrissy. All of the dear ones at the Ashram send much love to you.
Ajaib Singh

On the thirtieth of September, Sant Ji wrote me again. Beginning with, "*Te amo,*" He went on to say He was glad that things were going well at School, and reminded me that it was all due to the Grace of the Master. He mentioned that a group was then in Rajasthan, and that everyone was sitting together in the remembrance of God. The next day, responding to a request from Sant Bani School children that He visit again, Sant Ji wrote:

October 1, 1978

Dear Children,

I love all of you from all my heart. I will come to the School soon. If you want me to come to your school, obey your teachers and study wholeheartedly.
I send all of my love to all of you.
Ajaib Singh

On November sixth, another letter arrived for me. Sant Ji was very happy that Russell had returned to Sant Bani from Rajasthan – and that, once again, He was very glad to read that we were maintaining our friendship. He said that I should keep my love for the School and the

Ashram, and encouraged me to work hard for the progress of both. He
closed with a *"Te amo"* to the Bicknell family.

On the eleventh of January, 1979, Sant Ji wrote that He was very
happy to read that I would be coming to Rajasthan as the "Old Kent" –
because the old Kent was very loving. Karen was in 77 RB with the
January group, and He mentioned that she was His dear daughter. He
commented on the new book of bhajans, stating how pleased He was
with it.

On Master Kirpal Singh's birthday, the sixth of February, Sant Ji
sent another letter.

> *My dearly beloved Principal Sahib, Kent Bicknell,*
>
> *I received your letter. I will be very happy to be with the old
> Kent once again. That is because within the old Kent there was
> much, much love. For you also, it is very good to have become
> the old Kent. I am very pleased that you will be coming in the
> March group, and that you will be staying an extra week in
> Delhi with Pappu, to work on the translation of The Anurag
> Sagar.*
>
> *Do your Bhajan and Simran wholeheartedly. To Karen,
> Nicky, Chrissy – to the whole Bicknell Family – I send my love
> and best wishes.*
>
> *Ajaib Singh*

At the time I received Sant Ji's letter, I had little awareness of what
the work on the *Anurag Sagar* would entail. I knew that Sant Ji had
selected a particular variant of Sant Kabir's text, and that Pappu had
made an effort to translate it during the hot months of the summer and
fall. Progress stalled, and somehow it was decided that I could be
helpful. The plan was for me to stay in Delhi to work with Pappu – after
the March group had returned to the States. I was delighted at the prospect of helping – as Sant Ji had made it very clear that it was time to
make this key text of Spirituality available to the English-speaking
world. I had no idea, however, that our intense work on the *Anurag
Sagar [The Ocean of Love]* was to play a major role in my healing.

The big day in late February came. Christopher, now aged nine, and
I said our good-byes to Karen and Nick and headed off to the airport. We
had decided to be flexible in terms of Chris; that is, we left the decision
as to whether he would stay with me or go back with the group until we

saw how he was doing in India. He was excited to climb aboard the plane in Boston, accompanied by several favorite teachers from the Sant Bani School and me. He was a perfect traveling companion on the flight, and we laughed, ate, sang, joked, giggled, chatted, and slept our way through what Russell once referred to as "the time tunnel."

Saturday, the Twenty-fourth of February, 1979

After we had landed in Delhi and rested a few hours, we climbed aboard a rented tour bus to begin the twelve-plus hour journey to 77 RB. In less than three years, the overnight train as a means of travel to His feet had become relegated to the past. As we wove through the congestion of scooters, animals, cars, lorries, bicycles, rickshaws, and pedestrians that comprise Delhi "traffic," our bus slowed to a crawl. Chris and I looked out the window, and caught an image that burned into the memory cells. A young boy had just been struck and killed by a vehicle, and his body lay in the road right beneath us. As we inched by the fast gathering knot of onlookers, we saw the uncovered body, its very life having seeped onto the tarmac. The ankle of one of the outstretched legs was split down to the white bone. Chris and I pulled our heads in from the window, looked at each other soberly, and then talked quietly. We both felt somewhat sick to our stomachs – and we were very glad to be heading to the Feet of God Himself.

We arrived after dusk, and Sant Ji saw us briefly. He welcomed us all, saying that He could recognize the faces of those of us who had been there before. I could not make out any details of His face, however, as He was backlit by two powerful gas lanterns. Chris was very happy to be standing beside me – gazing upon the ethereal scene – and I was just as pleased to have Chris at my elbow.

Chris and I chose our beds in the large room that was the "men's dormitory," and, utilizing a glassful of boiled water from the earthen jugs, brushed our teeth under the night sky. Chris dropped right off, but as I lay there, I thought about a statement I had read in the latest *Sant Bani Magazine*. A fellow disciple, writing about his recent trip to Rajasthan, stated that as long as he could be filled with the sweet and innocent love for the Master, he would be quite content without inner spiritual experiences. That resonated with me – was I feeling the same? I wondered what my prayer should be for this trip, and it came: "O Sant Ji, fall me more in love with You!" I was very happy with the simplicity of that request, and started to drift off.

Suddenly a wicked thought entered my head – quite unannounced. The previous year I had come feeling "spiritually prepared," and had expected the floodgates to open. They had not. Now that I had been through some pain and suffering – and was my usual old "unprepared" self again – maybe now, I thought, I will really get some spiritual wealth. At once I remembered the story of the disciple who tried to recite the *Jap Ji* without being distracted.[5] The Guru had told him that if he could do that successfully, he would get anything he wished. The fellow began, and toward the end he wondered if he could have a fine horse owned by the Guru. When the disciple was finished, the Guru gave him the horse – but had been ready to give him complete liberation. Reflecting on that story, I was ashamed at my thought ("now I will really get some wealth"), but also glad to see that I was my old idiotic self – the old Kent. I sighed, content in the knowledge that the only way I would get anything would be if He gave it to me.

Sunday, the Twenty-fifth of February

Sant Ji did not ring the bell that first morning, as He had told us we could rest as needed after our long trip. Like most everyone else in the group, I arose early to meditate. Chris, who had been sleeping very well, awoke and needed to go to the bathroom. While we no longer used the fields, the latrines – thirty-foot narrow holes drilled deep into the earth, each surrounded by short mud walls – were at the far edge of the compound. Chris grabbed a flashlight, and was about to head out with nothing on his feet, when I whispered to him to get some shoes on. Sant Ji had been quite specific that we should wear footgear and dress warmly – so as not to get sick. Chris put on my shoes, and shuffle-clumped loudly out, then back – past all of the devotees sitting in meditation. We chuckled about it later, but I suggested to Pappu that perhaps Chris and I should squeeze our beds into his room. Pappu agreed.

At five o'clock, it felt wonderful to be holding a warm cup of chai in my hand, sipping the sweet, nourishing liquid, while gazing upon the red glow of a Rajasthani dawn once more. I was not certain how "at home" I

---

[5] The *Jap Ji* is the quite lengthy morning prayer of the Sikhs, written by Guru Nanak.

would feel this time – but the signs augured well.

Chris got up in time to see Sant Ji arrive for the meditation at 7:00 a.m., and then returned to the room until the hour was up. During the meditation, my mind wandered and then came back, but I worked hard, and quickly found more peace than I had experienced in months. The best part was to be sitting in front of Sant Ji once more, seeing Him, hearing Him gently clear His Throat. As we filed past Him at the door, He asked how I was doing. I responded enthusiastically, *"Teek hai! Gracias."* He answered, *"Te amo!"* and waved me on with a quick "whisht" of His folded hands. Chris was outside the door, and Sant Ji smiled to see him – and Chris beamed back at Sant Ji.

I tried to sit in the afternoon – but I was very tired. I began in the sun, and then moved into the shade. After a bit, I "found" myself on my bed – and before I knew it I was slumped over and sound asleep. I awoke with a giant headache – and, again, I could only chuckle when I compared my current state to the previous year. I would have sat ramrod straight without a backrest for the full two hours – completely lost in my own self. "Yikes, how the 'mighty' have fallen," I thought with relief.

Pappu presented his plan to me. He hoped that we could take as much time as we needed in Delhi to finish the *Anurag Sagar* and then come back up to 77 RB to review everything with Sant Ji. I loved the idea – who would not have wished to see Sant Ji again before going back? I began to anticipate returning to the Ashram with Pappu – and realized that I was back in the School of the Saints for another one of my apparently endless lessons: "Living in the Living Present – Basic Course #101." Whatever I was doing, whether I was enjoying it or not, I could be certain that part of me would be projecting ahead, thinking about what would happen when I finished. In meditation, I gazed into the Eye Focus and repeated *Simran*, but simultaneously I was waiting for the sitting to end – pondering over what I would do then.

Ever since I had met Master Kirpal in 1970, it had happened like that. I would be so happy to be having darshan, all the time wondering when it would be over. And as soon as it was over, I would be thinking about the next one! Sitting in meditation and enjoying it, while wondering when the meal was coming. It was as if I were in two places at once: fantasizing about the future while in the present moment. Again, it was like the disciple who thought about the Guru's horse – the gift at the end. It was so hard to do otherwise. The year before I had spent the first few days slipping under anesthesia, and several more coming out.

This trip, I thought, it would be wonderful if I could be more awake, a little sooner.

Christopher was really beginning to enjoy himself, fully in the moment of a nine-year-old boy. The crows were pests in the compound – alighting where they did not belong, and trying to steal bits and pieces of everything that glittered. To shoo the birds away, Harmel, one of Pathi Ji's sons, had whittled a simple bow, strung with twine, and some harmless crooked arrows. Chris gladly took over that "*seva*," and delighted in keeping the pesky crows at bay (with never a danger of actually inflicting any wound). At one point I came out of the room, and Jon Engle was helping Chris attach some paper feathers, so the arrows might fly more true. Shipp Webb came around the corner with an orange, and Jon jokingly suggested he balance it on his head as a target for Chris. It was a merry time, and Pappu and I told Chris several stories of the Masters that featured a bow: the lesson to keep looking into the center before you shoot, and the story of the boy who became a highly skilled archer by worshipping the statue of a real archer. The boy had created an idol of the master archer when the archer said he would not train him.

I felt that Sant Ji was sending me a great deal of love in a very quiet manner. In the first full day, I had not experienced the almost hysterical, intoxicated joy of the past, but there was a new, keener edged love, set in a backdrop of serious, hard, real work. I had had no interview or personal communication beyond glances and "*Te amo*," but everything seemed real and wonderful.

When Sant Ji had asked me to go back to being the old Kent, a long dormant wish had come to fruition. Since the age of thirteen or fourteen, I had been telling myself that if I wanted to play guitar, I could – no sweat – I simply had to practice and I'd get it. Year after year I said that, until the line became, "Well, if I had started playing guitar when I was fourteen, I could be really good now!" When I returned from India in 1978, I decided to try. I bought a vintage acoustic guitar made by the famed Martin Company, and spent a chunk of time almost every day learning the basics. I loved it – but hours spent plucking the strings were obviously not counted for meditation. I was fairly certain that before I returned to New Hampshire, I would talk to Sant Ji about how I was now spending my time, and I had a feeling that my priorities were going to be gently rearranged. I looked forward to that.

After lunch, Chris and I left the high walls of the compound through the main gate, and headed down the dirt road to visit the hut that Sant Ji had used for meditation in 1974. As we walked along, a couple of very young girls from the village saw us, and waved for us to stop. They called my name, "Keyn-tah" when they got close, and we all laughed. I foisted my Hindi on them, with some success. I told Chris he should get a picture of the two, which he preferred not to do. When I suggested that I could take the photo, and he should stand with them, he wanted that less – so he snapped the photo. They were very sweet.

We continued on until we got to the side path that led to the shelter. To describe Sant Ji's hut as simple does not begin to give a feel for that blessed spot. As we stood and looked at it – the thatched roof, the straw-daubed mud walls with holes for ventilation – the ceiling not high enough to stand in – it was overwhelming. Sant Ji sat there and sat there – not worrying about the birds, ants, rats, rain, wind, and heat – and remembered Great Master Kirpal. Sant Ji had received the Inner Orders from Master Kirpal to move to 77 RB a few weeks before the Master retired from His physical body on the twenty-first of August 1974. Unlike the majority of Master Kirpal's disciples, Sant Ji knew quite well what was coming – but His suffering on receiving the "official" news at that plain hut in 77 RB was enormous. The simple edifice was dressed in great and solemn dignity – a monument to obeying the Will of the Master and to the agony of physical separation from Him. Chris and I gazed in wonder, and slowly walked back to the compound.[6]

In the afternoon meditation my mind drifted more than in the morning, and sleep almost overtook me a couple of times. That was disappointing, but what could I do except follow Master Kirpal's advice to try my best and leave the rest to the Master Power? That thought was foremost in my mind when we went for a walk with Sant Ji – and, by His Grace, the effect was magnetic. Sant Ji did not say anything on that walk – no questions, no words. I was looking at Him, and He gave me such a glance that I was overwhelmed with an intoxicating sweetness, so much so that it almost made me nauseous. I felt so blessed to see Him in His glory, and to feel His power radiating forth in waves, as that was something that I had not ingested for quite a while. I remembered that I had just been thinking that such-like experiences were not happening on the trip, and laughed once more at my endless attempts to analyze.

The Satsang that evening captured the essence of old. The girls sang four or five bhajans in a row, all with the same tune, and then Sant Ji asked Pappu to sing a new one. Sant Ji was exquisitely beautiful, and as I looked at Him, I smiled and shook my head in wonder, and He looked

---

[6] *Cf.* A. S. Oberoi, *Support for the Shaken Sangat* (1984), pp. 287-290.

back at me and laughed as well. He was so kind, loving, and compassionate – so much the All Forgiving One. "We are foolish – You are wise and clever, O Satguru." The thought went through me that I was quite stained – perhaps damaged beyond repair. My heart sighed and I felt like weeping. What else could I do? I knew that He had forgiven me, yet a sadness had penetrated deep within. As the hour extended, and I bathed in the aural and visual waters of His Satsang, I understood that there was nowhere in the universe I would rather be. "Relax, relax," I told myself, "and feast upon Him with sweet remembrance."

I loved the bhajans – especially when sung by the village girls – but, as I had mentioned to Pappu that afternoon, my own enthusiasm for singing had waned some (no doubt connected with the period of my intense spiritual pride). At the end of Satsang, as I filed by Sant Ji, He said that Eric Perkins and I should learn all of the bhajans which the girls had presented – and that we should be prepared to sing them before the trip was over. These bhajans were all written by Brahmanand, and one of them quickly became an all-time favorite of mine: *Guru Bina Kaun Sahai Narak Me, Guru Bina Kaun Sahai Re* [Without the Guru, who will save you from hell?] That night, as I lay on my bed grinning, I realized that my enthusiasm for bhajans had returned with a vengeance – delivered straight into my heart by His Orders.

Monday, the Twenty-sixth of February

The bell rang at three, and the day began to unfold to the night noises of a rural area, steeped in agriculture. Dogs barked in the distance, pumps for irrigation ran, and the occasional call to prayer could be heard drifting across the chilled desert air. There was no meditation with Sant Ji that morning. He was busy giving Initiation to many hungry souls from near-by towns and villages. As the day passed, I thought how nice it would be to ask Sant Ji, "*Sacha hai ki mai purana Kent hu?*" [Sant Ji, is it true that I am the old Kent?] A quiet, confident voice told me that the time would come when He would address that without any query from me.

In those days, Sant Ji came to the dining room daily at lunch. He sat in a chair at the end of the serving tables, and greeted the devotees as they passed by, with their trays laden with food. When everyone was seated, He would fold His hands and retire to His quarters. When Chris passed through the line with his tray, Sant Ji looked at him and said,

Sant Ji leads the devotees to the meditation hut. The Ashram compound is in the distance.

A camel train makes its way along one of the many canals that bring life-giving water to the desert sands of Rajasthan.

"Sant Ji asked Chris to sing a bhajan. . . when Chris reached the line, 'without saying, You knew my pains and problems,' Sant Ji burst out laughing. He said 'Yes, without you even saying anything I knew all your pains and difficulties. I knew how you wanted to eat the sugar cane, so I had the sugar cane brought for you . . . and eating that, your pains and difficulties went away.'" (see p. 303).

The simple meditation hut used by Sant Ji is visible beyond the group. (see pp. 273, 282, 303)

"We walked back to the Ashram, following in the footsteps of the One Who 'knew our pain and difficulties without us even saying a word'. " (see p. 304)

Next Page
"When the sands of those sacred moments ran out, Sant Ji stood up and hugged Chris." (see p. 304)

"Later that afternoon, Chris and I went out for a walk, and we saw Sant Ji far away – checking the crops in a distant field." (see p. 302)

"Chrissy – Chris," and Chris was bubbling. Back in our room, Pappu called Chris over and handed him a box of chocolates. I looked at Pappu and asked, "*Kyo*?" [Why?], and Pappu explained. Sant Ji had given the box to Pappu, telling him to share the chocolates with Chris as well (and the two of them were kind enough to let me have some too).

Chris seemed totally "in his element." He was eating and drinking everything – on all levels. As I thought about it, I realized how good he was being. Occasionally my attention had to slip a little from Sant Ji, to see what he was up to – but generally he was doing an amazing job. Even on the walks, all I had to do was glance at him now and then – as he was quite adept at taking care of himself.

Meditation in the afternoon was real, and that felt very good to me. Perhaps my spiritual muscles had not atrophied after all. After the sitting, Sant Ji led us all on a walk out to the hut. Like the afternoon before, there were very few questions. We had extended opportunities to take in the delicious sight of Sant Ji standing amongst us, with the fields of tall sugar cane behind.

Toward the end, Mildred Meeh wondered what the village school at 77 RB was like. Sant Ji began by saying that the educational system was different in India. It was up to the parents and children to decide to attend – there was no law forcing anyone to go to school. He explained that the government paid the teacher. Further, there were no regulations that said the teacher could not beat the students if he felt they needed it – and this was very different from our system. Sant Ji added that the students saw the teacher coming in the same way that the soul saw the Lord of Death coming to take her. That is how much the children fear the teacher.

At that point, Sant Ji directed a sevadar to give sugar cane to everyone. We were handed short lengths of the bamboo-like stalk, and we all began to strip the bark back with our teeth, and then to chew the pulp to extract the surprisingly sweet juice. Out of the corner of my eye, I noticed that someone was still taping the session, and smiled at the thought of the recording: "CRUNCH! CRUNCH! CRUNCH!" We continued to work at consuming the parshad, and Sant Ji, with a smile and a hearty laugh, said that the sight of the group eating sugar cane was very beautiful to see.

At evening Satsang there were many bhajans once again. The girls sang, as did Pathi Ji, and Pappu. At the end, Sant Ji asked if Eric and I had learned any of the new bhajans of Brahmanand yet? Had we been practicing? I explained that we had just received the hand-written copies from Bant that afternoon, but that we would work to have one ready for the next evening. Sant Ji responded with a big, "*Aachaa!*" [Good!].

As I went to bed, I realized how much I had eaten that evening, and wondered if I would be sleepy in the morning. I had loaded up on fruit and the irresistible cashew nuts served to the Westerners. After gobbling those piles, I had joined Pappu in the Indian langar, where I consumed fresh chapattis and *palak* [spinach] stewed in *ghee* [clarified butter]. I resolved not to eat anything heavy the next morning, and closed my eyes for the night.

Tuesday, the Twenty-seventh of February

In the pre-dawn hours – surprise, surprise – I was terribly sleepy. It was awful. At the morning tea I avoided the cookies, and at last felt awake enough to be "ready" for the meditation sitting with Sant Ji at seven. He proceeded to show me what was what. Right after He told us to close our eyes and begin, a tremendous pain came in one of my legs, after which I began to feel faint. The session had barely started, and I was dying for it to end. It became so difficult to continue sitting in that room. The only thing that kept me going was that He had said, "Sit without moving, and do Simran without stopping." The fact that my mind would wander at first was not a new phenomenon – as that often happened until I had collected my scattered thoughts at the Eye Center. The day before had been pleasant – filled with gentle meanderings and good feelings prior to locking into the repetition of the Simran. But in this session I was barely holding on, doing Simran at a hundred miles an hour.

Then I thought, "Can't I even do this for one hour? I say I love Him, so can't I even sit for sixty minutes?" The idea that twelve months before I had considered myself ready for big spiritual tests seemed absurd, if not bizarre – especially since what I was dying to do was jump up, dash out of the room, and run off into the desert. It was much easier to sit and practice the guitar for long periods than to sit for one hour when one was fighting physical pain and the urge to move. By His Grace, I did not give up and, with renewed determination, continued to struggle.

Sant Ji chose to extend the sitting for five minutes beyond the hour – and that was exactly what I needed. In those final minutes, my body locked into its "statue" state, and peace and transcendence settled over me. Sant Ji was letting me know how "ready" I really was. At the end of the hour, I was exhausted, but thoroughly satisfied. I had come up against some very difficult parts of myself and, with Grace, had continued to do as He had asked. It had been hard, but necessary.

At the end of the sitting, Sant Ji sang His bhajan, *Charde Chet Har Chet Parani, Bina Simran Pachatayenga* [With the beginning of the New Year, O Soul, become conscious of the Lord, because without doing Simran you will repent.] – which was both beautiful and instructional: "When will you become humble in front of the Satguru, and get forgiveness for your sins?"

Sant Ji had asked us to bring our shoes inside prior to the session, as it looked liked it might rain – which it did. He walked over to the outer doors, while we gathered up our shoes and lined up to file by Him. When He opened the outer doors, there was a smiling Christopher, waiting to greet Him. Sant Ji patted him on the back and asked, *"Kya hal hai?"* [How are you?] Chris was very happy, and I was as well.

Later in the morning, Pathi Ji gave Chris an "official duty" – to keep the crows out of the Ashram. He headed off with his bow and arrows, very pleased to be recognized by so esteemed a figure as dear Pathi Ji. I lay back on my bed and reflected on the meditation. If I were a soldier in God's Army, how come I wanted to run at the first sign of trouble? A recent article in *Sant Bani Magazine* had a statement to the effect that there is no burden or pain in love. "Boy," I thought, "What a puny lover am I!" I realized that it was not easy to meditate for hours on end – something I had accomplished with seeming ease the year before. Had not Sant Ji Himself told us that He would have preferred to stand in front of cannons with His shirt open than to face the mind? I was a coward – a chicken at heart – but somehow it felt okay. I was reaching a starting point on which to build. And the meditation in the afternoon was real – with much less of a struggle.

The afternoon walk with Sant Ji was great fun. Chris was on his own, on the opposite side of the crowd that followed behind Sant Ji to the place where He stopped to talk to us. We took a different route than the days before, and a playful attitude infected many of us. Disciples were passing, darting, squeezing by one another – all in good humor. We were walking in a wide ditch with steep banks, and people would zoom up a bank to get ahead. At one point there seemed to be four "passing" lanes – and we were all giggling like happy children on a picnic with the loving parent.

Sant Ji stopped in a clearing, and we halted behind Him, fanning out into a semi-circle. He turned and glanced from person to person, giving darshan to each. When His eyes alighted upon Chris, He looked for a very long time. Chris stood there with folded hands, gazing back at Sant Ji. I was behind Sant Ji, but I could see that Chris did not even blink. His little face was glowing as if it had a light bulb inside of it. Children of that age often look angelic when they are sleeping – but he was wide-awake and shone like an angel. After the walk, Chris remarked, "Boy, when Sant Ji looked at me . . ." and he got into the position he had been in and began to gyrate backwards and forwards. I asked, "Did you feel like you were going to fall over?" He smiled and said, "Yeah, almost. Sant Ji kept looking and looking at me, and I just felt, kind of, 'whooooo-oooo' " and he continued to reel back and forth. The love fest was definitely beginning.

During the walk someone had wondered how to develop inside. Sant Ji answered that when one tasted the *Maha Ras* [the Divine Nectar] within, then the mind was subdued. A second disciple commented that he was so far away from that state – from tasting the *Maha Ras* – that he wondered what to do. Sant Ji said that we should never think that we were weak. We should never bow down before the five thieves of lust, anger, greed, attachment, and egotism, because we had the Satguru always standing behind us. The Satguru was strong, and He would help us defeat the passions. Being defeated was different than surrendering – and we should never surrender.

In Rajasthan, Sant Ji continued, the farmers were considered to be the strong ones, and the merchants were thought to be weak. The latter had weak hearts, but the farmers were strong. With much laughter, He related a story of a farmer who had gotten into a physical fight with a merchant. Somehow the merchant had managed to get the better of the farmer, and was sitting on top of his chest. The merchant suddenly became afraid of what would happen once he let the farmer up, so he yelled to a passerby, "Please, help me. I don't know what to do when this farmer gets up." The passerby asked, "Why? You are on top of him now." But, knowing how strong the farmer was, the merchant was still worried that he would end up defeated by that farmer pinned under him. The Satguru could not be defeated, so we must not surrender and we should not be afraid.

Someone asked if there were a danger in asking too many questions, adding that he had seen some people who asked a lot of questions fall into difficulty later on. Sant Ji laughed, and indicated that if that was what the questioner had seen, then he should accept his own experience. He added that, yes, if the people who asked all the questions would just meditate instead, then all of their questions would be answered from within.

Sant Ji did not call for as many bhajans during the Satsang that evening, but gave a discourse instead. There was no disharmony in this group, and we all went to bed while "visions of sugar cane danced in our heads." Pappu told me that several of us were to accompany Sant Ji to a portion of a wedding ceremony in a nearby village on Thursday (the first of March). And I was supposed to see Sant Ji in the morning.

Wednesday, February 28th

I had a good deal of trepidation in my heart as I went into my first private interview in a year. I was no longer "puffed up." Instead, the shame rose in me like blush on a cheek – and I really did feel as if I were wearing it on my sleeve. I bowed down at those great feet, and He scooped me back up and welcomed me with full love. I told Him how grateful I was for all that He had done for me – and that now I owed my life to Him. I had always loved Him, I explained, but when I had become so extreme, only His Grace and intervention saved me. Sant Ji gazed down at me with those huge beautiful eyes and quietly said, "You don't know how much this Saint loves you. And you don't know how much this Saint is praying for you, and is working for you." It was breath-taking, and I was overwhelmed.

He gently explained that it is the nature of the mind to do those types of tricks. Now my mind had been through all of that, so I could be careful to recognize and avoid it in the future. He smiled and said that He was so happy when I wrote and told Him that I had become "the old Kent." And now, He said, I should stay "the old Kent!"

I chose that moment to mention that, as my old self, I was now spending a couple hours a day learning to play the guitar. I asked if that was bad for me. With a look on His face of total patience, Sant Ji explained so kindly that, while it was all right to engage in those things, I should not leave off my meditations. I must be sure to do my spiritual practices side-by-side with whatever else I was doing.

Sant Ji asked me if Nicky were going to school yet and I said, "No, but he attends almost every day." Sant Ji said, "Oh, that is good. It will get him in the habit of going to school." We went on to talk about many other things – with much laughter throughout – and I felt much lighter when I walked out of His room.

On the afternoon walk, Sant Ji paused and asked, "Does anyone want to go get sugar cane?" Chris was nodding in the affirmative, so I tried to catch his eye to signal "No," as I was not sure he should go into the field. Then Sant Ji sent everyone in to get the cane, telling us to beware of our hands. He was laughing like anything while we all entered the thick rows to break off the stalks. When we returned and began to crunch, He told us again how we all looked very beautiful eating the sugar cane.

Someone asked if eating sugar cane was good for meditation? Sant Ji said that the juice was good for digestion, but that it had nothing to do with meditation. The row was narrow when we left that place, so we followed Sant Ji in a single file back to the main road. As He stood in the road, waiting for everyone to arrive, He turned to Chris and asked, "Do you like the sugar cane?" Chris said, "Yes!" Sant Ji laughed and said, "Eating sugar cane is your meditation!" I remarked, "Oh, if that is so then he is going to get to *Sach Khand* really soon!" And Sant Ji said, "*Zarur, zarur!*" [Surely, surely!]

Everyone was laughing by that point, and when we arrived back at the compound there was more divine hilarity in store. Anne Wiggins had noticed that people with cameras were given deferential treatment by most. The "photographers" were allowed to get close to Sant Ji, walk backwards in front of Him, step ahead of others, etc. Anne mimed her own "camera" of thin air – and acted the part perfectly. The result was very amusing to all – especially when Sant Ji laughed and laughed – and gave great darshan opportunities for Anne. As we turned off the road and walked through the Ashram gate, Anne stepped in front to snap a series of her magical photos – and we felt drunk with joy.

Sant Ji finally extricated Himself from the crowd, and stepped into a room to see a Westerner who was ill. Chris and I darted around to a spot we knew He would pass by. When He came, I said, "*Pita-Poot*" [Father-Son – also the name of a book about the relationship of Baba Sawan Singh to Master Kirpal – a text well known to Sant Ji]. Sant Ji folded His hands, laughed once again, and repeated, "*Pita-Poot.*"

At the evening Satsang, Eric and I sang a "new" bhajan of Brahmanand, *Guru Bina Kaun Sahai Narak Me* [Without the Guru, who will save you from hell?], as well as, *Satguru Ke Guna Ga Le Bande* [Sing the qualities of the Satguru, O man, and wind up the births and deaths].[7] Other Western disciples sang, and then Chris and I sang *Thakur Tum Sharnaee Aaya* [O Lord, I have taken refuge in You].

We filed out past Sant Ji, and gathered outside His door to hear Him say, "Good Night." Chris had told me that he had yet to hear Sant Ji speak those words in English, so we were set to make a special effort for Chris to be in earshot. The crowd was thick, however, so I hoisted him up and he sat on my shoulders. When Sant Ji saw Chris, He chuckled, and asked, "Shringi Rishi?" (a reference to the story of the great yogi who ended up with a wife and children clinging to him – see Chapter Six), and we burst into hearty laughter.

After Sant Ji closed the doors, Jon Engle approached us and asked, "Did Sant Ji say, 'Engi Rishi'?" I laughed and said, "No, Jon. He said 'Shringi Rishi.' " Jon smiled slyly and quipped, "Whew! I thought Sant Ji had revealed my secret – that I, Jon Engle, was 'Engi Rishi' – and I got nervous!" Again we laughed, caught up in the intoxication of the moment. Chris and I danced our way back to the room to the rhythm of a severe case of the giggles. We brushed our teeth and went to the bathroom and, as we lay in bed, Chris commented, "I do miss Nicky and his wild ways" – and we both burst out laughing once again.

Thursday, March 1st

At three a.m. the next morning – a time for tea made by Pathi Ji for several of the Westerners – I had a visitor. My old friend from Sanbornton, Anne Wiggins, dropped by with a message. She said that before the trip was over, I must take two photographs: one of Chris' face when He was getting darshan from Sant Ji, and the other of Sant Ji's face looking at Chris.[8] I told her that Sant Ji had said Chris' meditation should consist of eating sugar cane – and she commented that Chris has been a wonderful example for her. To see him simply being himself – no pretensions – a little sprite running along beside the Saint – that was extraordinary. It was exactly what she had needed. And, she added, at Satsang the evening before, Chris had helped provide one of the most important

---

[7] As explained in the footnotes of Chapters One and Six, Sant Ji actually wrote all of the songs attributed to Mastana Ji.

[8] I did take both of these photographs. The one of Chris as he looked at Sant Ji is quite blurry. The photograph of Sant Ji gazing at Chris graces the cover of this book.

moments of her life. She had been looking at Sant Ji, feeling so much love, and when she heard Chris singing *Thakur Tum* [O Lord, I have taken refuge in You], she wept and wept. I thanked her so much for those thoughts, and understood that they mirrored my own. After she left, I thought about how He had saved me – and I bowed my head and wept.

In the early afternoon, several of us traveled with Sant Ji to a near-by village to take part in a small portion of a wedding. We rode in Jeeps and, on arrival, climbed an outside staircase to enter a small living room. The room was jammed full of devotees, seated on the floor, awaiting the arrival of Sant Ji. They had reserved a special area for us, so Judith Perkins, Gene Dittmer, Anne Wiggins, Don Macken, Chris, and I squeezed in. Sant Ji sat in a chair and gave an informal discourse that sent ripples of laughter through the loving sea of faces. He drank some milk, distributed parshad, and then it was time to return. Several of us were snapping photos, so I suggested that Anne take one of her "special" ones. She jabbed me in the ribs with her elbow – but not before Sant Ji asked Pappu what I had said. When Pappu translated, Sant Ji laughed and said, "No. That is not for here. That is only for our group."

Chris was very excited to ride the tractor back to 77 RB – along with half a dozen other Ashram sevadars. When we had returned to the Ashram, Sant Ji again went to visit the Westerner who was ill. Stepping out of her room, Sant Ji saw us and asked, "Okay, Kent. Do you want Anne to take our photo now?" I nodded and said, *"Hunh Ji!"* [Yes!] Sant Ji and I proceeded to pose while Anne "took" a picture – spending plenty of time framing the photo and getting her non-existent camera into focus. It was a very jolly moment.

After the meditation sitting, I came back to the room and found a large pile of strips from sugar cane stalks – all spilling out of Chris' hat. He was nowhere to be seen. After a bit, he came running into the room. Pointing at his hat, I asked, "Chris, what are you doing?" He, of course, answered, "I have been doing my meditation!" Chris told Pappu that he had been eating so much sugar cane, he could go to *Sach Khand* twice. Pappu responded that if he went there once, he would not want to come back.

Sant Ji had invited us all to go walking again, so we got ready and followed Him out of the Ashram and down the road towards His hut. After a while, it began to drizzle. Sant Ji stopped and said, "Well, all of our clothes will get wet, so we should go back." As we were quite near the hut, Don Macken suggested that we could all squeeze inside. Sant Ji agreed, and somehow all forty of us managed to fit.

Sant Ji sat on the rope bed within, and the rest of us jammed around Him on the dirt floor, which was covered with empty burlap bags. Pappu sang *Thakur Tum*, and then Jonathan Powell sang Sant Ji's *Kya Hua Je Janam Liya* [What is the use of taking birth, if you have not appreciated it, and if you have not dyed it in the color of Satguru's devotion?]. The atmosphere was joyously electric, and we all felt intoxicated. Sant Ji asked if any others wished to sing, so I began the sweet Colombian hymn of praise, and everyone joined in: *San Yi, San Yi, San Yi – jubilosos Te esperamos* [Sant Ji, Sant Ji, Sant Ji – jubilantly we wait for You].

Shortly thereafter, Chris stuck his hand out the little window and observed aloud that it had stopped raining. Sant Ji wondered what Chris had said, so Pappu translated. Sant Ji asked, "Is it true?" Others answered that it was. *"Teek hai,"* said Sant Ji, "Then, let us go back to the Ashram." I thought, "Uh-oh. Chris is in for it now. If he had not said anything, we might have kept sitting forever, crammed into that blessed spot." But everyone was too happy to be upset with Chris' accurate meteorological observation, and we strode back to the compound to the vigorous pace set by our Leader.

In the evening Satsang, Sant Ji commented on a bhajan of Swami Ji Maharaj. He told a few stories that I had not heard before. He explained that Saints sometimes test the people who come to Them – using tools like criticism – to keep away those who are not really interested in the Teachings. The Masters may even do things that seem unbecoming in order to test the faith of the devotees.

One Saint had a disciple who was a king. When the Saint used to visit the king in his palace, he would get down from his throne and ask his Guru to sit upon it. One time the Saint came, bringing with him a bottle filled with colored water. The onlookers thought, "Ah, the cat is out of the bag now. This so-called saint is carrying a bottle of wine." They began to criticize the Guru, and the king felt the same way. At one point, the Saint began to pour the water onto the floor, and the king thought, "Hmmm. A drunkard would never pour his wine onto the floor. There must be some meaning behind all of this." The king asked the Saint what He was doing, and He replied, "Well, I am putting out a fire in some temple." The king sent someone to check, and sure enough, a fire had started in the temple and the Saint had appeared there to extinguish it. The king realized that he had been given a test, and failed.

Another Saint, in order to test the faith of His disciples, spent the night in the house of a prostitute. He sent people out to the market to buy food that resembled meat, and for drink that appeared to be wine. All of the disciples began to criticize the Master and, one by one, they left. In the morning the Guru came out of the house and found only one disciple remaining. The Master asked him, "Why are you still here?" The disciple answered, "Oh Master, if I left You I would not have anywhere to go. Who would I turn to? Where am I supposed to go?" The Master then gave that dear one the Successorship.

That night I lay on the rope bed, staring up at the forever moving shadows on the textured ceiling – brought into play by the kerosene lantern's small flame. I realized that I had no idea what it meant to be "tested" – and prayed with all my heart that I never would be, unless that was His Will. I recalled Sant Ji's advice for me at Sant Bani in May of 1977, when I expressed a desire for Him to call me a good meditator. He had strongly cautioned me against that, and suggested that my one prayer should be to maintain what I had been given.[9]

Friday, March 2nd

Sant Ji had told us that He wished to increase the time we were sitting for meditation in the mornings. On Friday we sat for an hour and a quarter, and it was very nice. The tremendous hurdles of physical pain and mental agony which I had faced the first day or two had dwindled to near non-existence, and now I was able to follow Sant Ji's advice and "not think of meditation as a burden." The only difficulty I faced was that I was "distracted" when I heard Him rustle in His chair, or clear His throat, and I had to smile as I fought the urge to pop open my eyes and stare.

I was scheduled to have an interview before lunch, but Pappu came in after breakfast to tell me that Sant Ji had changed the plans. I was disappointed for a moment, as I had been excited at the prospect of sitting in front of Him, but I quickly remembered Who was calling the shots. Chris and I laughed together as we talked about it. In the end I was glad for the delay, as a number of other items came to me that I wanted to discuss with Him. I realized that I was starting to enjoy the present moment and whatever it brought – rather than constantly playing the game of "O, I can't wait for this or that!"

During the walk that afternoon, Sant Ji paused, and requested Chris

---

[9] See May 6th, 1977, Chapter Four, above.

to come over and stand directly in front of Him. "Are you doing your meditation?" He asked. Chris said that he was. Then Sant Ji inquired, "Is your meditation coming along well?" "Yes, very well!" Chris responded, laughing along with Sant Ji. Anne Wiggins asked Sant Ji if eating sugar cane as a "meditation practice" was only for children – and Sant Ji, laughing even more, answered with an emphatic, "*Hunh!*" [Yes!]

Sant Ji told the very beautiful story about the disciple who carried water for Guru Gobind Singh. It was a time of war, and the emperor's forces were battling with the Sikhs of Guru Gobind Singh. The disciple whose seva it was to give water to the troops, served soldiers from both sides equally. Some of Guru Gobind Singh's soldiers complained, wondering why that disciple should be helping the enemy troops as well as his own. When Guru Gobind Singh asked the disciple why he was doing that, the latter humbly told the Guru, "I see You everywhere. I see You in everyone. It doesn't matter if the person is a friend or an enemy. So how am I supposed to refuse giving You the water?" Guru Gobind Singh was so pleased with that disciple, that He gave him bandages to help the enemy as well.

At Satsang that night, Chris and I sang *Dhun Ghat Vich Baj Rehi Ji* [The Sound is ringing within you, but you won't get it without the Beloved Guru]. When we were finished, Sant Ji said, "*Pita-poot bahot aacha!*" [Father and son, very good!] There was no doubt that Chris was a very happy little boy – completely at home halfway around the world from Sanbornton, New Hampshire. He loved to help with the seva whenever he could, and he was pleased when he was allowed to cut up carrots and other vegetables with Sardar Rattan Singh, Bhag Singh, Pathi Ji and others.

Pathi Ji was so kind to both of us. He and I sometimes talked for long stretches, as He gauged his Hindi to my level. He told me that when I was in America, Sant Ji and the sevadars of 77 RB had a lot of remembrance for me. People recounted different incidents involving me in some mishap or other, and they would all laugh. A favorite story was how I cried like a little child in Bogotá. Pathi Ji told me that sometimes Sant Ji would sing *Tati Vao Na Laga Di Ji* [The hot wind doesn't blow over one who has the Guru's protection], substituting my variant chorus: *Tandi Vao* [The cold wind . . .] – and that would bring more laughter to them. I received these tidbits like balm for my tender, but strengthening psyche. Last year Sant Ji had given me nothing but love – and it was just what I needed – but it hurt. This trip, it was as if the very sweetness of the atmosphere, rolling in like waves on a shore, wore gently at any residual walls of confusion. Slowly, slowly, the partitions were crumbling away, leaving a palace of peace in their stead.

Saturday, March 3rd

Before I headed off for the meditation, I noted that Chris was very well prepared. He sat on his bed, with a bhajan book in hand and a schoolbook near one knee, nibbling on parshad. A pile of sugar cane was in front of him, ready to be attacked. He looked up and smiled at me as I headed out the door to the meditation room. I was lucky enough to plunk myself right in front of the chair that Sant Ji would soon occupy. The hour and fifteen minutes went by very quickly. After Pappu had told us all, "Leave off, please," a devotee asked Sant Ji what He was doing while He sat there in front of us. She wondered if He were purifying our souls while He looked around the room – what exactly was happening.

Sant Ji spoke about the responsibilities of the Master. We were there, and He was working with us, but He also had souls very far away that He was purifying. The Masters have a great, great job. When They recline, They never really sleep. Their body does get some rest, but They go into the higher realms and continue to work for our salvation from within. When I returned to the room and told Chris what Sant Ji had said, he remarked, "And They do that job very well!"

The Final Day – Sunday, March 4th

At mid-morning on Sunday, Sant Ji held the monthly Satsang for the Indian Sangat. People came in droves – on foot, by camel, bike, scooter, by bus from Delhi – and via a few cars. Hundreds of pairs of shoes were checked in and placed carefully in a roped off area, and the devotees walked off, little numbered tags in hand, to sit cross-legged in the place of Satsang. A huge multi-colored canvas tent – with open walls – had been set up for that purpose, and it filled up completely. A special section up front was roped off for the Western guests. Prior to Sant Ji's arrival, there were many bhajans sung, utilizing a sound system powered by 12-volt batteries from the cars and tractor.

We followed Sant Ji in and took our places, as He climbed up on the dais, bowed His head down to the Great Masters, and sat in front of us. Pathi Ji sat to Sant Ji's left, with the sacred text from which he would chant cradled on a special wooden stand. After a couple more bhajans, Sant Ji indicated that Pathi Ji should begin to chant the opening lines of the hymn which Sant Ji had picked to discourse upon.

There was no translation for the Westerners – just straight, continuous darshan while the Punjabi flowed from Sant Ji to the Sangat – and the Love of the Saints reflected back to Him. I could not follow much of what was said, but the more I gazed, the more intoxicated I became. When Sant Ji would say something humorous, a ripple of soft laughter swept over the Indians all around me. Sitting in the midst of that experience was like nothing else on this earth.

After the Satsang, the crowds were all fed from the langar [free kitchen] of the Master. There were many people milling around: waiting to see Sant Ji; waiting to pick up their shoes; waiting to sit down for lunch. I sent Chris off to get some sugar cane so that we could run it through the juicer – a mill for the cane stalks that produced fresh, sweet juice in abundance. Chris ran off, and seemed to be gone a long time. He was very popular with the Indian Sangat – so I was not worried. Pappu and I finished the correspondence – which took a while – but Chris still had not returned. I decided to go looking. I walked out of the main gate and started down the road. From far, far away I saw a little, tiny, red-shirted figure coming across the field near Sant Ji's hut. And there came Chris with three stalks of cane. We ran them through the juicer, and delighted in the "fruits" of our labor.

The monthly Satsang always carried the sad reminder that the blessed days at His feet were quickly coming to an end. We were to leave well before dawn the next morning, and so the afternoon was dedicated to preparations for taking leave – sorting out all of those last minute snags and glitches that always take so much longer than one thought they would. Sant Ji was busy with the Indian Sangat, and the afternoon meditation was without His physical presence. We saw Him later in the evening, for a bhajan *mandli* [festival of bhajans] with the Indians.

On the twenty-eighth of February I had mailed a letter to Karen and Nick, explaining that Chris would probably be staying with me for the duration of my time in India. I had included a message to Debbie Asbeck as well, as she was helping Karen and Nick have fun in our absence. At the end I wrote that Sant Ji sent His Love to Nick, Karen, and Debbie, and signed it – and then Sant Ji had signed the letter as well: "*Love, Ajaib Singh.*"

By March third, the decision was clear that Chris would remain in Delhi, and then return with us to Rajasthan when Pappu and I had finished the work on the *Anurag Sagar*. The next morning, as we climbed aboard, we filed one more time past our beloved Guru – Who stood with folded hands at the door of the bus. We rolled out before the sun even rose, many of us weeping softly under the intense pain of that physical parting. Chris and I, at least, knew that, God Willing, we were going to come back up to see Sant Ji once more before we returned to New Hampshire.

Ten Days in Delhi with the *Anurag Sagar* [The Ocean of Love] March Fifth through Fifteenth

After the other Westerners had departed for their homes, we began in earnest the translation of Sant Kabir Sahib's sacred text the *Anurag Sagar* [*The Ocean of Love*]. The book is a poem that utilizes the format of dialogue to explain the creation and mysteries of the universe. Over and over again, Sant Kabir patiently answers the questions of His disciple, Dharam Das – along the way revealing the True Nature of Almighty God, and the various snares and deceptions of the Negative Power. The Great Master, Baba Jaimal Singh, had recommended the book in the highest terms to Baba Sawan Singh. The book helped to answer many of Sawan Singh's questions, and shortly after reading it, He took Initiation from Baba Jaimal Singh. Baba Sawan Singh later told a devoted disciple that, without studying the *Anurag Sagar*, "one cannot fully understand the difference between Kal (the Negative Power) and *Dayal Mat* (the Path of the True and Merciful God), nor can one fully grasp the teachings of Sant Mat."[10]

---

[10] From Rai Sahib Munshi Ram, *With the Three Masters*, Vol. II, p. 187, as quoted in Russell Perkins' "Introduction" to the *Anurag Sagar [The Ocean of Love]* [1982], p. xxxi. Much more information on the *Anurag Sagar [The Ocean of Love]* may be found in the introductory piece about Sant Kabir and Dharam Das by Sant Ajaib Singh, and the formal "Introduction" and copious notes throughout by Russell Perkins.

Sant Ji had examined a number of variant texts and chosen one in particular: a scholarly edition compiled in the early 1900's by a holy man, Swami Yugalananda. The language of the poem is Kabir Sahib's own *Braj* dialect – a far cry from modern Hindi, and a challenge to translate into English.[11] With the help of various people along the way, including a disciple of Sant Ji's, Partap Singh, a schoolteacher who was familiar with *Braj*, Pappu had started the translation. However, only ten to fifteen percent of the text had been translated (the English version is over 200 pages), and it had proved to be very slow going. We talked briefly about a strategy, but saw no shortcuts. As we had just been sitting at the feet of Sant Ji, and He had sent us to do this blessed work, our tanks were full, so we plunged right in.

What took place over the next nine days was not like any other time that Pappu and I had experienced before (nor have we since). We closed ourselves in a room and, before we knew it, the seva was doing us – rather than the other way. At every moment it was clear Who was really accomplishing all of the work – and we felt like happy puppets, delighted to have our strings pulled over and over again. The Bagga family actually worried about us at first – as we did not like to stop even to get something to eat. The work went on and on – as we logged up-wards of eighteen or more hours a day. Pappu sat on the bed, studying the next lines of verse, and I sat in a chair at a desk, pen in hand, poised to write on the blank page of my spiral notebook whatever he spoke. We would pause now and then to discuss a particular phrasing – or how best to render something into English – but mostly Pappu spoke and I wrote – both of us feeling the divine presence at every moment. I felt very privileged to be the divine stenographer.

After a few hours, we would switch positions. A gentle knock on the door might signal the arrival of chai or a meal – and we sighed, drank, ate, and hurried on – inexplicably driven by the seva itself. Our code words – that we still use today – became, *"Kya likha?"* [What did you write?] – from Pappu to me; and *"Kya bola?"* [What did you say?] – from me to Pappu.

The days went on and on, and the notebook began to fill. Along the way, we wrote down any questions that we had as to how best to render something into English. On the outside it was the time of *Holi* – a festive

---

[11] See Russell Perkins' "Introduction" to the *Anurag Sagar [The Ocean of Love]* [1982], pp. xxx-xxxii.

holiday honoring Prahlad.[12] On the second day of merry-making, people throw colored water and powder on each other (and complete strangers) – and celebrating groups went by our windows. We were startled when a water balloon burst on the grating, and its harmless red contents splashed within – but we laughed and kept on working. Chris was well occupied and cared for most lovingly by Pappu's younger siblings, so his joy continued. Both Chris and I suffered mild attacks of stomach ailments – and visited the doctor with good effect. But that was the only wobble in the wheel spinning the sacred text into English.

And what a text it was! It is not possible to capture the essence of the *Anurag Sagar* here, as the book must be experienced in its entirety. What Pappu and I found so fascinating was not just the amazing contents, but also the patience with which Sant Kabir dealt with the queries, doubts, and confusions of the disciple that would ultimately be His Successor, Dharam Das. Again and again, Kabir Sahib took Dharam Das to great heights within to reveal Inner Truths – and Dharam Das would be most grateful that all of His illusions had been removed. Yet, in the next few pages – sometimes in only a stanza or two – Dharam Das would raise more concerns and questions. This very human trait of Dharam Das made it easy to identify with him, as the same questions and doubts went through our minds. The format allowed many of the enormous Truths of the poem to be absorbed more easily.[13]

Kabir Sahib laid out the story of Creation in great detail. Kal, the Negative Power, was one of the original Sixteen Sons of Almighty God, *Sat Purush*. Kal did eons of devotional practices and, as a reward, asked for His own world – distinct from that of His Father. He wished to rule over a separate creation – and to do so He introduced passions such as impatience, anger, lust and greed. Using all of these, He created a world, and then trapped the souls there. The All Merciful Sat Purush, seeing the agony of the suffering souls, periodically sends another Son into this

---

[12] In ancient India, Prahlad was a devotee whose father, a king, wished that his son would worship only him – and not God. Prahlad refused, so his father tried to kill him. The king's sister had the boon that she could not be killed by fire. Her brother convinced her to sit in a fire with Prahlad in her lap – but she was consumed by the flames and Prahlad was untouched. *Holi* celebrates this event. On the first day, piles of wood are burned, and on the second, colors are scattered everywhere.

[13] As of this writing, I may safely add that I do not understand all of the Truths of this great book.

world, Kal's domain, to save the *jivas* [souls].

Kabir Sahib told Dharam Das how the various worlds came into being, and in what Forms the Almighty had manifested in different Ages or *Yugas*. He explained to Dharam Das that the powerful Lord Kal will stop at nothing to keep the souls locked in His realm – and will even create false paths that mimic the Path of the Masters. In a heartbreaking section of the book, Dharam Das struggled mightily with a reality presented by Kabir: that the Negative Power was destined to manifest in one of the physical sons of Dharam Das. Over and over, Kabir Sahib found ways to lovingly explain, cajole, joke, and otherwise direct His disciple's attention toward embracing the Truth.

Along the way, beautiful stories were told, most especially the saga of Queen Indra Mati and how she came to the Feet of the Saint for salvation of her soul, and of her husband's soul as well. The Queen was very devoted to Sat Purush, in His incarnation under the Name of "Karunamai." In the midst of her love for God, the Negative Power sent several extraordinary tests to her – including posing as the Satguru Himself. She recognized Kal, and told Him so – ordering the Negative Power to leave her presence. That great Power slapped her face, and, as she fell down, she cried out for her Guru, Gyani (again, "Karunamai" – Sant Kabir's name in His incarnation in the Copper Age – the *Dwapar Yuga*). In the passage that follows, Kabir Sahib details the liberation of the Queen and her arrival in the True Home of Her Father, Sat Purush – followed by her astonishment to find that God and her Guru are One and the Same. The extract – with its standard format of statement, explanation, quotation, hymn, and couplet – typifies the pithy lyrical beauty of the whole poem.

Kabir said to Dharam Das:

I couldn't stay away after hearing her call: Listen, Dharam Das, this is my nature.
When the Queen called me, in one moment I was there.
Seeing me, she became happy and from her mind the fear of Kal ran away.
When I came there Kal went away and the Queen's body was purified.

Then Indra Mati, folding her hands, said, "O God, listen to one request of mine:

Now I have recognized the shadow of Yama, and I will not live in
   this country anymore.
O Lord, take me to my own country, as here there are many
   sufferings of Kal."
After saying this she became sad and said, "Take me to the Sat
   Purush right now!"

Kabir said to Dharam Das:
First of all I took the Queen with me and finished the subject of
   the difficult Kal.
Right then her destiny karma was paid off, and then I went to Sat
   Lok, taking the Queen.
I took her to Mansarovar, which filled her with amazement.
I made her taste the Nectar from the Pool of Amrit, then I put
   her feet in the Kabir Sagar.
Beyond that is the Ocean of the Surat. Reaching there, the
   Queen became pure.
When I made her stand at the door of Sat Lok, the Queen became
   very happy looking at it.
The souls came and embraced her, sang the welcome song, and
   performed the Arti.
All the souls honored her and said: "You are a blessed soul who
   has realized the Satguru.
It is good that you are free from the snare of Kal, and all your
   pain and suffering is over.
Soul, come with us, have the darshan of Sat Purush, and bow
   your head to Him.
Indra Mati, come with us and have the darshan of Sat Purush."
Indra Mati joined the other souls and, in excitement, sang the
   happy song.
All the souls are walking and praying for the darshan of Sat
   Purush.
Then I requested Sat Purush, "Now give Your darshan to the
   souls who have come near.
Give them your darshan, O Din Dayal. Be gracious on them, O
   Liberator."
Then the Flower bloomed and these words were heard: "Listen,
   O Gyani, Yog Santayan!
Bring the souls and make them have darshan."

HYMN
Gyani then came near the souls and took all of them.
The souls became beautiful after having the darshan of Sat
   Purush.

*After bowing down, all of them put their attention on Sat Purush.
Then, He gave some fruit of Nectar which was received by all
the souls.*

COUPLET
*Just as the lotus blooms after getting the light of the sun,
In the same way the sufferings of the souls from ages and ages
are finished after having the darshan of Sat Purush.*

INDRA MATI'S AMAZEMENT, AFTER REACHING SAT LOK, TO FIND KARUNAMAI AND SAT PURUSH AS THE SAME FORM

*When the Queen saw the marvelous beauty of the Sat Purush,
and the wine of Nectar,
She became overwhelmed, and clung to His feet, as her soul was
wise and full of good qualities.
He put both His Hands on her soul, and she became happy as
the lotus blooms in the sunlight.*

*The Queen said, "Blessed are You, O Karunamai, Who brought
me here after finishing my illusion."*

Then Sat Purush told the Queen, "Go and call Karunamai."

Kabir said to Dharam Das:
*She came to me, and looking at my form, she, my servant, was
astonished.*

*The Queen said, "This is surprising! I can't see any difference.
Whatever qualities I saw in the Sat Purush, in Karunamai also I
see every single one!"
Running, she – the wise soul – touched the Feet and said, "O
Lord, now I know all Your character.
You are the Sat Purush and You call Yourself the servant. Where
did You hide this Glory?
In my mind I know this for sure: that You are the Sat Purush and
nobody else is.
I have seen this after coming here. I hail You, O Competent One,
Who woke me up.*

HYMN
*O Abode of Mercy, You are the Blessed One. Your wise Naam is
the remover of worries.
You are indescribable, unmovable, immortal, steady, pure, glorious, and endless.*

You are without doubts, selfless, the support of the world, name-
less, firm, and indestructible.
O Lord, You are the beginning of everything, and maker of all
the creatures.

COUPLET

You showered grace on me and woke me up, understanding me
as Your own.
You cut the snare of Yama and You brought me to the Ocean of
Happiness. "

Kabir said to Dharam Das:
Then the Lotus closed, and the souls all went to their abodes.[14]

As we came to the end of the book, our awe grew. We read about
path after path, designed to look like solid spiritual ways, but in fact
clever deceptions created by the Negative Power to ensnare the souls.
Kabir Sahib stated that the reach of the Negative Power, Lord Kal, and
His agents such as Yama, the Lord of Death, was so great that it could
even sow doubts in the Incarnations. In the end They would be saved by
Sat Purush, of course, but we could not help but wonder what hope there
was for poor mortals like us.[15] The answer rang out on every page
however – to us as it did to Dharam Das. The only means to salvation
was to take refuge in the holy shelter of the Master. It was the Grace and
Mercy of Sat Purush that would save us – no effort of our own.
Brahmanand had stated it so simply: *Guru Bina Kaun Sahai Narak Me,*
Guru Bina Kaun Sahai Re [Without the Guru, who will save you from
hell?].

After nine days we were finished, and ready to travel back to Rajasthan to go over our questions with Sant Ji. That night, completely wired
and intoxicated from the week and a half of intense seva, we allowed
ourselves a visit to the Volga Restaurant in Connaught Circle, where
Chris and I enjoyed the treat Pappu kindly bought us: "American Style
Pizza." We ordered grilled cheese sandwiches, with tomatoes, as well,
and ate a plate of french fries, washing it all down with Campa Colas and
Fanta Orange sodas. To top it off we had servings of "Qwality-brand"
pistachio and mango ice cream! Looking at the table full of delicious
items, I drowned any rising guilt by realizing that I was certainly "the old

---

[14] The *Anurag Sagar* [*The Ocean of Love*], pp. 123-126.
[15] *Op. cit.,* pp. 182 and 189.

Kent." Then I recalled Sant Ji's words about the *halvah parshad* the year before – how it was an expression of His Love for us – and I relaxed and enjoyed myself immensely. We went to bed that night, and the next thing we knew it was three in the morning. Our hired car and driver were outside waiting, ready for the long trip back to 77 RB.

Thursday, March Fifteenth – Back to Rajasthan

The drive from town to city to town, on ever-narrowing roads that finally dwindle into dust, was shorter by car than by bus. Pappu, Chris, and I were able to stop wherever we wished, and we had a good time on the ten-hour trip. We remembered Sant Ji, as well as various stories that made us laugh. Chris was very adept at listening unobtrusively to adult conversations. He had learned that if he were quiet, no one would particularly notice that he was nearby. One evening before we had come back to Delhi, Pappu and I were talking softly, assuming that Chris had fallen asleep. Pappu wondered if we should "get Chris a ball." Chris made a comment, so we asked him if he had heard. "Yes," he said, "Pappu was asking if 'Chris should be involved!' " We roared with laughter, and explained the joke to Chris – who also thought it was very funny. From then on, Pappu would frequently check with Chris to see if he was "involved."

We arrived at the Ashram around two in the afternoon. The compound was incredible – so different did it appear from ten days ago when we had left. I had trouble recognizing where I was. It was empty, empty – and appeared more like one of the mud-walled villages that we passed as we came into the area. When the groups from the West were there, the place was so well groomed that it sparkled. Now, it looked like a place in which a small number of people actually lived. I was astounded, and loved it. This was the Saint's home as it appeared on a day-to-day basis, and I bowed my head at the sight of it.

After a short time, a group of sevadars came in from watering the fields, and there was Sant Ji, right in the midst of everyone. He was dressed in a simple, gray Punjabi suit, and He looked wonderful. He appeared younger to me – like a man in his prime. It was as if He had relaxed, and shed some of that Mantle that we disciples expect – thus require – of Him. He was always in the role of a Saint, of course, because that is what He was and is. But somehow it seemed that He had contracted a portion of that enormous Power – pulled in some of the Bloom – so that He could function as a Rajasthani farmer. It was one of the most amazing sights I had ever seen in my life – and, again, I was totally thrilled to be experiencing that moment.

Sant Ji came over to greet us, and we bowed and touched His feet. He asked how the work had gone, "Had we been successful in our efforts?" We told Him that, with the Grace of the Master, we had finished the work. Pappu explained that we had a number of questions we needed to ask, in order to clarify certain confusing points in the translation.

Sant Ji asked for details on our journey, and Pappu mentioned how much more comfortable it had been to ride in a car all of the way – rather than a train, Jeep, or bus. Sant Ji considered that for a moment, and then, turning to me with a divine twinkle, queried, "Your bicycle? Your cycle?" I chuckled, and told Him that it was good. He looked at Chris and asked, "Do you want them to bring you some sugar cane?" and Chris said, "Yes, please." Sant Ji told us to rest, and went back to work.

In a short while, Bhag Singh, an elderly sevadar who lived at the Ashram, brought Chris a few really good cane stalks. We were outside on our rope beds, eating the cane, when Sant Ji appeared again. He looked at both of us and laughed. I asked Him if I could take His photo – as I really hoped to bottle the phenomenon I was witnessing. Sant Ji replied, "No. Wait until later. I have been out in the fields." I pleaded, "This won't be for publication in the magazine. Karen really likes that gray outfit." He looked at me, smiled, and said, "*Kal*" [Tomorrow]. He headed off to the fields again.

We were served a delicious simple supper, and Chris ate as much as I did. He had not been eating very much in Delhi, but the minute we were inside the compound he was ready to fill his plate. Perhaps the sugar cane was helping his digestion – as well as his spiritual progress.

As the sun sank, the moon rose, bright and full, but was ducking in and out of some large clouds. There was a lot of construction going on at the Ashram, and the bricks were arriving by the trailer load. At that moment, the focus was a new courtyard, and the night air was filled with the music of fired bricks clinking together as they were tossed off the trailer. I heard a commotion, and was able to figure out that one of the tractors hauling the bricks had gotten stuck a short distance from the Ashram. The Ashram tractor chugged out to assist, and the moon broke free just as it drove back through the compound gates. In the midst of it all, conducting as if from a chariot, came my beloved Sant Ji. When the tractor halted, Sant Ji jumped down to hurry on ahead of it – giving verbal direction and signaling with both hands where the load of bricks should go. The headlights cast His shadow on the wall.

Chris and I continued to watch quietly from the shadows, as Sant Ji grasped a kerosene lantern and held it up to light the work scene. Harmel brought a table, and Sant Ji finally placed His lamp alongside an Aladdin Lamp – that was soon pumped up enough to cast a bright light over all. After a while, Sant Ji sat in a chair, and continued to oversee the activity.

When all of the bricks were unloaded, a lull crept in, and Chris and I decided we had better get to sleep. Pappu had already retired. The dining room was serving as a dormitory for the many sevadars who had come to help with the construction. Chris and I entered quietly, closing the door behind us. Just as we reached our beds, the door opened again, and in came Sant Ji. He walked over to us, with a large flashlight in His hand. He asked where Pappu was, and I replied that he was sleeping. Sant Ji flashed the beam across Pappu's still form. He turned back to me, and asked me what aspect of the work we wished to go over with Him. I replied that it was *"saval"* [questions]. He asked, "What questions?"

I got out my notebook and showed Him our list of questions. He asked me what the first one was. In my broken Hindi, I explained that it was about our confusion over Kabir's description of the three Powers of the Satguru. *"Hunh!"* [Yes!] said Sant Ji. "And the second?" That is about the ceremony of the *chowka* – the coconut – and what the significance is of that. *"Aacha,"* He said. "And the next?" It was a question about how Kabir spoke of a turban – but I could not make the meaning clear to Sant Ji. He went on, pointing to the next question on my list with His forefinger, "And this one?" We came to the question about all of the different names of Kabir. I explained to Sant Ji that sometimes He was "Kabir," sometimes "Yog Jit" – and then He was "Nan Jit" – and then "Gyani." I asked if these names were *"sab eyk hai?"* [all one] Sant Ji nodded, and said, *"Hunh! Sab eyk hai!"* [Yes, They are all one!]

After looking over the list a bit more, Sant Ji said in English, "Okay." As He got up to leave, He said, "Good night!" Chris and I giggled and pinched ourselves at what had just occurred. It was nothing short of miraculous. Pathi Ji came in with two more roommates – the drivers of the hired tractors who, by that time, had stayed so late they needed to spend the night. Chris drifted off at once, but I stayed up, listening to the gentle breathing of a room full of sevadars, exhausted

after a long day in the fields of 77 RB. I worked for quite a while on the
notes and questions of the *Anurag Sagar* – to be certain that everything
was in order for our session with Sant Ji scheduled for the morning.
When I did blow out the flame of my lantern, I lay back on my bed, and
realized that I felt clearer than I had in a long, long time.

I was not at all sleepy – that is, I was not drifting off or anything of
the sort. Suddenly an intense feeling swept over me, impossible to
describe except in vague terms like I felt I was "half-way there." It was
such a state of peace and beauty, and I knew that it was very real. In my
mind's eye, I saw Sant Ji once again on the tractor – and then it was the
Form of Master Kirpal, Who became Baba Sawan Singh, and, then,
perhaps Kabir Sahib. I cannot say when I finally slept – but in the
morning I woke up to the sight of the sparrows over my head – darting in
and out of the room.

Friday, March 16th

On Friday morning, Pappu and I went in to see Sant Ji. I saw
immediately that He was dressed in shining white and I had to smile
inside at the absence of the gray work clothes. We bowed and touched
His feet, and then settled in for a long conversation. At first His beard
seemed a golden yellow, but then It became whiteness itself. I stopped
trying to analyze and began to drink. Sitting in the Ocean of Love, we
began to discuss the *Anurag Sagar*.

Sant Ji explained to us that Westerners would have a difficult time
understanding the book. He indicated that we would want to interpret the
events described, as myths and stories. The reality was, however, that
every word in the book was True. Everything that Kabir Sahib described
to Dharam Das had happened. The Westerners would have trouble
believing that, but it was true.

Sant Ji told us that Baba Sawan Singh had wanted to translate that
book into English, but had not done so because it was too complicated.
Sawan Singh quoted from the book often, and held it in very high regard,
but He ended up leaving its translation into English for a later time.
Master Kirpal used that book as well, but He also found it too complex
to translate. Even in its original language, it was a difficult text for
present day Indians to understand. Sant Ji laughed and added, "And now

it has been done under the direction of an illiterate!"[16]

We went through our list of questions. Most of Sant Ji's answers were later incorporated into the extraordinary notes, written by Russell Perkins, accompanying the published book. At one point we asked about one of the names of the Negative Power – as it seemed to be very similar to one of the Sacred Words. Sant Ji explained in a very matter-of-fact manner. The Five Charged Names are the Names of the Lords of the Five Inner Planes. If this were explained to the souls, then it would be difficult for them to understand that they were paying homage to Lord Kal in His Form as Lord of the first two Regions. But, Sant Ji continued, Sat Purush takes the soul through those five regions and protects it. And eventually the soul reaches the Lap of Sat Purush – guided by Sat Purush Himself in the Form of the Guru. The reality is that as the soul travels the inner journey, she has to pay respect to the Lord of each of the Five Planes.

Sant Ji proceeded to give us very specific instructions. With much strength He said that, first of all, we should not change anything on our own. We should not give our own interpretation. When a term came up that we did not understand, such as *Jambu Deep*, then we should not try to guess what Kabir Sahib meant by that. We should simply write "*Jambu Deep*" exactly as it was written in the edition we were using. It would not be good for people to think that we were interpreting things in our own manner.

He explained again that there were several editions, and this is the one that He chose. We should simply translate what was there as best as we could – without rewriting or changing the meaning of anything. He looked at the first part of the translation which had been written down by someone else, and then told me to rewrite it in the same manner as I had done the rest. He said I should not be impatient – that I must do a careful job. The whole transcript should then be typed, and a copy sent to Pappu for checking, as well as to Russell for publication.

Before it got published, He definitely wanted to see it and go over every single thing. And if any more questions about interpretation arose, we should check with Him – and not use our own judgment. In the end, He told me to convey all of what He was saying to Russell.

Sant Ji then gave me a cassette filled with new bhajans. I had

---

[16] In fact, Sant Ji was extremely literate. He was an excellent student in school and as a signalman in the army. His knowledge of the Sikh scriptures was breathtaking.

suggested a new approach to recording the songs. First, the title would be spoken, and then the bhajan would be sung – with the *Sangat* answering back – in just the way we should learn them in the West. Sant Ji asked me to listen to them to be certain that everything was acceptable (and they were wonderful!).

Sant Ji said that Pappu and I should communicate frequently – as much as we needed to – in order that the work on the *Anurag Sagar* be accomplished correctly. With a smile, He gave us permission to mail letters and packages back and forth once again. Using an old joke, He thanked us for our "good *kita*,"[17] and we bowed and left His presence. I was fairly singing as I left, knowing that I had been part of a cosmic conference that had much import – in spite of me.

The busy days and nights in Delhi, coupled with the long car ride the day before, made a mid-morning siesta seem most appealing. Chris, Pappu, and I stretched out on our rope beds, and soon fell into a deep sleep. I woke to a gentle tugging sensation on my toe – and I had a vague awareness that it had been going on for some time. When I opened my eyes, there was Sant Ji – standing, looking down at us. Pappu was sitting up on the bed next to me, and Chris was rubbing his eyes. Sant Ji said, "Campa Cola," and pointed to three bottles of the soft drink on a nearby table – cold bottles He had just brought to us. How kind of Him – and how wonderful for us. To awaken with the Saint standing over me – and then to drink a bottle of soda that He had brought – was a treasure that I hoped to hold forever. May He always wake me up when I am sleeping!

Chris and I roused ourselves and went out to observe the process by which the juice of the sugar cane is turned into *gur*, or raw sugar. Pathi Ji's brother, Darshan Singh, and his wife were hard at work over an outdoor stove, the fire of which was beneath the ground. As cotton plant twigs were fed into the flames, Darshan Singh used a large wooden paddle to stir and stir a huge vat of thick golden liquid from which water vapor arose as steam. In another part of the Ashram, two blindfolded oxen walked round and round a mill, turning the millstones to crush the cane and extract the juice. Chris and I each drank a glassful of juice, and thought about boiling down the sap from our sugar maple trees at Sant Bani in New Hampshire. To extract the essential sweetness – whether in the East or West – required a similar process. We then joked about the

---

[17] An elderly Satsangi had made Sant Ji laugh through his use of the combined English "good" and Punjabi, "*kita*" [work, job] – to mean "a job well done." Pathi Ji and others enjoyed using the phrase on occasion.

juice, calling it the "essence" of Chris' meditations.

Pathi Ji came over and we had a silly conversation with a sweetness of its own. He tried to tell me that while they were traveling in America, they had seen a sign for a city called "Kent Bicknell." I assured him that that could not be so: What they were seeing, I explained, was a billboard advertising Kent Cigarettes, and we both laughed. Pathi Ji had often made the chai on Tour – and continued to do so for the Western groups in the wee hours. When I was present, he would ask me to be sure that he was awake to do that seva. As we sat talking in Hindi, he began our old routine:

Pathi Ji: Whenever you want chai, just say, 'Pathi Ji! Chai!'
Kent: Like this? 'Pathi Ji! Chai!' (in a very strong, gruff tone)
Pathi Ji: *Hunh, like that! But not now!* (and he pulled the blanket over his head to feign sleep)
Kent: Pathi Ji. I want chai right now!
Pathi Ji: Not now – but at four o'clock!

We remembered that in Colombia I had asked him to wake me at two a.m. – and when he did, I had said, "No, wake me at three." At three when he shook me, I had changed it to four. And so we recalled those wonderful times we had had together in His presence.

In the early afternoon, Sant Ji came to walk around and check on the progress of various projects. As He headed out to the cauldron of hot *gur*, I returned to the room and grabbed my camera. Pappu was still resting, so Chris and I left him in peace. Sant Ji explained to me that it was very good to eat the raw sugar – the *gur* – when it was still warm. That would help the digestion and was a useful remedy for diarrhea. Sant Ji came close to Chris, who was dressed in a tee-shirt advertising the Cog Railway in the White Mountains of New Hampshire. I took a picture of the two of them. Sant Ji looked at Chris, smiled, and put His arm around him. He tousled Chris' hair – then pulled it back and caressed his fore-head. We joined Sant Ji as He went to check on the cows in the stable. He told us that He would have hot *gur* delivered to our room shortly.

When we returned to the room, I suggested to Chris that he wear his white Indian suit – the loose fitting cotton outfit known as *kurta-pajama* [shirt and pants]. Chris did, and when Sant Ji returned, I snapped another photo of the two together, explaining that it was "a group photo" – something very popular with the groups that visited Rajasthan each month. We all entered the dining room just as Bhag Singh came over with a big supply of the golden gur in a bucket.

Sant Ji looked at me, smiled, and said, "Kent Cigarettes." I said, "Yes, in India they advertise for the *Dsai Beede* cigarettes – but in the States they sell Kent cigarettes." Sant Ji turned to Chris and asked, "And what do you call your father – what is his name?" Chris answered, "Kent!" and we all laughed.[18] Then Sant Ji asked, "And what is he to you?" Chris said, "Father." He continued, "What is your little brother's name?" "Nick." "And your mother's name?" Chris answered, "Karen." Sant Ji laughed again, and said, "Nicky, Chrissy, Karen, Kent – Bick-a-nell Fam-i-lee!"

To cool the hot *gur,* Bhag Singh ladled some into a bowl and began to stir vigorously. We all watched as the spoon went round and round in the bowl. Chris commented that he did not think he could eat a whole lot – at one time. Sant Ji asked Bhag Singh to scoop more into the bowl – and then more. He watched carefully as Bhag Singh stirred, and suddenly a glob of the thickening gold slurped up and over the edge. Sant Ji caught it with His finger before it dropped to the floor, and carefully deposited it back in the bowl. Then He said we should go ahead and eat it – all of it. It was not too much, He added, and it would help us feel better – not cause more problems. Sant Ji left, and Pappu, Chris, and I shared the blessed treat.

Later that afternoon, Chris and I went out for a walk, and we saw Sant Ji far away – checking the crops in a distant field. I ran for the camera, and snapped some photos of His small, white form, shining against the lush green of the field. Pappu joined Him when He returned, and then He signaled for Chris and me to come over. He asked us if we wanted to go for a walk. I had put the camera back in the room, so I asked *"bina* camera?" [without my camera], and Sant Ji answered, "O, you may go get it." I did, thank God.[19]

Sant Ji, Pathi Ji, Pappu, Chris, and I walked out of the compound

---

[18] When Chris was four, we visited friends whose child called her parents by their first names. Chris picked up the habit, and never stopped. This was no doubt reinforced by the fact that students at the Sant Bani School had always called me "Kent." Later, Nick also called us "Kent" and "Karen." When Sant Ji first understood this, He found it most amusing – and often asked Chris and Nick to call us in their customary manner. This is a case in point.

[19] The series of photos I took on that walk are hauntingly beautiful – and have always been among my favorite shots of the Master.

gate, turned left, and headed down the road in the direction of the hut. When we reached the footpath on the right, Sant Ji led us in through the tall stalks of sugar cane. Arriving at the hut, Pathi Ji brought the bed out, and Sant Ji sat cross-legged on the woven rope. We four removed our shoes, and sat in front of Him.

Sant Ji asked Chris to sing a *bhajan*, but it took Chris a long time to decide on one. He said that he was thinking about it. Sant Ji looked lovingly down at Chris, and waited. At last Chris began to sing *Thakur Tum Sharnaee Aaya* [O Lord, I have taken refuge in You] – and Sant Ji sang along with him, conducting with His hands in an ever so radiant manner. When Chris reached the line, *Anbolat meri birtha jani, ji birtha jani* [Without saying, You knew my pain and problems], Sant Ji burst out laughing and said, "Yes, without you even saying anything, I knew all your pains and difficulties – I knew how you wanted to eat the sugar cane, so I had the sugar cane brought for you. You did not have to say even one thing. And eating that, your pains and difficulties went away." We all were in hysterics – with Sant Ji laughing the most. Then He told Chris, "And Kent used to sing *Tandi Vao Na Laga Di Ji*," and laughed even more.

After we stopped laughing, Sant Ji asked me about the School. He wondered how the recent graduates were doing, mentioning Carolyn Hammond and Evelyn Sanborn by name. He asked who was in college and where – so I brought Him up to date. Remembering the "cold winds," He asked about the winter. How did we keep the School warm? Were the shoes we had here good for the winter there? He asked if Eric Perkins and Gina Matty were graduating this year? He asked about other students He had met on the Tour, and I told Him that one girl who had been very devoted had gotten into trouble and had left the School. He was sympathetic toward her situation, and, shaking His head, commented that at that stage in a person's life, the mind is very strong, and has led many astray. The mind has thrown many a strong rider.

We then entered another moment of hilarity. Sant Ji asked me how much I paid to have my hair styled. I was confused. I told Him that it cost six or eight dollars to get it cut – and that I often had Karen cut it – or just did it myself. He said, "Ooh – that is a lot!" Still, He wondered how I got it to curl. It was confusing for a time – and then Pappu unraveled the secret. Someone in the previous group had mentioned that his wife, a Western devotee well known to Sant Ji, had recently got a permanent for her hair. The result was that her once straight hair was then very wavy. In order to explain to Sant Ji how it looked, the fellow had said, "Now her hair looks very curly – like Kent's!" So Sant Ji thought that I paid to have my hair "done." It was hard to stop giggling as I assured Sant Ji that what He saw was my natural "look."

When the sands of those sacred moments ran out, Sant Ji stood up and hugged Chris – a lot. I said, "Chris has been really happy here – happier than I have ever seen him." And Sant Ji said, "I am very very pleased with Chris. He is a good boy." We walked back to the Ashram, following in the footsteps of the One Who "knew our pains and difficulties without us saying even a word." That night we slept like babies.

Saturday the Seventeenth of March

I woke up early to meditate, but as I leaned against the wall, mostly I received sleepiness and a headache from my slumped posture. At five a.m. Sant Ji called to Pathi Ji through the window, "Gurdev Singh – Gurdev Singh Ji" and everyone woke up.[20] We ate a delicious breakfast of fresh chapattis stuffed with grated potatoes – all washed down by hot chai in glasses. Sant Ji called for us just before we were to leave, and we went into His room and knelt down to touch those Holy Feet once more. He asked, "Do you have anything to say?" and Chris and I, with tears in our eyes, shook our heads. "Nothing?" He asked – and then said, "*Hunh Ji!*" He looked so fondly at both of us, and then said, "Give my love to Karen and Nicky – and give my love to everyone at the Ashram – Russell and Judith and all the *premis*." [dear ones.] He looked into my eyes and said, "You have to be strong, and continue in your love at the Ashram like the old Kent."

I had thought of asking Him if I could continue to write Him my "sweet nothings" in Hindi – but He said it first, "And you should continue writing me the letters in Hindi as before. But don't write that you are the low and useless one. Don't write things like that. Just write the good things. Keep writing me the letters in Hindi, so that I may know about you. And you may continue communicating with Pappu like before." I wept more.

He gave me a big hug – a bear hug – and then hugged Chris for a long time as well. He patted us on the shoulder, said good-bye, and, wished us a safe journey for the remainder of the trip to our home. Just

---

[20] Pathi Ji's given name was Gurdev Singh.

as we were getting in the car, He looked deeply into me and said, "*Te amo!*" He stayed by the gate, waving to us, while we headed down the road. As we watched, His upraised hand become so small that It merged with His white form. After a time, Chris asked me what those final words meant. I told him, "They mean 'I love you' in Spanish."

****

About an hour from the Ashram, we stopped for a short time in the town of Raisinghnagar, and visited with Sant Ji's driver, Sathi. He was the son of Sardar Rattan Singh – and the fellow about whom Sant Ji told many amusing stories to Robert, Wendy and me in April of 1976. It was Sati who "used" the Master Power to drive the tractor that was broken – and who defeated a yogi in a sleeping contest.[21] Chris and I climbed three flights of stairs to the terrace on the roof, and took in the view. Cows wandered peacefully here and there in the streets, and a line of women filled their earthen jugs at the well below. The water vessels were large, but with the grace of constant practice, each woman swung the overflowing container up and onto her head. They walked off in pairs, and threesomes – chatting and laughing as they headed back to their homes – the jug balanced dead-center over their swaying forms.

India is a bazaar – a riot of multi-hued sights, smells, and sounds in a teeming environment. We were headed back to the snow-covered forests of central New Hampshire – where the cold winds awaited us. After a brief stop at the Bagga home, Chris and I headed for the airport to catch the midnight flight to London – to Boston – and home. On the plane to England, I looked at Chris, sleeping in the seat beside me, and the angelic face only seemed to glow brighter. My thoughts turned to the manuscript I carried with me. For God only knows what reason, Sant Ji had picked me to be the courier of an extraordinary book that the world needed: Sant Kabir Sahib's the *Anurag Sagar. The Ocean of Love* is nothing less than the true story of the creation, the fall, and the redemption of the souls, through the Grace, Mercy, and Love of Sat Purush – God Almighty, working though His Servants, the Saints.

I recalled how Sant Ji had hoped to begin translating that book back in 1977, laying great emphasis on its importance. I remembered that He had intended to start in earnest on His return from the first Tour – but the disharmony at Sant Bani Ashram – for which I carried perhaps the lion's

---

[21] See Chapter One.

share of responsibility – stopped Him. In March of 1978, I had come to His Feet, swelled with spiritual pride at my new self – the New Kent – the Meditator. Sant Ji had burst my bubble – with the Needle of Love – and set me back on course. He had told me that my strength was ruining the Ashram – and indicated that both the Ashram and the School might have failed if I had continued – and that would have been the worst trick that the Negative Power could have accomplished. And He told me to write at once when harmony had been re-established – so that He might start work on the *Anurag Sagar*. Now that book was translated – ready for the skilled editorial eye of Russell.[22]

I looked again at Chris, and thought of the plight of poor Dharam Das when Kabir informed him that his own son was a manifestation of Lord Kal. Dharam Das had to throw his son out of their home. I would never be ready for such tests – and what a fool I had been to think that I had actually made some inner progress. Growth on the Path was not mine to get – nor mine to measure. Sant Ji had made it abundantly clear, over and over again, that He preferred me as I had been – not as who I thought I should be. But what a painful lesson my undoing had been.

With a twinge of shame, I realized that there was a selfish reason I had wanted Chris to come with me. I had felt so tender from the year before, that Chris served me as a shield – a loving child behind whom I could hide. Yet, the healing had begun – and continued through Sant Ji's happiness to see *"Purane Kent"* [the old Kent]; the loving, sweet, hilarious, and deep therapy of difficult meditations; easy meditations; darshans; sugar cane; fake cameras; bhajans; my own son as un-pretentious messenger of what it meant to "live in the living present"; and the *Anurag Sagar – The Ocean of Love*. The core message of that book, as far as I could understand it, was the same as the bhajan of Brahmanand that Sant Ji asked Eric Perkins and me to learn: *Guru Bina Kaun Sahai Narak Me, Guru Bina Kaun Sahai Re* ["Without the Guru, who will save you from hell?"]. No one else could. He was the One.

Chris continued to sleep as our bodies hurtled northwest across the

---

[22] Over the next couple of years, Russell worked closely with Sant Ji to provide notes that explained – but did not misinterpret. The notes help bridge the chasm of Western incredulity that invariably looms in the face of the contents of the text. Even the format of the notes was designed with great care. There are no obtrusive numbers in the text itself, and the notes are placed artfully on the right-hand page only, to allow for an uninterrupted reading of the book.

cold, gray Atlantic – and then south over Newfoundland towards home. I closed my eyes, and thought of the old Shaker song about the simple gifts: "To turn, to turn will be our delight – 'til by turning, turning, we come round right." Sant Ji had succeeded in turning me around, so that, for better or worse, I was my old self again. I thought of those final words once more, "*Te amo!*" He loved me. He really, really loved me. And I felt whole again.

CHAPTER TEN

Epilogue

After my return from 77 RB in the spring of 1979, Sant Ji kept finding ways to tell me how pleased He was that I was my old self again. In a letter dated October 1st, 1979, He went into more detail as to why.

When you write that you have become the old Kent, I become very happy – because in the old Kent there were many good qualities. In becoming the new Kent, you know how the mind had become – and you know that the new Kent had become dry as far as Spirituality is concerned. That is why I become happy when you write that you are the old Kent.

Sant Ji continued to refer to my transformation until the time approached when I would receive the doctoral degree from Boston University – the summer of 1981. In June of that year, He wrote that He was very glad that I was close to completing the graduate work, as He wished to be able to call me, "Doctor Kent." In August, the salutation of His letter read, "*Mere bahut pyare beta doctor Kent*" [My dearly beloved son, Doctor Kent] – and He went on to say that He was very happy that I had succeeded in getting that degree. Subsequent letters often referred to me as "Doctor Kent." And while references to "the old Kent" faded away, almost every letter (through the last I received in 1997) was filled with "*Te amo,*" to which He began to add, "*mucho, mucho*" [a whole lot].

In the fall of 1979, one of the groups heading to Rajasthan was reserved for devotees whose native tongue was Spanish, and I began to accompany them on an annual basis. The rich spiritual lessons learned by all were taught in an atmosphere of profound love, which was filled with divine intoxication, tears and laughter – including moments of hilarity (as when Pappu's car keys were dropped into the gas tank by a careless pump attendant). Sant Ji distributed so much wealth that the account of those memorable events would fill another volume. This book, however, must draw to a close.

More waves of the love and protection of the Masters flowed over the Bicknell family, including when we faced some difficult moments. On Christmas Eve, 1979, my father passed away quite unexpectedly. He had had the good fortune to meet and appreciate both Master Kirpal and Sant Ji. While it was an emotionally wrenching time, Sant Ji was so supportive that my heart did not break. In a letter to me (and two to my mother), He made it very clear that my father had "gone to his Eternal Home," and would not be returning to this world again. He wrote us not to weep, as:

> " . . .one should weep only for the sakat (worldly one, who doesn't believe in God), who will take birth again in this world. The soul, who has the darshan of Master Power, or if the children are satsangis – even if he has not taken initiation, he is protected by Master Power. So, accept the Will of God and have patience. Teach the family also to be patient. Do your bhajan and simran."[1]

My whole family, especially my mother, deeply appreciated the love, sympathy, and support they received from Him.

The following April, Christopher, then aged ten, broke his leg while playing on a swing set at the Sant Bani School. It was a spiral fracture of the femur – the biggest bone in the human body. To heal, he spent a month in traction, flat on his back in the hospital, a second month in a full body cast (under which he contracted chicken-pox), and a final month in a walking cast. In several letters to me, Sant Ji sent much love and sympathy to Chris, as well as best wishes for his speedy, full recovery – with Master's Grace. As He said in the letter of May 29th, 1980:

> I hope that he will be all right when I come to Sant Bani Ashram. I pray to Master Kirpal to make dear Chris pay off his karmas and become all right soon. Please convey my love to him . . . I am very glad to know that Chrissy has been fine and his spirits have been really good.
> You know that all those who come into this world have to pay off their karmas before going back to their Real Home. You know how Master Power helps the dear ones. When Master Sawan Singh broke his leg, Baba Jaimal Singh helped him a great deal. Master Power always reduces the pain and helps

---

[1] Letters of Sant Ajaib Singh to me (January 6th, 1980), and to my mother (January 16th, 1980; February 3rd, 1980).

whatever amount is feasible. I will be happy to see you in Rio [de Janeiro] . . .

Right before Chris was to graduate from the body cast to the walking cast, Sant Ji, Pappu, Pathi Ji and his daughter, Bant, left India for the Second World Tour. They began in Ghana, and then flew to Rio de Janeiro for a night, prior to heading to Ecuador. I met them in Rio. From Ecuador we traveled to Colombia and Venezuela, and then came back to spend three wonderful weeks at Sant Bani. He invited me to stay in His house once again. On July 4th, 1980, Karen, Chris, Nick, and I were invited to see Sant Ji for a private session.

Nick, age five, entered the room first, and stuck out his hand for Sant Ji to shake. Sant Ji laughed, at which point Nick sat down and kept bowing to Sant Ji with folded hands. Sant Ji turned to Chris, who could maneuver quite well in his walking cast, and asked him all about the break. How did he do it? Which bone was broken? How was he feeling now? After listening carefully to all that Chris had to say, Sant Ji told a story from His childhood.

Once, when He was Chris' age, His friends and He decided to climb a tree together. There were fifteen of them – and they all crawled out on the same branch. It snapped under the combined weight, and no one escaped injury. Some had hurt their legs; others had fractured a wrist or arm. Sant Ji Himself had split open His lip with two teeth. All of them were afraid of what their parents would say – as they felt that they had been mischievous. So, they decided to hide. They went to Sant Ji's home and proceeded upstairs to His room, where they all hid. After a while the parents went out looking for the children, but could not find them, as Sant Ji and His friends stayed in that room all day. They got hungry, and thirsty, and, since they had no vessel for water, they used their turbans to transport some. In the evening the parents finally found them – and there was much relief all around. Sant Ji laughed, and added that the parents have to work and worry so much – but for the children, they just have to weep a little.

Chris definitely enjoyed this tale of Sant Ji and His naughty playmates – words and laughter that operated on several levels at once. He then told Chris that He hoped his leg would be better soon, and Chris said, "Me, too!" Until that moment, Sant Ji had been focusing on Nick and Chris. He suddenly looked intently at Karen and said to Pappu, "Oh, and tell Karen 'Hello!' " Pappu did and we all laughed. He let us know that this interview was primarily for Chris, and that He would see us later. I asked if He would come to our house, and He said, "Surely!" and a few days later, He came to sit with us again in our home.

After Sant Ji returned to India, I thought about all that I had been through. I began to see the events in my life – especially my trips to India and time with Him – as non-linear. That is, they did not occur on a straight line of past, present, and future. Rather, they were cyclical in nature – but not repetitious. More precisely, they seemed to be spirals – and each time I would revisit something, it was from a changed perspective – hopefully from a somewhat higher level. I wrote earlier that the Saints have a naturally elevated point of view – but mortals like me count on the passage of time to be able to see things more clearly. In the fall of 1981, an event occurred that brought me to a deeper understanding of the Saints and Time.

On a crisp Saturday in October, a few weeks before I was to head to Rajasthan with the Spanish-speaking group, I was the recipient of a fracture. I had been playing soccer, and an opponent's kick caught my fibula with such force that a piece of bone was knocked out. I wrote Sant Ji about the injury, and just before I was supposed to travel to India, I received a reply. I remembered His 1977 letter to Karen, asking her not to come to 77 RB and, as I was in a cast, I prepared myself to accept whatever His Will might be.[2]

With Hindi dictionary in hand, I poured over His letter to me, reading it again and again. As the words on the page fell into coherent sentences, the essential Truth of my Beloveds, Great Master Kirpal Singh and Sant Ajaib Singh, shone through. Sant Ji informed me that I was to have endured six months of intense suffering but, through the Grace of the Masters, my debt had been reduced to almost nothing. He had prayed to Kirpal for me, and the Master Power had manipulated both my fate and Time itself. I was in awe.

November 12, 1981

My dearly beloved Doctor Kent,

I received your loving letter. Your injury caused me limitless pain. My dear, you had six months of very heavy suffering over

---

[2] The cast came off in time, and the doctor said I was free to travel, so I did go to Rajasthan in November of 1981. When I arrived at the Ashram with the Spanish-speaking group, Pathi Ji told me that, on hearing about my broken leg, he had expressed doubt to Sant Ji as to whether I would be able to come. Sant Ji had answered, rather enigmatically, "Let us see." So Pathi Ji had been watching carefully as each person got off the bus, until he saw me step gingerly down.

you. But after listening to my prayers, Kirpal changed the gallows into something like the prick of a thorn. May the Grace of Anaami Kirpal reach you.

You must follow strictly the regimen given you by the doctor. Surely do your bhajan and simran regularly. To Nicky, Chrissy, Karen, and everyone, I send much much love and best wishes.

Ajaib Singh

Time, Love, and Grace were at the core of the mystery. Speaking of the theme of the *Anurag Sagar*, Russell wrote, "The poem centers around the impact of Time on Eternity, and Eternity's response. It is Eternity which is the Anurag Sagar or "Ocean of Love," and it is Time's perversion of that part of Eternity which it touches that produces the *bhav sagar*, "ocean of the world" – the only reality most of us know, the mock world we are trapped in."[3] The Grace and Mercy of Master Kirpal and Sant Ji had freed me – if momentarily – from the "mock world" that trapped me – virtually eliminating the intense suffering I should have received. "Time" in Hindi is "kal" – and "kal" can mean "yesterday" or "tomorrow" – depending on the tense of the verb form accompanying it. "Kal" is also another name for the Negative Power. And Who could defeat the Negative Power – Who could defeat Time – except the Masters?

I realized that the lovely blue air letter from Rajasthan spread out on the table in front of me carried a precise message, impossible to ignore. Time, that bugbear of all humanity – that great machine that rolls on in spite of the efforts of gods and kings – was in the Hands of the Masters. I felt caught in the Ocean of Love. With a tremendous sense of relief, I understood that no one – especially my own self – could save me from hell except the Guru. I put the letter down, and glanced up at a large framed composite photo of Master Kirpal and Sant Ji. I smiled, feeling very happy to be exactly where I was – sitting in the lap of the Lord with God's rainbow on my heart.

THE END

---

[3] Russell Perkins, "Introduction," *The Ocean of Love: The Anurag Sagar of Kabir*, p. xxvii.